SUSTAINABILITY, SOCIAL RESPONSIBILITY, AND INNOVATIONS IN TOURISM AND HOSPITALITY

Advances in Hospitality and Tourism

SUSTAINABILITY, SOCIAL RESPONSIBILITY, AND INNOVATIONS IN TOURISM AND HOSPITALITY

Edited by
H. G. Parsa, PhD

Vijaya "Vi" Narapareddy, PhD
Consulting Editor

SooCheong (Shawn) Jang, PhD, Marival Segarra-Oña, PhD, and Rachel J. C. Chen, PhD, CHE
Associate Editors

Apple Academic Press Inc. | Apple Academic Press Inc.
3333 Mistwell Crescent | 9 Spinnaker Way
Oakville, ON L6L 0A2 | Waretown, NJ 08758
Canada | USA

©2015 by Apple Academic Press, Inc.

First issued in paperback 2021

Exclusive worldwide distribution by CRC Press, a member of Taylor & Francis Group
No claim to original U.S. Government works

ISBN 13: 978-1-77463-295-6 (pbk)
ISBN 13: 978-1-926895-67-3 (hbk)

Library and Archives Canada Cataloguing in Publication

Sustainability, social responsibility, and innovations in tourism and hospitality / edited by H.G. Parsa, PhD ; Vijaya "Vi" Narapareddy, PhD, consulting editor ; SooCheong (Shawn) Jang, PhD, Marival Segarra-Oña, PhD, and Rachel J.C. Chen, PhD, CHE, associate editors.

(Advances in hospitality and tourism book series)
Includes bibliographical references and index.
ISBN 978-1-926895-67-3 (bound)
1. Tourism--Environmental aspects--Case studies. 2. Sustainable tourism--Case studies.
3. Hospitality industry--Environmental aspects--Case studies. 4. Social responsibility of business--Case studies. I. Parsa, H. G., author, editor II. Series: Advances in hospitality and tourism book series

G156.5.E58S98 2015   338.4'791   C2015-901051-9

Library of Congress Cataloging-in-Publication Data

Sustainability, social responsibility, and innovations in tourism and hospitality / editor, H.G. Parsa ; Vijaya (Vi) Narapareddy, consulting editor ; SooCheong (Shawn) Jang, María de Val Segarra-Oña, and Rachel J.C. Chen, associate editors.

pages cm
Includes bibliographical references and index.
ISBN 978-1-926895-67-3 (alk. paper)
1. Sustainable tourism. 2. Tourism--Environmental aspects. 3. Hospitality industry--Environmental aspects. 4. Social responsibility of business. I. Parsa, H. G., editor of compilation.

G156.5.S87S93 2015   910.68'4--dc23   2015004462

Apple Academic Press also publishes its books in a variety of electronic formats. Some content that appears in print may not be available in electronic format. For information about Apple Academic Press products, visit our website at **www.appleacademicpress.com** and the CRC Press website at **www.crcpress.com**

ADVANCES IN HOSPITALITY AND TOURISM BOOK SERIES

Editor-in-Chief:
Mahmood A. Khan, PhD
Professor, Department of Hospitality and Tourism Management,
Pamplin College of Business,
Virginia Polytechnic Institute and State University,
Falls Church, Virginia
email: mahmood@vt.edu

BOOKS IN THE SERIES:

Food Safety: Researching the Hazard in Hazardous Foods
Editors: Barbara Almanza, PhD, RD, and Richard Ghiselli, PhD

Strategic Winery Tourism and Management: Building Competitive Winery Tourism and Winery Management Strategy
Editor: Kyuho Lee, PhD

Sustainability, Social Responsibility, and Innovations in the Hospitality Industry
Editor: H. G. Parsa, PhD
Consulting Editor: Vijaya "Vi" Narapareddy, PhD
Associate Editors: SooCheong (Shawn) Jang, PhD, Marival Segarra-Oña, PhD, and Rachel J. C. Chen, PhD, CHE

Managing Sustainability in the Hospitality and Tourism Industry: Paradigms and Directions for the Future
Editor: Vinnie Jauhari, PhD

Management Science in Hospitality and Tourism: Theory, Practice, and Applications
Editors: Muzaffer Uysal, PhD, Zvi Schwartz, PhD, and Ercan Sirakaya-Turk, PhD

Tourism in Central Asia: Issues and Challenges
Editors: Kemal Kantarci, PhD, Muzaffer Uysal, PhD, and Vincent Magnini, PhD

Poverty Alleviation through Tourism Development: A Comprehensive and Integrated Approach
Robertico Croes, PhD, and Manuel Rivera, PhD

Chinese Outbound Tourism 2.0
Editor: Xiang (Robert) Li, PhD

ABOUT THE EDITORS

H. G. Parsa, PhD, FMP

H. G. Parsa holds the Barron Hilton Chair in Lodging and is a Professor of Hospitality Management at the University of Denver, Colorado, USA. He earned his PhD in hospitality management from Virginia Tech as well as two MS degrees and a Food Management Professional (FMP) diploma. He is also a recipient of a prestigious Fulbright Visiting Scholar Fellowship in 2005. Currently he serves as an Associate Editor of the *Journal of Hospitality and Tourism Research (JHTR)*. He was the founding editor-in-chief of the *Journal of Foodservice Business Research*. In 2013, he became the Guest Editor for the *Cornell Hospitality Quarterly* special issue on sustainability and innovation. He has published numerous research papers in business and hospitality journals and serves on the editorial boards of several academic journals. Dr. Parsa's research has appeared in many refereed journals. He has presented papers nationally and internationally in 16 countries, including Germany, Canada, Australia, India, Korea, Curacao, Switzerland, Hungary, Serbia, France, Netherlands, Puerto Rico, Turkey, Taiwan, Caribbean Islands, and China. His research has been quoted in the popular press, including radio, television, and the *Wall Street Journal, New York Times*, *Chicago Tribune, Forbes, USA Today*, *Fortune*, and many others.

Dr. Parsa is a member of the Council of Hotel, Restaurant, and Institutional Education (CHRIE), Western CHRIE, and American Marketing Association. In 2013, he received the Michael D. Olsen Award for research and mentoring graduate students. In 2011, he received John Wiley & Sons Lifetime Research Achievement award from the International CHRIE. He also received Best Published Paper awards at International CHRIE and also at the Euro-CHRIE. He received the John Wiley & Sons Teaching Innovation Award and the Bradford Wiley Excellence in Research Award in 2006 and 2000. Earlier he received the President's Award for Excellence in Research and Creativity presented by the State University of New York College—Buffalo. Dr. Parsa also received the Faculty of the Year award three times from two major universities. He was awarded Educator of the Year–2007 by the Ohio Restaurant Association.

His research interests include strategic marketing in hospitality, managing employee turnover for profitability, sustainability and green practices in hospitality, entrepreneurship in hospitality, revenue management and pricing strategies in restaurants, franchising and multiunit management, and changing American food habits.

Vijaya (Vi) Narapareddy, PhD, MBA

Vi Narapareddy holds a PhD in Business Administration from the University of Illinois, Urbana-Champaign, Illinois, USA. Currently, she is Associate Professor and a Fellow of the Institute of Enterprise Ethics, Daniels College of Business, University of Denver, where she teaches traditional and online courses in business policy and strategy, international management, and global social entrepreneurship. A gold medalist from Sri J.C.B.M. College, India, Vi Narapareddy is a recipient of several awards for her teaching, case research, and reviewing.

Dr. Narapareddy has published articles and numerous unique case studies in corporate governance, global strategy, and global social entrepreneurship in leading journals in the U.S., Europe, and India. She is a member of the Academy of Management, the Academy of International Business, the Strategic Management Society, the North American Case Research Association, and the CASE Association. She has offered workshops on teaching with cases, developing theory from case studies, and writing publishable cases in the U.S. and overseas. She was the keynote speaker at two international conferences and is an invited speaker at several professional associations and colleges.

Vi Narapareddy is the President and cofounder of ITBC, an international technology and business consulting firm and also serves on the Advisory Board of Lutz-Lutz, a Franco-Chilean company. She serves as a reviewer for several professional associations, journals, and foundations in the U.S. Additionally, she serves on the editorial review boards of the *Case Research Journal, Journal of Case Research and Inquiry*, and *Journal of STEM (Science, Technology, Engineering, and Math)*

Education: Innovations and Research. She is the Immediate Past President of the North American Case Research Association and has been elected to serve as the Representative-at-Large of the Teaching Community, the Strategic Management Society. She is the co-guest editor of a special issue of the *European Journal of Cross-Cultural Competence and Management* (EJCCM) on building theory from case research and case methodologies in cross-cultural contexts.

SooCheong (Shawn) Jang, PhD

Dr. SooCheong (Shawn) Jang is currently Professor of Hospitality and Tourism Management (HTM) at Purdue University, USA. Dr. Jang's research is focused on business strategies in the hospitality and tourism industries. His secondary area of research investigates consumer subjects such as consumer values, service quality evaluation, and consumer experiences. Dr. Jang has received the W. Bradford Wiley Best Published Research Paper of the Year Award (2009) from the International CHRIE. During the past 15 years, 17 of his papers were selected as among the best papers at international conferences. Earlier Dr. Jang organized the TOSOK International Tourism Annual Conference, and he currently serves as one of chairs for the APTA (Asia Pacific Tourism Association) Annual Conference. Dr. Jang was Coeditor-in-Chief of the *International Journal of Tourism Sciences* and Research Note Editor of *Journal of Hospitality Marketing and Management.* He also serves on the editorial boards of top-tier HTM journals such as *Journal of Travel Research, Tourism Management, Journal of Hospitality and Tourism Research, International Journal of Hospitality Management, International Journal of Contemporary Hospitality Management, Journal of Travel and Tourism Marketing,* and *Tourism Analysis.*

Marival Segarra-Oña, PhD

Dr. Segarra-Oña is an Associate Professor of Innovation and Competitiveness, Business School, Technical University of Valencia, Spain. Dr. Segarra holds a PhD in management and BS degrees in industrial engineering and mechanical engineering. Professor Segarra is also a Research Associate of the Center for Hospitality Research, CHR, Cornell University, USA, and was member of the Jury of the 40th Anniversary contest of Sustainable Innovations of the European Patent Office in 2013. She currently teaches at the Universitat Politècnica de València. Dr. Segarra also teaches MBA classes at the Spanish Deloitte executive master since 2008 and has published several articles in prestigious journals such as *Cornell Hospitality Quarterly, Journal of Cleaner Production, Marine Policy*, among others. Her research interests include sustainability, eco-innovation, and strategy. Dr. Segarra has served as an associate editor of the special issue on sustainability at the *Cornell Hospitality Quarterly*. She is also a visiting scholar at the University of Bath (England).

Rachel Chen, PhD

Dr. Rachel J. C. Chen is the Director of the Center for Sustainable Business and Development at the University of Tennessee (UT), where she is also a Professor in Retail, Hospitality, and Tourism Management. Dr. Chen has conducted various types of research projects in the areas of tourism, hospitality, and service management, including sustainable development, economic impact assessments, forecast model evaluations, tourist behavior analyses, and geographic information system (GIS) applications in business development. She serves as an associate editor, guest editor, editorial board member, paper reviewer, and track chair for 23 refereed journals and four national/international associations. Recently, she has concentrated her research and outreach on valuing sustainable business, eco-tourism, and environment. During 2009–2010, Dr. Chen was appointed as Visiting Associate Professor in the School of Forestry and Environmental Studies at Yale University, New Haven, Connecticut. Dr. Chen is a Fulbright Senior Scientist.

CONTENTS

LIST OF CONTRIBUTORS

Nunzia Auletta
Professor Entrepreneurship and Marketing Departments, Instituto de Estudios Superiores en Administración (IESA), Caracas, Venezuela. PhD. in Political Science and MBA. Professor Auletta has carried out research on entrepreneurship, family businesses and innovation, and locally coordinated the Global Entrepreneurship Monitor (GEM) and the Successful Trans-generational Entrepreneurship Practices (STEP) research teams at IESA. AV. IESA, Edf. Iesa, San Bernardino, Caracas, 1010, Venezuela.Tele: 0058 2125554210 - nunzia.auletta@iesa.edu.ve

Robin M. Back
Department of Hospitality and Tourism Management, Isenberg School of Management, University of Massachusetts, Amherst, Massachusetts 01003, E-mail: rback@som.umass.edu

Angelo A. Camillo
School of Business, Woodbury University, 7500, Burbank, CA 91510, USA, Email: angelo.camillo@woodbury.edu

Lourdes Canós-Darós
ROGLE Research Group, Grao de Gandia, Universitat Politècnica de València, Valencia, Spain, Email: loucada@omp.upv.es

Roberto Cervelló-Royo
Faculty of Business Administration and Management, Universidad Politécnica de Valencia, Camino de Vera s/n, 46022, Valencia, E-mail: rocerro@esp.upv.es

JaeMin Cha
The School of Hospitality Business, Broad College of Business, Michigan State University, East Lansing, MI 48824, E-mail: jcha@broad.msu.edu

Rachel J. C. Chen
The University of Tennessee, 311 Conference Center Building, Knoxville, Tennessee 37996-4134, USA, E-Mail: **rchen@utk.edu**

Ronald F. Cichy
The School of Hospitality Business, Broad College of Business, Michigan State University, East Lansing, MI 48824, cichy@broad.msu.edu

Nicole Darnall
School of Public Affairs and School of Sustainability, Arizona State University, Phoenix, AZ 85004-0687, USA, ndarnall@asu.edu.

Karen Delchet-Cochet
ISC Paris, 75017 Paris, France, Email: karen.delchet-cochet@iscparis.com.

Thierry Delecolle
ISC Paris, 75017 Paris, France, tdelecolle@iscparis.com

María del-Val Segarra-Oña
Globalisation, Service Economy, Tourism and Heritage Microcluster, Management Department, Universitat Politècnica de València, Valencia, Spain, Email: maseo@omp.upv.es

María del-Val Segarra-Oña
Management Department, 7D building, Camí de Vera s/n, 46022, Universitat Politècnica de València Valencia (Spain), Email: maseo@omp.upv.es

Blanca de-Miguel-Molina
Globalisation, Service Economy, Tourism and Heritage Microcluster, Management Department, Universitat Politècnica de València, 46022 Valencia, Spain, Email: bdemigu@omp.upv.es

María de-Miguel-Molina
Associate Professor, Globalisation, Service Economy, Tourism and Heritage Microcluster, Management Department, Universitat Politècnica de València, 7D Building, Camino de Vera s/n, 46022 Valencia, Spain, Email: mademi@omp.upv.es

Ioana Dollinger
Department of Hospitality and Tourism Management, Pamplin College of Business, Virginia Tech, Blacksburg, VA, USA.

Raphaël Dornier
ISC Paris, 75017 Paris, France, rdornier@iscparis.com

Sarah Goudeau
Alumni ISC PARIS, 75017 Paris, France, sarah.goudeau@iscparis.com

Svetlana Holt
Department of Management, School of Business, Woodbury University, Burbank, CA 91510, E-mail: svetlana.holt@woodbury.edu

María Helena Jaén
Professor Management and Leadership Department, Instituto de Estudios Superiores en Administración (IESA), Caracas, Venezuela. PhD. in Development Studies in Social Sciences, and Master in Public Health (MPH). Social Enterprise Knowledge Network General Coordinator since 2014. Professor Jaén's research focuses on business ethics and social responsibility, leadership & change management, and management education and learning. AV. IESA, Edf. Iesa, San Bernardino, Caracas, 1010, Venezuela. Tele: 0058 2125554210 - maria.jaen@iesa.edu.ve

Dae-Young Kim
Hospitality Management, University of Missouri, 220 Eckles Hall, Columbia MO, USA, E-mail: kimdae@missouri.edu

Kathleen Jeehyae Kim
Hospitality Management, University of Missouri, Columbia MO, USA, E-mail: jhkznb@mail.missouri.edu

MiRan Kim
The School of Hospitality Business, Broad College of Business, Michigan State University, East Lansing, MI 48824, E-mail: kimmi@broad.msu.edu

Seung Hyun Kim
The School of Hospitality Business, Broad College of Business, Michigan State University, East Lansing, MI 48824, E-mail: kimseung@broad.msu.edu

Sung-Bum Kim
Hospitality Management, University of Missouri, Columbia MO, USA, E-mail: sk7w2@mail.missouri.edu

Tanvi Kothari
School of Global Innovation and Leadership, Lucas College and Graduate School of Business, San Jose State University, San Jose,CA 95192-0164

Linda L. Lowry
Department of Hospitality and Tourism Management, Isenberg School of Management, University of Massachusetts, Amherst, Massachusetts 01003, E-mail: llowry@isenberg.umass.edu

Mark B. Milstein
Samuel Curtis Johnson Graduate School of Management, Cornell University, Ithaca, NY 14853-6201, USA, E-mail: mm462@cornell.edu

Antonio Minguzzi
Department of Tourism Research Center, University of Molise, Via Duca Degli Abruzzi, 86039 Termoli, (CB), Italy, Email: minguzzi@unimol.it

Lluís Miret-Pastor
Social Sciences Department, Universitat Politècnica de València, Valencia, Spain, Email: luimipas@esp.upv.es

José Mondéjar-Jiménez
Dean of the Social Sciences School, Edificio Cardenal Gil de Albornoz, Universidad de Castilla La Mancha, Email: Jose.Mondejar@uclm.es

H. G. Parsa
Knoebel School of Hospitality Management, Daniels School of Business, 337 Joy Burns Center, University of Denver, Denver, CO (303) 871-3693. E-mail: hparsa@du.edu

Ángel Peiró-Signes
Management Department, Universitat Politècnica de València, Camino de Vera s/n, 7D Building, 46022,Valencia (Spain), Email: anpeisig@omp.upv.es

Angelo Presenza
University "G. D'Annunzio" of Chieti-Pescara, Tourism Research Center, University of Molise, Via Duca Degli Abruzzi, 86039 Termoli, (CB), Italy, Email: presenza@unich.it

Francisca Ramón Fernández
RE-FOREST Research Group, Escuela Técnica Superior de Ingeniería Agronómica y del Medio Natural (ETSIAMN), Universitat Politècnica de València, Valencia-Spain, Email: frarafer@urb.upv.es

Virginia Santamarina-Campos
Globalisation, Service Economy, Tourism and Heritage Microcluster, Department of conservation and Restoration of Cultural Heritage, Universitat Politècnica de València, Valencia, Spain, Email: virsanca@crbc.upv.es

Cristina Santandreu-Mascarell
IGIC Research Group, Grao de Gandia, Universitat Politècnica de València Valencia, Spain, Email: crisanma@omp.upv.es

Murray Silverman
College of Business, San Francisco State University, E-mail: msilver@sfsu.edu

Manisha Singal
Department of Hospitality Management, Pamplin College of Business, Virginia Tech, Blacksburg, VA 24061-0429, Email: msingal@vt.edu

Helle Sorensen
Department of Hospitality, Tourism and Events, Metropolitan State University of Denver, Denver, CO 80217, E-mail: sorenseh@msudenver.edu or (303) 556-3241

Michael L. Wray
Department of Hospitality, Hospitality, Tourism and Events, Metropolitan State University of Denver, Denver, CO, E-mail: wraym@msudenver.edu or (303) 556-3393

LIST OF ABBREVIATIONS

AHLA	Hotel and Lodging Association
ATES	Association pour le Tourisme Equitable et Solidaire
ATR	Agir pour un Tourisme Responsable
AWWPS	Advanced Waste Water Purification System
CA	Conjoint Analysis
CFL	Compact Fluorescent Lights
CI	Conservation International
CLIA	Cruise Line Industry Association
CLIA	Cruise Line Industry Association
CMAA	Club Managers Association of America
CO2	Carbon Dioxide
COOs	Chief Operating Officers
CPA	Principal Component Analysis
CSR	Corporate Social Responsibility
CVP	Customer Value Proposition
DMC	Destination Management Companies
EMS	Environmental Management System
FA	Factor Analysis
FCC	Fuel Conservation Committee
FOMIT	Tourism Infrastructures Modernisation Fund
FTC	Federal Trade Commission
GDP	Gross Domestic Product
GEO	Golf Environmental Organization
GMs	General Managers
GSTC	Global Sustainable Tourism Council
HACCP	Hazard Analysis of Critical Control Points
HAL	Holland America Line
HAWT	Horizontal Axis Wind Turbine
HFO	Heavy Fuel Oil
HVAC	Heating, Ventilation and Air Conditioning
IMO	International Maritime Organization
ISEAL	International Social and Environment Accreditation and Labelling
IT	Information Technology
IWC	The International Whaling Convention
LEED	Leadership in Energy and Environmental Design

MARTI	MesoAmerican Reef Tourism Association
MCI	Marine Conservation Institute
MSD	Marine Sanitation Devices
NGO	Nongovernmental Organization
NOX	Nitrous Oxide
PCA	Principal Component Analysis
PM	Particulate Matter
QCS	Quality of Commercial Services
QPS	Quality of Public Service
RMHC	Ronald McDonald House Charities
RSC	Restaurant Support Center
SBP	Sustainable Business Practices
SIDS	Small Island Developing States
SMEs	Small and Medium Businesses
SOX	Sulfur Oxide
TIES	The International Ecotourism Society
TO	Tour Operators
UNCED	United Nations Conference on Environment and Development
UNCLOS	United Nations Convention on the Law of the Sea
UNWTO	United Nations World Tourism Organization
VAWT	Vertical Axis Wind Turbine
VEP	Voluntary Environmental Program
VOC	Low Volatile Organic Compound
WCED	World Commission on Environment and Development
WTO	World Tourism Organization

PREFACE

Sustainability and corporate social responsibility (CSR) have become competitive strategic tools for the business world in the twenty-first century. Sustainability is no longer a desirable trait, but a necessary activity that holds organizations accountable to their actions and makes them socially responsible to their stakeholders. According to many scholars, dwindling natural resources and ever increasing human demands are soon bound to clash. It is not meant to be a doomsday prediction but an informed caution against an impending eventuality. Corporations have the responsibility to sustain and preserve the finite pool of available resources while minimizing the rate of utilization for their own long-term financial and operational survival. The *'tragedy of commons'* doesn't have to be a reality when organizations behave in a socially responsible manner. Thus, the importance of sustainability cannot be overemphasized when social burdens continue to outpace the economic benefits.

With the introduction of the Sustainability Accounting Standards Board (SASB) in July 2011, it is becoming increasingly imperative for corporations and nonprofit institutions to report their sustainability activities. Similar to the Financial Accounting Standards Board (FASB), the role of the SASB is also expected to evolve gradually in the business community from a reporting choice to a business requirement that affects net social and financial value of an organization. To meet the SASB guidelines, it is no longer sufficient to merely report sustainability scores or present a list of green accomplishments; organizations must integrate sustainability practices into the organizational procedures and operational processes. Sustainability cannot be treated just as a tool of public relations, but it must be considered as earnestly as the basic human resource practices of an organization. We do not need another Love Canal and Occidental contamination, Exxon Valdez accident, or BP Oil explosion to become socially responsible to the stakeholders and the greater community.

According to George Scott (2012), "Landfills are unsustainable. There is only so much land in the world, and every year about 175 million tons of refuse enter landfills. While some matter will decompose in landfills, some materials, like plastic and Styrofoam, will last millions of years." The colonial era strategies of transferring waste from the industrialized nations to the developing countries is no longer sustainable as developing nations, including BRICS countries, are also contributing extensively to world pollution and solid waste. Moreover, recent Tsunami in Japan and volcano blow up in Iceland are some of the good examples of air and water pollution issues becoming global challenges as they can no longer be treated as local concerns. It is unfortunate that eventually future generations have to pay the price for our excessive consumption and lack of urgency for environmental stewardship and CSR.

Tourism and hospitality are truly global in nature. This industry is the second largest employer in the world with one in 11 jobs being related to tourism. According to UNWTO (2014), over 1 billion tourists have contributed over $1.3 trillion in exports. The U.S. Travel Association (2014) estimates that tourism in the U.S. contributes $2.1 trillion in economic impact and about $133.9 billion in taxes. In the U.S. alone, tourists spend about $28,154 every second and $2.4 billion per day. With nearly 1,000,000 restaurants generating about $680 billion in sales annually, the tourism sector is a net exporter worth $180.7 billion per year. One in three Americans have worked in this industry once in their lifetime. With this impressive economic, social, and cultural impact in the global place, the tourism-hospitality has the moral obligation to show leadership in sustainability and CSR.

The current book takes a global view of sustainability and CSR from hospitality and tourism perspective. We are pleased to share with you that this book is conceptualized as a scholarly resource, with cases and research articles from Asia, Europe, Latin America, and North America. The case study co-authored by Darnall and Milstein discusses sustainability strategies in a resort from Asia – Bali Island. The general manager of the resort ponders the issue of return on investment for sustainability initiatives in a resort. He begs the quint essential question of this book 'can *we do well while doing good.*"

Then moving on to Europe, Sorenson, Wray, and Parsa address the commonly held myth that Vikings are "….. brutal, destructive, and superhuman warriors who pillaged and raped wherever they went. This case study offers an ethnographic account of how a Viking Village near Copenhagen uses sustainable techniques to combat this misunderstood and misrepresented culture." Here is a good example of using sustainability tools to correct a commonly held myth about the past. This paper shows how ethnographic tools can be used to better understand the role of sustainability.

Traveling to the US, Lowry and Mack demonstrate how a social movement, Slow Tourism, that started in Italy is slowly embracing and affecting human habitat from the sustainability perspective. The second article on this topic comes from Europe. Miret-Pastor, Peiro-Signes, and Segarra-Ona describe how Slow Tourism is consistent with sustainability principles. They stated that "The commitment to protect biodiversity, cultivation and processing methods, and to maintain the traditions, the wisdom of local communities and the ecosystems that surround them have offered sustainable prospects for the future." Later, Singal, Kothari, and Dollinger presented a review of current eco-friendly practices and made constructive suggestions for the future. It is a conceptual paper worthy of reading.

From the hospitality perspective, Kim, Kim, and Kim explored corporate social responsibility in restaurant settings. Going beyond conceptual abstracts, they have provided real world examples from the restaurant industry. This paper discusses

"CSR case exemplars in restaurant settings."Considering the important role played by hotels in sustainability, de-Miguel-Molina, de-Miguel-Molina, Segarra-Oña and Santamarina-Campos explain "how to detect the value proposition of hotels by analysing the value offered by luxury hotels in the Seychelles."

The idea of extending sustainability to the country club industry sounds almost like an oxymoron. But Cichy, Cha, Kim, and Kim present a well-articulated case for sustainability for the country club industry with numerous industry examples and a conceptual map for country club managers. It is a good example of extending sustainability to a new area that is not known for being green.

From the tourism perspective, Chen explains how a simple love story blossomed into a major regional tourist attraction. Ruby Falls of Tennessee, USA, is striving to become not only a regional attractions but a truly sustainable regional attraction. Moving on to the Mediterranean coast line, Cervelló-Royo and Peiró-Signes describe the impact of tourism on the coastline of Spain and present constructive suggestions to achieve a balance between economic incentives for growth and the need for sustainability for future generations. Staying on the theme of protecting our ocean lines, Silverman delves into the topic of cruise lines and their responsibility "for ensuring that the company and fleet complied with safety and environmental regulations and policies." Later in the book, Camillo, Miguzzi, Presenza, and Holt describe a microdestination and its struggle to balance among the need for economic growth, maintaining the purity of the nature, water, and the coastline and the needs of the locals for a good quality of life. As they describe, "Results show that the quality of the environment, its uniqueness and integrity are of greatest satisfaction for all three destinations and are key to maintaining tourist satisfaction." Continuing on this theme, Fernández, Canós-Darós, and Santandreu-Mascarell, describe the case of heritage tourism and the need for controlled growth to preserve the historic monuments for future generations.

Moving into the arena of public policy, Delchet-Cochet, Delecolle, Goudeau, and Dornier investigated the role certifications in promoting sustainable tourism. In France, AFNOR Certification was introduced in 2010, and it "….consists in four major commitments: involving and respecting local people in the development process, minimizing the environmental impact, being customer friendly and applying to oneself what is recommended to others. The aim of this study is to evaluate the impact of this certification on tour-operators."

Putting all together, Auletta and Helena Jaén, scholars from Venezuela, were able to blend hospitality and tourism as a part of a master plan for a Caribbean Island of Dominican Republic. They describe a grand vision for this island with sustainability in the heart of it. As they describe, "The overall Tropicalia's sustainability approach is guided by the ten UN Global Compact principles and the concept of shared value creation."

In summary, this book presents a comprehensive view of sustainability from various aspects of hospitality and tourism. Studies range from restaurants, hotels, country clubs, resorts, heritage tourism, microtourism, resort development, public policy, responsible coastline development, slow tourism, to a regional destination tourism. The cases and articles selected for this book are truly global in nature with research contexts that covered Asia, Europe, Latin America, and North America. We have considered uniqueness of research methodologies while selecting articles for this book to include ethnographic studies, case studies, research articles, empirical papers, conceptual papers, and review papers.

We sincerely thank the authors for patiently working with us in making the necessary revisions. We are indebted to the invaluable contributions they made to this book. Most importantly, we can't thank Dr. Mahmood Khan enough for encouraging us to pursue this project, and Mr. Ashish Kumar of Apple Academic Press for his incredible patience in working with authors' copyright forms and the revisions. Many a time, we received emails from him Sunday nights after 10.00 PM—thanks Ashish. We truly appreciate the staff of the AAP for their cooperation and assistance in this project.

H. G. Parsa
Vijaya "Vi" Narapareddy
Senior Editors

CHAPTER 1

CAN ECO-STANDARDS AND CERTIFICATION CREATE COMPETITIVE ADVANTAGE FOR A LUXURY RESORT?

N. DARNALL and M. B. MILSTEIN

Doctoral Program Director, School of Public Affairs
Associate Professor of Management and Public Policy, School of Public Affairs & School of Sustainability, Arizona State University, 411 N Central Avenue, Suite 400, Phoenix AZ 85004-0687, +1 602.496.0445, E-mail: ndarnall@asu.edu

CONTENTS

Earlier versions of this case were awarded The Case Association's Best First Case, in addition to the oikos Sustainability Case Writing Competition's Honorable Mention. The original case (and instructor's manual) were published as Darnall N., Milstein M.B. 2014. Damaí *Lovina Villas: can eco-standards and certification create competitive advantage for a luxury resort? Case Research Journal 34(3), 1-20.*

1.1   INTRODUCTION

Glenn Knape, general manager of Damaí Lovina Villas, wandered the small luxury hotel's grounds looking out over the property's rice paddy fields located on the island of Bali, Indonesia. His gaze was drawn to the property's gardens full of organic produce destined for the resort's restaurant. He turned to see the hotel's outdoor spa, which was surrounded by waterfalls that captured and reclaimed fertile topsoil for use by neighboring farms. In the four years since his arrival in 2002, Knape had strived to make Damaí more sustainable by building on his experience as food service manager at the 2000 Sydney Olympics. The experience had taught him how to promote high quality service delivery and enhance operational efficiency through waste reduction. In applying that knowledge to Damaí, Knape introduced significant changes that had made the resort more efficient than many of its competitors. Additionally, many of his innovative initiatives – from sourcing food to preventing erosion – were benefitting employees and the local community in ways he had not anticipated.

Now, in 2006, Knape wondered whether his efforts to address a host of social and environmental issues could be leveraged to brand Damaí as a "green" hotel to improve its competitiveness. Toward that end, Knape considered whether participating in a voluntary environmental program (VEP) would help Damaí gain external recognition for the hotel's sustainability efforts and improve revenues. These programs used standards and certification to improve business' environmental performance, and had become increasingly popular in Europe, Asia, the United States (US), and his own native Australia. But Knape wondered whether Damaí's existing sustainability practices would need to be expanded significantly to qualify the hotel for membership in those programs. He also questioned whether the programs were worth the investment, and if they would persuade additional guests to stay at the hotel. Moreover, if he chose to participate in a VEP, he had questions about which one (or which combination) might offer Damaí the greatest benefits.

1.2   DAMAÍ LOVINA VILLAS & RESTAURANT

Damaí Lovina Villas & Restaurant was situated 3.2 km from Lovina Beach on the northern part of Bali, Indonesia (see Exhibit 1.1) among spice plantations, tropical jungles, and terraced mountainsides. Secluded on a hillside, views from the hotel stretched from the former Balinese capital, Singaraja, in the east to the volcanoes on the neighboring island of Java in the west. A panorama of jungle and hills lay to the south, and to the north was the hotel's eternity pool that seemed to spill into the ocean below. The hotel's motto was "hard to find, hard to leave." The property consisted of 8 romantic villas with 57 hotel staff to pamper its guests.

EXHIBIT 1.1   Island of Bali and Damaí Lovina Villas[a]

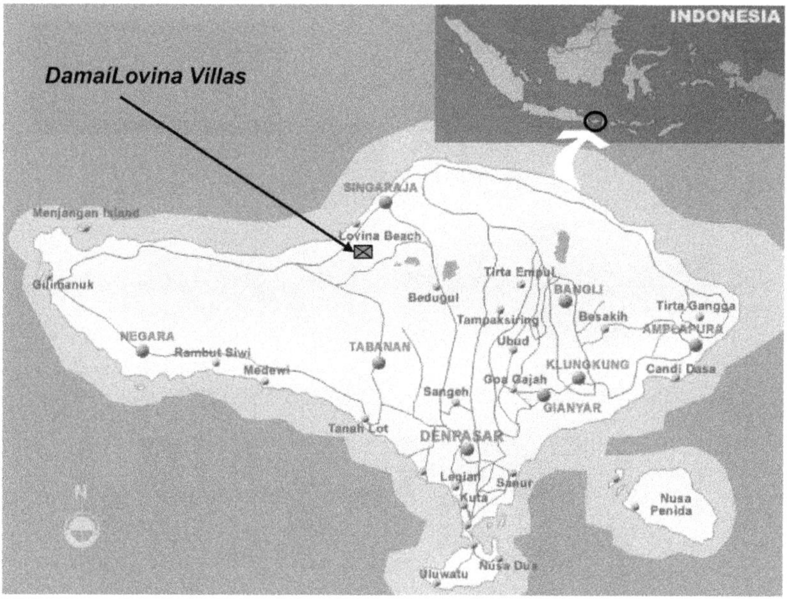

[a]Source: http://www.retire-asia.com/qvbali.shtml, with permission, and adapted by the authors.

Upon check in, guests were treated to welcome drinks, a 10-min massage, sparkling wine, fresh exotic fruit, and a bouquet of tropical flowers. Villas were furnished with four-post beds, handcrafted furniture, and a sunken lounge with a floor-level dining table (see Exhibit 1.2). Hand woven local textiles hung on guest room walls. Freshly cut flowers from the grounds were placed in the rooms daily. Bathrooms featured private outdoor showers in a garden setting, whirlpools, and massage tables for in-room spa treatments. Guests also had the option of receiving spa treatments at two private outdoor "bales" with views of rice paddies and waterfalls.

EXHIBIT 1.2   Damaí Lovina Villas & Restaurant[a]

DamaiLovina Restaurant and Bar   Pool-side dining

In-room dining   Organic restaurant cuisine

Guest bed, natural linens & mosquito netting Garden bath, organic soaps & natural whirlpool
[a]Source: Hotel documents, with permission, and author photos.

Damaí's open-air dining room and restaurant was one of the hotel's foremost features. Fodor's wrote that the restaurant was "not to be missed under any circumstances" [1]. Similarly, Rough Guide claimed the restaurant was "the most exquisite gourmet dining experience in northern Bali, if not the Entire Island" [2]. Daily menus were created based on available spices and seasonal organic produce from local markets and the hotel's own private gardens. Dinner typically consisted of five set courses. Meals were designed with a creative flair and a strong focus on presentation. That attention to detail kept most hotel guests dining at the hotel rather than venturing into one of Lovina Beach's many cafes and bistros. The hotel offered spa treatments that were exclusive to hotel guests. It also arranged daily excursions for guests to snorkel, dive, golf, and shop, in addition to programs for guests to learn Balinese cooking, yoga, meditation, and Tai Chi. Damaí's target guest was the urban professional. Guests came from all parts of the world, however, most traveled from Western Europe and the US. Many visitors were honeymooners or couples celebrating other special occasions. With 8 villas, Damaí's maximum occupancy was 16 guests, and about 39 percent were repeat visitors. Most guests booked their stays using either an Internet search engine (e.g., Expedia.com, Hotels.com) or the hotel website.

Room sales accounted for approximately 40 percent of Damaí's total revenues (see Exhibit 1.3, which summarizes Damaí's revenues and costs). The restaurant's food and beverage sales accounted for approximately 43 percent of the hotel's revenues. While guests from other hotels sometimes dined at Damaí's restaurant, restaurant revenues from outside guests were negligible (<2%). Spa treatments accounted for approximately 7 percent of total revenues and excursions and other hotel programs accounted for the remaining 10 percent. Damaí's average annual costs of operations were approximately 40 percent of total revenues.

EXHIBIT 1.3 Damaí's Revenues and Operating Costs[a]

Occupancy	Revenues					Costs
	Rooms	**Restaurant**	**Spa**	**Excursions**	**TOTAL**	
	40%	**43%**	**7%**	**10%**	**100%**	
65%	$306,053	$329,006	$53,559	$76,513	$765,131	$306,052
70%	$329,595	$354,315	$57,679	$82,399	$823,988	$329,595
75%	$353,138	$379,623	$61,799	$88,284	$882,844	$353,138
80%	$376,680	$404,931	$65,919	$94,170	$941,700	$376,680
85%	$400,223	$430,239	$70,039	$100,056	$1,000,556	$400,222
90%	$423,765	$455,547	$74,159	$105,941	$1,059,413	$423,765
95%	$447,308	$480,856	$78,279	$111,827	$1,118,269	$447,308
100%	$470,850	$506,164	$82,399	$117,713	$1,177,125	$470,850

[a]All figures in USD. Calculations assumed hotel was open all year. Nonroom revenue sources grew proportionally to occupancy. Average occupancy was 65 percent. Cost was 40 percent of total revenue. Nonhotel guests accounted <2 percent of restaurant revenues and were not included in the calculations. Spa services and excursions were only available to hotel guests.

The hotel's strong operating margins were bolstered by Bali's low cost of labor and Damaí's compensation structure. A good paying wage for a waiter was about $350 per month, and this wage could sustain a family of four with no additional income. Gardeners and cleaning staff were paid less. Knape's salary was less than Western standards because of market factors, but also because the hotel provided him with on-site accommodations, transportation, and meals. Food production costs in Bali were also quite low (again because of low labor costs), and Damaí's on-site gardens reduced the hotel's food costs even further. All these factors, in addition to Damaí's strong emphasis on operational efficiency, contributed to the hotel's overall profitability.

In spite of its strong margins, Damaí's average occupancy rate was only 65 percent. Knape therefore was eager to improve this rate. He hoped that the hotel's sustainability initiatives might be a vehicle to brand Damaí as a sustainable retreat, which might, in turn, improve occupancy and increase revenue. Knape believed that no other hotel in Bali offered Damaí's level of environmentally friendly experience and services. He knew that those that had come close lacked the hotel's luxury offerings and were recognized largely as "backpacker" hotels that were frequented by budget-minded eco-travelers, who were not Damaí's core customer. Hotels that offered amenities rivaling Damaí's—Alila Ubud, Puri Bagus, and Matahari Beach Resort—were significantly larger, and thus lacked the same level of intimacy as Damaí. Damaí's competitors also had higher room prices (see Exhibit 1.4). Only one of these competitors, PuriBagus, was located in Lovina. Other smaller Lovina hotels, while significantly cheaper, could not compare toDamaí for comfort. Damaí therefore occupied a unique niche of being the only boutique luxury hotel in Lovina.

Damaí's website (www.damai.com) was the primary vehicle for marketing the hotel's various sustainability efforts. The website directed environmentally conscious customers to an "organic resort" link to learn about the hotel's sustainability vision. Potential guests were guided to a statement describing the hotel's organic restaurant. There was no additional information about the hotel's sustainability activities on the website.

EXHIBIT 1.4   Competitor Hotels[a]

| | HOTEL | | | |
Characteristic	Damaí Lovina Villas	PuriBagus Lovina	Alila	Matahari Beach Resort
City	Lovina Beach (2 mi)	Lovina Beach	Ubud	Pemutaran
Region	North Bali	North Bali	Central Bali	Northwest Bali
Number of Rooms	8	40	56	32
Room Rates[b]				
Superior	$150	$183	$200–315	$225–306
Deluxe	$165	$256	$230–333	$355–564
Additional high season cost	–	$25/room	$30/room	10%

EXHIBIT 1.4 *(Continued)*

	HOTEL			
Characteristic	Damaí Lovina Villas	PuriBagus Lovina	Alila	Matahari Beach Resort
Breakfast included?	✓	✓	✓	✓
Spa facilities?	✓	✓	✓	✓
Organic focus?	✓	–	–	–
Sustainability focus?	✓	–	–	–
VEP Participation?	–	–	Green Globe Affiliate	–

[a]As of July 6, 2006.
[b]Rates were based on double occupancy, exclusive of 21 percent tax and service fees. All figures in USD.

1.3 POSITIONING DAMAÍ'S AS A GREEN BRAND

As Knape became interested in potentially leveraging Damaí's sustainability investments to build brand awareness and drive revenues, he began to look into how sustainability was being marketed in the hotel industry. By 2006, 16 percent of consumers in Europe, Asia and the US showed a strong preference to purchase goods and services from eco-friendly businesses, and indicated they were willing to pay price premiums for these goods and services [3]. Additionally, 25 percent of consumers were committed to achieving personal health, and while not committed to environmental concerns, sought out products and services that were perceived as health-conscious.

Knape learned that in response, many hotels were putting forward claims that they were environmentally friendly. However, the lack of verifiable information was creating opportunities for businesses to disclose misleading information about their environmental status or display superficial or insincere concern for the environment. This deception prompted the US Federal Trade Commission (FTC) in 2006 to consider fast-tracking review of its 1998 regulations on green marketing. The FTC saw the largely unregulated area of "green advertising" as being riddled with misinformation [4]. Misleading information also caused consumers with a strong preference for purchasing eco-friendly goods and services to distrust hotels' green marketing claims.

For instance, by 2006, 10 percent of all environmentally misleading claims were attributable to the travel/vacation industry [5]. Similarly, a 2005 survey by Ipsos

Mori indicated that 4 out of 5 consumers believed companies pretended to be ethical just to sell more products and services [6]. Because of their distrust, consumers were less likely to act on companies' unsubstantiated sustainability claims, and often avoided purchasing their products and/or services altogether [7].

Nongovernmental organizations had responded to these market conditions by developing a range of voluntary environmental programs (VEPs) to inform potential guests about hotels' sustainability activities. A VEP is any program, code, agreement or commitment that encouraged organizations to voluntarily reduce their environmental impacts *beyond* that required by the environmental regulatory system [8]. VEPs fostered environmental improvements by way of environmental standards and certification. By 2006, more than a dozen VEPs targeted the hotel industry, with a handful of those extending membership to small-scale Indonesia hotels.

Knape determined that the most widely known programs were: Best Green Hotels, Eco Lodge, Green Globe 21, Green Hotel Initiative, and ISO 14001 (see Exhibits 1.5–1.9). While each of these VEPs shared the common goal of using environmental standards to identify and promote environmentally superior hotels, Knape noticed that there was significant variation among their sustainability requirements. VEPs also offered varying levels of credibility for their sustainability approach, in that most VEPs required hotels to self-report their adherence to program guidelines while others required third-party certification of participants, which enhanced the legitimacy of member hotels' environmental claims [8]. For example, participation in the Best Green Hotels program (Exhibit 1.5) required that participating hotels evaluate their environmental performance across 29 "green" attributes, whereas participants in CERES' Green Hotel Initiative completed a longer "Best Practice Survey." Best Green Hotels (Exhibit 1.5), Eco Lodge (Exhibit 1.6), and CERES' Green Hotel Initiative (Exhibit 1.7), all asked member hotels to self-assess their environmental performance. By contrast, Green Globe (Exhibit 1.8) and ISO 14001 (Exhibit 1.9) relied on independent third parties to verify members' environmental practices.

EXHIBIT 1.5   Best Green Hotels[a]
The Best Green Hotels website described itself as providing participating lodging properties with the opportunity to demonstrate commitment to the environment and greening of the hospitality industry. By participating in the program, hotels identified themselves as being sustainable and provided specific information about what environmental action they have taken. Participating hotels were included in an online database that was searchable by location and other identifiers. Registration was free. Hotels used an online submission form to provide information about their environmental activities. Responses were then summed and ranked based on the number of "green" attributes they designate. Between 1 and 6 green triangles were assigned to participating hotels to indicate their level of "greenness." A rating of 6 indicated that a hotel had all the green attributes deemed important by Best Green Hotels.

Participation Survey

No: X   Yes: ✓   Unknown: ?   Promised but not provided: #

	X ✓ ? #		X ✓ ? #
Towel Program	OOOO	Fresh Air	OOOO
Sheet Program	OOOO	Allergies	OOOO
Cotton Towels/Sheets	OOOO	Nonsmoking Rooms	OOOO
		Environmental Cleaning	OOOO
Alternative energy	OOOO	Water Conservation	OOOO
Maintenance for Conservation	OOOO	Xeric Garden	OOOO
Energy Conservation	OOO	Gray-Water Recycling	OOO
Bulk Soap & Amenities	OOOO	Recyclable Disposables	OOOO
Bonus	OOOO	Compostable Disposables	OOOO
Newspaper Program	OOOO	Durable Service Items	OOOO
Composting	OOOO	Guestroom Recycling Bins	OOOO
Organic Food Served	OOOO	Hotel Recycling Bins	OOOO
Eco-friendly Food Served	OOOO	Donations to Charity	OOOO
Promote "Greenness" in PR	OOO	Conference Center/Rooms[b]	OOOO
Educate Staff to "Green"	OOOO	Transportation[b]	OOOO
Educate Guests to "Green"	OOOO	Fitness Center[b]	OOOO
Participate in "Green" Program(s)	OOOO	Internet[b]	OOO

[b]The nongreen (business related) attributes are not included in the rating system.

Best Green Hotels Rating System

- **1 green triangle**—▲ = 1-4 checks
- **2 green triangles**—▲▲ = 5-9 checks
- **3 green triangles**—▲▲▲ = 10-15 checks
- **4 green triangles**—▲▲▲▲ = 16-22 checks
- **5 green triangles**—▲▲▲▲▲ = 23-28 checks
- **6 green triangles**—▲▲▲▲▲▲ = 29 checks

Bali Participants

Risata Bali Resort & Spa, Tuban

Bali Hilton International, Nusa Dua

Udayana Eco Lodge, Denpasar

Melia Bali Villas & Spa Resort, Nusa Dua

Melia Benoa, Tanjung

Le Meridien Nirwana Golf and Spa Resort, Kedri

[a]Source: http://www.bestgreenhotels.com, July 6, 2006

EXHIBIT 1.6   Eco Lodge[a]

Eco Lodge website described participating properties as being in harmony with their surrounding environment and utilizing local businesses and labor. The program characterized member hotels as being generally in remote locations but still often luxurious and always comfortable. Eco Lodge reported that most participating hotels celebrate and preserve native vegetation in their gardens and are usually good spots for watching wildlife. Staying at one offers guests' easy contact with local people and the opportunity to become familiar with their traditional way of life, and guests can take part in sponsored activities that are low-impact on the environment. The program described itself as being designed to promote environmental protection through education of guests and staff, recycling of water and waste as well as efficient use of electricity, solar heating, rainwater, and composting. A lodge was considered an "eco-hotel" when it fulfilled the six main components of ecotourism, namely that it:

— Depended on the natural environment
— Was ecologically sustainable
— Was proven to contribute to conservation
— Featured an environmental training program
— Incorporated cultural considerations
— Provided a net economic return to the local community.

Participation involved hoteliers self-registering their property. Once the application was approved, the property would appear on the Eco Lodge website. Eco Lodge allowed owners of hotels to reach potential customers through its searchable website featuring over 620 retail travel agencies. Eco Lodge also had an agreement with over 670 travel agencies (employing over 7000 travel agents and independent contractors). Properties listed on the website were networked to all participating travel agencies. The travel agents then promoted these properties to their clients. Travel agents contacted the property owners directly about bookings.

Listing properties on the Eco Lodge website was free. Hotel owners paid 10 percent commission on accommodation charged (exclusive to sales tax) to Eco Lodge for each sale as a result of the lead received from its website. If a travel agent booked a client, the travel agent collected 10 percent commission on accommodation charge (exclusive to sales tax) directly from the property owner. In this case, the hotel did not pay an Eco Lodge commission (Eco Lodge had a separate arrangement with travel agents in the network).

Bali Participants

As of October 2005, no hotels in Bali were Eco Lodge Hotels.
[a]Source: http://www.infohub.com/Lodgings/eco_lodge/, July 6, 2006

EXHIBIT 1.7   Green Globe 21[a]

The Green Globe 21 (GG21) website characterized this VEP as a global benchmarking, certification, and improvement program that encouraged sustainable travel and tourism. GG21 was developed using Agenda 21 and principles for sustainable development, which were endorsed by 182 Heads of State at the United Nations Rio de Janeiro Earth Summit. Its website indicates that GG21's goals were to provide companies, communities, and consumers with a path to sustainable travel and tourism. Participation in GG21 was open to businesses across the travel and tourism industry, including accommodations.

According to GG21, its International Ecotourism Standard was designed to facilitate environmentally sustainable ecotourism by promoting a core set of principles which included:

— Conservation & management
— Design of environmentally sensitive products
— Energy efficiency
— Environmentally sensitive purchasing policies
— Hazardous substances
— Involving staff, customers, and communities in environmental issues
— Land-use planning and management
— Management of fresh-water resources
— Noise control
— Partnerships for sustainable development
— Protection of air quality
— Reuse and recycling
— Transport
— Waste minimization
— Waste-water management

GG21 provided participants a report indicating where the member hotel performance was positioned relative to environmental and social benchmarks. Each year advice was provided as to whether a participant had improved or maintained its performance based on the original benchmarking assessment.

The GG21 program involved three steps or levels—Affiliation, Benchmarking, and Certifying—which had to be renewed annually to maintain status. Hotels were encouraged to work toward higher levels and track progress in achieving targets over time, thus committing to a process of continual improvement. Operations had to meet all of the requirements of the relevant level and undergo an independent audit in order to use the GG21 logo. According to GG21, certification to the International Ecotourism Standard helped to provide ecotourism businesses with:

— A benchmark of their ecotourism performance through Ecotourism Benchmarking and encourages continual improvement of their product
— Recognition and reward for best practice performance through the Standard
— A blueprint for ecotourism development
— A means of recognizing genuine ecotourism product for primary consumers—the visitors—and secondary consumers such as local communities, protected area managers, and tour wholesalers
— A means of protecting local and global environmental quality
— Encouragement to contribute to local communities and conservation
— Improved profitability by being less wasteful and more efficient

Participation fees were based on the hotel's entry level into the program and the number of full time equivalent employees or the number of rooms (accommodation properties only) a hotel had. Hotels seeking Awareness (Affiliate) status paid $220 USD per site and 50 percent of the Benchmarking & Certification base costs. Benchmarking and Certification base fees were a function of hotel size. Micro hotels with <5 employees or <10 rooms pay $395 USD, small enterprises (<50 employees or <70 rooms) paid $695 USD. Large sites (>50 employees or >70 rooms) paid $1,610 USD. Benchmarking and Certification fees did not include the cost of onsite independent assessment for GG21 Certification, which typically cost $2000–$3000 (total) for large sized hotels.

BALI PARTICIPANTS

Level	Requirements	Participants
Affiliated	Required gathering information about sustainable tourism practices and principles and preparation of an Environmental and Social Sustainability Policy.	Alila Manggis Alila Ubud Amandari Amankila Bali Dynasty Resort Conrad Bali Resort & Spa Kayumanis Private Villas & Spa Maya Ubud Resort & Spa Nikko Bali Resort & Spa Novotel Coralia Benoa Bali Nusa Dua Beach Hotel & Spa Sanur Paradise Plaza Hotel & Suites Sofitel Seminyak Bali The Bale The Legian The Ritz Carlton Bali Resort & Spa The Westin Resort Nusa Dua Uma Ubud Waka Gangga

Bench- marked	Required an independent assessment of measurements against key indicators, the development of an Environmental and Social Sustainability Policy, and annual collection of measures in key environmental and social performance areas.	Discovery Kartika Plaza Hotel The Oberoi
Certified	Required implementation of an integrated Environmental Management System. The logo was only used once the operation has been successfully benchmarked AND passed an independent on-site assessment/ audit.	Bali Hilton International Melia Bali Villas and Spa Resort Meliá Benoa All-Inclusive Resort Meliá Purosani Hotel Udayana Lodge

[a]Source: http://www.greenglobe21.com/, July 6, 2006

EXHIBIT 1.8   CERES' Green Hotel Initiative[a]

Launched in 2001, the Coalition for Environmentally Responsible Economies' (CERES') Green Hotel Initiative (GHI) was designed to catalyze the market demand for, and supply of, environmentally responsible hotel services. CERES was a worldwide coalition of environmental, investor, and advocacy groups working together for a sustainable future. Its network included a community of forward-looking companies and multinational corporations that endorsed CERES' codes of environmental conduct.

The goal of GHI was to raise awareness about environmental and social concerns in the hospitality industry and to encourage meeting planners and travel buyers to demand green services. According to the CERES website, GHI came about by collaborating with consumers and industry members, with the aim of demonstrating the economic savings that resulted from environmentally responsible operations and facility maintenance. The program was designed to address two major obstacles that typically frustrated hotel guests from communicating their preference for environmentally responsible hotel services: (1) a lack of information about environmental options and (2) a lack of time to research the environmental performance of hotels. While many guests were inclined to use green hotel services, they needed improved access to environmental information in order to include such considerations in their purchasing decisions.

GHI's goals were to:

— Educate the purchasers of hotel services, particularly large buyers such as corporate meeting planners and travel buyers, about what they can ask from lodging providers
— Create vehicles for these purchasers to express their demand for these services
— Provide mechanisms for hotels to communicate their environmental performance

To participate in GHI, hotels completed the online Best Practice Survey, which allowed potential guests to assess a hotel's environmental performance. There was no cost to hotels to follow GHI practices. While CERES did not actively promote participants, because no information was collected on hotels which completed the GHI Best Practices Survey, hotels were encouraged to self-promote their adherence to GHI goals.

Bali Participants

Because CERES did not track participating hotels, Knape was uncertain how many Bali hotels (if any) were following GHI practices.

[a]Source: http://www.ceres.org/industryprograms/ghi.php, July 6, 2006

EXHIBIT 1.9   ISO 14001[a]

ISO 14001 was a certified standard for environmental management systems (EMS) that was developed in 1996 by the International Organization for Standardization (ISO). Any type of organization could adopt an ISO 14001 EMS. In addition to hotels, government offices, administrative companies, and manufacturing facilities could certify to ISO 14001. Because of this broad applicability, ISO 14001 had quickly become one of the most widely recognized environmental certification program in the world. According to its website, more than 129,000 companies worldwide had certified to ISO 14001.

A requirement for ISO 14001 certification was the adoption of an externally audited EMS, which involved the adoption of a formal management system that required companies to evaluate and manage the environmental aspects of their operations. Sustainability management systems broadened this objective by also considering the organization's impacts to the community. Both management systems emphasized compliance with environmental regulations, involvement of external stakeholders in environmental activities, and pollution prevention.

To adopt ISO 14001, businesses were required to undertake six steps and commit to continuously lowering the environmental impact of their goods, products, and services:

— Develop an environmental policy
— Assess environmental aspects and impacts
— Establish objectives and targets
— Develop an implementation strategy
— Monitor and correct for problems
— Undergo management review

While many companies had employed EMSs for years, ISO 14001 was the first international standard certified by an independent third-party auditor.[1] According to ISO's website, most companies that certified to ISO 14001 reported that obtaining registration was the main reason for their interest in ISO 14001, because for the first time they could market their environmental management processes as a means to reach environmentally conscious purchasers.

Certification required that businesses hire independent external auditors to review and verify that their EMS conformed to the ISO 14001 standard. Adoption of an ISO 14001 EMS cost between $270 and $1,370 USD per employee, depending on the extent to which the company had already instituted proactive environmental and continual improvement procedures prior to implementing a formalized EMS and seeking external certification [10].

Bali Participants
Because ISO did not have a central list of ISO 14001 certified companies, Knape was uncertain how many Bali hotels (if any) were ISO 14001.
[a]Source: http://www.iso.org/iso/en/iso9000-14000/index.html, July 6, 2006

Knape also observed that there was significant variation in VEP costs. For instance, participating in Best Green Hotels and CERES' Green Hotel Initiative was free. Eco Lodge charged a percentage of bookings through its website. Green Globe 21 had a graduated fee system that began at $220 per year, whereas ISO 14001 certification cost between $270–$1,370 USD per employee, depending on the extent to which the business had instituted pollution prevention and product stewardship procedures prior to implementing the environmental management system (EMS).

The gold standard in the hotel industry was the certified eco-hotels located in Costa Rica, a country which had gained an international reputation for sustainability. Costa Rica had more than 75,000 acres of natural parks, and 87 percent of tourists reported that these parks were the most important place to visit in the country [9]. Many lodges and hotels in Costa Rica had participated in a third-party certified VEP called Certification for Sustainable Tourism. Any hotel within the country could have participated in the VEP, however, hotels that demonstrated highest verifiable levels of superior environmental performance had built reputations as sustainability havens, and eco-minded tourists were paying price premiums of $30 above other hotels to stay in them [9]. However, travelers to Costa Rica might have differed significantly compared to travelers to other countries. For instance, travelers to India indicated that while they preferred to patron more eco-conscious lodging, they were not willing to pay extra to do so [10].

In considering the prospect of Damaí receiving premium prices associated with VEP participation, Knape wondered whether Bali could command a price premium similar to Costa Rican hotels or whether Damaí's patrons were more like those traveling to India, who was unwilling to pay a price premium. Bali lacked the nature preserves that had drawn so many eco-minded tourists to Costa Rica in the first place. Additionally, Knape perceived that nonluxury eco-hotels appealed to budget-minded travelers in a way that a luxury hotel might not. Perhaps a segment of the market would have been likely to seek out a visit to a luxury eco-hotel, but would the individuals comprising this segment be willing to pay a premium to stay at Damaí? Would VEP membership influence their decision for selecting a hotel?

Knape thought VEPs might be a way to establish Damaí as a green brand to overcome consumer skepticism. But given the variations in VEP requirements, he decided to conduct an internal audit of the hotel's sustainability practices to better understand the procedure. Coincidentally, about that time, a friend and sustainability consultant persuaded Knape to implement his internal audit with the assistance of a broader sustainability framework (see Exhibit 1.10). The consultant explained to Knape that the framework would encourage him to assign each of Damaí's individual activities into one of four sustainability categories —cost/risk reduction, reputation/legitimacy, innovation/repositions, and vision/opportunity framing. In viewing the categories, Knape saw that companies which tended to emphasize cost/risk reduction and/or reputation/legitimacy were in a good position to address present day environmental concerns related to existing services. But they still could be vulnerable to unanticipated shifts in the operating environment, consumer preferences, etc. On the other hand, hotels which placed greater emphasis on innovation/repositioning and vision/opportunity framing tended to have stronger sustainability visions but lacked the foundational capabilities or analytical skills necessary to implement that vision. Knape further observed that hotels focused internally were more inwardly concerned with activities they could control, which could lead to myopia and a lack consideration for critical external constituencies. On the other hand, hotels that fixated externally were more concerned with stakeholder concerns and external opinions, and could fail to nurture their internal capabilities. These hotels, Knape surmised, were especially vulnerable to external claims of "green washing."

Knape saw that the framework would also help him think about the activities the hotel did (or could do). By utilizing the framework, Knape hoped to determine whether Damaí's sustainability activities were balanced both in terms of their focus on short- and long-term goals, and the degree to which these goals engaged internal or external stakeholders. Finally, the framework would encourage Knape to consider the organizational value of the hotel's sustainability activities, and what skills or capabilities would be associated with each category.

EXHIBIT 1.10   Sustainable Value Portfolio and Definitions

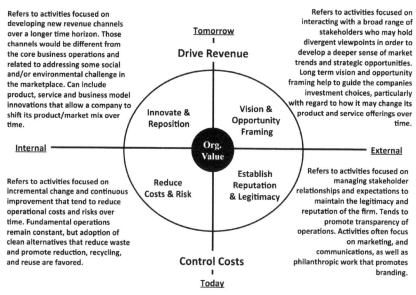

Refers to activities focused on developing new revenue channels over a longer time horizon. Those channels would be different from the core business operations and related to addressing some social and/or environmental challenge in the marketplace. Can include product, service and business model innovations that allow a company to shift its product/market mix over time.

Refers to activities focused on interacting with a broad range of stakeholders who may hold divergent viewpoints in order to develop a deeper sense of market trends and strategic opportunities. Long term vision and opportunity framing help to guide the companies investment choices, particularly with regard to how it may change its product and service offerings over time.

Tomorrow

Drive Revenue

Innovate & Reposition

Vision & Opportunity Framing

Org. Value

Internal   External

Reduce Costs & Risk

Establish Reputation & Legitimacy

Refers to activities focused on incremental change and continuous improvement that tend to reduce operational costs and risks over time. Fundamental operations remain constant, but adoption of clean alternatives that reduce waste and promote reduction, recycling, and reuse are favored.

Refers to activities focused on managing stakeholder relationships and expectations to maintain the legitimacy and reputation of the firm. Tends to promote transparency of operations. Activities often focus on marketing, and communications, as well as philanthropic work that promotes branding.

Control Costs

Today

Adapted from Hart & Milstein (2003), "Creating Sustainable Value"

Knape was keen to apply the portfolio framework to determine how Damaí's various activities linked to value creation. He also believed that the results of the portfolio analysis would offer a basis upon which to compare Damaí's sustainability program to the activities required by the various VEPs, to determine what additional activities the hotel would need in order to qualify for VEP participation.

1.4   DAMAÍ'S SUSTAINABILITY PROGRAM

Knape began inventorying Damaí's sustainability program and noticed that it focused on three areas: organic and locally sourced services, operational efficiency, and employees/community.

1.4.1   ORGANIC AND LOCALLY SOURCED SERVICES

By 2006, Damaí was growing approximately 80 percent of its organic produce in the gardens surrounding the hotel. What Damaí could not grow onsite was purchased from local farmers who also utilized organic farming principles.

Knape made a concerted effort to purchase the restaurant's supply from local farmers rather than farmers in South Bali or the neighboring Indonesian islands.

Wines and cheeses were examples of two exceptions to the restaurant's "buy local" policy. Bali had only two wineries—Hatten Wines and the organic Bali Fruit Drink. The restaurant stocked wines from both producers, but neither were of premium quality. There also were no cheese makers on Bali. As such, Knape imported wines and cheeses from Australia. The hotel had not established an organic purchasing policy for these imported food items.

Damaí's villas contained furniture made of plantation grown wood from neighboring Java that was handcrafted in Bali. Stains were organically based. Cotton bed linens and towels were woven with natural—but not organically grown—cotton. Guests were provided with organically produced massage oils, perfumes, soaps, lotions, and shampoos developed especially for Damaí. Knape purchased all body products in bulk and placed them in refillable ceramic dispensers in guest rooms. In partnership with a local nonprofit, Damaí had also developed a line of spa products, which consisted of organically produced natural botanicals.

Knape maintained a chemical free policy by using nontoxic organic sanitizers. These products were cheaper than conventional chemical-based detergents and sanitizers. In its gardens, pests were managed using biological controls. Through strategic planting of crops, indigenous insects helped limit the population of unwanted insects. Pests were also controlled by using botanicals made of citronella and lemongrass. Inside guest rooms, mosquito nettings canopied the beds.

All of the hotel's natural wastes were composted, including pre- and postpreparation food scraps, spoilage, excess product, cooking oil, paper, flowers, and natural packaging (e.g., crates and boxes). Animal-based wastes were treated using nontoxic and environmentally safe microorganisms, which reduced bacteria development that created odor. The treated wastes were then composted and used as fertilizer in Damaí's gardens, which had increased crop production by 20 percent.

1.4.2 IMPROVING OPERATIONAL EFFICIENCY

To increase operational efficiency, Knape had focused on energy and water conservation, in addition to reducing solid waste generation. As a first step, Knape had swapped the property's halogen lighting and 40-watt incandescent bulbs with compact fluorescent lights (CFL), which consumed a quarter of the energy and lasted up to 10 times longer. Garden lights were changed from 100 volts to 12 volts by purchasing a new transformer. Knape installed one-way valves and sensors in the hotel's water system so that the hotel's water pumps would operate only when water pressure fell below a specified threshold instead of operating 24 hrs a day. Hotel staff lowered shades in the guest rooms during the hottest times of the day to help keep the rooms cooler. By implementing these measures, Damaí had reduced its electric bill by 65 percent.

The hotel's practice of paying a Denpasar contractor to drive to Lovina, pick up the hotel's solid waste, and transport the waste back to Denpasar (which hosted

Bali's only landfill, 3.5 hrs away by car) had proved very costly. Knape decided to send plastic and bottle containers back to their respective (local) suppliers for reuse or recycling. Guest rooms contained drinking cups made of recycled glass rather than plastic or paper, and the restaurant used linen napkins and bamboo drinking straws that were washed and reused. Rather than using plastic waste bin liners (and since there was no local manufacturer of paper bags), the hotel found a reliable source for large unbleached paper envelopes. The staff cut off the tops of the envelopes and the remainder was used to line the waste bins. These natural fiber "bags" were composted with all other natural waste from guest rooms. Combined, these efforts eliminated the need to send solid waste to the Denpasar landfill.

Damaí did not heat its pool since the tropical temperatures kept it warm year-round. The pool's water was maintained at 1/7th the salinity of sea water to inhibit biological growth. Even so, it still required a 2 percent chlorine solution to further reduce algae development. To eliminate the need to purchase chlorine, Damaí switched to iodized water. The new system converted noniodized salt into pure chlorine. Once the chlorine oxidized dead bacteria and algae, it was recycled back into salt—ready to be converted to chlorine again. While the system was not chemical free, it was a closed loop process and eliminated stabilizers and calcium byproducts that were associated with conventional chlorine systems.

Damaí utilized a water recycling system that directed "gray water" from sinks and showers to on-site tanks. This wastewater was filtered through a series of tanks containing volcanic rock, porous rubber, and sand. Treated water was tested once a month by government officials who communicated to Knape that Damaí's water rating was the best in North Bali. Treated water was used in agricultural production. Even waste from the toilets, or "black water," was collected and treated using natural enzymes to break down the organic waste. Black water was then passed through a series of filters and reused in the hotel's fields. In aggregate, Damaí's water conservation efforts reduced hotel water use by 75 percent.

Permaculture was used to lower water consumption in hotel gardens and to increase healthy crops. It created a closed loop system by which Damaí's farmers collected leaves and other natural garden waste and distributed them among the crops. Like mulch, the natural waste reduced water evaporation. The permaculture also prevented weed growth and eventually become compost that nourished the fields. To further sustain its garden, Damaí's farmers allowed a portion of their crops to go to seed. In other instances, plants were grafted. The result of these efforts was high quality, high yield fruit and vegetable production, which had reduced Damaí's crop production costs by 90 percent.

In early 2006, Knape was in the process of installing a solar energy system with storage capacity. The first step in this conversion had begun in November 2005 when Damaí converted its hot water systems to solar power-based heating. A new solar electric system was anticipated to further reduce the hotel's electric costs. As the hotel moved all its electrical systems toward solar power, Knape anticipated that surplus electricity would be sold to the state-operated electricity authority, and yield a return on investment within 3 months.

The hotel's eight villas were not constructed with green design principles. The rooms, for example, lacked vents for natural air flow. As a consequence, guests had to rely exclusively on air conditioning for temperature control. Looking ahead, Knape hoped to renovate the villas so that they utilized natural thatching and venting to keep the rooms cool. While, the hotel's owner was reluctant to undertake the renovations, a new investor might change this, and some discussions were underway.

Knape did not promote Damaí's sustainability focus in guest rooms, restaurant, and gardens and did not seek to involve guests in activities such as optional linen reuse programs which had gained popularity in the US and European hotel industry. These efforts seemed to him unbefitting of Damaí's luxury status.

1.4.3   EMPLOYEES/COMMUNITY

Knape provided transportation, telephone service, and two meals per shift to Damaí employees. The hotel employed a doctor to address the health concerns of both the staff and their families. To accommodate the religious needs of its workers and their families, the hotel offered transportation for monthly visits to the region's largest temple. Private temples constructed on the hotel's grounds and communal temples in nearby villages met religious needs at other times.

Additionally, Knape had instituted a preferred purchasing policy with its hotel staff. Staff relatives made employee uniforms and guest room curtains. The hotel gave preference to hiring the staff's family when booking musical performances and traditional dances. Damaí did not have an official incentive program that encouraged continual improvement of the hotel's environmental and community practices; however departments that operated most efficiently were recognized with bonuses.

Related to the broader community, conventional farming practices in nearby villages had involved farmers burning their agricultural waste at the end of the growing season to generate ash that fertilized the land. However, burning impaired air quality and human health—an issue compounded by the hundreds of small farms that operated locally. Poor air quality also had a negative impact on tourism. In response, Damaí partnered with local farmers to teach them about composting their leftover plant material, and utilizing microorganisms to increase the pace of decomposition, thereby eliminating the need for burning.

Knape had also sought to address some of the environmental problems facing the fishing industry. Fish farms were common in North Bali and one of the biggest concerns was limiting the growth of blue/green algae. High algae growth produced harmful toxins, emitted strong sulfurous odors, and depleted dissolved oxygen in water causing fish to die. Conventional fishing methods typically relied on harmful chemicals to control algae development. These methods also limited Damaí's access to organically farmed fish. By encouraging fishermen to use microorganisms to temper blue/green algae growth and forego the need for harmful chemicals, fish farms were able protect their revenue streams while at the same time increase their availability of organically farmed fish.

Damaí was also working with local farmers and village leaders to reclaim eroded topsoil. Bali's terraced landscapes, coupled with monsoon rains, caused fertile topsoil to flow from the rice paddies and drain into the ocean. The topsoil loss prompted more farmers to rely on chemical fertilizers to grow their crops. As a means to address the issue, Damaí built a series of large rock wall filters in the river that ran through the hotel's property. The filters created a series of waterfalls, the base of which captured much of the topsoil lost from the seven villages surrounding the hotel. Damaí encouraged the local farms to reclaim their topsoil from the hotel pools to reduce the need for chemical fertilizers. Damaí's guests appreciated the waterfalls as a tranquil place to relax and enjoy nature.

Finally, Damaí had partnered with the area leaders to help them develop a fire preparedness strategy. Damaí was especially concerned about the lack of fire preparedness procedures because fires were commonly used in agricultural practices, and were one of the greatest threats to the community. Knape had collaborated with the fire department to write detailed fire procedures to ensure the safety of local residents and businesses.

1.5   NEXT STEPS

Moving forward, Knape faced three nested decisions to determine whether participating in a VEP could leverage Damaí's sustainability efforts to achieve the company's competitive goals of increasing guest occupancy and its related revenues. First, having undertaken his internal audit of Damaí's existing sustainability practices, he had to decide whether or not they would be enough to qualify for one (or more) of the five VEPs related to the hotel industry. Next, Knape had to decide whether the hotel needed to invest additional resources to qualify for VEP participation, and if so what investments were required. Finally, he needed to decide whether or not VEP participation would achieve Damaí's broader strategic objective to enhance its external profile, increase bookings, and lead to premium prices.

KEYWORDS

- **Ecotourism**
- **Sustainability branding**
- **Sustainability program**
- **Voluntary environmental program**

ENDNOTES

1. Foder's.; Foder's Bali and Lombok (first edition): Where to Stay, Eat, and Explore On and Off the Beaten Path, Smart Travel Tips from A to Z. New York: Foder's Travel Publications; **2001**.
2. Reader, L.; and Ridout, L.; Rough Guide to Bali & Lombok (fourth edition). London: Rough Guides; **2001**.
3. The Natural Marketing Institute.; Excerpts from the 2006 understanding the LOHAS market report. In: Environmental Management: Readings and Cases (Ed.) Russo, M. V., Los Angeles: Sage; **2008**.
4. Bastile, G.; and Skierka, K.; Greenwashing: A Perfect Storm. Bite Communications Group; **2008**. http://zicklin.baruch.cuny.edu/centers/zcci/downloads/greenwashing/bite-greenwashing-perfect-storm.pdf (accessed 25 July 2013).
5. Futerra Sustainability Communication. The Greenwash Guide. London, UK: Futerra Sustainability Communication; **2008**.
6. Rizkallah, E. G.; Brand-consumer relationship. *J. Bus. Eco. Res.* **2012**, *10*(6), 333–344.
7. Hall, E.; U.K. consumers catch companies committing "Green Murder." *Advertis. Age.* **2007**, *78*(40), 3–4.
8. Carmin, J.; Darnall, N.; and Mil-Homens, J.; Stakeholder involvement in the design of U.S. voluntary environmental programs: Does sponsorship matter? *Pol. Stud. J.*, **2003**, *31*, 527–543.
9. Rivera, J.; Assessing a voluntary environmental initiative in the developing world: The Costa Rican certification for sustainable tourism. *Pol. Sci.* **2002**, *35*, 333–360.
10. Darnall, N.; and Edwards, Jr. D.; Predicting the cost of environmental management system adoption: the role of capabilities, resources and ownership structure. *Strat. Manag. J.* **2006**, *27*(2), 301–320.

APPENDIX 1: INSTRUCTOR'S MANUAL

A1.1   CASE SUMMARY

Located in northern Bali, Damaí Lovina Villas and Restaurant was a boutique hotel with a generous staff to room ratio of 57:8 that ensured a guest's experience would be more personal, luxurious, and secluded than could be offered by the island's typical large-scale beach resorts. Damaí's general manager, Glenn Knape, wanted to strengthen the hotel's competitive position and increase utilization rates beyond the hotel's 65 percent occupancy. Knape wondered whether his prior efforts to address a host of social and environmental issues could be leveraged to brand Damaí as a "green" hotel and attract additional customers. Specifically, Knape was considering whether participating in a voluntary environmental program (VEP), which relied on eco-standards and certification, could leverage Damaí's sustainability efforts by increasing its external profile and guest bookings. Knape had to decide whether or not Damaí's existing sustainability practices would be enough to qualify for one of the VEPs under consideration. He also needed to decide whether the hotel had to invest additional resources to qualify for participation, and if so what those investments would be. At a more strategic level, he needed to decide whether membership in a VEP would achieve Damaí's competitive goals—to increase guest occupancy and its related revenues—and if so, which VEP (or combination of VEPs) would make the most sense?

A1.2   LEARNING OBJECTIVES & THEORETICAL FOUNDATIONS

The case facilitates classroom discussion in three areas of importance to management in general and sustainability in particular:

1. **Evaluate corporate sustainability options**. Businesses are presented with a host of challenges and opportunities when considering complex issues related to poverty, climate change, and ecosystem degradation. Increasingly, managers are being asked to consider these factors when developing their strategic business goals. The case allows students to consider what sustainability means in the context of a specific company, including the extent to which an organization focuses on issues related to value creation stemming from efficiency and productivity, reputation and legitimacy, innovation and repositioning, and strategic visioning opportunity framing. The case presents an assessment framework with these dimensions, which enables students (1) to learn how to evaluate a firm's environmental and social activities, (2) assess activities of various VEPs, and (3) compare the two to determine whether and how the company's programs align with the choices of VEPs under consideration.

   Going further, students can consider how some sustainability activities impact costs while others impact revenue, and whether investments in one or the other may be more or less likely to lead to greater financial outcomes (see suggested readings Hart & Milstein, 2003 and Kurapatskie & Darnall, 2013).

2. **Understand the strengths and limitations of VEPs and articulate a business case for VEP participation**. VEPs are becoming more prolific and are part of a larger trend toward standardization and certification. Increasingly, managers are faced with deciding whether the returns for participating in such programs are worth the investment. Specifically, many managers struggle to articulate the business case for VEP participation, because it is often unclear whether VEPs should be considered either a cost of doing business, a valuable marketing/branding opportunity, or an opportunity to establish strategic distinction in the marketplace. The case provides students with an opportunity to consider the merits and limitations of these programs from the perspective of a general manager who must consider the idiosyncratic nature of business competition for his business. It enables readers to assess managerial decisions related to standards and certification programs

and consider whether VEPs advance industry standardization, strategic competitive advantage, or both. In doing so, students can consider whether a business with distinct (sustainability) capabilities benefit from participating in programs with varying programmatic and conformance expectations (see suggested reading Darnall & Carmin, 2005).

3. **Evaluate managerial decisions from the perspective of a small firm in an emerging economy**. Much of the past decade of global economic and population growth has occurred in emerging economies. Firms from developing countries have targeted emerging economies for growth while successful firms in emerging economies are extending their global reach into developed countries. The case provides a rare opportunity to evaluate managerial decisions from the point of view of a small firm in an emerging economy where the operating environment can present unfamiliar challenges to the decision-maker steeped in Western business traditions. Particularly relevant for this case is that social and environmental issues are framed much differently in emerging economies where poverty, climate change, and ecosystem degradation directly impact the social, economic, and environmental resilience of people on a daily basis. The case encourages readers to consider the impacts of and different ways in which a company can approach these issues, including balancing the company's internal cost saving activities with activities that make meaningful contributions to community capacity and growth (see suggested reading Porter & Kramer, 2011).

A1.3   CLASSROOM UTILIZATION

The Damaí case may be employed in a core strategic management or marketing course at the MBA level (or a similar upper-level undergraduate class) to explore the issues around strategic differentiation and standardization and strategy-environment fit. It could also be employed in any one of a number of specialized business or tourism courses dealing with topics that include sustainable enterprise, corporate social responsibility, international management, hospitality or hotel management, and ecotourism.

Sample Teaching Plan for a 90 Min Session:
1. Distribution of case and discussion questions 2–7 days before class
2. Discussion of ecotourism and changing consumer preferences   10 min
3. Analysis of Damaí's sustainability strategy   15 min
4. Analysis of voluntary environmental programs   15 min
5. Evaluation of recommendations for Damaí   35 min
6. Summarize key learning objectives   10 min
7. Damaí update & wrap up   5 min

A1.4   SUGGESTED READINGS RELATED TO CASE

The following articles are strongly recommended for their ability to provide background information about the key themes and theories explored in the Damaí case. They may be useful for the instructor preparation and/or can be assigned to students in concert with the case.

— Darnall, N.; and Carmin, J.; Cleaner and greener? The signaling accuracy of U.S. voluntary environmental programs. *Pol. Sci.* **2005**, *38*(2–3), 71–90.

— Hart, S. L.; and Milstein, M. B.; Creating sustainable value. *Acad. Manag. Exec.* **2003**, *17*(2), 56–69.

— Hart, S. L.; and Milstein, M. B.; Global sustainability and the creative destruction of industry. *Sloan Manag. Rev.* **1999**, *41*(1), 23–33.

— Kurapatskie, B.; and Darnall, N.; Are some corporate sustainability activities associated with greater financial payoffs? *Bus. Strat. Environ.* **2013**, *11*(1), 49–61.

— Porter, M. E.; and Kramer, M. R.; Creating shared value. *Harvard Bus. Rev.* **2011**, *89*(1–2), 62–-77.

— Rivera, J.; Assessing a voluntary environmental initiative in the developing world: The Costa Rican certification for sustainable tourism. *Pol. Sci.* **2002**, *35*(4), 333–360.

For tourism management courses, the following articles are also recommended:

—Font, X.; and Tribe, J.; Promoting green tourism: the future of environmental awards. *Int. J. Tour. Res.* **2001**, *3*, 9–21.

—Perez-Salom, J. R.; Sustainable tourism: emerging global regional regulation. *Georgetown Int. Environ. Law Rev.* **2001**, *13*(4), 801–836.

A1.5   DISCUSSION QUESTIONS

In the case, general manager Glenn Knape faces a number of nested decisions to determine whether participating in a VEP could leverage Damaí's sustainability efforts to achieve the company's competitive goals—to increase guest occupancy and its related revenues. These decisions and the corresponding discussion questions are as follows:

1. Deciding whether or not Damaí's existing sustainability practices would be enough to qualify for one (or more) of the five VEPs related to the hotel industry.

    a. How balanced was Damaí's approach to generating value from sustainability?

    b. How balanced were the various VEPs under consideration to generating value from sustainability?

    c. What were the similarities and the differences between the hotel's activities and the various VEPs?

      d. If cost were not a consideration, which VEP(s) (if any) would you rec-
        ommend Knape pursue?

2. Deciding whether the hotel needed to invest additional resources to qualify
   for VEP participation, and if so what investments were required.

      a. What was the membership costs associated with participation in each
        VEP?

      b. Calculate Damaí's breakeven occupancy (the level of occupancy that
        Knape would need to realize in order to cover VEP participation costs).
        Next, calculate the percent increase above existing occupancy needed to
        cover VEP participation costs. Note that some VEPs will have a range of
        costs (e.g., Green Globe 21 affiliate, Green Globe 21 Certification, and
        ISO 14001).

      c. If participation in any given VEP led to a subsequent 20 percent increase
        in occupancy, would it cover the cost of Damaí's VEP participation?
        What if occupancy increased by only 5 percent?

3. Deciding whether or not VEP participation would achieve Damaí's broader
   strategic objective to leverage its sustainability efforts to enhance its external profile, increase bookings, and lead to premium prices.

      a. Should Knape expect that VEP participation will improve his ability to
        brand Damaí as a green hotel?

      b. Should Knape expect that VEP participation might increase bookings
        and potentially lead to premium prices?

      c. Are there other options Knape might consider leveraging Damaí's sus-
        tainability efforts?

A1.5.1   DECISION 1:

To understand whether or not Damaí's existing sustainability practices would be
enough to qualify for one of the VEPs under consideration, it is important to make
sense of the hotel's existing sustainability efforts. Managers often understand the
sustainability-related investments and activities they have undertaken over time, but
lack clarity on the strategic nature of those activities. The sustainable value framework presented in the case provides a way to organize Damaí's efforts.

A1.5.1.1   ASSIGNMENT (GIVEN PRIOR TO CLASS):

*Using case Exhibit 1.10, map Damaí's environmental and social activities to the
sustainable value framework by listing each of the hotel's sustainability activities
that are relevant to each quadrant. Next, separately map the activities of each VEP
(case Exhibits 1.5–1.9) onto the same framework. Finally, compare the two sets of
maps for similarities and differences.*

A1.5.1.2   ASSIGNMENT/CLASSROOM DISCUSSION QUESTIONS:

1a. How balanced was the hotel's approach to generating value from sustainability?

1b. How balanced were the various VEPs under consideration to generating value from sustainability?

1c. What were the similarities and the differences between the hotel's activities and the various VEPs?

1d. If cost were not a consideration, which VEP(s) (if any) would you recommend Knape pursue?

A1.5.1.3   CLASSROOM DISCUSSION:

1a. Damaí's Sustainability Profile
Figure A1.1 illustrates how the sustainable value framework can be used to evaluate Damaí's sustainability activities based on the definitions provided in Exhibit 1.10 of the case. The portfolio can be used to sort Damaí's environmental and social activities into four categories: cost/risk reduction, reputation/legitimacy, innovation/reposition, and vision/opportunity framing.

1. **Cost/Risk Reduction**—Through incremental improvements, Damaí had reduced costs and risks to become a more efficient hotel. Its focus on waste reduction and the adoption of cleaner alternatives—from energy consumption to water use—saved the business money, improved its environmental footprint, and boosted profits. Organic sanitizers and biological controls were purchased in lieu of more risky toxic chemicals.

2. **Reputation/Legitimacy**—By integrating value chain stakeholders into business processes, Knape was able to develop strong relationships with the extended families of staff and surrounding communities. These relationships, in turn, provided Damaí with unique resources that further enhanced guest experiences. Local materials purchasing, preferred purchasing programs with hotel staff, and supplier take-back were all initiatives that extended Damaí's business practices beyond the hotel's boundaries into the community.

3. **Innovation/Repositioning**—Damaí's organic onsite farming and its development of a new organic spa botanical line were innovations that departed significantly from widely accepted industry routines and knowledge. They repositioned the hotel for future business opportunities, especially those related to increasing consumer preferences for organic and healthful products and services.

4. **Vision/Opportunity Framing**—Knape was guided by his strategic vision in which the hotel was a catalyst for local economic development that ex-

tended beyond the hotel property and typical industry practices. Consistent with that vision, Knape had developed an unusual business model that involved working with community members to improve their quality of life, which, in turn, benefitted the hotel. The hotel's farming partnership increased compost activities among area farmers, while decreasing the use of chemical fertilizers and burning of plant refuse (which had been diminishing guest experiences). The hotel's fishing partnership reduced the growth of blue/green algae and chemical controls along Lovina Beach, while increasing the supply of organically farmed fish. Damaí's soil reclamation program restored topsoil to area farms, and reduced the need for chemical fertilizers, while offering a tranquil retreat for hotel guests. Partnership with area leaders to develop a fire preparedness program increased fire safety for all members of the community, including the hotel.

Summary: Damaí had developed a fairly balanced portfolio of sustainability activity. In the short-run, the hotel had reduced costs and risks and enjoyed strong support from the community. In the long-run, the company was launching innovative ventures built around a vision of stimulating regional economic development.

1b. VEP Profiles

Figures A1.2–1.6 illustrate how the sustainable value framework can be used to evaluate the VEPs described in case Exhibits 1.5–1.9 based on the definitions provided in case Exhibit 1.10. The portfolio can be used to sort VEPs' requirements into four categories: cost/risk reduction, reputation/legitimacy, innovation/reposition, and vision/opportunity framing.

1. **Cost/Risk Reduction:** All five VEPs under consideration included or implied that they value activities that make operations more efficient. Best Green Hotels was the most detailed. Eco Lodge and Green Globe required specific elements—such as rainwater collection, solar heating, water recycling and waste minimization—but contained more general guidelines as well—such as protection of air quality and land use planning. CERES and ISO 14001 were the broadest, articulating general principles, and processes rather than specific activities.

2. **Reputation/Legitimacy:** Four of the five programs under consideration included or implied at least some basic activities oriented toward stakeholders. Most VEPs focused on educating staff and guests, communicating green activities, or some combination of both. Best Green Hotels was one of two VEPs that required external certification. Green Globe required engagement with suppliers via designing more environmentally sensitive products. It also asked participants to develop an environmentally sensitive purchasing policy, and involve staff, customers, and community members in participants' environmental issues but did not provide details on how that should occur or what it should consist of. ISO 14001 certification which

was focused on the establishment of clear environmental policies and procedures—provided no, specific guidelines with respect to external stakeholder relationships. However, as part of ISO 14001 certification, businesses could emphasize external stakeholder relationships if they choose, and many do.[I] So while students may not indicate that this VEP does not include basic activities oriented toward external stakeholders, it is worth noting that in practice, ISO 14001 adopters typically do.

3. **Innovation/Repositioning:** Of the five VEPs presented in the case, none of the specified activities meant to create new sources of revenue through innovative products and services. So, while innovation/repositioning may be an outgrowth of VEP participation, the VEPs under consideration do not require it.

4. **Vision/Opportunity Framing:** Of the five VEPs presented in the case, only Eco Lodge and Green Globe 21 included language addressing the importance of strategic vision for future growth. Eco Lodge expects participants to serve as catalysts for local economic growth while Green Globe 21 recognized the value of working in partnership to achieve sustainability although the number and ambitiousness of those partnerships were left up to participating hotels to decide. Neither of the programs provided specific guidance on which programs or activities would be appropriate toward those ends.

Summary: All of the VEPs touched on cost/risk reduction activities, which were comparatively easier to measure and evaluate over time. Most of the programs explicitly recognized the value of stakeholder connections. However, most were also ambiguous in specifying best practices related to revenue generation, innovation, and strategic visioning, in large part because these factors tend to be firm-specific. Additionally, compared to the other VEPs, Eco Lodge, Green Globe, and ISO 14001 allowed for more idiosyncratic implementation of hotels' sustainability activities.

1c. Comparing Damaí to VEPs

Table A1.1 compares Damaí's sustainability activities to VEP requirements. Students may likely recognize that many of Damaí's activities exceeded the programs' requirements. Damaí had more extensive sustainability initiatives related to cost/risk reduction and reputation/legitimacy activities. Additionally it emphasized more complex initiatives that involved innovation/repositioning and shared vision. Yet in a few instances, in order to qualify for the program, Knape would have to expand the hotel's existing activities. For example, Best Green Hotels specifically emphasized linen programs and educational efforts geared toward guests—activities Knape saw as undesirable given the hotel's emphasis on luxury branding. Figure A1.7 contains some areas students may suggest Knape could have elected to bring the hotel more in line with various VEP requirements.

1d. Which VEP?

Given the comprehensiveness of Damaí's sustainability activities, Knape could have elected to do any of the VEPs in question with little expansion of the hotel's existing programs. Limiting factors would include the managerial time and attention required to enroll or apply to a given program, as well as any associated costs for certification.

Astute students might raise the point that the market did not have much information about VEPs, and the proliferation of VEPs had made it difficult for consumers to distinguish one from another. However, these same students should be able to assess which VEPs (those with external certification) might have greater credence with some potential customers.

In general, some key considerations related to each VEP include:

Best Green Hotels: offered perhaps the lowest barrier to entry—a self-reporting survey—or which the company was already doing most activities and could indicate intentions to do more.

Eco Lodge: a more complicated VEP that required submission of an application that would be vetted by program staff. Criteria for the program are broad in nature, but in most cases, Damaí's activities are aligned with overall program goals. Once accepted into the program, Damaí would benefit from marketing through the program's network of travel agents and independent contractors.

Green Globe: A more general benchmarking and certification program, which charged a fee for participating that, was based on the level of participation. A number of properties in Bali had received certification, most of which lacked the extensiveness of Damaí's program and activities.

CERES' Green Hotel Initiative: was built around a code of conduct determined by a set of multinational operators, this program required completion of a Best Practice Survey which focused on environmental criteria.

ISO 14001: an international environmental management system standard focused on establishment of clear policies and procedures for continuously improving and managing environmental impacts over time. Hotels had significant autonomy in how they implemented the VEP. Because ISO 14001 was a process standard, to obtain certification companies needed only to demonstrate the existence of management processes that could lead to continual environmental improvement. Each business decided for itself how ambitious it wished to be in establishing its environmental goals. In principle, Damaí could have applied such a system to all dimensions of value creation. In practice, businesses typically had focused on cost/risk reduction. ISO 14001 was also typically used as a means to enhance reputation/legitimacy, by implementing supplier purchasing programs [I].

A1.5.2   DECISION 2:

To determine the extent to which the hotel needed to invest additional resources to qualify for VEP participation students can compare activities needed to fulfill obligations for a specific VEP, determine whether or not Damaí was already doing them, and if not, estimate what it might have cost to implement those new programs. Additionally, students should assess the direct membership costs associated with each VEP.

A1.5.2.1   ASSIGNMENT (GIVEN PRIOR TO OR DURING CLASS):

— 2a. Determine the membership costs associated with participation in each VEP. Then assume Damaí is open all year and that guests have no preference between deluxe and superior rooms. For each occupancy increase of 5 percent, calculate the hotel's profit after subtracting VEP costs.
— 2b. Calculate Damaí's breakeven occupancy (the level of occupancy that Knape would need to realize in order to cover VEP participation costs). Next, calculate the percent increase above existing occupancy needed to cover VEP participation costs. Note that some VEPs will have a range of costs (e.g., Green Globe 21 affiliate, Green Globe 21 Certification, and ISO 14001).
— 2c. If participation in any given VEP led to a subsequent 20 percent increase in occupancy, would it cover the cost of Damaí's VEP participation? What if occupancy increased by only 5 percent?

A1.5.2.2 CLASSROOM DISCUSSION:

2a. Damaí's Profits Net VEP Participation Costs

Column five of Table A1.1 summarizes the various costs associated with each VEP. Because of the comparative strength and robustness of Damaí's existing programs, the cost to adopt any one of the five VEPs largely related to upfront participation costs (for those VEPs that have one).

Students are likely to have noted in the earlier discussion that there are several opportunities for Knape to expand or extend Damaí's existing sustainability activities (see Figure A1.7 for examples). Developing these additional programs might further improve the hotel's operational efficiencies, but would also entail some capital investment and staff time, even if such costs are small.

Table A1.2 contains a breakdown of expected revenue, costs, and profit associated with various increases in occupancy rates. Calculating these values is necessary to determine the extent to which Damaí's occupancy would have needed to increase to justify VEP participation.

In examining Table A1.2, students might note that Damaí was quite profitable for a small hotel (operating with a 60% profit margin). This was largely due to Bali's low cost of labor and Damaí's compensation structure. A good paying wage for a waiter was about $350 per month, and this wage could sustain a family of four with no additional income. Gardeners and cleaning staff were paid less. Knape's salary was less than Western standards because of market factors, but also because the hotel provided him with on-site accommodations, transportation, and all meals. Food costs in Bali were also quite low (again because of low labor costs), and Damaí's on-site gardens reduced the hotel's food costs even further. All these factors, in addition to Damaí's strong emphasis on operational efficiency, contributed to the hotel's overall profitability.

2b. Breakeven Occupancy

The breakeven analysis in Table A1.3 illustrates the increase in occupancy needed to cover the costs of VEP participation, and offers a basis for determining whether the hotel should participate in a particular VEP.

In assessing the breakeven occupancy rates, since participation in Best Green Hotels and CERES' Green Hotel Initiative was free, the hotel did not need to increase occupancy to cover its VEP participation costs. For participation to justify costs in the highest level of Green Globe 21 (certification), Knape needed Damaí's occupancy to increase between .51–.72 percent (depending on the cost of onsite independent assessment, which was expected to be at the low-end because of weak labor costs in the region). Similarly, in order to justify participation in Eco Lodge, Knape would have needed to see an occupancy increase of .5 percent to cover costs associated with each 5 percent increase in occupancy. Since the costs of participating in this program only accrued as occupancy increased, the decision to join Eco Lodge would have carried little risk. Given the low costs of VEP participation (and assuming that the costs of certifying to ISO 14001 were at the lower bound) Knape could have considered participating in *all* the VEPs.

2c. Occupancy Increases to Cover the Cost of Damaí's VEP Participation

Table A1.3 shows that if participation in any given VEP led to a subsequent 20 percent increase in occupancy, Damaí's revenues would have exceeded its VEP participation costs. Additionally, if participation in one or more VEPs increased occupancy 5 percent or more, annually, the hotel's revenues would have exceeded the cost of participation, except for ISO 14001. ISO 14001 costs typically varied based on whether or not a business had already adopted activities required by an environmental management system. An assessment of the hotel's sustainability activities indicated that Damaí was in good position to adopt ISO 14001 at a lower cost. If Damaí's certification costs were closer to $270 per employee, a 5 percent increase in occupancy would have covered the cost of ISO 14001 certification. The breakeven occupancy associated with Damaí's participating in all VEPs was between 3.85–17.78 percent, and most likely was closer to 3.85 percent given the hotel's prior sustainability investments.

Summary: Table A1.3 illustrates that Damaí's VEP participation costs were quite trivial, and Knape could have elected to participate in any one of these VEPs with only a small investment.

A1.5.3   DECISION 3:

To decide whether or not VEP participation would achieve Damaí's broader strategic objective to enhance its external profile and increase bookings it is important to establish a connection between VEP participation and increased reservations. Managers assume that participation in a standard or certification program will lead to competitive advantage. However, that notion should be evaluated based on evidence.

A1.5.3.1   CLASSROOM DISCUSSION QUESTION:

3a. Should Knape expect that VEP participation will improve his ability to brand Damaí as a green hotel?

3b. Should Knape expect that VEP participation might increase bookings and potentially lead to premium prices? What evidence supports your conclusion?

3c. Are there other options Knape might consider to leverage Damaí's sustainability efforts?

A1.5.3.2   CLASSROOM DISCUSSION:

3a. Green Branding

This discussion draws on material introduced in the beginning of the case, which indicated that 16 percent of consumers in Europe, Asia, and the US showed a strong preference to purchase goods and services from eco-friendly businesses [II]. These individuals were referred to in the marketing literature as LOHAS consumers (an acronym for Lifestyles of Health and Sustainability). Additionally, 25 percent of consumers were committed to promoting personal health. Referred to as Naturalizes, these consumers were not committed to environmental concerns, but sought products and services that were health-conscious.

In general, both LOHAS consumers and Naturalizes were also less trusting of companies' self-promoted sustainability claims. Lack of consumer trust was further fueled by concerns that the travel/vacation industry was developing a reputation for being a source of increasingly misleading environmental claims [III]. As a consequence, eco-conscious consumers generally distrusted firms' unsubstantiated sustainability claims [IV]. For Knape, who was seeking to brand Damaí as a "green" hotel, consumer distrust was particularly problematic because his self-promoted sustainability efforts would likely have little effect. In order to gain credibility for his environmental claims, Knape needed a source of external legitimacy, and his options were limited. VEP participation—especially in one requiring external certification—might therefore have been a reasonable mechanism for Damaí to develop a green brand, and because the cost of membership was so low, participation was feasible.

However, one point that students should be made aware of is that the market did not have much information about VEPs, and the proliferation of VEPs had made it difficult for consumers to distinguish one from another. Moreover, no single standard had emerged as one recognized widely across a variety of consumer markets. Lack of VEP differentiation made Knape's task of creating a green brand more difficult, and was another reason for Knape to consider participating in all the VEPs.
Whether VEP participation would actually help Damaí create a green brand was uncertain. It was also unclear whether VEP participation might detract from the company's brand given that consumers had been expressing growing distrust for hotels' green claims.

3b. Increasing Bookings and Premium Pricing

Developing a green brand may appeal to LOHAS and Naturalize consumers. Branding therefore had the potential to have increased bookings. However, there is no way to know for certain that establishing a green brand would enhance Damaí's hotel reservations.

Some consumers (especially LOHAS) had demonstrated a willingness to pay more for environmentally friendly products and services. These individuals also tended to be less sensitive to price [II], which created a possibility for Knape to charge a price premium. While Naturalizes were more likely to pay more for healthful products and services (such as organic food), none of the VEPs under consideration focused exclusively on organic foods and services. Best Green Hotels included organic/eco-friendly food in its checklist of sustainability activity options. However, it was not required for participation and so Naturalizes likely would not associate this VEP with health/wellness. As a consequence, these consumers would likely forego paying a price premium to hotels participating in this (or any other) VEP.

While the case indicates Costa Rican eco-hotels participating in VEPs were able to charge premium pricing, [III] suggesting that similar dynamics could occur in Bali is debatable. Bali lacked the nature preserves that drew so many eco-minded tourists to Costa Rica in the first place (87% of tourists to Costa Rica reported that national parks were the most important place to visit in the country). There also was no evidence that tourists visiting Bali were driven by the same market dynamics as tourists who visit Costa Rica, or possessed the same economic utility curves with respect to pricing. This issue was especially salient since consumers traveling to India indicated that while they preferred to patron more eco-conscious lodging, they were not willing to pay extra to do so. [IV].

Assuming some LOHAS consumers were already visiting Bali, and willing to pay a price premium, Knape needed to balance this possibility with the other possibility that increasing room price may diminish bookings made by Damaí's non-LOHAS guests (who comprised the majority of the hotel's reservations). The prospect of charging price premiums in the short-run therefore had considerable risk.

In the long-run, if Knape's branding efforts were effective, the proportion of LOHAS guests staying at the hotel may increase and thus comprise a larger share of hotel occupancy. Additionally, non-LOHAS guests might feel that they have had a better experience because they know their luxury stay was contributing to sustainability in Bali in multiple ways. Under these circumstances, Knape would have been in a better position to charge a premium price. However, given that the LOHAS market segment was quite small, and that an individual's willingness to pay more was not always consistent with actual behavior, the likelihood that customers would accept price premiums was uncertain.

Summary: It is unclear whether VEP participation would have improved Knape's ability to brand Damaí as a green hotel and increase bookings. However, given consumers' distrust of hotels' green marketing claims, if Damaí had pursued a green brand, some sort of external legitimacy likely would have been required. Additionally, the low cost of VEP participation somewhat buffered Damaí's risk of pursuing this approach.

In the event that Damaí's was successful at establishing a green brand and increasing bookings, it was still uncertain whether the hotel could have charged price premiums. Bali's tourists differed significantly from other more recognized eco-destinations, and while LOHAS consumers tended to be less price sensitive, the possibility of charging price premiums remained ambiguous.

3c. Additional Considerations

VEPs promoted best practices and raised awareness of sustainability for both hotels and customers. Operationally, many of the activities associated with VEPs reduced costs and risk and also improved reputation and legitimacy which could provide businesses a stronger basis for marketing and communication efforts.

Less clear, however, was whether customers would make preferential decisions favoring hotels with various VEP certification or membership. Moreover, the proliferation of VEPs made it more difficult for consumers to distinguish one VEP from another. This concern was increasingly relevant because of issues related to increasing numbers of misleading claims that were attributable to the travel/vacation industry [V], and intensifying distrust among consumers about firms' unsubstantiated sustainability claims [VI]. As such, there was no guarantee that consumer interest in sustainability and wellness would enhance, diminish, or have no impact on a participating company's sustainability reputation or whether those effects would attract, repel, or have no effect on hotel bookings.

Some students might suggest that Knape should forego VEP participation altogether, since there was no clear evidence linking VEP membership to increased hotel bookings. Damaí's sustainable value portfolio also was more balanced than the portfolios emphasized by most VEPs, suggesting that VEP participation would offer little additional value to the hotel [VII]. However, it is important to note that whereas most VEPs were focused more on sustainability goals rather than the business outcomes, Eco Lodge was the only VEP explicitly focused on linking membership to preference in promotion and bookings through a cultivated network. This more direct link to business outcomes might make it worthy of greater consideration.

Other students might suggest that a complement or substitute for VEP participation is the active pursuit of press coverage (e.g., a story in Conde Nest or similar travel magazine about how luxurious and sustainable the resort is) and/or other recognitions of its sustainability efforts. Whatever approach Knape takes, the sustainability marketing literature is clear—the hotel will need to communicate both the core value of its offering (here luxury) with its sustainability message.

ENDNOTES

1. Arimura, T.; Darnall, N.; and Katayama, H.; Is ISO 14001 a gateway to more advanced environmental action? The case for green supply chain management. *J. Environ. Econ. Manag.* **2011**, 61(2), 170–182.
2. The Natural Marketing Institute.; Excerpts from the 2006 understanding the LOHAS market report. In: Environmental Management: Readings and Cases (Ed.) Russo, M. V.; **2008**, Los Angeles: Sage.
3. Rivera, J.; Assessing a voluntary environmental initiative in the developing world: The Costa Rican certification for sustainable tourism. *Pol. Sci.* 35(4): 333–360.
4. Manaktola, K.; and Jauhari, V.; Exploring consumer attitude and behavior towards green practices in the lodging industry in India. *Int. J. Contemp. Hospital. Manag.* **2007**, *19*(4), 364–377.
5. Futerra Sustainability Communication.; The Green wash Guide. London, UK: Futerra Sustainability Communication, **2008**.
6. Hall, E.; U.K. consumers catch companies committing "Green Murder." *Advertising Age.* **2007**, *78*(40), 3–4.
7. Darnall, N.; and Carmin, J.; Cleaner and greener? The signaling accuracy of U.S. voluntary environmental programs. *Pol. Sci.* **2005**, *38*(2–3), 71–90.

A1.7   RESEARCH METHODS

Data for this case were collected during two site visits to Damaí Lovina Villas. The authors interviewed Glenn Knape, the general manager, and the on-site assistant manager, in addition to Nyoman Sutarya, owner of Institute Pengembangan Sumber Daya Alam, one of Damaí's strategic partners that encouraged the hotel's use of low-input agriculture technologies. Follow-up correspondence with Knape continued through 2013.

Other data was collected from the hotel's internal documents and financial reports. Data related to the VEPs were sourced from websites developed by VEP sponsors. Other VEP data were collected from scholarly literature, as was information related to green marketing.

A1.8 EPILOGUE

New Investor. According to Knape, in 2006, Niklas Zennström, cofounder of Skype Internet, became an investor in Damaí, creating more opportunities for expanding the hotel's sustainability pursuits. Additional capital allowed Damaí to expand its guest facilities from 8 villas to 14. Each new villa had its own private pool. The capital infusion created an avenue for Damaí to pursue VEPs that otherwise might have been viewed as cost prohibitive.

VEP Participation. In 2006, Damaí joined the Best Green Hotel program where it earned five green triangles—the highest rating of any hotel on Bali. Implementation of guest education programs would qualify Damaí for the highest rating offered by Best Green Hotels. By 2013, however, other hotels were also seeking a green brand. Ten Bali hotels were recognized by Best Green Hotels, and a new eco-hotel, Surinbuana Eco-Lodge, had the highest rating in Bali. Surinbuana was able to surpass Damaí's rating because it had adopted guest education programs and a linen reuse program.

Cost/Risk Reduction. Damaí completed its solar conversion, which began in November 2005 when hot water systems were transitioned to solar power-based heating. By 2007, all electrical systems were solar powered and surplus electricity was being sold to state-operated utilities.

Innovation/Repositioning. Damaí began raising its own animals for use in the hotel's restaurant. Development of the farm came about as a quality measure so that Damaí could control of all parts of its food service, and further advance the hotel's sustainability practices. The hotel raised free-range pigs, rabbits, pigeons, and ducks, as well as more exotic livestock such as frogs and snails, and fresh-water lobsters. All operations were 100 percent organic.

Vision/Opportunity Framing. Knape helped raise funds to refurbish the King's Palace in the historic capital of Singaraga, which was becoming a significant tourist attraction in North Bali. Damaí sponsored a European tour of a traditional Balinese dance and gamelan troupe that was chronicled by Discovery Channel. These efforts increased Damaí's recognition, especially among Europeans.

Loss of a Leader. In January 2008, Knape left his position as Damaí's general manager. With his departure, questions emerged about whether the hotel's sustainability initiatives would continue. However, these concerns dissipated. In 2009, Damaí was chosen by the regional government to be a role model for other hotels and resorts of North Bali, and to serve as a field laboratory for new concepts related to sustainable resort operation. The government recognized Damaí as the exemplar for other resorts to follow in an effort to encourage other North Bali hotels to operate more sustainably.

Oversight. Concern about the prevalence of deceptive environmental claims was increasing globally. Within the US, in 2007, the US Federal Trade Commission announced that it would accelerate revisions to its green marketing guidelines to discourage businesses' deceptive environmental claims. The guidelines had not been updated since 1998, when environmental marking claims were far less prevalent. On October 1, 2012, the new guidelines were released. They were expected to discourage businesses' deceptive environmental claims.

Accolades. In 2012 Damaí received Trip Advisor's Traveler's Choice Award for being one of Indonesia's Top 25 Spa and Leisure hotels. It was also recognized by Trip Advisor as being one of Indonesia's Top 25 Best Small Hotels, in addition to being one of Indonesia's Top 25 Hotels for Service. Trip Advisor's Travelers' Choice winners are selected based on travelers' reviews and opinions. In 2013 the hotel also received recognition among property experts. A judging panel of over 50 experts covering every aspect of the property business honored Damaí with the Asia Pacific Property Award's 'Best Small Hotel' in Indonesia.

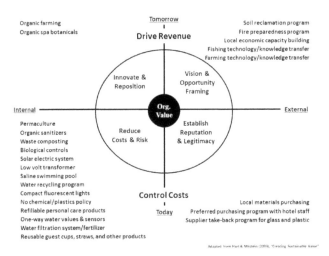

FIGURE A1.1   Damaí's sustainable value portfolio.

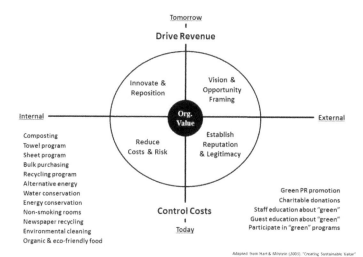

FIGURE A1.2   Best Green Hotels sustainable value portfolio.

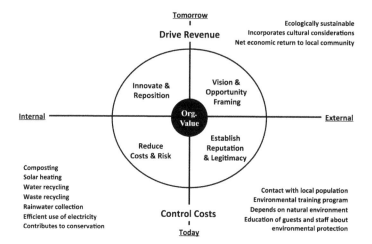

FIGURE A1.3   Eco Lodge sustainable value portfolio.

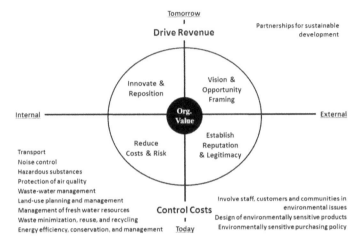

FIGURE A1.4   Green globe 21 sustainable value portfolio.

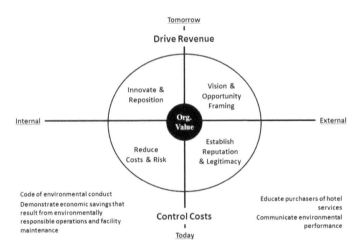

FIGURE A1.5   CERES' green hotel initiative sustainable value portfolio.

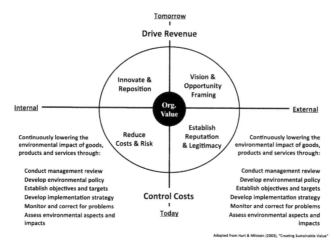

FIGURE A1.6   ISO 14001 sustainable value portfolio.

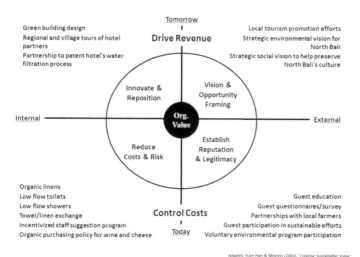

FIGURE A1.7   Potential damaí investments & activities.

TABLE A1.1 Comparison of VEP requirements and costs, and Damaí's existing sustainability program

VEP Name	VEP Key Environmental Element	Existing Element at Damaí?	Monitoring of Participants' Performance	Damaí's Participation Cost	Comments
Best green hotels	Linen program Energy conservation Bulk purchasing Composting Organic Food Education of guests and staff Water conservation Recycling	X ✓ ✓ [a] ✓ ✓ X ✓ ✓	Self-report via online submission form	Free	Case information illustrates that Damaí would likely earn 20–25 points, making it the highest rated hotel in Bali
Eco Lodge	Education of guests and staff Recycling of water and waste Efficient use of electricity Solar heating Rainwater collection Composting	X ✓ ✓ ✓ X ✓	Self-report	Free website listing, 10% commission on rooms booked on website	While the program is not free, hotels are only charged for bookings made on the Eco Lodge website
Green globe 21	Waste minimization, reuse & recycling Energy efficiency, conservation & management Management of fresh-water resources Waste-water management Hazardous substances Transport Land-use planning and management Involving staff, customers and communities in environmental issues Design of environmentally sensitive products Partnerships for sustainable development Protection of air quality Noise control Environmentally sensitive purchasing policy	✓ ✓ ✓ ✓ ✓ ✓ [b] ✓ Some [c] ✓ ✓ ✓ X ✓	Self-report & 3rd party certification	Varied fee structure	Relatively inexpensive—at least for affiliate or benchmarking status; costs are significantly greater for 3rd party certification, although they are not prohibitive; third-party certification reduces free-riding opportunities

CE-RES' Green Hotel Initiative	Commitment & awareness ✓ Energy efficiency ✓ Solid waste minimization ✓ Air & water quality ✓ Water conservation ✓ Environmental purchasing	Self-report via online survey	Free	VEP is de-centralized. CERES does not promote participants, since it do not know which hotels participate
ISO 14001[4]	Environmental policy ✓ Environmental aspects and ✓ impacts X Objectives and targets X Implementation strategy X Monitor and correct for X problems Management review	3rd party certification	$270–$1,370/ employee; depends on whether hotel has to start from scratch to develop its EMS	Widely recognized in manu-facturing sectors and increasingly in service industries; certifica-tion restricts free-riding opportunities

Notes:[a]Relates to purchases of guests' refillable toiletries.

[b]Relates to efforts to minimize solid waste transportation. Hotel fleets are SUVs because of Bali's poor road conditions.

[c]Damaí involved communities in environmental issues but does not have a strong emphasis on staff or customer involvement.

TABLE A1.2   Damaí's estimated profits from occupancy increases[a]

Occu-pancy	Revenues[b]					Costs –40% of Revenue	Profits	Profit Increase	Percent Profit In-crease
	Rooms[c]	Restau-rant	Spa	Excur-sions	TOTAL				
	40%	43%	7%	10%	100%				
65%	$306,053	$329,006	$53,559	$76,513	$765,131	$306,052	$459,079	–	–
70%	$329,595	$354,315	$57,679	$82,399	$823,988	$329,595	$494,393	$35,314	8%
75%	$353,138	$379,623	$61,799	$88,284	$882,844	$353,138	$529,706	$70,628	15%
80%	$376,680	$404,931	$65,919	$94,170	$941,700	$376,680	$565,020	$105,941	23%
85%	$400,223	$430,239	$70,039	$100,056	$1,000,556	$400,222	$600,334	$141,255	31%

TABLE A1.2 *(Continued)*

Occupancy	Revenues[b]					Costs Profits −40% of Revenue	Profits	Profit Increase	Percent Profit Increase
	Rooms[c]	Restaurant	Spa	Excursions	TOTAL				
	40%	43%	7%	10%	100%				
90%	$423,765	$455,547	$74,159	$105,941	$1,059,413	$423,765	$635,648	$176,569	38%
95%	$447,308	$480,856	$78,279	$111,827	$1,118,269	$447,308	$670,961	$211,883	46%
100%	$470,850	$506,164	$82,399	$117,713	$1,177,125	$470,850	$706,275	$247,196	54%

Notes:[a]All figures in USD; calculations assumed hotel was open all year, nonroom revenues grew proportional to occupancy. Existing occupancy was average occupancy was 65 percent.

[b]Since restaurant revenues from outside guests were negligible (<2%), they have been omitted from the calculations. Spa treatments and excursions and other hotel programs were used exclusively by guests.

[c]Since rooms accounted for 40 percent of total revenue, restaurant, spa, and excursion revenue was calculated by (room revenue / 40%) * % revenue from each respective source.

In submitting this case to the *Case Research Journal* for widespread distribution in print and electronic media, I (we) certify that it is original work, based on real events in a real organization. It has not been published and is not under review elsewhere. Copyright holders have given written permission for the use of any material not permitted by the "Fair Use Doctrine." The host organization has assigned a release authorizing the publication of all information gathered with understandings of confidentiality.

TABLE 1.3 VEP breakeven analysis[a]

VEP Name	VEP Cost Explanation	Actual VEP Cost	Net Profit by Occupancy After Subtracting VEP Costs							Breakeven Occupancy[b]	Percent Increase Above Existing Occupancy
			70%	75%	80%	85%	90%	95%	100%		
Best green hotels	Free	$0	$35,314	$70,628	$105,941	$141,255	$176,569	$211,883	$247,196	65.00%	0.00%
Eco Lodge[c]	10% ($16.13) per additional booking	$2,354 per 5% occupancy increase	$32,960	$68,274	$103,587	$138,901	$174,215	$209,529	$244,842	65.50%	0.50% per 5% occupancy increase
Green globe 21 Affiliate[d]	$220 in year 1; $198 per year thereafter + 50% of Benchmarking base fee	$396 >1 yr 1; $418 yr 1	$34,897– $34,919	$70,210– $70,232	$105,524– $105,546	$140,838– $140,860	$176,152– $176,174	$211,465– $211,487	$246,779– $246,801	65.08%– 65.09%	0.08%–0.09%
Benchmarking	$395 per year	$395	$34,919	$70,233	$105,546	$140,860	$176,174	$211,488	$246,801	65.09%	0.08%
Certification[e]	Benchmarking base fee + onsite independent assessment	$2,395– $3,395	$31,524– $32,524	$66,838– $67,838	$102,151– $103,151	$137,465– $138,465	$172,779– $173,779	$211,488– $209,093	$246,801– $244,406	65.51%– 65.72%	.51%–.72%
CERES' green hotel initiative	Free	$0	$35,314	$70,628	$105,941	$141,255	$176,569	$211,883	$247,196	65.00%	0.00%

TABLE 1.3 *(Continued)*

VEP Name	VEP Cost Explanation	Actual VEP Cost	Net Profit by Occupancy After Subtracting VEP Costs							Breakeven Occupancy[b]	Percent Increase Above Existing Occupancy
			70%	75%	80%	85%	90%	95%	100%		
ISO 14001[f]	$270–$1,370 per employee for third-party ISO 14001 EMS certification	$15,390–$78,090	($42,776)–$19,924	($7,462)–$55,238	$27,851–$90,551	$63,165–$125,865	$98,479–$161,179	$133,793–$196,493	$169,106–$231,806	68.27%–81.58%	3.27%–16.56%

Notes: [a]All figures in USD. Calculations assumed that nonroom revenues grew proportionally to occupancy. Figures were derived by subtracting VEP participation costs from profit increases estimated in Table A1.1.

[b]Breakeven occupancy referred to the increased occupancy that equaled the cost of VEP participation. Calculations were based on [65% occupancy profit + VEP cost]/100 **percent** occupancy profit (see Table A1.2).

[c]Eco Lodge calculations were based on profit increase—[(room revenue at 5% higher occupancy—room revenue at current occupancy) * .10 to account for the 10 **percent** travel agent commission on room bookings].

[d]Affiliate calculations were based on $220 in year 1, $198 per year thereafter +50 **percent** of the $395/year (Benchmarking base fee).

[e]Certification calculations were based on $395/year for Benchmarking base fee +$2,000 to $3,000 for independent assessment expenses for a medium sized hotel.

[f]Calculations were based on $270 to $1,370 per employee to implement and certify an EMS * 57 employees; most likely Damai's profit increases would have been in the higher range since the hotel had already implemented aspects of an, thereby making the cost of adopting this VEP less.

CHAPTER 2

ECO-INNOVATIONS IN A VIKING VILLAGE: AN ETHNOGRAPHIC INVESTIGATION FROM DENMARK

H. SORENSEN[1], M. L. WRAY[2], and H. G. PARSA[3]

[1]Professor of Tourism Management, Metropolitan State University of Denver, Department of Hospitality, Tourism and Events, Campus Box 60, P.O. Box 173362,Denver, CO 80217, 303 556 3241, E-mail: sorenseh@msudenver.edu

[2]Professor of Restaurant Management, Metropolitan State University of Denver, Department of Hospitality, Tourism and Events, 1190 Auraria Parkway, Suite B, Denver, CO 80204, 303 556 3393, E-mail: wraym@msudenver.edu

[3]Barron Hilton Chair in Lodging & Professor, Knoebel School of Hospitality Management, Daniels School of Business, 337 Joy Burns Center, University of Denver, 2044 E. Evans Ave., Denver, CO 80208, (303) 871-3693, E-mail: hparsa@du.edu

CONTENTS

2.1   INTRODUCTION

The understanding of the history of Vikings in the Scandinavian countries is much different from what is commonly known outside of Scandinavia. To address this, one of the authors of this paper met the leaders of the Viking Village, a reproduction Village that uses its natural environment and cultural landscape to tell the story of Vikings. During these discussions with these leaders, they explored the potential of the Village to utilize the ecotourism design to influence cultural awareness of Viking life that is contrary to popular lore. The leader invited the author and her students to visit the Village, work with the Village residents and volunteers, and spend 3 days and two nights living the Viking life. Cultural understanding of any ethnic group can be best studied using ethnographic method of research. Thus, to better understand the life of the Vikings as recreated in the Viking Village, an ethnographic method of investigation was found to be most appropriate. One of the authors is a qualified researcher in ethnography.

Before commencing the current project, one of the authors, visited the Viking Village on three different occasions and developed an understanding of the growth and changes of the Village over the years. In addition, the authors have visited Viking Village and participated in the Viking Village living activities, visited the gravesites and museums, took part in rowing an authentic Viking ship, and eventually experienced an overnight stay in the Village living the life of Vikings. Through this cultural immersion over repeated visits, the authors have gained strong insights about the life of the Viking Village. After gaining expertise about the Viking life styles, the authors took several groups of students as a part of study abroad program. The students and the authors have conducted numerous interviews with the locals, officials and tourist to gain deeper understanding and perception of various groups about the Viking Village This case study employs the rich stories of students, in depth interviews with Village workers and experiences of students to provide readers with a means to determine the feasibility of ecotourism to foster an understanding of cultural significance of Vikings contrary to popular lore. The Viking world is brought into realization from the travel logs of students as they engaged in participatory activities and interactive simulations that were true to the latest Viking archeological sites and historical research. Experiences in the Village hope to demonstrate how most Vikings were peaceful and self-sufficient farmers and traders. Readers of this case may determine for themselves the feasibility of the Viking Village to enhance cultural awareness of Vikings and its ability to function as a sustainable ecotourism Village.

This case study presents some of the challenges of developing community-based tourism without compromising the high quality authentic experience that people come to experience in the first place. Community-based tourism has demonstrated an ability to maintain a balance between a healthy environment and a maximum number of visitors [1]. Community based tourism has been further clarified as "community participation in the tourism planning process" [2].

The main goal of the Village is to maintain tourism at a community-based grass-roots level. Therefore, its ability to adjust from a K-12 school environment to an adult ecotourism experience is assessed according to the community-based tourism model. This model has helped the Viking Village identify appropriate ecotourism development strategies for the Village as a destination. A bottom-up community development project is feasible in Denmark due to the legislative provision for "public right of access". In Denmark this right is also referred to as the *"freedom to roam."* This concept grants the general public the right to access uncultivated public or privately owned land for recreation and exercise [3, 4]. The drawing of the Viking Village location in Figure 2.1, demonstrates how the Village is situated on public land where anyone is welcome to walk through the Village at any time as long as the Village activities are not disturbed.

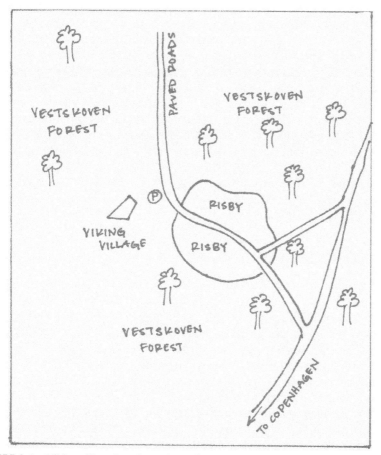

FIGURE 2.1   Viking village location—drawn by the author.

The challenge of the students was to evaluate how the Village may become successful at offering overnight stay accommodations for small groups of ecotourists. This challenge would demonstrate the progression from a K-12 environment to a sustainable community Village for both children and adult groups. Towards this goal, students visiting the Viking Village as a part of their study abroad program have helped in developing programs to ensure that the tourism experience is maintained at a sustainable small-scale level. The students were trained to apply concepts related to ecotourism to their reflections regarding the strengths and weaknesses of the Village experience in enhancing their cultural awareness of true Viking life. A frequently quoted definition of ecotourism is provided by The International Ecotourism Society [5] as "responsible travel to natural areas that conserves the environment and improves the well-being of local people." However, this case study takes the view that the definition from Wallace and Pierce [6], is a better fit, wherein, "ecotourism is traveling to relatively undisturbed natural areas for study, enjoyment, or volunteer assistance… It views natural areas both as 'home to all of us' in a global sense ('eco' meaning home) but 'home to nearby residents' specifically. It is envisioned as a tool for both conservation and sustainable development" (p. 848).

The case study concludes by discussing the challenges and implications of developing ecotourism in a country where ecotourism does not yet seem to be fully embraced. It is curious to note that Kaae [7] determined that "Visit Denmark (formerly the Danish Tourist Board) has not wholeheartedly embraced the concepts of ecotourism and sustainability" and it views ecotourism as a "passing trend" (p. 12). Another challenge is the limited research and studies on ecotourism throughout the Scandinavian countries [8 and 9]. However, the largest challenge presented to the researchers was whether or not experiences in the Viking Village could correct the romanticized and popular images of warrior Vikings who dominated Northern Europe through destructive military conquests.

2.2 ECOTOURISM IN DENMARK

The tremendous growth of tourism over the last 20 years has functioned as an agent of change [10 and 11]. If this growth is managed effectively, tourism has the potential for becoming a sustainable industry that does not impose major and drastic changes to the landscapes of a destination area. Koning [12] recognized that "an imitation-American culture of commerce has covered the landscape" (p. 8). Smith [13] further insinuated the possible early beginnings of ecotourism by stating that "host destinations must consciously control or restrict tourism in order to preserve its economic or cultural integrity" (p. 8).

A myriad of ecotourism definitions have surfaced since the early 1970's. A frequently quoted definition is from The International Ecotourism Society (TIES) which was the first international nonprofit organization dedicated to ecotourism as a tool for conservation and sustainable development. TIES [5] defines ecotourism as "responsible travel to natural areas that conserves the environment and improves the well-being of local people." Even though this is a popular definition, Björk, [8] saw ecotourism as an "elusive concept" (p. 304) 15 years ago. Soon afterward, Hvenegaard and Dearden [14] lamented that "a standardized definition of ecotourism does not yet exist" (p. 700). One major flaw with ecotourism is that there still is no one universally accepted definition. Another flaw lies with the modern TIES definition because it assumes local people are in need of help. This definition also insinuates that ecotourism only takes place in impoverished areas that seem to be in dire need of help. However, more developed destinations in all corners of the world may share an equal interest in protecting their environments. A third flaw is the word conservation. When comparing ecotourism definitions, the words conservation and preservation are used either interchangeably or exclusively, indicating a lack of consistency of terminology in ecotourism literature.

Perhaps strength of ecotourism lies in the ambiguity identified in the literature, because it allows people with different opinions about development issues to search for common ground without appearing to compromise their positions. Ironically, the weakness of the concept is also its ambiguity, such as the difficulty in determining whether its policies will enhance environmentally and sociocultural sensitive developments [15]. Another weakness is also that stakeholders often don't seem to agree on what needs to be sustained and for whom, such as nature or humans [16]. To eliminate this kind of confusion in this case study, neither preservation nor conservation words are used to describe ecotourism concepts.

Since few types of tourism in Denmark fulfill all the criteria of ecotourism [7], the definition of Wallace and Pierce [6] is a much better fit for this case study, but specifically this description: "It [ecotourism] views natural areas both as 'home to all of us' in a global sense ('eco' meaning home) but 'home to nearby residents' specifically" (p. 848). Kaee [7] seems to agree, stating that "The inclusion of 'culture' in many ecotourism definitions is highly relevant to Denmark, where nature experiences are often interwoven with cultural elements" (p.19). More recently, it has been determined that little has been written about ecotourism in Scandinavia and that statement still holds true as searches for keywords in common database yield no recent results [7, 17].

For the current case study, there are two major challenges regarding ecotourism's community-based model. The first challenge concerns the assumption of negative growth over time if a community-based tourism model is not implemented. Such negative growth may include physical landscapes being replaced by development projects, culturally sophisticated visitors being replaced by less sophisticated ones, and tourism eventually could become self-destructive [18]. Destination areas carry with them the seeds of their own destruction, as they allow themselves to become commercialized and lose their qualities which originally attracted tourists [19]. Such negative growth trends seem to contradict tourism planners' assumption that tourism products promise unlimited growth opportunities, with a continuous increase in tourist arrivals [20]. The second challenge has to do with sustainable development, because sustainability is often a grossly overused and abused concept. The whole idea of sustainability may be a paradox, since the goal is to protect the very thing (tourism sites) we want to use. The diversity of definitions reflects the enormous differences in social, economic, and ecological expectations [16].

The dilemma with the mainstream community-based approach is that it offers a too simplistic explanation of a highly dynamic and interconnected development challenge. The mainstream approach often reflects personal or political agendas and is therefore hard for a destination to follow as a model. Okazaki [2] argues that community-based tourism projects may not always be realistic due to high project implementation and maintenance costs. The advantage of the Viking Village is that it is funded nearly entirely by the county. The workforce has low turnover rate, the Viking Village had nearly the same group leaders from 1992 to 2013, and there is high morale and an excellent work ethic among employees. The growth and the development of the Village has been rather slow however, as it has taken more than 10 years to complete the five Village structures (see Table 2.1). This can be explained by the nature of the work and limited resources available.

TABLE 2 1   Timeline of Viking village construction

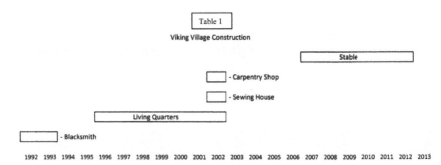

With the high level of bottom-up community support and participation, the Viking Village does not seem to encounter the same problems faced by the other community-based projects. All stakeholders were consulted at every major step. Contrary to other community projects identified by others [21], they have been able to develop from the bottom-up, efficient and effective models of Viking life. The operation of the Village involves stakeholders from both the community and Village participants. The Village operates consistent with recommendations from Choi and Murray [22] where the residents and their perceptions of the Village is important aspect of further development. Before growing further and taking on the role of overnight stays in the Village, both the residents and their Village leader seek the feedback from the American students that stayed overnight in the Village.

2.3 METHODOLOGY

To develop this case study, a review of ecotourism and Viking-related literature were conducted. However, published histories of the Viking era are often contradictory and very limited research has been done on ecotourism in Scandinavia [7, 17]. Therefore, the ethnographic qualitative method of participant-observation and semi-structured interviews have been conducted by the author and her students during repeated visits to the Viking Village since 2006. This case study relies heavily on the author's own personal knowledge and her student experiences. One of the authors grew up in Denmark, where the Viking culture was introduced in early childhood education. Since then, she has read, observed, and investigated the Viking era and the lifestyles of Vikings. Much of her Viking knowledge comes from this inner familiarity, awareness, and understanding.

During the pilot project, the goal was to show the students how to embrace and appreciate the Viking Village as a completely different lifestyle that most likely would remove them from their comfort zone. Agar's [23] and Geertz's [24] anthropological model of "being there" [23, 24] was heavily relied on for the current study, which means the students began their cultural experience with passive observations first. After a few hours, the students raised their level of attention and actively engaged in Village activities. The students adapted the definition of holistic recognition: "That an isolated observation cannot be understood unless you understand its relationships to other aspects of the situation in which it occurred" [23]. Students then evolved from being passive learners into active participants in the Village lifestyle. The students' task was not to observe the Village as an isolated place in history, but to experience and understand the Village's relationship with the larger world. At the Village, students had to adjust and "go with the flow" as the days unfolded.

Informal interviews were conducted with various members of the Viking Village culture. The informal ethnographic interview style [23] was adopted, because not having a written list of questions worked better in a busy Village life environment. Rather, having a repertoire of questions-asking strategies from which to draw upon at the moment seemed appropriate. An informal inquiry method enabled the author and students to casually chat with Village workers. The data collecting strategy fostered informality and minimized harm to the natural flow of events into which formal questions could have intruded. Combining observation and interview through simultaneous or sequential questions fit very well in the Village atmosphere [23].

Students were required to record data and take notes in a journal, which are referenced in this case study. The students took notes at irregular occasions, because they were asked to follow the participatory "hanging-out" method of collecting data [25]. They recorded information in their journals during many informal conversations with the Village workers. They were required to express themselves through pencil sketches. This paper contains quotes from student journals where they have given written permission to reproduce their work.

The procedure to secure students' anonymity and to completely de-identify them was possible through a coding system. In a notebook, each person was assigned and referred to as a code followed by a number. For example, the first student was assigned the code STU1, while the second was referred to as STU2. All full-time and volunteer workers from the Village have granted permission to the author to use their quotes and materials. The Village leader was proud of their Village and wished to share their community-based project with the world so that future investigators may research the Village and contact the Village for future learning experiences. Permission has also been given to use their website and utilize pictures and drawings from the Village.

2.4   THE VIKING VILLAGE

The tourism industry is often depicted as a win-win situation for both tourists and locals 19). The idealistic cliché that "tourists should take nothing but pictures and leave nothing but footprints" (p. 253) was taken very seriously. In the Village, they made sure that the footprints left behind by their visitors are not too many. Even though a greater number of visitors would translate into more tourist dollars at an extremely rapid rate [10], the Village wishes to maintain the balance of delivering a high quality educational experience and managing visitor numbers. The Viking Village works hard to avoid "commercialization of [its] natural and cultural resources, [where] the result [may be] a contrived and inauthentic representation of, for example, a cultural theme or event that has been eroded into a distant memory" [26]. The Village attempts this through authentic re-creation of Viking stories, myths, legends, and way of life through means that are true to the core principles of ecotourism.

Albertslund County originated the idea of the Viking Village in 1992. The vision was to reconstruct a Village with a strong focus on cultural authenticity and active participation [27, 28]. This historical workshop approach was used by educational institutions, especially grades K-12, from the Albertslund County. The county runs the Village and organizes school visits. All other visitors are charged an entrance fee. This is not just another reconstructed medieval Village that is built to please masses of tourists. Here, there is no souvenir shop or happy-hour bar. Visitors make their own festivities through participatory work. As STU1 (2010) wrote in her journal:

> *"This cultural experience is truly unique, because it is completely authentic to the Viking era and is ran as identical as possible to the time period. Since the Village is tucked away, it separates you from reality and really places you in another time to be immersed in the   Viking era."*

As can be seen in Figure 2.2, the Viking Village is situated on 2 hectares (about 5 acres) of public land, ½ hectare of which is fenced. The Village borders the Village of Risby and is surrounded by Vestskoven State Forest. Albertslund County leases the land from the State Forest service. Two hectares of forest immediately north of the Village has the purpose of growing tall straight oak trees that are used for all construction needs, including structures, fence, and tools. This technique of a selective logging forest was also used in the Viking era [29]. Southwest of the Village, 13 hectares has been leased, some of which is used for Village cows and sheep to graze. Due to the concept of freedom to roam, anyone is welcome to walk through the Village at any time as long as the activities are not disturbed. Anyone who happens to pass by is welcome to be a fly on the wall for a few minutes. The Village is only partially fenced with no locked entrance door.

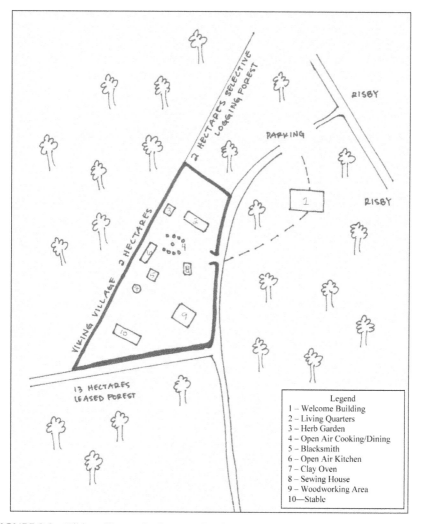

FIGURE 2 2   Viking village—Redrawn and updated from Poulson and Draiby (2005).

The idea of the freedom to roam has deep historical roots. It has been traced back to the Viking Era in the early Middle Ages [3]. Kaltenborn [3] explains, "the purpose then was to ensure people's ability to move around the countryside unrestricted, provided that one did not disturb or damage the property of local inhabitants" (p. 419). The Village is built on an 850 C.E. Viking farmer's site in a beautiful meadow, where the Vikings had access to plenty of water, timber, and fertile soil. The stunning rural landscape has sweeping views of creeks, rolling hills, and open fields. STU2 (2010) made it clear that:

> "The Viking Village is unique and different from other cultural experiences because it truly puts you into a state of mind where you feel like you are a part of the culture. We were not lectured about the history of the Vikings. We were not dragged around the site simply just to look at what a Viking Village might have looked like, but quite the opposite. We were split up into groups where we got hands-on experience with everything that Vikings used to do."

The entire Village was reconstructed with Viking tools and techniques, using local materials. STU5 (2012) noticed an interesting reconstructed detail:

> "The art in the Village is very subtle, but very intricate at the same time. The first piece of art I noticed was Maria's pendants on the top of her dress. We have seen these molds all over in the different museums. It was really cool to see that the Village truly is being authentic and real to the Viking ages."

Village houses were reconstructed in collaboration with the three main stakeholders: museums, archeologists, and historians [28]. They used excavated Viking sites from the Copenhagen area as models. No modern construction technology or tools were allowed. Only reconstructed Viking tools, techniques, materials, and knowledge were implemented, with very few compromises [28, 29]. The largest of the Village structures was a living quarters and was the center of Viking life. The experiences inside this house were the essence of the pilot project (see Figure 2.3). The house has wattle-and-daub walls in a timber framework. The walls were constructed of horizontal logs with lapped corners. The floor was smooth pounded earth. There was one long central living room with two small rooms at the end. In one of these small rooms, flour was hand milled on a circular grindstone. The majority of the light inside this house came from a fire in the central hearth. A few tiny windows add only a little light. Since there was no chimney, the smoke escaped through gaps in the roof, which was covered with wooden shingles. The long open hearth was the focus of the room. Here, life was carried out around the hearth, and the fire rarely went out. An iron caldron was suspended from the ceiling on a chain. Benches ran along the walls closest to the hearth. There was little other furniture, so the benches were used for sitting during the day and for sleeping at night.

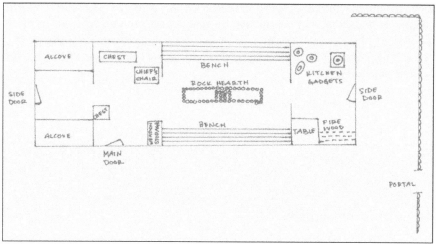

FIGURE 2.3 Living quarters—Redrawn from Poulson and Draiby (2005).

Seeing the rustic and minimalistic living conditions, STU7 (2012) was thrilled:

"We walked around and made sleeping plans while wondering where and how we are going to fit into two long flat pieces of wood with no privacy and only sheep skins laying all over the place. It was one of the most amazing nights I had in a long time, no blankets, no pillows, no fancy sheets and everything was just basic as Professor have said to us many times 'sometimes you have to go back to basics...' and that is what made the entire trip enjoyable."

2.5 ECOTOURISM PRESENCE

The organization and operation of the Viking Village appears directly related to the ecotourism definition of Wallace and Pierce [6] that, "Ecotourism is traveling to relatively undisturbed natural areas for study, enjoyment, or volunteer assistance .... It views natural areas both as 'home to all of us' in a global sense ('eco' meaning home) but 'home to nearby residents' specifically" (p.848). The idea of a county managed Viking Village with priority for its own county's educational institutions clearly fits with the ecotourism notion *of traveling to relatively undisturbed natural areas for study.* The *volunteer assistance* aspect is evident in that the Village relies on 130 members of the "Friends of Viking Village" organization [27].

The members are private citizens from all over Denmark. Most volunteers are from the Copenhagen area, only about 30 miles from the Village, which fits well with Wallace and Pierce explanation *that natural areas [are] home to all of us in a global sense .... but home to nearby residents specifically.* Some volunteers contribute to the Village through private donations. Others volunteer a few days each year to help with construction, maintenance, and activities. The volunteers take great pride in attempting to create objects with the same high quality standards as the Vikings [28]. As can be seen in Table 2.2, the volunteers are an important part of the Village operations and management, because the county only employs a few fulltime people.

TABLE 2 2   Tenure of Viking village employees

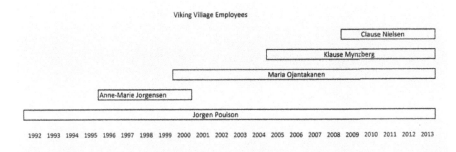

2.6   CULTURAL AUTHENTICITY

It is no coincidence that the Viking Village location of bordering Risby Village was chosen. Since *"eco" means home,* the name Risby has been traced to the Viking era, where Village names were commonly created with functional syllables [29]. Many Village names end with the syllable "by", which means Village. The first syllable of "ris" means grain. Thus, each Village was then identified with a functional characteristic. The first syllable could also indicate geographical location or feature. However, "ris" could also indicate the type of road that the Viking built over the nearby boggish landscape [29]. This road was built with branches and grain that were held together with sand and resources took up major space in the students' journals dirt. It is easy to take the modern interpretation of *"eco" means home* literally, because a few of Risby's 200 residents regularly volunteer in the Viking Village. However, almost more importantly, since the Viking Village has no locked gates or security cameras (see Figure 2.4), many more show their support by keeping an eye on the Village and guarding the Village like a neighborhood watch. Clearly, tourism at the grassroots level has become an important part in many of the 200 Village people's lives [30].

FIGURE 2 4 Viking village entrance—Redrawn from Poulson and Draiby (2005).

The idea of ecotourism development does not involve running around like a warrior with big swords. More realistic life of Vikings was that of farmers. Indeed, the Viking Village simulates a small version of a vast 850 hectare ancient farm that had a sparse population. At the height of the Viking Empire, relatively small number of Scandinavians could never have supported large armies of ships, although this is what was often acclaimed by tenth century monks throughout coastal Europe [31, 32]. The Scandinavian population numbers have not changed much since 800 CE, "even today the Scandinavian landmass supports a population of little more than 17 million people. In the Viking Age ... there were many fewer people" [33]. By 1,000 CE Scandinavia's population was less than 2 million [34]. Since most Vikings were farmers [28, 33, 35], this leaves very few men in their prime age to pillage all of Europe. Therefore, it seems absurd to claim that "by the end of the ninth century, large parts of Europe were so devastated by Vikings that the countryside was a desolate place" [36]. While some Vikings indeed were attacking and pillaging, it is not realistic to envision an estimated few hundred thousand men scattered all over Europe, West Asia, Northern Africa, and North America decimating an entire continent.

2.7 PILOT PROJECT

The objective of the pilot project was to gauge the feasibility of overnight stays in the Viking Village, and to determine what degree of immersing in the Village life would improve cultural understanding of Vikings. It was determined that a stay that spanned 3 days and two nights in the Village would allow the students to have ample time to prepare ecotourism feedback and suggestions. The visit started by walking backward into the Village, an act which simulates walking 1,200 years back in time.

This is an excellent way to get a clearer view of the early Middle Ages. It is also an excellent way to walk-the-talk of ecotourism. Walking backward brings the experience to life because it forces the visitor to slow down and begin to understand the Village on its terms instead of on modern terms.

The right to freely roam around could provide a great opportunity for ecotourism in the Viking Village, because it allows Village visitors to walk to Vestskoven State Forest to pick nettles. One Village worker summed it up nicely: "*It is important to use what the land gives you.*" She walked us into the forest to show us how to collect a big basket full of wild growing nettles, without getting stung. STU4 (2012) explains, "*You must pick the nettle leaf when the plant is young. Older plants can be bitter and fibrous. We must make sure that they haven't flowered.*"

The main ingredients in the soup were chicken and nettles. The recipes used by the Vikings were simple and straightforward as the ingredients come from their surroundings. The rustic cooking techniques created an entirely new challenge as STU13 (2012) witnessed;

> "*It took all afternoon to prepare our meal. I felt a bit irritated that it took so long to prepare and cook the food and it was devoured in minutes.*"

To make their meals, students worked experientially with Viking chisels that were used to make bowls and spoons for cooking. The challenge of medieval utensils was made clear by STU6 (2012): "*We drank out of a horn. The horn is like drinking out of a boot. You have to spin it or it splashes all over your face.*"

Another food related use of the forest was demonstrated by Poulsen, (2012), who said, "*First you are serfs, then you can eat lunch.*" STU8 (2012) enjoyed being serf, as he stated:

> "*We picked branches off maple trees in order to make stakes to hold down the salmon. We picked branches that were shaped in a certain way. The straight end would go into a peg board. The two slanted pieces would hold the fish down. Once we broke the branches off, we cut the pieces so they were the right shape and fit in the peg board. To carve the pieces to the right size, we used actual reconstructed Viking knives. Once we had carved eighteen pieces to the right size, we pegged the fish down to the boards.*"

Students experienced the right to freely roam a second time. Learning efficient use of forest resources was a frequent topic in the students' journals. This experience clearly made a deep impression on them. Chopping down two trees with a reconstructed Viking axe and dragging them back to the Village was a major accomplishment. They roamed around freely in the forest north of the Village to choose the right tree. The optimal tree must be between 20 and 30 years old. The shape must be as straight as possible. Then they learned which side of the forest to choose from and to alternate between the east and west side of the forest to keep nature in equilibrium. They needed to feel the direction of the wind so that it helps take down the tree. It is very important to choose the right side and start the chopping from the opposite site as to avoid a tree fall near people or structures.

The tree chopping ordeal began with a lesson on how to use and swing the axe the right way. The Village workers then studied the area where the tree was going to fall. Suddenly one of them said, "this is the one." He started swinging the axe effortlessly while big chunks of bark flew away in all directions. Students describe this venture in a very amusing way. STU7's (2012) journal entry is quite detailed:

"As soon as I first swung the axe and touched the trunk, then I got a vibration that began in my fingers and traveled to my entire body and with an assuring inner-voice I said 'ooooops I hit the wrong part, no maybe it was the wrong angle, let's try it again'. After a few swings, I realized that no matter how hard you swing, only small pieces jump here and there. Then Claus tells us, the first part was the part where all the water condensates and is the softest area of the tree and once that two to three inches of bark goes away, then you start on the real trunk. The hard work starts now and we started taking turns swinging again and again taking one hit at a time. We started showing each other the number of blisters in our hands, bragging how tough our hands are. Ryan gets the last few hits and the tree goes down, breaking the silence rained over the forest exactly where and how Claus said it would. Then Claus says the easy part is done and now we have to get it ready to drag back to the Village. Claus starts taking measurements and decides the length of the trunk. Then more swinging was done until we cleaned the trunk from the branches. We started hauling the big trunk using a chain and a long rope all the way to the Village."

STU8 (2012) wrote,

"It felt good to do some hard work and help out the Village." And helping the Village, it truly did. The trees were used as a cross beam in the stable (see Figure 2.2) which was finished a few months after we left. The bark was used to braid rope, and the scrap wood was used for cooking fire. There was absolutely no waste.

The third experience of the right to freely roam was playing games within the 13 hectares. Students were taught the value of Viking games as a part of their daily life. They learned quickly that they are not just fun games. The games were designed to prepare them to fight to defend their family, home, Village, and kingdom [2, 35]. As the Village leader said, *"Some enemies may have bigger people or more people than you, but it shouldn't matter, you have to try your best and your region anyway."* It took many years of training to build up the strength to fight man-to-man using only a sword and a shield [28]. Some of the games in the Village simulate strength building activities. One such game is called Gleena and is explained by STU13 (2012):

"Gleena is a great game to practice wrestling the enemy. Two people wrap their arms around each other, lock hands behind their backs, and circle in a dancing motion. When Jørgen yells "Gleena" the two people who are circling begin to wrestle to try and bring the other to the ground. Whoever lands on the ground first is the loser ... What stuck out to me the most was how Jørgen stressed the importance of shaking hands and having eye contact as a sign of respect after the game is over."

2.8 FEASIBILITY OF OVERNIGHT STAYS

The main point of the pilot project was to test the idea of an overnight stay in the Village. Spending two nights did present some challenges. Having students sleep on wood and animal skins in one large common room was difficult to prepare them for, as noted in STU6's (2012) comment:

"I hate spiders, spiders everywhere. How are we going to sleep? No way will I be comfortable. Look up, and there are spiders all around, every corner. I lay down and already I can tell this is going to be a bad night. Starting to get dark. I can't sleep. Ryan sounds like a train. I really have to pee. I can't find the door. I ran my hand along the wall and touched ten spider webs. How am I going to get out of here?"

STU9 (2012) wrote:

"Sleeping in the Viking house was quite an experience. You are not on a mattress. It makes me wonder why we complain for what we have. Maybe life is much easier out here if we try to adapt."

In a sustainable Village that follows the principles of being "bypassed by tourism" [30], overnight visitors truly need to adapt, because there are no accommodations, shops, restaurants, or bars in Risby Village. Other than the pilot study, Viking Village visitors traditionally stay overnight in nearby Copenhagen and drive 30 miles to the rural Village.

Despite a few complaints about the sleeping arrangements, overall Village satisfaction was high. Through the method of learning by doing, the experience in the Village managed to correct all sorts of stereotypical and grossly exaggerated myths about the Vikings. STU5 (2012) wrote:

"I learned more in the Village than in the three museums we visited"

and STU7 (2012) commented,

"We don't have a sense of place and time when looking at an exhibit in a museum."

The authors were surprised to learn that the most high-risk part of the project, the overnight experience, ended up being very popular. It was a huge risk to dare be different from the traditional type of participatory experience. The risk of low trip evaluation, unhappiness, and complaints by truly implementing the core ecotourism concepts was very real.

A much more negative student feedback was expected. It was daring to take students into the medieval era, with rough minimalistic sleeping conditions, and far removed from modern conveniences. The author knew she was testing their limits with no recourse for alternative housing within miles. They eventually raved about how much fun it was to be in the Village. They loved participating in and completing various chores. The "mishaps" during the Village nights somehow added a fun dimension to the overall experience that could never have been imagined. STU7, (2012) attests to the overall success:

"I truly believe that this project was a total success from my standards. I couldn't believe how much knowledge and experience these people have and are willing to share. Life is not always flowers and happy moments, but it is what you make of it is what define a true life warrior."

STU9 (2012) agrees:

"I personally got so involved I started believing and feeling like I am a Viking. Honestly, with only two nights and three days I haven't even scratched the surface of what these people really sacrificed their lives for and are working so hard to share with the rest of the world to taste the Viking era."

Students identified another challenge. They agreed that the Viking Village may be a tough sell in the United States, because there is no similar tourism experience here that people can identify with. Some students had a difficult time visualizing the experience before we arrived. However, the counter question could be: isn't that what ecotourism is all about? We discussed different ways to get people to slow down to adopt the slower travel concept of ecotourism. STU10 (2012) admitted that

"Americans are more interested in where we are going instead of where we have been," while STU12 (2012) noted that

"We are always on the move."

STU11 (2012) brought up an interesting issue that completely surprised the author:

"The real obstacle in bringing people from far away countries has nothing to do with the Village itself. It's the question us Americans got constantly asked: 'Why are you in Denmark?' or 'What's in Denmark?' If Denmark wants visitors, the country will have to answer those questions—why Denmark? Most people I know couldn't locate Denmark on a map, or tell me anything about Denmark."

Even though the rights to freely roam around could provide great opportunities for ecotourism in Denmark, it also presents some challenges. One student had a hard time getting used to a few local people walking through the Village and observe for a few minutes what they were doing. This student didn't appreciate their ability to make a shortcut through the Village on the way to a hiking trail, a freedom that all Danes take for granted and don't really think about. STU11 (2012) explained in her journal:

> *"I didn't like being watched by passing visitors like we were on display. I really didn't like feeling like a zoo animal. I know they didn't mean anything by it, however it was uncomfortable."*

2.9   ENHANCED CULTURAL AWARENESS

Chief among the pilot project's conclusions is that of the distorted images of brutal and vicious Viking lore. Even though, the Village works hard to recreate a realistic environment, the question remains whether an ecotourist would appreciate and welcome the contradiction to their previous impressions of Vikings. The dilemma is that "the image of the Vikings as traders and merchants is less romantic that their image as warriors, invaders and pirates" [33]. Furthermore, contradictions and disagreements abound among authors, scholars, historians, archeologists, and medieval chronicles. Thompson, [36] contradicts himself by describing the Vikings as "the Norse pirates" and that all of Europe felt "the icy grip of the Vikings" (p. 161). The stereotype is completed by stating, "the ruddy, blue-eyed, merciless pirates swooped through like Vandals… spreading terror through Europe" [36]. However, he also admits that the "images of Viking brutality have overshadowed many positive aspects of their culture" and that "most Vikings were farmers" [36].

Viking culture as farmers is more true to what their lives were centered upon. Medieval farming involves not being allowed to use any gadgets that were not used in the early Middle Ages, such as sun glasses and cell phones. To facilitate an awareness of Viking life, visitors (including the students) were required to dress in Viking outfits that were made with fabrics that closely resembled the textiles that were available 1,200 years ago [28, 29]. The textiles were weaved, dyed, and sewn by hand. When students put on headgear, their image of the warrior Viking helmet was shattered. The worst truth offender always has been this helmet. The Viking helmet did not have horns! We spent 3 days in these outfits as STU3's (2010) comment is worth noting:

> *"The whole experience takes people completely out of their element and has the potential of really changing how a person thinks. When we first got to the Village and starting putting on the dresses it seemed like such a silly thing to be doing, but the second we stepped out of that first 'welcome building' I was no longer a college student in 2010, I was a Viking woman in 800CE."*

STU10 (2012) concludes his experience of the pilot project:

> *"After the three days and two nights of activities were over, the group met to debrief with workers at the Viking Village to evaluate the successes and the oppor-*

tunities. All students brought fresh ideas to the table in order to encourage new visitors and to advertise multiple day visits. This pilot project helped promote a historically accurate site that also encourages ecotourism. One would hope that the efforts of [us] is witnessed and expanded upon because, if we wish to preserve our future we must understand our past."

2.10   FEASIBILITY OF ECOTOURISM IN THE UNITED STATES

It is curious to ponder whether the surprising success of this small pilot project could be used as a model for a similar tourism experience in the United States. If STU10 is correct that our future is dependent on our understanding of our past, then we should not hesitate to find better ways to connect with the past. For example, students suggested that in their home state of Colorado, many have forgotten the 1850s gold mine experiences that could be re-created similar to the Viking Village experience. One method would be to utilize one of the over 300 ghost towns. How about having visitors spend 2 days and one night in a reconstructed wagon train before arriving in the resurrected town? Of course it would involve dressing the pioneer way. The cooking experience will come to a new level of appreciation when realizing the challenge of cooking entirely outdoors with rustic utensils. The Viking Village had many herbs and plants to collect, while the wagon train caravans did not. The true lesson here is to learn how they survived across the plains without urban conveniences and without much shelter from the elements, surviving on what they carried with them.

Just like the Viking Village was built using only reconstructed tools, perhaps ghost town buildings could be reconstructed in their original locations using only materials that were available in the 1850's. Perhaps the Viking Village leader could demonstrate the most effective way to use existing core resources of a specific site. In this former ghost town, visitors could be engaged in authentically recreated 1850s activities. One often overlooked fact is how some women would walk for miles to care for and feed sick miners. Perhaps a day hike in traditional clothing to one of the many abandoned mines would solidify impressions of the daily lives of gold miners. How about spending the morning cooking and then bring the food on an afternoon hike to a mine? Some of the visitors could play the role of miners, while others re-enact the lives of townspeople.

Whether it is the Viking Village or the life of Gold Miners, it is apparent from the student reflections in this case study, that the more authentic connection the experiences are with the past the better the opportunity to understand the cultural significance and truth of those that came before us. Like the Viking Village, authentic Gold Miners Town would best practice ecotourism principles by freely roaming around and avoid channeled lines and fences found in commercial Wild West exhibits. To be truly sustainable, such a town would leave few footprints and need to sustain itself with the resources available to the townspeople in the 1800's. Perhaps

American enterprise and stakeholders of ecotourism destinations may not have the patience to wait for several years for a single structure to be constructed by hand, as was the case with the Viking Village's newest stable structure (see Table 2.1). Indeed commitment to ecotourism principles would require investors, communities and all stakeholders to take the time to locally and authentically resource clothing, foods, and structures.

2.11   DISCUSSION QUESTIONS

To assist the reader in understanding the principles of ecotourism and sustainability in authentic Village settings, the authors have prepared discussion questions. The references listed in this case study and the data collected from student and Village resources will assist you in formulating your response:

1. How did the students in this pilot study change their impressions of traditional Viking lore? What activities and experiences contributed to their viewpoint?
2. How is the Viking Village practicing the principles of ecotourism? Could they do more to practice sustainability?
3. What is the feasibility of multiple small group visits to the Viking Village for overnight stays? What are the implications regarding the environment, physical limitations, health and welfare, and legal aspects of participants in overnight stays?
4. What are the positive and negative implications of freely roaming in and out of the Viking Village? How feasible is such a free roaming structure in the United States?
5. How might American perceptions of the Gold Mining age change over the next 1200 years? If what we remember of Vikings is horned hats and murderous raids, what then will we remember of Gold Miners?
6. How would participation in an authentic ecotourism Gold Miner Town change traditional viewpoints of life in the Gold Mining age?

2.12   BENEFITS TO THE READERS, TEACHERS, AND STUDENTS

By participating in a study abroad trip to the Viking Village, students learned how to apply the theoretical concepts of ecotourism to the practical on-site learning experience of the Viking Village. Student activities and observations brought a sense of understanding for the role of ecotourism in preservation and conservation of cultural and natural tourism resources. Students observed and recorded their impressions of the complex importance of blending decision-making processes of the private sector with government processes toward effective application of ecotourism planning, design, and management. Student reflections included rich stories and impressions of how Vikings lived. The hands-on approach to learning in an authentic setting allowed for a deeper understanding of the challenges and benefits of implementing ecotourism principles into a working cultural complex.

The authors expected the students to prepare a field experience question through critical analysis, synthesis, and logical thinking. They were expected to synthesize data collected through the review of literature and primary data collected during the field experience. Students recorded their field notes in a Viking Village note-book. Students recorded their impressions and observations of daily activities and life in the Village. From their observations and record of experiences, they were asked to explain how their participation in the Village experience related to their understanding of the challenges to maintain an authentic cultural experience while implementing ecotourism principles.

Readers of this article may also be able to gauge the level of viability for the Viking Village to be an ecotourism facility for daily and overnight stays. Readers may be able to help evaluate how well the Village experience fostered understanding of ecotourism principles in both daily activities and overnight stays.

2.13 SUGGESTED FURTHER READINGS

—Andkjær, S.; A cultural and comparative perspective on outdoor education in New Zealand and *friluftsliv* in Denmark. *J. Advent. Edu. Outdoor Learn.* **2012**, *12*(2), 121–136.

—Bentsen, P.; Mygind, E.; and Randrup, T.; Towards and understanding of *udeskole*: education outside the classroom in a Danish context. *Education.* **2009**, *37*(1), 29–44.

—Clarke, H.; and Ambrosiani, B.; Towns in the Viking Age. Leicester. England: Palgrave Macmillan, **1991**.

—Roesdahl, E.; Viking Age Denmark. London, England: British Museum Publications, **1982**.

—Salazar, N. B.; Community-based cultural tourism: issues, threats and opportunities. *Journal of Sustainable Tourism.* **2012**, *20*(1), 9–22.

—Sawyer, B.; and Sawyer, P.; Medieval Scandinavia: From Conversion to Reformation, circa 800–1500. Minneapolis, MN: University Of Minnesota Press, **1993**.

ACKNOWLEDGEMENT

This article is dedicated to Jørgen Poulsen, the Viking Village leader. His passion and dedication to provide superior high quality and accurate Viking educational and historical experiences has enriched the lives of all of our students. This Viking Chief retired in 2013 and will be greatly missed.

KEYWORDS

- ecotourism
- ethnography
- freedom to roam
- Viking Village
- culture

REFERENCES

1. Mason, P.; Tourism Impacts, Planning, and Management. New York: Butterworth & Heinemann; **2009**.
2. Okazaki, E.; A community-based tourism model: its conception and use. *J. Sust. Tour.* **2008**, *116*(5), 511–529.
3. Kaltenborn, B.; Haaland, H.; and Sandel, K.; The public right of access—some challenges to sustainable tourism development in Scandinavia. *J. Sust. Tour.* **2001**, *19*(5), 417–433.
4. Højring, K.; The right to roam the countryside—law and reality concerning public access to the landscape in Denmark. *Landscape Urban Plan.* **2002**, *59*, 29–41.
5. The International Ecotourism Society (TIES).; What is Ecotourism. http://www.ecotourism.org (accessed 10–20 January 2013).
6. Wallace, G. N.; and Pierce, S. M.; An evaluation of ecotourism in Amazonas, Brazil. *Ann. Tour. Res.* **1996**, *23*(4), 843–873.
7. Kaae, B.; Ecotourism in Denmark. In: Ecotourism in Scandinavia: Lessons in Theory and Practice. Cambridge, England: Cab International, **2006**.
8. Björk, P.; Marketing a finnish resort. *J. Vacat. Market.* **1997**, *3*(4), 303–313.
9. Wurzinger, S.; and Johansson, M.; Environmental concern and knowledge of ecotourism among three groups of Swedish tourists. *J. Trav. Res.* **2006**, *45*, 217–226.
10. Greenwood, D. J.; Tourism as an agent of change: a Spanish Basque case. *Ethnology.* **1972**, *11*, 80–91.
11. Williams, P. W.; and Gill, A.; Tourism carrying capacity management. In issues in global tourism. Boston: Butterworth Heinemann, **1998**, pp. 229–246.
12. Koning, H.; Travel is destroying a major reason for travelling. The New York Times, 17 November, Section TR, **1974**, p. 590.
13. Smith, V.; Hosts and Guests: The Anthropology of Tourism. Philadelphia: University of Philadelphia Press [original 1979]; **1989**.
14. Hvenegaard, G. T.; and Dearden, P.; Ecotourism versus tourism in a Thai National Park. *Ann. Tour. Res.* **1998**, *25*(3), 700–720.
15. Lele, S. M.; Sustainable development: a critical review. *World Develop,* **1991**, *19*(6), 607–621.
16. Puntenney, P. J.; Solving the environmental equation: an engaging anthropology. In: Global Ecosystems: Creating Options through Anthropological Perspectives. Arlington: NAPA Bulletin; **1995**, pp. 4–17.

17. Gössling, S.; and Hultman, J.; An introduction to ecotourism in Scandinavia. Ecotourism in Scandinavia: Lessons in Theory and Practice. Cambridge, England: Cab International; **2006**.

18. Butler, R. W.; The concept of a tourist area cycle of evolution: implications for management of resources. *Canad. Geog.* **1979,** *1*, 5–12.

19. Plog, S.; Why destinations preservation makes sense. In: Global Tourism. (Eds.) William F. Theobald, Boston: Butterworth Heinemann; **1997,** pp. 251–266.

20. Cooper, C.; and Jackson, S.; Destination life cycle: the isle of man case study. *Ann. Tour. Res.* **1989**, *16*, 377–398.

21. Chiabai, A.; Krassimira, P.; and Lombardi, P.; e-Participation model for sustainable cultural tourism management: a bottom-up approach. *Int. J. Tour. Res.* **2013,** *15*, 35–51.

22. Choi, H.; Murray, C.; and Murray, I.; Resident attitudes toward sustainable community tourism. *J. Sust. Tour*. **2010**, *18*(4), 575–594.

23. Agar, M.; The Professional Stranger: An Informal Introduction to Ethnography. San Diego: Academic Press; **1996**.

24. Geertz, C.; Being there: anthropology and the scene of writing. In: Works and Lives: the Anthropologist as Author. Standford: Stanford University Press; **1988**, pp. 1–24.

25. De Munck, V. C.; and Sobo, E. J.; Participant observation: a thick explanation of conflict in a Sri Lankan village. In: Using Methods in the Field: A Practical Introduction and Casebook, Walnut Creek, CA: Alta Mira Press; **1996**, pp. 39–53.

26. Fennell, D.; Ecotourism. New York: Routledge; **2008**.

27. Vikingelandsbyen; Vikingelandsbyen [Viking Village]. **2012**. http://www.vikingelandsbyen.dk/ (accessed 1 May 2012).

28. Poulsen, J.; Personal interviews and visits to Vikingelandsbyen (Viking Village). Albertslund, Denmark, various dates and years; **2008–2012**.

29. Poulsen, J.; and Draiby, B.; Salshuset—Fra Drøm Til Virkelighed [Main House—The Construction] Albertslund, Denmark: Paedagogisk Center Albertslund; **2005**.

30. Connell, B.; and Rugendyke, B.; (Eds.) Tourism at the Grassroots: Villagers and Visitors In the Asia Pacific. London: Routledge; **2008**.

31. Gabrielsen, K.; A Short History of the Vikings. Copenhagen, Denmark: Aschehoug Dansk Forlag; **2000**.

32. Brøndsted, J.; The Vikings. London, England: Penguin Books; **1987**.

33. Batey, C.; Clarke, H.; Page, R. I.; and Price, N.; Cultural Atlas of the Viking World. New York: Facts in File; **1994**.

34. Russell, J. C.; Medieval population. *Social Forces.* **1935**, *15*(4, May), 503–511.

35. Roesdahl, E.; Vikingernes Verden [The Viking World]. Viborg, Denmark: Norhaven Bogtrykkeri a/s; **1991**.

36. Thompson, J. M.; The Medieval World. Washington DC: National Geographic Society; **2009**.

CHAPTER 3

SLOW FOOD, SLOW TOURISM, AND SUSTAINABLE PRACTICES: A CONCEPTUAL MODEL

L. L. LOWRY[1] and R. M. BACK[2]

[1]Associate Professor, Department of Hospitality & Tourism Management, Isenberg School of Management, University of Massachusetts, 90 Campus Center Way Amherst, Massachusetts 01003, 413-545-4041, E-mail: llowry@isenberg.umass.edu

[2]Doctoral Student, Department of Hospitality & Tourism Management, Isenberg School of Management, University of Massachusetts, 90 Campus Center Way, Amherst, Massachusetts 01003, 413-545-5376, E-mail: rback@som.umass.edu

CONTENTS

Slow Tourism, a new type of tourism that originated in Italy, has the potential to change how we travel and how we embed sustainable practices within our destinations. The aim of this chapter is to trace its evolution, critique existing definitions, and develop a conceptual model of Slow Tourism that focuses on sustainable practices. We argue that Slow Tourism is both an outgrowth of and is inextricably tied to the Slow Food Movement, can occur in both urban and rural settings, and is much more than a state of mind or form of mobility.

As an emerging phenomenon, Slow Tourism has been studied on a limited basis. Currently, it lacks a universally agreed upon definition and, in some cases, authors choose to use it interchangeability with Slow Travel. We do not subscribe to the notion that Slow Tourism and Slow Travel are one in the same. Instead, we treat them as distinct entities that may or may not be linked together. In addition, most of the available data are of the case study [1], place specific variety [2, 3], or provide critical or interpretive analysis of different aspects of Slow Tourism such as mobility [1, 4–6, 7] or activities and experiences [1, 8]. At this juncture, two conceptual frameworks—one for the Development of Slow Tourism [9] and the other on Slow Travel [10]—have been suggested, and no empirically tested scales for Slow Tourism have been reported in the literature.

The conceptual model suggested in this chapter builds on the frameworks proposed by Lowry and Lee [9] and Lumsdon and McGrath [9] and incorporates the ethical dimension of sustainable tourism suggested by Hughes [11] and the political dimension suggested by Butler [12] (p. 224). A critical interpretive critique of the extant literature [13] is used to identify the salient features of Slow Tourism, and to locate this new genre of tourism within the context of sustainable practices. This type of framework is appropriate for investigating "what" and "how" [14] and provides a richer understanding of a type of tourism that has evolved from a sociopolitical movement [8–10, 15, 16]. Three overarching questions drove our inquiry and shaped our conceptual model: How did it emerge? What is it? How does it fit with sustainable practices and development?

3.1   THE EMERGENCE OF SLOW TOURISM

3.1.1   A PANACEA FOR THE ILLS OF MASS TOURISM

Long before Slow Tourism had a name, Krippendorf [17] envisioned an alternative type of tourism that was softer, more environmentally friendly than mass tourism, and advocated for tourism practices with a slower pace that featured relaxed enjoyment while simultaneously engaging with local people and places. Various authors argued the virtues of "soft" versus "hard" tourism [18–22] and described types of tourism such as rural, eco, green, agricultural, individual, and small-scale that were preferable alternatives to large-scale, mass tourism. The quest to identify and implement an "alternative," more "sustainable" type of tourism consumed most of the

1990s and continues to the present. The following is a vignette of a few of the influential writings that define the genre:

In 1990, Nash and Butler [23] reported on papers presented at the Academy for the Study of Tourism's first meeting in 1989, which focused on the theoretical perspectives on alternative tourism as well as the differing opinions and lack of agreement on how to define "alternative."

Smith and Eadington [24] provided an introduction to emerging alternatives and presented both theoretical perspectives and case studies. By 1993, the more environmentally friendly, alternative type of tourism was firmly captured under the umbrella of "sustainable tourism" with the launch of the first edition of the *Journal of Sustainable Tourism* by co-editors Bramwell and Lane and their seminal article [25] in that first edition.

Over the next 5 years numerous scholarly articles were produced, numerous definitions were suggested, and little agreement was achieved—with the exception that tourism's connection with sustainable development was important and necessary. What followed this exploratory phase was a series of articles admonishing the tourism research establishment for not moving forward regardless of agreement on the definition [26, 27]. Nonetheless, major work [28, 29] continued to define and conceptualize the genre. More recent articles focused on various aspects of sustainable tourism such as the unknown impact of greater global awareness of environmental problems on travel [30], travel consumer behavior and climate change [31–35], development issues [36], policy issues [37], research issues [38, 39], a debate on mass tourism and sustainability [40–42], and a recap of the past 30 years [12].

3.1.2 A QUEST FOR A NEW SOCIAL ORDER

Much of the debate and search for answers can be attributed to "Our Common Future," more commonly called the Brundtland Report [43], the seminal document that called for a new way of thinking and acting on a global scale. This report called for four broad initiatives which are shown in Table 3.1:

TABLE 3 1   Four broad initiatives from "Our Common Future"—The Brundtland report

- "to propose long-term environmental strategies for achieving sustainable development by the year 2000 and beyond;
- to recommend ways concern for the environment may be translated into greater cooperation among developing countries and between countries at different stages of economical and social development and lead to the achievement of common and mutually supportive objectives that take account of the interrelationships between people, resources, environment, and development;
- to consider ways and means by which the international community can deal more effectively with environment concerns; and

- to help define shared perceptions of long-term environmental issues and the appropriate efforts needed to deal successfully with the problems of protecting and enhancing the environment, a long-term agenda for action during the coming decades, and aspirational goals for the world community" (52) (p. 11).

The first globally acknowledged definition of sustainable development came from this document through its suggestion that "humanity has the ability to make development sustainable to ensure that it meets the needs of the present without compromising the ability of future generations to meet their own needs" [43] (p. 24). Focusing global attention on the environment and sustainable development continues to be the pressing agenda of the United Nations and they have provided three additional global forums for addressing these urgent needs. In 1992, they held the Earth Summit [44], which led to the Earth Summit Agreements. The first, "Agenda 21," was a global action plan for all aspects of sustainable development. The second, the "Rio Declaration on Environment and Development," provided a guiding set of 27 principles that defined the rights and responsibilities of states and placed at the forefront the role of women in sustainable development [44] (p. 7, Principle 20). Another prominent principle in the "Rio Declaration" was the need for the reduction and elimination of unsustainable patterns of production and consumption while simultaneously promoting appropriate policies and practices [44] (p. 4, Principle 8).

In 2002, the United Nations hosted the World Summit in Johannesburg, South Africa [45], which focused on the challenges still faced, issues of globalization, and the pressing need for change in production and consumption. More recently, they hosted RIO+20. The outcome document produced by RIO+20, "The Future We Want—Our Common Vision" [46], reaffirmed commitment to achieving sustainable development by saying that eliminating poverty, changing unsustainable practices and replacing them with sustainable patterns of production and consumption, and protecting and managing resources for economic and social development are the all-encompassing objectives of and vital requirements for sustainable development (p. 2).

These politically charged United Nations initiatives and the global calls to action that they invoked have shaped the discourse of sustainability since the late twentieth century. Simultaneously, a grass-roots type of political activism emerged in opposition to modern industrial society. The characteristic of modern industrial society that these activists found most troubling was globalization; particularly, its ever-increasing fast pace and the consumption of resources without regard to the environmental and social costs it produced in the pursuit of economic gain by an elite few. It is this second type of activism that gave a life to Slow Tourism.

3.2   FROM LOCAL TO GLOBAL AND BACK AGAIN—A "SLOW" MOVEMENT THAT LAUNCHED A REVOLUTIONARY WORLDWIDE CHANGE AGENDA

Who would have imagined that a protest staged by actors and intellectuals [47] outside the first McDonald's restaurant in Italy would launch a revolution? Perhaps it was their unique form of protest [47, 48], which was highlighted by a lunch consisting of pasta and wine at a large dining table set up in the middle of the Piazza di Spagna which was the antithesis to fast food that garnered interest. At any rate, as a more permanent form of protest, Carlo Petrini, a "left leaning" food and wine writer, and fellow Italian epicureans formed a gastronomical society known as ARCI Gola which was later named Slow Food [49–51]. In 1998, co-founder and poet, Folco Portinari, wrote the Slow Food Manifesto which was presented and signed by delegates from 15 countries and gave voice to the new International Slow Food Movement [52].

Political activism was and continues to be the foremost goal of the Slow Food Movement. The political nature of the International Slow Food Movement is explicit in its Slow Food Manifesto [53] shown in Table 3.2 and the numerous initiatives it takes and activities it encourages [52, 54].

TABLE 3 2   Slow food manifesto

"We are enslaved by speed and have all succumbed to the same insidious virus: *Fast Life*, which disrupts our habits, pervades the privacy of our homes and forces us to eat Fast Foods. To be worthy of the name, *Homo Sapiens* should rid himself of speed before it reduces him to a species in danger of extinction. A firm defense of quiet material pleasure is the only way to oppose the universal folly of *Fast Life*. May suitable doses of guaranteed sensual pleasure and slow, long-lasting enjoyment preserve us from the contagion of the multitude who mistake frenzy for efficiency. Our defense should begin at the table with *Slow Food*. Let us rediscover the flavors and savors of regional cooking and banish the degrading effects of *Fast Food*. In the name of productivity, *Fast Life* has changed our way of being and threatens our environment and our landscapes. So *Slow Food* is now the only truly progressive answer. This is what real culture is all about: developing taste rather than demeaning it. And what better way to set about this than an international exchange of experiences, knowledge, projects? Slow Food guarantees a better future. *Slow Food* is an idea that needs plenty of qualified supporters who can help turn this (slow) motion into an international movement, with the little snail as its symbol" (69) (p. 1).

Today, Slow Food characterizes itself as a global, nonprofit organization with more than 100,000 members in 1,500 convivia (i.e., local chapters) located in 150 countries that are "linking the pleasure of good food with a commitment to their community and the environment" [55] (para. 1). They posit the notion that "every-

one has a fundamental right to the pleasure of good food and consequently the responsibility to protect the heritage of biodiversity, culture and knowledge that make
this pleasure possible" [55] (para. 1).

It is this call to action and embodied activism that led to the Italian based Cittaslow (Slow Cities) Movement, an outgrowth of Slow Food, which was established
in 1999 by Carlo Petrini, the president of Slow Food, and the mayors of four Italian
towns (Bra, Greve, Orvieto, and Positano) that became the first Cittaslow certified
towns. Cittaslow's goal has always been "to enlarge the philosophy of Slow Food
to local communities and to government of towns, applying the concepts of ecogas-
tronomy at practice of everyday life" [56] (para. 2). From a local organization consisting of four Italian cities in 1999 to a global network of 177 cities in 27 countries
in 2013 [57], Cittaslow brings the local to the global and back again in the form of
certified "Slow Cities."

3.2.1   DEFINING SLOW TOURISM

Against the backdrop of global calls for living a more sustainable lifestyle that produces sustainable patterns of production and consumption, the expanding worldwide lived experience of the relentless fast pace of modern life, and the sociopolitical movements of Slow Food and Cittaslow that call for changes in lifestyle values
and both production and consumption practices, Slow Tourism emerged as a new
form of tourism. But, what makes it new or different from other forms of tourism?
The following five questions frame the scholarly discourse and provide a critical
lens for its examination: Is it an "alternative" type of tourism; and, if so, an alternative to what other type(s) of tourism? Is it a form of political consumption; and, if
so what are its tenets?

Are Slow Tourism and Slow Travel different, potentially connected, or one and
the same? Is it a subgenre of Sustainable Tourism; and, if so, what kind? Is it related
to the broader umbrellas of sustainability and sustainable development; and, if so,
what is its relationship?

3.2.2   SLOW TOURISM AS AN "ALTERNATIVE" TYPE OF
TOURISM

If we use the myriad of possibilities identified in the writings of authors in Smith
and Eadington's [24] seminal work on alternative tourism, then Slow Tourism provides a new "alternative." The nuances of "alternative" tourism and the continuing
scholarly discourse on the topic is extensive and beyond the scope of this chapter.
However, the following vignette exemplifies the antithetical dichotomies suggested
by scholars examining the genre of Slow Tourism:

In the general sense, Slow Tourism is the antithesis of Fast Tourism, which could
be viewed using the literal meanings of pace or speed [4, 7, 10, 58]. On the other

hand, it could be viewed in a more metaphorical way, with "fast" exemplifying the ills of the increasing pressures of modern life and its trappings such as "fast food" and "time poverty" and "slow" symbolizing a different way of conceiving personal values, interacting with others, and taking back some control over one's way of living and being [2, 8, 9, 59, 60]. To extend the metaphoric transfer, if Mass Tourism is the spawn produced from the ideology and praxis of modern life, then Slow Tourism is its antithetical rival.

As not only an "alternative" but also a rival perspective, Slow Tourism can be viewed as an alternative to Mass Tourism in a number of different ways. The first point of difference is its explicit treatment of development policies and practices that are locally based, locally controlled, locally appropriate, and that benefit the local people. Conway and Timms [2] (p. 330) say that it exemplifies a "development-from-below" model that makes tourism planning, management and benefits accessible to everyone. They [61] (p. 73) also say that its theoretical basis is "soft growth," which affords qualitative efficiency by developing local resources and improving efficiency levels of production, consumption and qualitative returns, instead of "hard growth," which calls for increases in size and scale as well as increased production and consumption. Hall [62] (p. 55) characterizes this efficiency approach as "degrowth" or "rightsizing" that produces a steady state economy. The actual dichotomy of large scale and small scale has a caveat of place appropriateness that focuses not only on the positive economic benefits to the community but also positively impacts the environment, the climate, and the social fabric of the community —the "quadruple bottom line" [63] (p. 24). Secondly, it provides a foil to Mass Tourism's commodification of culture by providing the traveler with an in-depth, authentic, and meaningful connection to people and places through active engagement and immersion in the unique aspects of place such as its culture, heritage, food, and its environment that is made possible by the slowness (e.g., lack of haste) of the travel experience [1, 4, 8, 10, 58, 59, 64, 65].

3.2.3 SLOW TOURISM AS A FORM OF POLITICAL CONSUMPTION

Without doubt, Slow Tourism can be viewed as a form of political consumption [6–9, 62]. Not only does it exhibit the tenets of its Slow Food Movement roots, but also takes a firm stand, draws a hard line, and uniquely, shows a gentle hand. It is this mindful, deliberate, and sustainable set of consumption practices that stands in opposite to the mindless consumption practices associated with Mass Tourism. Or as Dickinson et al. [6] frame it, this type of vacation requires the power to act instead of ambivalence (p. 485). Hall [62] simply calls this mindful type of consumption "slow consumption," which he views as a necessity for the achievement of sustainable consumption.

Some other issues with the construct of Slow Tourism, as a focused type of consumption, are related to consumer markets. A number of authors suggest that Slow Tourism may be perceived as elitist and only for a wealthy clientele [10, 58, 65]. Other authors suggest that it is exclusionary or only for particular niche market segments [2, 4, 8, 58]. Additional authors say that consumers may select a Slow Tourism type of holiday for its status enhancing potential [5, 9, 60].

3.2.4 SLOW TOURISM AND SLOW TRAVEL: DIFFERENT, POTENTIALLY CONNECTED, OR ONE AND THE SAME?

There is ongoing dissension in both scholarly and popular discourse about the relationship between Slow Tourism and Slow Travel. Key proponents of the "one-and-the-same" philosophy [4, 5, 10] choose to call the phenomenon Slow Travel and derive their perspective from a holistic view point that places the journey to and from the destination and the time spent at the destination as the sum total of the travel experience. Dickinson et al. [5] even argue that separating the two can substantially increase the carbon foot print of the vacation and suggest that vacations that include long-haul air travel are little more than ruses (p. 293). Another "one-and-the-same" approach [1] is more semantic in that Slow Travel and Tourism are used interchangeably to mean the same thing and while most of the work they present is focused on mobility, they choose to use Slow Tourism to represent their perspective.

Other scholars [8, 9, 58, 61] argue that while they both emerged from the same political discourse and practices, they are inherently different and may or may not have the potential to be linked. Two particular rationales for their separation have to do with focus and practicality. In the first case, Slow Travel is linked to the transport or journey and is therefore a demand-focused perspective while Slow Tourism is linked to the destination and subsequently is supply-focused [8, 58, 63]. Definitions shown in Table 3.3 provide examples of this demand/supply dichotomy.

TABLE 3.3 Definitions showing demand and supply dichotomy of slow travel and slow tourism

Slow Travel	Slow Tourism
"Holiday travel involving shorter trips (distance) and longer stays (time) where air transport is rejected in favor of less environmentally damaging forms of overland transport which become incorporated as part of the holiday experience" [66] (p. 1).	"This new version of tourism includes not only accommodation (which must be simple), but also diet (healthy), leisure (peaceful), culture (local), services (provided in a peaceful atmosphere), and respect for the natural environment" [59] (p. 96).

TABLE 3.3   *(Continued)*

Slow Travel	Slow Tourism
"Slow travel can therefore be best described as a different type of holiday which has the potential to reduce environmental impact" [10] (p. 276).	"Tourism which involves making real and meaningful connections with people (i.e., local community, your companions, yourself), places, culture, food, heritage, and the environment" [64] (slide #11).
"Slow travel results in lower carbon emissions due to modal choice" [5] (p. 285).	"…slow tourism is a 'development–from-below' initiative that has ecological sensitivity as well as human capacity building potential…" [61] (p. 75).

Secondly, treating both transport and destination as inextricably tied together as suggested by Dickinson et al. [5] creates a problematic situation [8, 9, 61, 67] that we argue is very different than a ruse. If the rejection of all long-haul air transport and short stay holidays are essential to the "slow" concept, then for many places and countries in the world, staycations (i.e., vacationing at home) [8] would be the only holiday option, as there are no other feasible ways to access the location other than by long-haul air travel. In addition, many places do not have a widely available low-carbon transport infrastructure (i.e., public rail and bus systems). Another constraint is that available vacation time is also place dependent. If extended stay holidays are the only ones that qualify as "slow," then only travelers who have extensive vacation time can enjoy this form of holiday. In other words, this type of tourism would truly be exclusive in nature as it is only possible in places such as Europe, Japan, New Zealand, and South Korea that have an affluent population, with sufficient number of vacation days, living in proximity to numerous destinations which can be accessed using excellent public transport [61] (p. 72). We take the position that more people and places across the globe have the potential to benefit from the new ways of consumption and production exemplified in these two tourism paradigms if they are treated as separate and potentially linked.

3.3   LOCATING SLOW TOURISM IN THE DISCOURSE OF SUSTAINABLE TOURISM AND THE BROADER CONTEXTS OF SUSTAINABILITY AND SUSTAINABLE DEVELOPMENT

A number of the scholars investigating the genre of Slow Tourism believe that it is a form of Sustainable Tourism [1, 4, 5, 6, 10, 58, 61, 68] and/or sustainable development [8, 9, 59, 61]. And, if this is the case, then the foremost issue that must be addressed is: sustainable for whom and in what ways?

With all issues regarding tourism in general and sustainable tourism, sustainability and sustainable development in particular, there are political, ethical, and practi-

cal considerations. Each of these focal areas has been addressed in the tourism literature; however, even a brief coverage is beyond the scope of this chapter. Instead,
we used the discourse of Hughes [11] and the concluding vision of Swarbrooke [29]
(pp. 358–360) as a departure point for the consideration of ethical issues and the
discourse of both Butler [12] and Hall [15, 62] to frame the political critique. We
used both the Buckley notion for assessing the sustainability of tourism "through
its contributions to five global-scale social processes, summarized as: population,
peace, prosperity, pollution and protection" [12] (p. 227) and the "quadruple bottom
line" (i.e., economic, social, environmental, and climate considerations) found in
the Davos Declaration [67] (p. 24) to locate Slow Tourism within the parameters of
Sustainable Tourism. Finally, we used the insights of McCool [12] to systemically
locate both the discourse and praxis of Slow Tourism within the global outcome
goals identified by the United Nations [43, 44, 46], while simultaneously retaining
the sense of commonality and purpose with the highly political and consumption
based Slow Food Movement (see www.slowfood.com).

Figure 3.1 shows the nature of Slow Tourism's embedded position within the
continuous push-back/reinvigoration cycle that occurs in the Slow Food and Citta-

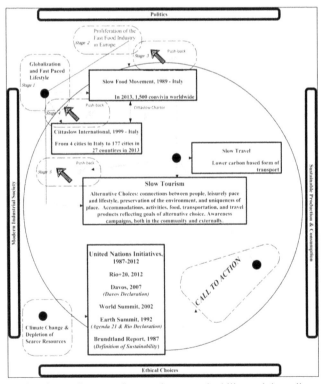

FIGURE 3.1   Time is running out: slow tourism, sustainability and the call to action.

slow Movements, which was adapted from Lowry and Lee [9] (p. 8), as well as the continuous calls to action initiated by the United Nations. It also locates the resultant contentious discourse within the relentless demands of modern industrial society, the idiosyncrasies of politics, the problematic conundrums of ethical choice, and the pressing need for sustainable production and consumption practices. The systemic cycle that is depicted never stops; as one action triggers another, connects to other subsystems and perpetuates the system. The cacophony of voices just grows louder and more urgent as the clock continues to tick and the possibility for global sustainable solutions has a finite future.

3.3.1 SLOW TOURISM AS AN EXEMPLARY OF SUSTAINABLE TOURISM

A preamble: Firstly, if we adopted Dodds'[68] viewpoint that Slow Tourism is just one of the various subtypes of Sustainable Tourism and not particularly new or different, then our critique would be over. Secondly, if we viewed Slow Tourism as primarily a promotional identity or brand [2], albeit a positive one [2, 8, 59], we would need to temper our linkage of Slow Tourism to sustainable issues of any kind with skeptical caution. And, if we chose to privilege Hall's premonition of "…its seemingly inevitable commodification as yet another marketing slogan for screwing the Earth" [16] (p. 65), then we would proverbially pack our bags and go home. More importantly, if we believed Wheeller [12] (pp. 235, 238) who suggested that Slow Tourism is "nonsense" that eludes common sense and that it is one among other idealistic versions of sustainable tourism (which he views as just a "buzzword"), then we would not have written this chapter.

Instead, we, like McCool [12] (p. 240), take an optimistic perspective and believe that human passion has the power to overcome seemingly insurmountable obstacles. We find sufficient evidence in the political underpinning and tenets of Slow Tourism as well as its praxis to make the argument that the spark of human passion is part and parcel of this new tourism genre. More specifically, we believe that it is the aggressive pushback against the representations of an unsustainable world order that gives Slow Tourism its promise for achievable sustainable development. Will it supplant mindless mass tourism? Will all peoples and places embrace it? Is it even possible in all locations?—probably not. On the other hand, it needs to be viewed in the context of a grass-roots movement that takes a firm stand (through mindful consumption, production, and lifestyle choices), draws a hard line (holds everyone responsible and accountable for its success), and that keeps a gentle hand (remains inextricably connected to both the pleasures of living a life—being human—as well as the protection of resources, both environmental and social, that make this good-life possible—being humane). We find it odd and disheartening that Wheeller [12] (p. 235) considers being human and humane to be mutually exclusive conditions as this would preclude the possibility of "doing well" while also "doing good."

Metaphorically—taking a firm stand and drawing a hard line while keeping a gentle hand—militant consumption with a soul—might not be so different than staging a protest using a dinner table loaded with good pasta and wine. If a protest against a McDonald's restaurant in Rome can launch a global movement that continues to grow and evolve, then Slow Tourism has the potential to positively contribute to sustainable practice.

The conceptual model we propose aims to capture a snapshot of the constantly morphing essence of Slow Tourism and locate it in the equally changing landscape of sustainability. Figure 3.2 presents our emergent conceptual model of Slow Tourism as Sustainable Practice.

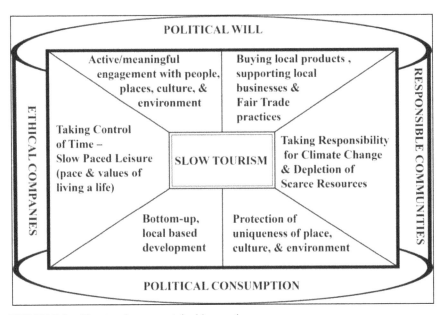

FIGURE 3.2   Slow tourism as sustainable practice.

Political Will is the first and foremost construct in our proposed model. Without global political will, sustainability will not be achievable. Secondly, companies need to both embrace and actually practice corporate social responsibility. Thirdly, global communities of people need to take responsibility for their actions. And lastly, without a growing number of people who make very targeted and mindful choices (i.e., engage in political consumption), neither companies nor communities and the political masters they serve will change their current extractive and exploitive practices that serve today's gain at tomorrow's expense. In other words, political consumption is the wake-up call that impacts the economic bottom line and causes a ripple effect that serves as change agent that opens new possibilities and potential for positive economic, social and environmental practices. Slow Tourism, a gem in the rough, is an emerging type of tourism that is both an example of political consumption (i.e., mindful traveler choices with regards to time, meaningful engagement, purchases, and carbon footprint) as well as sustainable patterns of production, policies and practices (i.e., local-based tourism development that benefits the community and protects its uniqueness of place, culture and the environment).

3.4   IMPLICATIONS AND CONCLUSIONS

3.4.1   MARKETING IMPLICATIONS

Is it a marketing ploy or does it have sufficient and discernible practices that guarantee a genuine and unique experience? While there are naysayers such as Hall [16] and Wheeller [12], two works [2, 8] provide extensive insight on the value of the "slow" brand and suggest ways in which the "slow" brand can be used as both an external and internal marketing device. For example, it shares the philosophy and praxis of both the Slow Food and Slow City movements and could benefit from the growing global consumer interest in both Slow Food and Slow Cities and potentially appeal to market segments that already identify with the "slow" concepts such as environmentally, culturally, or gastronomically conscious consumers [8, 69]. Internally, it could be used as a way to focus rejuvenation efforts, encourage local participation, and create synergisms emanating from uniqueness of place [2, 8].

Another marketing consideration is the use of the word "slow" and its plethora of both positive and negative connotations [8, 58, 59, 65]. The most worrisome aspect of the use of "slow" in marketing initiatives is the potential for people or places to be perceived as backwards [8, 58, 59, 65] or perhaps boring. As a result of the ambiguities of the meaning of slowness, destinations may be reluctant to brand themselves as "slow" [58].

3.4.2   RESEARCH IMPLICATIONS

This chapter provides a critical interpretive critique of the current literature on Slow Tourism and the first conceptual model of Slow Tourism that focuses on sustainable practices. Together, these artifacts aim to fill the knowledge gap and illuminate the divergent opinions about this emerging type of tourism. Its trustworthiness or credibility is based on a close reading and synthesis of extant literature. The new insights are transferable and the connections to sustainable practices are relevant and achievable. More importantly, this chapter increases both catalytic and tactical authenticity (i.e., stimulation and empowerment to act) [70] with regards to the evolving development of Slow Tourism and sustainable destinations. Empirical researchers will also be able to use concepts identified in this chapter to begin the process of building scales; and developing and testing new hypotheses.

3.4.3   PRACTICAL IMPLICATIONS

Figure 3.1 provides a dynamic systems perspective that locates Slow Tourism within the broader context of the Slow Food and Cittaslow movements and the global call for sustainable action. Figure 3.2 depicts the emergent conceptual model of Slow Tourism as Sustainable Practice and lays out the parameters for engaging in sustainable actions. Together, these two figures make explicit the complex components of Slow Tourism and make it more understandable for communities, consumers, and academics.

For example, governments and community organizations will have more comprehensive information about Slow Tourism and its implications for both economic gain as well as sustainable practices for their particular destination. Individual travelers will become more aware of how their travel consumption practices impact the globe. In addition, marketers will have a better understanding of how the "slow" brand could provide a unifying concept for clustering sustainable lifestyle practices.

3.4.4   CONCLUSIONS

The critical interpretive critique provided in this chapter makes a valuable contribution to the fields of hospitality and tourism by offering a comprehensive synthesis of the divergent definitions of Slow Tourism. It differentiates Slow Travel from Slow Tourism and proposes a conceptual model of Slow Tourism that focuses on sustainable practices that are suitable to both travelers and destinations across the globe.

In addition, we argue that Slow Tourism is definitely not about staying in a chain-based, island resort compound and mindlessly sitting at the beach, reading a book, and drinking a piña colada. While this may be a touristic activity that involves little movement (i.e., is slow paced), it belongs to Mass Tourism's commodification of island life. As such, it neither supports active, meaningful engagement with local people, their culture, and environment nor provides economic benefit to the community. We also take the position that it is not just a restful state of mind or body. Instead, we place political will, corporate social responsibility, responsible communities, and political consumption at the forefront of Slow Tourism. It is about sustainable change—real actions, not just talk about actions. It is also about taking control of one's time and being responsible for actions and choices.

If we are what we eat (e.g., fair trade, organic, locally grown and prepared vs. mass produced, genetically modified or sprayed with pesticides, sourced from food jobbers and served in fast food restaurants), then the same could be said of our travel choices. How we choose to live our lives, who we share them with, how much or how little time we spend in active engagement with others, and what type of world we privilege are all part and parcel of who we are and how we get on in life. Our worldview and consumption practices ultimately influence whether we choose an extractive and exploitive type of holiday or one that exemplifies sustainable practices. Choices are often complicated and the real work of sustainability is not easy. Slow Tourism is an opportunity for sustainable change that is simultaneously enjoyable and actionable.

3.5 DISCUSSION QUESTIONS, TEAM EXERCISES AND ADDITIONAL READING MATERIAL

3.5.1 DISCUSSION QUESTIONS

— What steps could you take to reduce your carbon footprint when you travel?
— In what ways do you control your time and in what ways does time control you?
— How would you go about engaging with people, places, culture, and the environment when you travel?
— Under what circumstances would you stay in locally owned (not chain-type) accommodations, eat in local restaurants serving local types of food, or buy locally made products?
— How do you use your consumption practices to influence change?

3.5.2 TEAM EXERCISES

— Identify locations (both urban and rural) that have the potential to develop Slow Tourism; justify your reasons for selecting these places; and describe specific ways that they could use Slow Tourism to stimulate "development-from-below" policies, plans, and development agendas.
— Design a "slow" based marketing campaign for a particular destination that showcases the positive aspects of a Slow Tourism type of holiday while simultaneously negating the "backwards" or "boring" connotations of the word "slow."
—Use the WorldChanging website (http://www.worldchanging.com/) to identify various sustainability trends and issues and then discuss ways that tourism is, is not, or could be contributing positively or negatively to the trends and issues that were identified.

3.6 ADDITIONAL READING MATERIAL

— Dodds, F.; Schneeberger, K.; and Ullah, F.; Review of implementation of Agenda 21 and the Rio Principles: Synthesis—Sustainable development in the 21st century *(SD21)*. **2012**, January. Retrieved from http://sustainabledevelopment.un.org/content/documents/641Synthesis_report_Web.pdf

— Drexhange, J.; and Murphy, D.; Sustainable development: From Brundtland to Rio 2012. United Nations International Institute for Sustainable Development. **2010**, September. Retrieved from http://www.un.org/wcm/webdav/site/climatechange/shared/gsp/docs/GSP1-6_Background%20on%20Sustainable%20Devt.pdf

— Steffen, A.; (Ed.); World Changing: A User's Guide for the 21st Century. New York: Harry N. Abrams, **2006**.

KEYWORDS

- **Mass Tourism**
- **New Social Order**
- **Slow Tourism**

REFERENCES

1. Fullagar, S.; Markwell, K.; and Wilson, E.; (Eds.); Slow Tourism: Experiences and Mobilities, *54*. Bristol: Channel View Publications; **2012.**

2. Conway, D.; and Timms, B.; Re-branding alternative tourism in the Caribbean: the case for 'slow tourism'. *Tour Hos Res.* **2010**, *10*(4), 329–344.

3. Timms, B.; and Conway, D.; Slow tourism at the Caribbean's geographical margins. *Tour Geog.* **2012**, *14*(3), 396–418.

4. Dickinson, J.; and Lumsdon, L.;. Slow Travel and Tourism. London: Earthscan; **2010**.

5. Dickinson, J.; Lumsdon, L.; and Robbins, D.;. Slow travel: issues for tourism and climate change. *J. Sust. Tour.* **2011**, *19*(3), 281–300.

6. Dickinson, J.; Robbins, D.; and Lumsdon, L.; Holiday travel discourses and climate change. *J. Trans. Geog.* **2011**, *18*(3), 482–489.

7. Molz, J.; Representing pace in tourism mobilities: staycations, slow tourism and The Amazing Race. *J. Tour. Cul. Chan.* **2009**, *7*(4), 270–286.

8. Heitmann, S.; Robinson, P.; and Povey, G.; Slow food, slow cities and slow tourism. In: Research Themes for Tourism (Eds.) Robinson, P.; Heitmann, S.; and Dieke, P.; Wallingford, UK: CABI; **2011**, pp. 114–127.

9. Lowry, L.; and Lee, M.; CittaSlow, slow cities, slow food: Searching for a model for the development of slow tourism. In: Travel & Tourism Research Association, 42nd Annual Conference Proceedings: Seeing the Forest and the Trees–Big Picture Research in a Detail–Driven World, June 19–21, London, Ontario, Canada. Retrieved from http://works.bepress.com/lowry_linda/3/, **2011**, pp. 1–13.

10. Lumsdon, L.; and McGrath, P.; Developing a conceptual framework for slow travel: a grounded theory approach. *J. Sust. Tour.* **2011**, *19*(3), 265–279.

11. Hughes, G.; The cultural construction of sustainable tourism. *Tour. Manag.* **1995**, *16*(1), 49–59.

12. McCool, S.; Butler, R.; Buckley, R.; Weaver, D.; and Wheeler, B.; Is concept of sustainability utopian: Ideally perfect but impractical? *Tour. Recreat. Res.* **2013**, *38*(2), 213–242.

13. Denzin, N.; and Lincoln, Y.; (Eds.); The SAGE Handbook of Qualitative Research (4th Ed.). London: Sage; **2011**.

14. Janesick, V.; The dance of qualitative research design. In: Handbook of Qualitative Research London: Sage; **1994**, pp. 209–219.

15. Hall, C. M.; Researching the political in tourism where knowledge meets power. In Fieldwork in Tourism: Methods, Issues and Reflections. (Ed.) C. M. Hall , . London: Routledge; **2011**, pp. 39–54.

16. Hall, C. M.; The contradictions and paradoxes of Slow Food: Environmental change, sustainability and the conversation of taste. In, Slow Tourism: Experiences and Mobilities (Eds.) Fullager, S.; Markwell, K.; and Wilson, E.; Bristol: Channel View Publications; **2012**, *54,* pp. 53–68.

17. Krippendorf, J.; The Holidaymakers: Understanding the Impact of Leisure Travel. London: Butterworth Heinemann; **1987**

18. Lane, B.; What is rural tourism? *J. Sust. Tour.* **1994,** *2*(1/2), 7–21.

19. Slee, B.; Farr, H.; and Snowdon, P.; Soft tourism and rural development in Badenoch and Strathspey. *Scottish Agric. Eco. Rev.* **1995** (8), 53–62.

20. Slee, B.; Farr, H.; and Snowdon, P.; The economic impact of alternative types of rural tourism. *J. Agric. Eco.* **1997,** *48*(1–3), 179–192.

21. Snowdon, P.; Slee, B.; and Farr, H.; The economic impacts of different types of tourism in upland and mountain areas of Europa. In: Tourism and Development in Mountain Regions (Eds.) Godde, P. M.; Price, M. F.; and Zimmermann, F. M; New York: CBI International; **2000,** pp. 137–145.

22. Williams, F.; and MacLeod, M.; Tourism development: hard core or soft touch? In: Managing Tourism and Hospitality Services: Theory and International Application (Eds.) Prideaux, B.; Moscardo, G.; and Laws, E.; Oxford: CAB International; **2006,** pp. 126–144.

23. Nash, D.; and Butler, R.; Towards sustainable tourism. *Tour. Manag.* **1990**, *11*(3), 263–264.

24. Smith, V.; and Eadington, W.; (Eds.); Tourism Alternatives: Potentials and Problems in the Development of Tourism. Philadelphia: University of Pennsylvania Press; **1992**.

25. Bramwell, B.; and Lane, B.; Sustainable tourism: an evolving global approach. *J. Sust. Tou.* **1993**, *1*(1), 1–5.

26. Garrod, B.; and Fyall, A.; Beyond the rhetoric of sustainable tourism? *Tour. Manag.* **1998**, *19*(3), 199–212.

27. Hunter, C.; Sustainable tourism as an adaptive paradigm. *Ann. Tour. Res.* **1997**, *24*(4), 850–867.

28. Butler, R.; Sustainable tourism: a state of the art review. *Tour. Geog.* **1999**, *1*(1), 7–25.

29. Swarbrooke, J.; Sustainable Tourism Management. Wallingford: CAB International; **1999**.

30. Butler, R.; Tourism in the future: cycles, waves or wheels. *Futures.* **2009**, *41*(6), 346–352.

31. Budeanu, A.; Sustainable tourist behavior—a discussion of opportunities for change. *Int.J. Con. Stud.* **2007**, *31*(5), 499–508.

32. Hares, A.; Dickinson, J.; and Wilkes, K.; Climate change and the air travel decisions of UK tourists. *J. Trans. Geog.* **2010**, *18*(3), 466–473.

33. Hergesell, A.; Climate friendly tourist behavior. *Tour. South East Europe.* **2011**, *1*(1), 95–105.
34. Sharpley, R.; Ecotourism a consumption perspective. *J. Ecotour.* **2006**, *5*(1), 7–22.
35. McKercher, B.; Pridaux, B.; Cheung, C.; and Law, R.; Achieving voluntary reductions in the carbon footprint of tourism and climate change. *J. Sust. Tour.* **2010**, *18*(3), 297–317.
36. Sharpley, R.; (Ed.); Tourism Development and the Environment: Beyond Sustainability. London and Washington, DC: Earthscan; **2009**.
37. Dodds, R.; and Butler, R.; Barriers to implementing sustainable tourism policy in mass tourism destinations. *Tour. Int. Multidiscipl. J.* **2010**, *5*(1), 35–53.
38. Bramwell, B.; and Lane, B.; Editorial towards innovation in sustainable tourism research. *J. Sust. Tour.* **2012**, *20*(1), 1–7.
39. Buckley, R.; Sustainable tourism: research and reality. *Ann. Tour.Res.* **2012**, *39*(2), 528–546.
40. Peeters, P.; A clear path towards sustainable mass tourism? Rejoinder to the paper 'Organic, incremental and induced paths to sustainable mass tourism convergence' by David B. Weaver. *Tour. Manag.* **2012**, *33*(5), 1038–1041.
41. Weaver, D.; Organic, incremental and induced paths to sustainable mass tourism convergence. *Tour. Manag.* **2012**, *33*(5), 1030–1037.
42. Weaver, D.; Clearing the path to sustainable mass tourism: a response to Peeters. *Tour. Manag.* **2012**, *33*(5), 1042–1043.
43. United Nations World Commission on Environment and Development; Report of the United Nations World Commission on Environment and Development: Our Common Future, A/42/427. **1987**, August 4. Retrieved from http://daccess-dds-ny.un.org/doc/UN-DOC/GEN/N87/184/67/IMG/N8718467.pdf?OpenElement
44. United Nations Conference on Environment and Development; Report of the United Nations Conference on Environment and Development, Rio de Janeiro, Brazil, A/CONF.151/26/Rev.1 Vol.1. **1992**, June 3–14. Retrieved from http://daccess-dds-ny.un.org/doc/UNDOC/GEN/N92/836/55/PDF/N9283655.pdf?OpenElement
45. United Nations World Summit on Sustainable Development; Report of the United Nations World Summit on Sustainable Development, Johannesburg, South Africa, A/CONF.199/20. **2002**, August 26–September 4. Retrieved from http://daccess-dds-ny.un.org/doc/UNDOC/GEN/N02/636/93/PDF/N0263693.pdf?OpenElement
46. United Nations Conference on Sustainable Development; Report of the United Nations Conference on Sustainable Development, Rio de Janeiro, Brazil, A/CONF.216/16. **2012**, June 20–23. Retrieved from http://www.uncsd2012.org/content/documents/814UNCSD%20REPORT%20final%20revs.pdf
47. McDonald's Go Home; United Press International. **1986**, April 20, p. 1. Retrieved from www.lexisnexis.com/hottopics/lnacademic
48. Reuter; Fast-food outlets under attack as Rome fights to preserve city. The Toronto Star. **1986**, May 2. p. B8. Retrieved from www.lexisnexis.com/hottopics/lnacademic
49. Leitch, A.; Slow food and the politics of 'virtuous globalization'. In: Globalization of Food (Eds.) Inglis, D.; and Grimlin, D.; Oxford: Berg; **2009,** pp. 45–64.
50. Morrison, J.; Slow food creed gains momentum; savor, don't slam-dunk food, proponents say. Palm Beach Post (Florida), **1992**, October 29. p. 1FN. Retrieved from www.lexisnexis.com/hottopics/lnacademic

51. O'Neill, M.; Barbarians at the plate. New York Times. **1997**, June 8. Retrieved from http://www.nytimes.com/1997/06/08/magazine/barbarians-at-the-plate. html?pagewanted=all&src=pm

52. Slow Food International; History. **2013**. Retrieved from http://www.slowfood.com/international/7/history

53. Portinari, F.; Slow Food Manifesto. **1989**. Retrieved from http://www.slowfood.com/about_us/eng/manifesto.lasso

54. Slow Food International; ABC of Slow Food. **2013**. Retrieved from http://www.slowfood.com/international/8/abc-of-slow-food

55. Slow Food International; About Us. **2013**. Retrieved from http://www.slowfood.com/international/1/about-us

56. Cittaslow International; About Cittaslow Organization. **2013a**. Retrieved from http://www.cittaslow.org/section/association

57. Cittaslow International; Cittaslow List. **2013b**. Retrieved from http://www.cittaslow.org/download/DocumentiUfficiali/CITTASLOW_LIST_september_2013.pdf

58. Caffyn, A.; Advocating and implementing slow tourism. Tour. Recreat. Res. **2012**, *37*(1), 77–80.

59. Matos, R.; Can slow tourism bring new life to alpine regions. In: The Tourism and Leisure Industry: Shaping the Future (Eds.) Weiermair, K.; and Mathies, C.; Binghamton, NY: Haworth Hospitality Press; **2004,** pp. 93–103.

60. Woehler, K.; The rediscovery of slowness, or leisure time as one's own and as self-aggrandizement. In: The Tourism and Leisure Industry: Shaping the Future (Eds.) Weiermair, K.; and Mathies, C.; Binghamton, NY: Haworth Hospitality Press; **2004,** pp. 83–92.

61. Conway, D.; and Timms, B.; Are slow travel and slow tourism misfits, compadres or different genres? *Tour. Recreat. Res.* **2012**, *37*(1), 71–76.

62. Hall, C. M.; Degrowing tourism: Décroissance, sustainable consumption and steady-state tourism. *Anatolia: Int. J. Tour. Hosp. Res.* **2009**, *20*(1), 46–61.

63. United Nations World Tourism Organization; From Davos to Copenhagen and Beyond: Advancing Tourism's Response to Climate Change. **2009**. Retrieved from http://sdt.unwto.org/sites/all/files/docpdf/fromdavostocopenhagenbeyondunwtopaperelectronicversion.pdf

64. Caffyn, A.; Slow tourism. In: Paper presented at the Slow Tourism Workshop, Tourism Partnership North Wales, **2007**, October. Retrieved from http://www.tpnw.org/newfiles/Slow%20Tourism%20-%20NWTP.ppt

65. Caffyn, A.; The Slow Route to New Markets. **2009**, September. Retrieved from http://www.insights.org.uk/articleitem.aspx?title=The%20Slow%20Route%20to%20New%20Markets

66. Dickson, J.; Slow tourism travel for a lower carbon future (non-technical report). Bournemouth University—U.K.: International Center for Tourism & Hospitality Research. **2009**. Retrieved from http://www.bournemouth.ac.uk/icthr/PDFs/rgsnontech.pdf

67. Hall, C. M.; Introduction: culinary tourism and regional development: from slow food to slow tourism? *Tour. Rev. Int.* **2006**, *9*(4), 303–305.

68. Dodds, R.; Questioning slow as sustainable. *Tour. Recreat. Res.* **2012**, *37*(1), 81–83.

69. Hall, C. M.; Sharples, L.; Mitchell, R.; Macionis, N.; and Cambourne, B.; (Eds.); Food Tourism around the World: Development, Management and Markets. London: Butterworth Heinemann; **2003**.

70. Guba, E.; and Lincoln, Y.; Fourth Generation Evaluation. Newbury Park, CA: Sage; **1989**.

CHAPTER 4

PERSPECTIVES OF ECO-INNOVATION IN THE HOSPITALITY INDUSTRY

M. SINGAL[1], T. KOTHARI[2], and I. DOLLINGER[3]

[1]Assistant Professor of Hospitality Management, Pamplin College of Business, Virginia Tech, Blacksburg, VA 24061-0429, msingal@vt.edu

[2]Assistant Professor, San Jose State University, College of Business, Department of Organization & Management Department, San Jose, CA 95192-0070

[3]PhD Student, Department of Hospitality and Tourism Management, Pamplin College of Business, Virginia Tech, Blacksburg, VA 24061-0429

CONTENTS

4.1   INTRODUCTION

Hospitality businesses, including restaurants and hotels, have a significant impact on the sustainability of the natural environment in which they function due to their obligatory consumption of considerable amounts of natural resources. Despite the fact, that the bulk of the restaurant sector consists of small establishments employing fewer than 50 employees each, there are nearly a million such establishments in the U.S. alone employing over 13 million employees and constituting 4 percent of GDP. Given the overall size of this sector in the economy, strategic, and operational changes in activities in this industry that affect sustainability deserve attention [1]. Even though attention to eco-innovation practices (i.e., those practices that help the environment) appears to be a relatively novel phenomenon in the hospitality sector, there is an incipient debate about the responsibilities of the industry with reference to the reduction of solid waste, water consumption, energy use, and air pollution [2–4].

Industry associations like the American Hotel and Lodging Association (AHLA) and the National Restaurant Association (NRA) make substantial efforts to provide resources to their members and disseminate knowledge regarding eco-innovations and sustainability initiatives. Not only are green initiatives encouraged but they have spawned a certification industry like the Green Restaurant Association, Sustainable Restaurant Association, Green Key Global, Green Global International, Energy Star, LEED, Audobon Green Leaf and several others that provide certification based on environmental impact parameters which can attract and accommodate not only "green" consumers but all stakeholders.

Stakeholder pressures and the increasing awareness of environmental damage have driven businesses and consumers into doing more with less as the new normal. The general opinion that in order to successfully cater to the environmental and socially aware patrons one must no longer view people as mere "customers" with an unquenchable appetite for material goods, but rather as human beings trying to lead full, healthy lives is increasingly gaining ground [5]. In parallel we have the ambiguous effects of environmentally driven investments on the financial future of companies and whole lists of difficulties in transitioning toward corporate sustainability [6, 7]. The contemporary environmental problems such as soil erosion, climate change, water pollution and loss of bio-diversity are characterized by delocalization (the separation of production and consumption centers), insecurity (of supplies), irreversibility (depletion of natural resources), and tremendous complexity in terms of consequences, such that only innovation can provide a solution [7, 8].

The traditional approach to sustainability viewed a trade-off between environmental performance and economic performance such that regulation was aimed toward social welfare and firms were required to pay for negative externalities imposing costs that detracted from financial performance. However, the modern approach views a dynamic and circular relationship between sustainability and competitive performance. Porter and Van Linde [9] hypothesized two decades ago that environmental regulations can spur innovation and result in an increase in efficiency and productivity leading to a competitive advantage. Currently, the literature reflects an evolved perspective, suggesting that many firms proactively innovate for sustainability not only for compliance and competitiveness, but because they are motivated by a wider system to adopt responsible positions in terms of the triple bottom line for profits, people, and planet and are cognizant of the social and environmental impacts of their business activities. It should be apparent then to large and small hospitality firms that in order to improve the quality of the environment without restricting economic activity, intensive efforts must be made to promote eco-innovations—innovations that improve environmental performance, and use sustainability efforts as a core driver of business activity.

Few attempts to conceptualize eco-innovation and provide structured approaches for its management and governance have been made not only in the hospitality industry but also in the general academic literature. The term has been used in many contexts with various underlying connotations. An outline of the concept of eco-innovation seems valuable from both an academic and managerial standpoint—there is no clear framework, nor unanimous definition of the concept, yet the term is being manipulated with multiple variations. A better understanding and framing of eco-innovation can benefit future hospitality empirical research as well as practitioners—perhaps particularly through an overview of existent practices within the industry and their revealed meaning as "lessons learned" for the latter. This chapter attempts to discuss some conceptions of eco-innovation and "green" terms, explaining their motivations/antecedents. It further provides examples of eco-innovative practices in restaurants and hotels from different parts of the world while also listing some barriers to eco-innovation that hinder the widespread initiation, adoption, and adaptation of sustainable practices

4.2 CONCEPTUALIZATION OF "GREEN" TERMS AND ANTECEDENTS TO ECO-INNOVATION

Following the line of thought of scholars who still consider sustainability itself as an innovative idea [through environmental conservation and/or stewardship of natural resources aspects in particular] [10], the dominant stream of research regards "environmental innovation" or "green innovation" as any "environmental/green practice" incorporated into a company's policies (Bartlett, 2010) [11] by which owners and managers demonstrate assumption of environmental responsibility and response to green trends. These trends have great significance, since, according to the National Restaurant Association, as much as 62 percent of consumers declare that they are more likely to spend their money at a restaurant if they know it is "green" [12]. Similarly, Deloitte [13] reports that in a recent survey it conducted, 95 percent of respondents stated that they believed that lodging companies should be undertaking green initiatives, and adopting operational practices like recycling, and energy saving. This sentiment was similar across gender, age and income groups underlying the widespread desire of consumers to see companies doing their duty toward the environment.

The conceptualization and definition of green initiatives and of eco-innovation varies, and ranges from the short "[Eco-] Innovation, that is able to extract green rents from the market" [14], to the more comprehensive, such as "Eco-innovation is the production, assimilation or exploitation of a novelty of products, production processes, services or in the management and business methods which aims, throughout its lifecycle to prevent or substantially reduce environmental risk, pollution, and other negative impacts of resource use including energy (European Commission, 2008 as cited in [15]). In general for the purpose of this chapter, and as consistent with prior understanding, eco-innovation refers to the adoption of programs and practices that are *novel to the firm* that improve environmental performance. We do not distinguish the practice based upon the intent of the initiative (i.e. whether the practice is undertaken for regulatory compliance, motivated by cost reduction, or fosters competitive advantage), but rather that it attempts to reduce environmental impact.

The evolution of green practices within hospitality is traced back to sustainable tourism matters, and the differentiating point for such practices within hospitality when compared to other industries is the provision of food in a sustainable manner and the reduction of waste—that is, businesses ensuring that their customers' choices positively contribute to the environment [11]. Other green practices adopted by the restaurant and hotel world include water efficiency and conservation solutions, waste reduction through reusing and recycling, energy efficiency applications, the adoption of "eco-friendly" and biodegradable products (such as green heat chafing fuels, environmentally sustainable cleaning products, refrigerator temperature sensors, etc.) and green designs for furnishings and buildings, Leadership in Energy and Environmental Design (LEED) certifications, and pollution prevention applications [11, 16–19]. The majority of the above-mentioned practices are further broken down and categorized as standards that restaurants need to comply with if they wish to be certified as "green" by the Green Restaurant Association [18]. The Green Restaurant Association is the largest American nonprofit organization that promotes the implementation of green practices in restaurants and offers, besides actual certifications, guidance, and training for employers and employees regarding green practices. Similar and numerous green certifications for hotels are available based on comparable parameters, but may also include linen and towel reuse programs, high efficiency plumbing, complete smoke-free building requirements, and evaluation even based sometimes on size of amenity dispensers with guests being advised to take the remainder of their bathroom amenities home or donate them to homeless shelters (e.g., see Greenseal.org).

The contribution that service production and consumption in hospitality has on the carbon footprint increasingly preoccupy researchers and the larger public [20,

Makover and Pike, 2009, 21, 22]. Gössling et al. [21] outline the relationship between food production, consumption, and climate change and attempt to alarm readers about the fact that emissions from food production in particular are expected to increase in the future given both the growing global population demands for food and the changes occurring in dietary preferences toward higher-order food. They make recommendations for "buy less" and "buy more" type of policies in particular for the food-service industry in a tourism context in their study, but several such policies are transferable to the restaurant and hospitality service industry in general—buy more local produce so transportation can be maintained to a minimum, or buy less to reduce water and energy consumption for example.

Green practices appear clearly crucial to the contemporary hospitality industry, particularly given their increasing role in brand design and management; engaging in such practices has been shown to have a positive effect on corporate brand image, and bring additional financial benefits while simultaneously contributing to the economic sustainability of local communities [23, 24]. Rennings and Zwick [25] identify five drivers for eco-innovation; regulation compliance, customer demand, desire to capture new markets, cost reduction, and finally to reap reputational benefits. While compliance with environmental regulations is more important for pollution control innovations needed primarily in chemical and manufacturing industries, improving firm image, achieving accreditation, meeting customer demand, and increasing market share seem more relevant to the hospitality industry.

"Green restaurants" and the "farm to table" or the preference for "locally sourced food" appeals to an ever more environmentally aware public [16, 26] and stands out among competitors [16, 19]. The difference between green and regular restaurants apparently agreed upon in the literature is that the first focus on the three Rs—reduce, reuse, recycle—and the two Es—energy and efficiency [27]), while the latter do not. Lorenzini [28] defines green restaurants as "new or renovated structures designed, constructed, operated, and demolished in an environmentally friendly and energy-efficient manner." Even though the actual food-service is intangible in nature, food-service operations depend upon physical components which are considered tangibles with major environmental impact [29]. According to [4] the food-service industry is being gradually more recognized for its capabilities to reduce a multitude of environmental factors, amongst which solid waste and energy consumption are focal. Their research shows that consumers' environmental concerns and knowledge about sustainable practices amongst restaurants have a significant impact on intentions to patronize green restaurants. Several studies show that customers who care about protecting the environment are willing to pay more to offset any additional costs triggered by the green practices [13, 18, 25] (Laroche, Bergeron, Barbaro-Forleo, 2002).

Research with respect to the lodging industry has yielded almost parallel results. While conceptions of green lodging vary [30], identified components that included fixtures, facilities, amenities, supplies, consumables, and practices are adopted to lessen externalities. Motivation for adopting eco-innovative and green practices were derived from manager's personal values and organizational competitive orientation (El Dief and Font, 2010), regulation compliance [31], commercial benefits [32]), and enhanced firm image [33]. Higher consumer willingness to pay for a "green" hotel, a positive effect on financial performance, and greater customer satisfaction and loyalty were also reported as positive outcomes of sustainability efforts (Choi et al, 2009) [34–36]. Independent certifications from third parties like ISO 14001, LEED and Green Building Council added to firm reputation, enabled firms to charge higher prices, and also conferred a competitive advantage, although this was not considered universally true across all hotel categories [2, 37, 38]. When considering the antecedents to the environmental proactivity of hotel operations, Park and Kim [39] report that stakeholder pressure is the most dominant predictor for changing managerial attitudes when adopting environmental programs, followed by the incentive to reap economic benefits, and finally top management's personal environmental concern. The authors also suggest that managerial discretion, such as that prevalent in independent hotels rather than chain-owned hotels, plays an important role in the relationship between managerial attitudes toward the environment and organizational commitment to adopt environmentally friendly practices. Figure 4.1 summarizes the drivers and antecedents of eco-innovation.

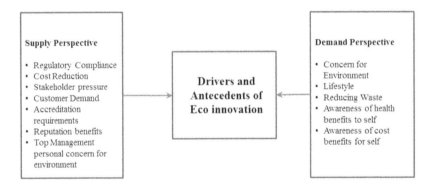

FIGURE 4.1   Drivers and antecedents of eco-innovation.

4.3 ECO-INNOVATION

Research revolving around the issue of innovation within the hospitality industry has worked under the premise that innovation is "anything new" that a company does—new for the company itself, not necessarily new to the world—[40–42] and even if no highly structured way is necessary in order to carry out innovations, companies should try to adopt the novelties through systematic processes. This view sheds light on why the majority of the hospitality and tourism subindustries consider any new green practices a company adopts as equivalent to eco-innovation. Even though the hospitality industry is primarily a service-based one, the fact that most innovation involves the advancement of an idea that has both product and service attributes needs to be taken into account for the development process [40].

The high failure rate attributed to hospitality innovations in general [43, 44] and to food-service ones in particular [45] is thought to be most likely due to the limited knowledge on ways of achieving success with innovations; as a result, hospitality managers tend to rely on speculation, gut feeling, and personal experience when prospects for innovation are involved [42, 46]. Research shows that there are other sources which lead to innovation failure within the hospitality industry: managers may develop personal favorite ideas without conducting market research, incorrectly position new offers, conduct faulty communication to the customers about new offer, pay insufficient attention to the dimensions of chosen market niches, and perceive unfavorable imbalance in the costs versus financial returns equation. On the other hand, approaches shown to lead to successful innovation within the hospitality industry include management focusing on specific strategies varying by goals to be attained via innovation (increasing market performance versus increasing financial performance versus customer relationship enhancement versus employee relationship enhancement), management making sure that both the market and the customer are understood before deciding on the specific innovation and approach, that tangible quality is offered while implementing well-planned and employee-driven development processes, and investing in superior human resource management practices [42]. Regarding the human resource aspect, some believe that a "hire for skill, train for skill" approach should replace the "hire for attitude, train for skill" mantra in the case of companies looking to implement hospitality innovations [47]. Different implementation strategies are shown to affect innovation success differently depending upon whether the innovation is cost-based or quality-based. Execution strategies such as leader intervention, participation, and implementation by persuasion have a strong connection with innovation success, especially when applied in a mix, and participative employee-centered implementation strategies appear as the most critical for the diffusion of hospitality innovations [48].

Rennings [49] presents eco-innovation by addressing three kinds of changes toward sustainable development; technological, institutional, and social innovation. Environmental technological measures can be curative or preventative, resulting in substitution of harmful inputs like effluents in the air or substitution of primary resources for secondary resources. Consumer changes in life-style to reduce waste and conserve energy can be considered social innovation, while management instruments at the firm level like eco-audits can be examples of institutional innovation. Eco-innovations are known to produce spillovers both in the innovation and diffusion phases, a phenomenon known as "the double externality problem." Positive spillovers from the diffusion phase are possible due to a smaller amount of external costs than competing services [or goods] from the market—clearly visible in the case of hospitality operations "going green" (even when it only involves simple practices)—but the double externality problem is known to overall reduce incentives for companies to invest in eco-innovations [49]. Due to the fact that both externalities produce suboptimal levels of investment, the double externality problem leads to another peculiarity—"the regulatory push-pull effect": the importance of the regulatory context as key determinant for companies engaged in eco-innovative practices.

According to Rennings [49], the novel eco-efficient technologies seen as technology push factors and the preferences for environmental friendliness seen as market pull factors, need to be placed in a regulatory framework because of the externality problem inherent to eco-innovations. Cleff and Rennings' [50] work distinguishes between ecological product- and process- innovation and shows that the first is mostly guided by the strategies of the companies present in the market—market pull effect—while the latter is more driven by regulations—the regulatory push-pull effect. This framework is transferable to the hospitality industry while considering differences between countries with regard to the varying values attributed and applications chosen in the management of environmental practices. The third peculiarity of eco-innovation is the increasing importance of social and institutional innovation, again very visible when considering environmentalist issues revolving around the hospitality industry.

[Eco]-innovation is often mapped by a mix of dimensions [7, 42] such that it is useful to identify veritable occurrences of innovation distinguished from mere practices. Using a five-point Likert scale, Carrillo-Hermosilla et al. [7] propose a dashboard of eight dimensions in three parts, the design dimension, the user dimension, and the product service dimension for the analysis of eco-innovations that is designed to determine the environmental impact of each innovation. If we consider the success of hospitality eco-innovations in providing new opportunities and contributing to changes toward sustainability as dependent on the interplay of different dimensions, mapping eco-innovations on Carrillo-Hermosilla et al.'s [7] dashboard can serve as a practical tool for the management of such innovations. It must be kept in mind though that eco-innovations are being defined both as sustaining or incremental innovation, and disruptive innovations—the latter referring to discontinuous changes that cause existing structures and systems to become obsolete [51].

In the next section we describe some examples of both incremental changes as well as discontinuous or radical changes effected in the eco-innovation practices of restaurants and hotels.

4.4   EXAMPLES AND OVERVIEW OF CONTEMPORARY PRACTICES

In the most general sense, the hospitality industry understands any green practice newly adopted by an entity as an eco-innovation. Famous restaurants adopting such practices range from scarce to "100% green." The vast majority of American restaurants are involved in at least some kind of green practice, most commonly waste reduction through recycling and eco-friendly or biodegradable products; the commonality of these two practices appears to have resulted in a terminological transformation however—that is, these practices are no longer addressed as innovations, but rather environmentally conscious policies. Not even the "Zero Waste restaurants" (such as Hannah's Bretzel in Chicago (hannahsbretzel.com), or Ecco in Atlanta (eco-atlanta.com) are publicized as innovative. Hannah's Bretzel introduced composting in addition to biodegradable packing and 100 percent organic food, but had the no-waste title before adopting this course of action [52]. Declared "the greenest restaurant in America" [53], the Grey Plume in Omaha (thegreyplume.com) markets itself first and foremost through its innovative cuisine rather than the zero-waste policy.

It is worth noting that specific associations or opinion groups within the hospitality industry are less prevalent in some parts of the world [19, 54], and as Chen et al. [54] note, the institutional strain from within lacking, the perceived societal demand and stakeholder pressure sensed by restaurateurs/hoteliers with regard to adopting green practices are insignificant there. In such countries, restaurants are more likely and willing to change their business model in order to align with wellness or vegetarian philosophies rather than green or environmental ones; recommendations are thus made for managerial education and training to be intensified in an attempt to enhance organizational learning, and for governmental policies and strategies to be undertaken in order to encourage intentions to accept green practices [54].

The niche of ecological gourmet restaurants emerged more or less contemporaneously with molecular gastronomy that appears to have transformed into a diffusing trend from a wowing innovation. Places like Maaemo in Oslo (maaemo.no) or BioM in Copenhagen (biom.dk) that run on policies like 100 percent organic, no-waste, and farm-to-fork or on-site grown produce are more and more popular and numerous.

Given their radicalism and world-level impact, some extremely unusual examples however do stand out and appear to legitimately qualify as eco-innovations at the moment. The Cube by Electrolux (electrolux.co.uk/Cube/) is such an example, and so is the Waterfalls Restaurant at Villa Escudero (villaescudero.com/waterfalls-restaurant.php). The Cube by Electrolux is a unique dining concept created to celebrate 90 years of expertise along with the fact that almost 50 percent of the European Michelin-Starred Chefs use Electrolux appliances in their kitchens; the Cube seeks to offer a unique perspective on Europe's most prominent cities by touring and setting camp in unusual locations—such as the top of the Parc du Cinquantenaire in Brussels or overlooking Piazza del Duomo in Milan [55]. The cube is built from lightweight materials with a small footprint and is exceedingly innovative in terms of eco-sustainability, energy saving, and technology; it is reusable as it can be torn apart and rebuilt as it travels around Europe and is set upon rooftops, cliff sides and important monuments; it can be transported in a number of different ways (including by ship—supposedly the least harmful to the environment) [56]. Michelin-starred world-class chefs are employed to prepare signature dishes from locally sourced ingredients [55].

The Waterfalls Restaurant at Villa Escudero serves Philippine cuisine at the foot of the Labasin Falls; it is an example of light impact on the environment with great impact on the mind of the customer who gets to dine on locally sourced produce with feet in the running water, sitting at bamboo tables [57]. The concept is similar to that of European resorts and restaurants built on top of flowing streams or portions of rivers without affecting the course or flow of the water, however not yet popularly adopted worldwide.

Just like restaurants, hotels, as important members of the global tourism value chain, have adopted eco-innovation to mitigate negative impacts on the environment. While most eco-friendly hotels strive for the LEED and Green Building certification, several examples of local and sustainable material use in construction, energy saving programs and recycling and waste-reduction practices from around the world can be found.

In the U.S. the Las Vegas strip, home to the world's best-known casino hotels and where luxury and excess, an integral part of its core identity and business model, is reinventing itself as a model of sustainability over the last few years in an effort known as "greening of the strip." Taking advantage of the generous green building incentive package passed by the Nevada Legislature in 2005, the strip now has one of the highest concentrations of LEED certified buildings in the world. Water conservation and waste repurposing are other efforts initiated by companies like MGM and Las Vegas Sands; although considering the extent of the carbon footprint of the city, it appears to be a herculean task [58].

In Germany, the Premier Hotel Victoria, Freiburg (EMAS) has built up energy-generating systems based on renewable sources, including sun, wind, water and timber, supplying itself with emission-free power. The hotel has implemented a solar power plant on the roof of the hotel generating approximately 7000 kwh of solar power per year supplying a quarter of the hotel's rooms around the year. This hotel invested in a local wind power plant to ensure constant supply of renewable energy, while the solar plant ensures a constant supply of hot water on sunny days for the entire hotel guests' requirements. A wood-pellet heating system that was installed in 2002 to meet central heating and hot water requirements of the 63-room hotel consists entirely of wood pellets from the local sustainable Black Forest timber production.

In Estonia, the Waide Motel Elva (Green Key certified) actively promotes its waste management activities and informs guests of their active role in reducing, reusing and recycling waste. Similarly, the Scandic Lübeck was renovated with sustainable, natural and recyclable materials—low volatile organic compound (VOC) paints and finishes were used which improve air quality and prevent health hazards. The Ökotel Hamburg eliminated all Polyvinyl chloride (PVC, one of the most profitable materials for the chemical industry and a health hazard that requires vast amounts of nonrenewable resources) in pipes and electric circuits.

In the Netherlands, respect for the environment and responsibility have been the core value at the Beaumont Hotel in Maastricht for three generations. The family-run business recently earned a Green Globe recertification based upon its sustainable operations that sources products and services only from certified contractors and suppliers. Energy use and reduction goals are strictly monitored and specified on a monthly basis. Solar panels installed on the hotel roof provide electricity for all LED lighting fixtures and heat water. In addition other practices which include a heat retrieval system in the shower drains and air circulators, low-flow toilets and tabs, use of locally-produced furniture and refurbished furniture, use of non-toxic and eco-labeled cleaning products, own line of eco-friendly amenities are also prevalent. The hotel even encourages guests to use public transportation, bicycles, or e-scooters.

While a clear and defined understanding of sustainability may be less common among the general public in Asia, as U.S. companies like LV Sands expand their operations globally, and especially in the growth markets like Singapore and Macao, they institute policies that are applicable throughout the corporation, although they may be implemented differentially within countries and properties, for example Sands Eco360 program [59].

Similarly, achieving sustainable operations can be a major goal for large chains that are based in Asia but operate worldwide like Shangri-La International Hotel Management Ltd., which manages 78 hotels and will open 36 more over the next three years, including 23 hotels in mainland China. Its environmental and conservation achievements a 20 percent reduction in potable water consumption per guest night and 13 percent reduction in energy consumption per guest night across the group compared with 2010 levels. Even with an increase in the total number of hotels, Shangri-La reduced CO_2 emissions by 16 percent per guest night over the two-year period. In addition, Shangri-La's Sustainable Seafood Policy does not allow its operated restaurants to serve shark fin, and the Shangri-La Supplier Code of Conduct incorporates criteria aligned with the ten principles of the United Nations Global Compact [60].

The conclusion thus drawn is that for the hospitality industry from a terminological point of view, green practices are equivalent to eco-innovations, and the longer and the wider these practices have been established, the less used the term "innovation" can be used in referring to them. Environmental practices can thus be placed on a continuum depending on the length of time they have been known to the world and the extent to which they have been adopted throughout the industry; the longer on the market and the wider accepted, the greater the loss of carried [eco-]innovation load attributed. It may be useful to truly evaluate eco-innovations based on the hospitality service development range proposed by Ottenbacher and Gnoth [43] that may distinguish between "true innovations," totally new to the world, with an entirely new market, at one end, and fairly minor modifications of existing services at the other.

4.5   BARRIERS TO ECO-INNOVATION

Notwithstanding the examples cited above, and despite the pressures from the marketplace, certain barriers to eco-innovation have been identified. Ashford [61] offers several categories of barriers like technological barriers (lack of availability for specific applications, process inflexibilities); financial barriers (lack of capital investment flexibility, short-term profitability considerations); labor-related barriers (lack of skilled labor to implement waste-reduction or other sophisticated technologies); regulatory barriers (uncertainty about future environmental regulation, depreciation tax laws); consumer related barriers (product-service expectations and specifications, unwillingness to bear additional cost); supplier related barriers (lack of supplier or supply chain inputs); and managerial barriers (lack of top management commitment, lack of expertise in supervision).

These barriers are interrelated and can often stymie or delay the process or adoption of even simple eco-innovative practices [62]. Bohdanowicz et al [63] find that despite years of environmental training and performance at a Scandic hotel that seemed essential to the development of the tourism industry, the biggest barriers preventing the setting up of green hotels was the perception of such measures being extremely expensive. In other research, Erdogan and Baris (2001) when studying hotels in Turkey, find that managers did not have the knowledge or interest in environmental matters; Kasim [64] finds that education and availability of a good support system was necessary for wider acceptance of the environmental responsibility in small and medium hotels in developing countries; Scanlon (2000) finds that many hotel managers were unaware of the cost reduction attributes of environmental management programs; and Ayuso [46] finds that managers in Spanish hotels in his study had little awareness of the sustainability concept or the contribution of business to environment protection. From the consumer angle, Baker et al [65] identify barriers to participation in sustainability efforts such as inconvenience, perceptions of cost cutting, and decreased luxury. The authors also report that customers behave with greater environmental responsibility at home than they do in a hotel, and that the hotel's communications and actions must consider guests' concerns by educating customers, increasing convenience to participate in green programs, and decreasing perceptions of cost cutting.

In short, weaknesses in information and training, unclear regulations or standards, economic barriers of high cost of investment and its perceived risk, along with a lack of understanding and demand from consumers for certain environmental innovations can serve as barriers to not only the firm's but also the industry's efforts at sustainability oriented innovations.

4.6   CONCLUSIONS AND SUGGESTION FOR FUTURE RESEARCH

Global realities and exigencies like climate change, media reports, government regulations, and an increasingly aware-of-environmental-problems public, pressure the hospitality service industries to "turn green," however unevenly amongst countries. The majority of hospitality industry members define eco-innovation as "any" environmentally aware/conscious/friendly practice, and innovation in general as "any" impacting novelty adopted by a company—even if the novelty is perhaps null to the rest of the world. Our proposed explanation for this phenomenon is the association of eco-innovation with sustainability and the dominant trend within sustainability literature to personalize approaches in response to operational circumstances [as opposed to "one solution fits all" advances] [66].

Hotel and restaurant operations that adopt green practices can range from just a few to "100% green" with top-notch certifications. Most businesses that earn low scores in number/amount of practices adopted tend to only be involved in recycling and use of some biodegradable materials, and cannot claim to be innovators. In addition, as a certain practice gains wide acceptance and becomes standard, the less associated it becomes with innovation—from a terminological point of view. Thus it would be interesting and potentially valuable to study when and what innovations turn into practices and dominant design at the environmental-friendly level, as it would appear that all green practices can be considered eco-innovations at one point or another within the hospitality industry. Frameworks like Carrillo-Hermosilla et al.'s [7] dashboard may be of relevance here.

The hospitality industry is very large and diverse; it consists of many small businesses but, is increasingly being dominated by large multinational corporations both in the restaurant and hotel sector. While it is growing geographically diverse, it strives to balance the tension between standardization of practices for ease of coordination with the desire to remain authentic to local conditions, tastes, and cultures. The industry operates at multiple levels like unit establishment or property level, the brand level, the corporate level, and the industry sector level—each having its own challenges for environmental management. Thus an attempt to have a clearer conceptualization of eco-innovation and the provision of more structured approaches for managerial purposes will prove very useful. This is especially relevant considering the industry attribute of perishability which necessitates the need to manage revenue while also making an investment in eco-innovation to meet market demand. Examining the process of introducing eco-innovations to hospitality operations, noting differences in implementation strategies, and developing business relevant criteria for the relevant issues also appears important, as no such studies exist and, as Krozer [67] [for example] notes—perplexity at the corporate strategic level is quite elevated.

Information dissemination regarding successful practices at the industry and trade association level spurred by incentives at the county and state levels, and education via outreach by research institutes will go a long way in successful eco-innovation. Adopting best practices and learning from other industries in the information technology or chemical industries using Big Data to identify consumer preferences and choices actions can help spur innovation efforts and measure success. Exploring cocreation and coproduction idea with consumers and suppliers for eco-innovative products and practices can go a long way to create a sustainable eco-system in the hospitality industry. Please see Figure 4.2 for an overview of some current practices and suggestions for the path forward.

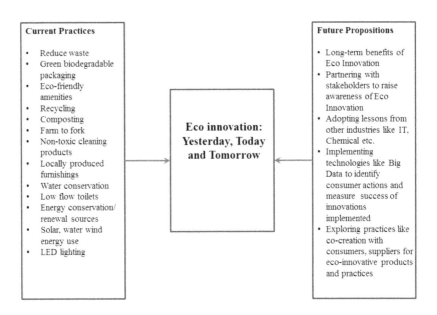

FIGURE 4.2   Current practices of eco-innovation and suggestions for path forward.

At the corporate level programs like Darden's "People, Planet, Plate," McDonald's "Global Corporate Social Responsibility, Sustainability, Philanthropy," Marriott's "Global Green Council," IHG's "Green Engage," and Wyndham's "Wyndham Green" to name just a few, seek to provide leadership, information, resources, and standards across the portfolio of locations, properties, and brands of these companies.

Furthermore, given the known different approaches to measuring innovation performance, it appears useful to determine which dimensions are in fact relevant in measuring an eco-innovation's success within the hospitality industry with known and acceptable common metrics and standards.

Last but not least, it appears fundamental to consider the role of culture at all levels, country, industry, corporate, brand, unit, and individual decision-maker [54] when determining the feasibility of adopting particular eco-innovation management practices, along with the economic one, as they both appear crucial for the advancement of knowledge and comprehension of innovation processes toward sustainability.

4.7   DISCUSSION QUESTIONS:

1. How would you describe the concept of eco-innovation?
2. What are the barriers to eco-innovation and how can these barriers be overcome in the hospitality sector?
3. As an individual identify some of your own consumption practices that are currently not sustainable.
4. Identify some of the challenges you anticipate in implementing a change to the practices identified in question 3. Prioritize this list and pick the top five.
5. How can you use your consumption practices to influence change in ecological impact?
6. What steps could you take to reduce your carbon footprint when you travel? Identify some proactive and reactive approaches.
7. How would you go about engaging with people, places, culture, and the environment when you travel? Do you think this will vary drastically in different countries?
8. Under what circumstances would you stay in locally owned (not chain-type) accommodations, eat in local restaurants serving local types of food, or buy locally made products?
9. Based on your experiences in other industries (e.g., retail, Information technology, chemical, etc.), are there any eco-innovations that can be adopted in the tourism and the hospitality industry? Is there something we can do differently as members of this industry?
10. Assume you have a chance to develop a cool Eco-Innovation App that can be used on your Apple or Android devices. What would you like to see in such an App that will enable you to enhance sustainability in the hospitality industry?

4.8   TEAM EXERCISES

1. As a young tech savvy individual assume that Mr. Mark Zuckerberg, the CEO of Facebook, has given you an opportunity to use the medium to spread the word for a special eco-innovation initiative that is being implemented in your town/city. As a group come up with a marketing campaign that can be used on a social media platform like Facebook. Identify how you would measure the impact of such a campaign.

2. Use the World Changing website (http://www.worldchanging.com/) to identify various sustainability trends and issues and then discuss ways that hospitality/tourism is, is not, or could be contributing positively or negatively to the trends and issues that were identified.

3. Think of your town/city as a tourist destination. If you were the head of the local destination marketing organization what are some eco-innovation proposals you would try to implement to make your town/city a sustainable tourist destination. Think of how the various stakeholders (restaurant, hotels, tourist attractions, etc.) can participate. First brainstorm all the different ideas and then prioritize five such initiatives that can be both, implemented in the short run and can have the maximum impact.

4. Identify locations (both urban and rural) that have the potential to develop Slow Tourism; justify your reasons for selecting these places; and describe specific ways that they could use Slow Tourism to stimulate "a development-from-below"™ policies, plans, and development agendas.

5. Design a "slow" based marketing campaign for a particular destination that showcases the positive aspects of a Slow Tourism type of holiday with low ecological impact, while simultaneously negating the "backwards" or "boring" connotations of the word "slow"

4.9   SUGGESTED FURTHER READING:

—Aschehoug, S. H.; Boks, C.; and Støren, S.; Environmental information from stakeholders supporting product development. *J. Clean. Product.*2012, *31*, 1–13.

—Ayuso, S.; Rodríguez, M. Á.; Castro, R. G.; and Ariño, M. Á.; Does stakeholder engagement promote sustainable innovation orientation? *Indust. Manag. Data Syst.* 2011, *111* (9), 1399–1417.

—Dodds, F.; Schneeberger, K.; and Ullah, F.; Review of implementation of Agenda 21 and the Rio Principles: Synthesis—Sustainable development in the 21st century (SD21), 2012, January. Retrieved on December 22, 2013 from http://sustainabledevelopment.un.org/content/documents/641Synthesis_report_Web.pdf

—Drexhange, J.; and Murphy, D. ; Sustainable Development: From Brundtland to Rio 2012, United Nations International Institute for Sustainable Development, 2010, September. Retrieved on December 22, 2013 from http://www.un.org/wcm/webdav/site/climatechange/shared/gsp/docs/GSP1-6_Background%20on%20Sustainable%20Devt.pdf

—Könnölä, T.; and Unruh, G. C.; Really changing the course: the limitations of environmental management systems for innovation. *Bus. Strat. Environ.* 2007, *16*(8), 525–537.

—Barton, D. L.; Core capabilities and core rigidities: a paradox in managing new product development. *Strat. Manag. J.* 1992, *13*(Special Issue), 111–125.

—Loorbach, D.; Van Bakel, J. C.; Whiteman, G.; and Rotmans, J.; Business strategies for transitions towards sustainable systems. *Bus. Strat. Environ.* 2010, *19*(2), 133–146.

—Low, M. K.; Lamvik, T.; Walsh, K.; and Myklebust, O.; Manufacturing a green service: engaging the TRIZ model of innovation. *IEEE Transact. Electronics Packag. Manufactur.* 2001, *24*(1), 10–17.

—Magnusson, T.; Lindström, G.; and Berggren, C.; Architectural or modular innovation? Managing discontinuous product development in response to challenging environmental performance targets. *Int. J. Innovat. Manag.* 2003, *7*(1), 1–26.

—Maxwell, D.; and Van De Vorst, R.; Developing sustainable products and services. *J. Clean. Product.* 2003, *11*, 883–895.

—McDonough, W.; and Braungart, M.; Cradle to cradle: remaking the way we make things. London: North Point Press, 2002.

—Melnyk, S. A.; Sroufe, R. P.;and Calantone, R.; Assessing the impact of environmental management systems on corporate and environmental performance. *J. Operat. Manag.* 2003, *21*, 329–351.

—Nidumolu, R.; Prahalad, C. K.; and Rangaswami, M. R.; Why sustainability is now a key driver of innovation. *Harvard Bus. Rev.* 2009,(September), 57–64.

—Nohria, N.; and Gulati, R.; Is slack good or bad for innovation? *Acad. Manag. J.* 1996, *39*(5), 1245–1264.

—Porter, M. E.; & Van Der Linde, C.; Green and competitive. *Harvard Bus. Rev.* 1995 (September/October), 120–134.

—Prahalad, C. K.; and Hart, S. L.; The fortune at the bottom of the pyramid. *Strat. Bus.* 2002, *26*, 54–67.

—Prahalad, C. K.; The fortune at the bottom of the pyramid: eradicating poverty through profit. Upper Saddle River, NJ: Pearson Education, Inc., publishing as Wharton School Publishing, 2010.

—Pujari, D.; Wright, G.; and Peattie, K.; Green and competitive: influences on environmental new product development performance. *J. Bus. Res.* 2003, *56*(8), 657–671.

—Radjou, N.; Prabhu, J.; and Ahuja, S.; Jugaad innovation: think frugal, be flexible, generate breakthrough growth. Jossey–Bass, 2012.

—Ramus, C. A.; Organizational support for employees: encouraging creative ideas for environmental sustainability. *California Manag. Rev.* 2001, *43*(3), 85–105.

—Reay, T.; Berta, W.; and Kohn, M. K.; What's the evidence on evidence-based management? *Acad. Manag. Perspec.* 2009, *23*(4), 5–18.

—Rennings, K.; Redefining innovation: eco-innovation research and the contribution from ecological economics. *Ecol. Econ.* 2000, *32*(2), 319–332.

—Sandström, G.; and Tingström, J.; Management of radical innovation and environmental challenges. *European J. Innov. Manag.* 2008, *11*(2), 182–198.

—Schiederig, T.; Tietze, F.; and Herstatt, C.; Green innovation in technology and innovation management: an exploratory literature review. *R&D Manag.* 2012, *42*(2), 180–192.

—Shrivastava, P.; and Hart, S.; Creating sustainable corporations. *Bus. Strat. Environ.* 1995, *4*(3), 154–165.

—Steffen, A.; (Eds.); World changing: a user's guide for the 21st century. New York: Harry N. Abrams, 2006.

—Sukhdev, P.; The corporate climate overhaul. *Nature*. 2012, *486*, 27–28.

—UN Global Compact & Rockefeller Foundation.; A framework for action: social enterprise and impact investing. Global Compact Office, United Nations, 2012.

KEYWORDS

- **Eco-innovations**
- **Environmental innovation**
- **Implementation strategies**

REFERENCES

1. NRA (National Restaurant Association); **2013**. Available at http://www.restaurant.org/ retrieved December 7, 2013.

2. Butler, J.; The compelling "hard case" for "green" hotel development. *Corn. Hosp. Quar.* **2008**, *49*, 234–244.

3. Johnson, R.; Organizational motivations for going green or profitability versus sustainability. *Bus. Rev.* **2009**, *13*(1), 22–28.

4. Hu, H.-H.; Parsa, H. G.; and Self, J.; The dynamics of green restaurant patronage. *Corn. Hosp. Quar.* **2010**, *51*(3), 344–362.

5. Ottman, J. A.; The New Rules Of Green Marketing: Strategies, Tools, and Inspiration For Sustainable Branding. San Francisco, CA: Berrett-Koehler Publishing; **2011**.

6. Sharma, S.; Aragon Correa, J. A. A.; and Manzanares, A. R.; The contingent influence of organizational capabilities on proactive environmental strategy in the service sector: an analysis of North American and European ski resorts. *Canad. J. Admin. Sci.* **2007**, *24*, 268–283.

7. Carrillo Hermosilla, J.; Río, G. P.; and Könnöla, T.; Eco-Innovation: When Sustainability and Competitiveness Shake Hands. Houndmills, Basingstoke: Palgrave Macmillan; **2009**.

8. Mazzanti, M.; and Montini, A.; Environmental Efficiency, Innovation and Economic Performances. Abingdon, Oxon: Routledge; **2010**.

9. Porter, M.; and Van der Linde, C.; Green and competitive: ending the stalemate. *Harvard Bus. Rev.* **1995**, September/October, 120–134

10. Gössling, S.; Hall, C. M.; and Weaver, D. B.; (Eds.); Sustainable Tourism Futures: Perspectives on Systems, Restructuring and Innovations. , New York: Routledge,**2009**.

11. Chou, C. J.; Chen, K. S.; and Wang, Y. Y.; Green practices in the restaurant industry from an innovation adoption perspective: Evidence from Taiwan. *Int. J. Hosp. Manag.* **2012**, *31*, 703–711.

12. NRA.   National Restaurant Association, Recycling for all the right returns–Meeting Demands of Consumers, Nature–and Restaurants' Bottom Lines, **2011**. Retrieved from: http://www.restaurant.org/Downloads/PDFs/Conserve/Library/Recycling,-Composting,-and-Zero-Waste/recycling_full_survey_results-0511-pdf.pdf (12.07.13)

13. Deloitte.; The Staying Power of Sustainability: Balancing Opportunity and Risk In The Hospitality Industry, **2008**. Retrieved from http://www.deloitte.com/assets/dcom-united-states/local%20assets/documents/us_cb_sustainability_190608(1).pdf (accessed 7 December 7 2013).

14. Andersen, M. M.; Organizing Inter-firm Learning- as the market begins to turn green. In Partnership and Leadership: Building Alliances for a Sustainable Future (Eds) de Bruijn, T. J. N. M.; and Tukker, A.; Dordrecht: Kluwer Academic Publishers; **2002**, pp.103–119.

15. Carrillo Hermosilla, J.; del Río, P.; Könnölä, T.; Diversity of eco-innovations: Reflections from selected case studies. *J. Clean. Product.* **2010**, *18*(10), 1073–1083.

16. Stys, B.; Green Restaurants. Commercial kitchens face unique challenges as well as opportunities for saving energy and materials. *Environ. Design Construct.* **2008**, *11* (5): 64.

17. GRA.; Certification Standards for All Food-Service Operations. **2012**. Retrieved from: http://dinegreen.com/restaurants/standards.asp (accessed 12 July 2013).

18. Namkung, Y.; and Jang, S.; Effects of restaurant green practices on brand equity formation: do green practices really matter? *Int. J. Hosp. Manag.* **2012**.

19. Tan, B. C.; and Yeap, P. F.; What Drives Green Restaurant Patronage Intention? *Int. J. Bus. Manag.* **2012**, *7*(2), 215.

20. Billen, G.; Barles, S.; Garnier, J.; Rouillard, J.; and Benoit, P.; The food-print of Paris: long-term reconstruction of the nitrogen flows imported into the city from its rural hinterland. *Region. Environ. Change.* **2009**, *9*(1), 13–24.

21. Gössling, S.; Garrod, B.; Aall, C.; Hille, J.; and Peeters, P.; Food management in tourism: reducing tourism's carbon 'foodprint'. *Tour. Manag.* **2011**, *32*(3), 534–543.

22. Stoessel, F.; Juraske, R.; Pfister, S.; and Hellweg, S.; Life cycle inventory and carbon and water foodprint of fruits and vegetables: application to a Swiss retailer. *Environ. Sci. Technol.* **2012**, *46*(6), 3253–3262.

23. Choi, G.; and Parsa , H. G.; Green practices II: measuring restaurant managers ' psychological attributes and their willingness to charge for the 'green practices. *J. Foodserv. Bus. Res.* **2006**, *9*(4), 41–63.

24. Schubert, F.; Kandampully, J.; Solnet, D.; and Kralj, A.; Exploring consumer perceptions of green restaurants in the US. *Tour. Hosp. Res.* **2010**, *10*(4), 286–300.

25. Rennings, K.; and Zwick, T.; Employment impact of cleaner production on the firm level: empirical evidence from a survey in five European countries. *Int. J. Innovat. Manag.* **2002**, *6*(3), 310–342.

26. Jang, Y. J.; Kim, W. G.; and Bonn, M. A.; Generation Y consumers' selection attributes and behavioral intentions concerning green restaurants. *Int. J. Hosp. Manag.* **2011**, *30*(4), 803–811.

27. Gilg, A.; Barr, S.; and Ford, N.; Green consumption or sustainable lifestyles? Identifying the sustainable consumer. *Futures.* **2005**, *37*, 481.

28. Lorenzini, B.; The green restaurant, part II: systems and service. *Restaurant Institut.* **1994**, *104*(11), 119–136.

29. Ismail, A.; Kassim, A.; and Zahari, M. S.; Responsiveness of restaurateurs towards the implementation of environmentally-friendly practices. *South Asian J. Tour. Heritage.* **2010**, *3*(2), 1–10.

30. Jackson, L. A.; Toward a framework for the components of green lodging. *J. Retail Leisure Prop.* **2010**, *9*(3), 211–230.

31. Revilla, G.; Dodd, T. H.; and Hoover, L. C.; Environmental tactics used by hotel companies in Mexico. *Int. J. Hosp. Tour. Admin.* **2001**, *1*(3–4), 111–127.
32. Tzschentke, N.; Kirk, D.; and Lynch, P.A.; Reasons for going green in serviced accommodation establsihments. *Int. J. Hosp. Manag.* **2004**, *17*, 284–313.
33. Lee, J. S.; Hsu, L. T.; Han, H.; and Kim, Y.; Understanding how consumers view green hotels: how a hotel's green image can influence behavioral intentions. *J. Sust. Tour.* **2010**, *18*(7), 901–914.
34. Han, H.; Hsu, L. T. J.; and Lee, J. S.; Empirical investigation of the roles of attitudes toward green behaviors, overall image, gender, and age in hotel customers' eco-friendly decision-making process. *Int. J. Hosp. Manag.* **2009**, *28*(4), 519–528.
35. Kassinis, G. I.; and Soteriou, A. C.; Greening the service profit chain: the impact of environmental management practices. *Product. Operat. Manag.* **2003**, *12*(3), 386–403.
36. Singal, M.; The link between firm financial performance and investment in sustainability initiatives. *Corn. Hosp. Quarter.* **2013**. doi:1938965513505700.
37. Peiró-Signes, A., Segarra-Oña, M., Verma, R. Mondéjar-Jiménez, J. and Vargasvargas, M.; The impact of environmental certification on hotel guest Ratings, *Cornell Hospitality Quarterly*, 2014, 55 (1) 40–51.
38. Sanchez Ollero, J. L; Pozo, A. G.; and Mera, A. M.; How does respect for the environment affect final prices in the hospitality sector? A hedonic pricing approach. *Corn. Hosp. Quarter.* **2013**. doi:10.1177/1938965513500709.
39. Park, J.; and Kim, H. J.; Environmental proactivity of hotel operations: antecedents and the moderating effect of ownership type. *Int. J. Hosp. Manag.* **2014**, *37*, 1–10.
40. Jones, P.; Managing hospitality innovation. *Corn. Hotel Restaurant Admin. Quarter.* **1996**, *37*(5), 86–95.
41. Victorino, L.; Verma, R.; Plaschka, G.; and Dev, C.; Service innovation and customer choices in the hospitality industry. *Manag. Serv. Qual.* **2005**, *15*(6), 555–576.
42. Ottenbacher, M. C.; Innovation management in the hospitality industry: different strategies for achieving success. *J. Hosp. Tour. Res.* **2007**, *31*(4), 431–454.
43. Ottenbacher, M.; and Gnoth, J.; How to develop successful hospitality innovation. *Corn. Hotel Restaurant Admin. Quarter.* **2005**, *46*(2), 205–222.
44. Kotler, P.; Bowen, J.; and Makens, J.; Marketing for hospitality and tourism. Upper Saddle River, NJ: Prentice Hall; **2006**.
45. Parsa, H. G.; Self, J. T.; Njite, D.; and King, T.; Why restaurants fail. *Corn. Hotel Restaurant Admin. Quarter.* **2005**, *46*(3), 304–322.
46. Ayuso, S.; Adoption of voluntary environmental tools for sustainable tourism: analysing the experience of Spanish hotels. *Corp. Soc. Respons. Environ. Manag.* **2006**, *13*(4), 207–220.
47. Chang, S.; Gong, Y.; and Shum, C.; Promoting innovation in hospitality companies through human resource management practices. *Int. J. Hosp. Manag.* **2011**, *30*(4), 812–818.
48. Enz, C. A.; Strategies for the implementation of service innovations. *Corn. Hosp. Quarter.* **2012**, *53*(3), 187–195.
49. Rennings, K.; Redefining innovation—eco-innovation research and the contribution from ecological economics. *Ecol. Econ.* **2000**, *32*(2), 319–332.
50. Cleff, T.; and Rennings, K.; Determinants of environmental innovation-empirical evidence from the Mannheim innovation panel and an additional telephone survey. In: In-

novation- Oriented Environmental Regulation: Theoretical Approaches and Empirical Analysis (Eds.) Hemmelskamp, J.; Leone, F.; and Rennings, K.; Heidelberg, New York: Physica Verlag; **1999**.

51. Christensen, C.M.; The Innovator's Dilemma: When New Technologies Case Great Firms to Fail, Boston, MA: Harvard Business School Press; **1997**.
52. Mazzoni, M.; Zero-Waste Restaurants: Is it Possible? **2012**. Retrieved from: http://earth911.com/news/2012/10/11/hannahs-bretzel-chicago-zero-waste-restaurant/ (accessed 12 July 2013).
53. Meinhold, B; The Greenest Restaurant in America is in Omaha, Nebraska, **2010**. Retrieved from: http://inhabitat.com/the-greenest-restaurant-in-america-is-in-omaha-nebraska/ (12 July 13).
54. Chen, R. X. Y.; Cheung, C.; and Law, R.; A review of the literature on culture in hotel management research: what is the future? *Int. J. Hosp. Manag.* **2012**, *31*, 52–65.
55. Electrolux.; **2012**. Retrieved from: http://www.electrolux.co.uk/Cube/ (12 July 2013).
56. Meinhold, B.; Cube Pavilion: Mod Green Restaurant to Pop Up on Top of European Cliffs and Famous Monuments, **2011**. Retrieved from: http://inhabitat.com/cube-pavilion-mod-green-restaurant-to-pop-up-on-top-of-european-cliffs-and-famous-monuments/ (12 July 2013).
57. Cotter, M.; Villa Escudero's Waterfall Restaurant Serves Philippine Cuisine at the Foot of the Falls, **2012**. Retrieved from: http://inhabitat.com/villa-escuderos-waterfall-restaurant-   serves-philippine-cuisine-at-the-foot-of-the-falls/ (12 July 2013).
58. Walshe ,S.; Las Vegas: the Reinvention of Sin City as a Sustainable City, **2013**. Retrieved from: http://www.theguardian.com/sustainable-business/las-vegas-sin-city-sustainable?goback=%2Egde_4420455_member_5809363132182732804#%21 (accessed 7 December 2013).
59. Tesarova, K.; and Singh, A. J.; Implementing sustainable practices in Asia. **2013**. Retrieved from: http://www.hotelnewsnow.com/Article/9375/Implementing-sustainable-practices-in-Asia (accessed 7 December 2013).
60. Shangri La Asia Ltd.; Sustainability Report, **2012**. Retrieved from;http://hospitalityleaders.com/2013/05/03/shangri-la-asia-limited-issues-second-sustainability-report/ (accessed 7 December 2013).
61. Ashford, N.; Understanding technological responses of industrial firms to environmental problems: implications for government policy. In: Environmental Strategies for Industry: International Perspectives on Research Needs and Policy Implications (Eds.) Fischer, K.; and Schot, J.; , Washington, DC: Island Press; **1993**, pp. 277–307.
62. Arundel, A.; and Kemp, R.; Measuring eco-innovation. *United Nations University Working Paper Series.* **2009** (2009/017), 1–40.
63. Bohdanowicz, P.; Simanic, B.; and Martinac, I.; Environmental training and measures at Scandic hotels, Sweden. *Tour. Rev. Int.* **2005**, *9*(1), 7–19.
64. Kasim, A.; Towards a wider adoption of environmental responsibility in the hotel sector. *Int. J. Hosp. Tour. Admin.* **2007**, *8*(2), 25–49.
65. Baker, M. A.; Davis, E. A.; and Weaver, P. A.; Eco-friendly attitudes, barriers to participation, and differences in behavior at green hotels. *Corn. Hosp. Quarter.* **2013**. doi:1938965513504483.

66. Van Marrewijk, M.; and Werre, M.; Multiple levels of corporate sustainability. *J. Bus. Ethics.* **2003**, *44*(2), 107–119.

67. Krozer, Y.; Innovations and the Environment. Springer; **2008**.

68. Bartlett, D.; and Trifilova, A.; Green technology and eco-innovation: seven case-studies from a Russian manufacturing context. *J. Manufactur. Technol. Manag.* **2010**, *21*(8), 910–929.

69. El Dief, M.; and Font, X.; Determinants of environmental management in the Red Sea hotels personal and organizational values and contextual variables. *J. Hosp. Tour. Res.* **2012**, *36*(1), 115–137.

70. Erdogan, N.; and Baris, E.; Environmental protection programs and conservation practices of hotels in Ankara, Turkey. *Tour. Manag.* **2007**, *28*(2), 604–614)

71. Laroche, M.; Bergeron, J.; and Barbaro-Forleo, G.; Targeting consumers who are willing to pay more for environmentally friendly products. *J. Cons. Market.* **2001**, *18*(6), 503–520.

72. Scanlon, N. L.; An analysis and assessment of environmental operating practices in hotel and resort properties. *Int. J. Hosp. Manag.* **2007**, 711–723

73. Myung, E.; McClaren, A.; and Li, L.; Environmentally related research in scholarly hospitality journals: current status and future opportunities. *Int. J. Hosp. Manag.* **2012**, *31*, 1264–1275.

CHAPTER 5

AN EXTENDED FRAMEWORK FOR UNDERSTANDING CORPORATE SOCIAL RESPONSIBILITY: STRATEGIC IMPLICATIONS IN RESTAURANT SETTINGS

K. J. KIM[1], S.-B. KIM[2], and D.-Y. KIM[3]

[1]PhD Student, Hospitality Management, University of Missouri, 220 Eckles Hall, Columbia MO, USA, E-mail: jhkznb@mail.missouri.edu

[2]PhD Candidate, Hospitality Management, University of Missouri, 220 Eckles Hall, Columbia MO, USA, E-mail: sk7w2@mail.missouri.edu

[3]Associate Professor, Hospitality Management, University of Missouri, 220 Eckles Hall, Columbia MO, USA, E-mail: kimdae@missouri.edu

---

CONTENTS

5.1   INTRODUCTION

Given their increasing consideration for the socially conscious market environment, major companies across industry sectors have implemented managerial practices based on the concept of corporate social responsibility (CSR) [1]. Many definitions of CSR are available, but the term is generally used to describe how businesses go beyond economic criteria to meet their broader societal and environmental expectations and responsibilities [2]. Individuals around the world are increasingly concerned about such issues as global warming, child labor, and poverty, leading companies to engage with problems that they once would have considered irrelevant [3]. Companies have generally confined their responsibility to issues of safety and social welfare. Within that framework, they have become involved active in human rights, labor, and employment reform (e.g., health and well-being), environmental protection (e.g., pollution of the environment) and local community development. In related veins, restaurants focus on providing food that is safe and sustainably grown or raised (e.g., meat and seafood) as well as on their relationships with the individuals who grow and provide the food. These companies then communicate their social responsibility aims and achievements to educate their target audiences about their good corporate performance.

To better understand the consumer's perception of CSR, it is necessary to look into how companies effectuate this CSR communication within the restaurant context. CSR-related marketing communication is an opportunity to shape consumer perceptions through a company's differentiation strategy. Corporations have a plethora of channels at their disposal when disseminating CSR information (e.g., their own sustainability reports and all manner of multimedia) [4]. Concern for CSR has especially grown in the hospitality industry, with restaurateurs focusing on the consequences of the customer's perception of their restaurants' CSR [5]. Yet despite the importance of CSR to positioning and marketing strategies, both current research and marketing activities in restaurant settings still deal with only limited aspects of socially responsible efforts. To understand CSR's impact on both market positioning and communication to customers, it is imperative to understand the overall structure of CSR activities themselves.

Thus, this chapter extensively reviews and synthesizes the existing CSR literature and actual restaurants' own reports and websites on CSR in order to shed light on its implementation. Specifically, the chapter proposes an extended conceptual framework considering company characteristics, some salient dimensions of CSR practices, communication channels, and CSR outcomes within the restaurant context. In addition, this chapter discusses CSR case exemplars in restaurant settings. Through its conceptual research endeavor, the chapter is anticipated to provide insights into how companies can harness their CSR activities to market and position themselves more effectively. Consequently, the specific research questions for this chapter are: a) What are the unique and most important CSR attributes in the restaurant setting? b) How do restaurant firms communicate their CSR activities? and c) How does CSR communication affect customers' responses?

5.2   LITERATURE REVIEW

5.2.1   GROWTH AND POPULARITY OF CORPORATE SOCIAL RESPONSIBILITY (CSR) INITIATIVES

CSR research and studies in the hospitality industry have been increasing recently. Companies can benefit from the competitive advantage created by CSR, an area of corporate activity whose positive effects have been well documented in the hospitality literature [6]. For instance, some relevant studies have shown that CSR is positively linked to the financial performance of organizations (e.g., revenue, return on assets, and brand equity) [5]. This has led to a growing number of companies' becoming involved in CSR as a long-term business strategy. Many Fortune 500 companies consider CSR an important commitment that they should sustain and expand. These companies invest heavily not only in performing good works but also in communicating these works to consumers [7]. In the 2010 Annual Corporate Social Responsibility Perceptions Survey released by Penn Scheon Berland, Landor Associates, and Burson-Marsteller, more than 75 percent of consumers said that examining companies' CSR strategies was important. This survey also showed that consumers prioritized social responsibility across business sectors, and that 55 percent were more likely to purchase from and 70 percent were willing pay premium prices for products from a socially responsible company [8].

Still, companies do need to be careful about communicating their CSR undertakings to the public if they are to reap the benefits of CSR status. Recent initiatives by nonprofit organizations (NGOs) demonstrate the enormous impact of calling on companies to act responsibly. Their campaigns receive attention from consumers that can translate into a demand for better CSR from companies. With consumers the world over concerned about global warming, poverty, child labor, and so forth, many companies engage with such problems by sponsoring events, donating to appropriate causes, and adopting sustainability programs [3]. By advertising this engagement to the customer base, companies at once quell consumer discontent and build their brand identities.

This acceleration correlates with a growing number of hospitality companies' implementing socially responsible practices to show their commitment toward CSR [9]. Hospitality-service providers like Starbucks and Panera Bread are examples of firms increasingly engaging in CSR activities. The main reasons for this growing interest are several fold. Restaurant-industry research suggests that corporate engagement in CSR is positively associated with better customer assessments [10], meaning a restaurant company's CSR performance positively influences its consumers' willingness to reward that restaurant. CSR activities enhance the image of the company to overcome the hesitation customers may have to support a restaurant when they are unsure whether it harbors a genuine concern for the social good. That effect reverberates to the bottom line as well.

5.3   COMPANY CHARACTERISTICS

Proposition 1. Company characteristics such as corporate reputation, types of service, and firm size influence CSR activity.

Company characteristics such as corporate reputation, types of services, and firm size influence the choice of CSR activities [11]. A company's reputation affects the success of its CSR strategy, in that reputation can be thought of as an independent variable that influences the effects of CSR communication [3]. The reputation of a company is the result of all the perceptions that individuals have of that company, whether positive or negative [3]. Companies with good reputations often experience successful CSR communication because they have formed higher source credibility, whereas companies with poor reputations may experience backfire effects from their social initiatives [12]. According to the research of Yoon, Gurhan-Canli, and Schwarz (2006), companies with poor reputations participate in CSR activities in order to reform their negative public images. For example, companies in the oil industry have highlighted environmental and social activities, successfully improving their corporate images (e.g., Monsanto and Exxon) [12]. Within the restaurant industry, fast-food restaurants have sometimes been accused of ignoring health concerns, leading companies to engage in health- and obesity-related issues as one of their CSR activities [13].

In addition to corporate reputation, the types of services associated with a company also influence CSR activities. Certain dimensions of CSR may differ depending on the industry. It is reasonable to assume that the choice of CSR activities would vary depending on the type of service a firm provides, particularly in restaurant market segments (e.g., fast food, family restaurants, and etc.) [14]. While some studies (e.g., Cowen, Ferreri, & Parker, 1987) [15] report that CSR disclosure does not differ by industry type, most research (e.g., Simpson & Kohers, 2002) [16] has found great differences in CSR disclosures across industries. For instance, Deegan and Gordon's (1996) [17] finding is reinforced by a study conducted by Ness and Mizra (1991) [18], which found companies in the oil industry—a sector beset by public-relations woes—were disclosing more CSR information than companies in other industries. From the customer side of the interaction, Melo and Garrido-Morgado (2012) have documented that consumer responses depend on the type of industry as well [19]. In addition, relevant research has documented that in the interaction between corporate reputation and CSR, industry-type effects are a determinant of consumer responses [20].

Key studies have found that company size relates to CSR activity as well. The size of the company is treated as an independent variable on CSR activities in CSR research [19], with firm size being operationalized based on a firm's number of employees (10–250 = small; 251–500 = medium; 501+ = large) [21]. Baumann-Pauly and his colleagues (2013) found that firm size seems to trigger a specific CSR implementation pattern [22]. Since most companies have limited resources, they choose different CSR activities as determined by the allocation and combination of those resources. The majority of academic studies on CSR focus only on large or multinational companies; research regarding the CSR of small and medium enterprises (SMEs) remains scarce. In the case of large enterprises, their greater financial, technical, and human resources available for CSR initiatives and communication are critical [23]. With this enhanced corporate ability, large enterprises can approach CSR more strategically. In other words, they engage in CSR initiatives in order to ameliorate negative occurrences such as boycotts, suspicion, and bad rankings by instead focusing attention on their efforts to mold a better society [24].

Additionally, since large enterprises are more easily exposed to public inspection and receive greater political and social pressure to act in a socially appropriate way, such companies tend to take on more formal CSR activities and provide more information to the public regarding their CSR practices [25]. Large corporations pay keen attention to their various stakeholders' matters of concern (e.g., their customers, employees, suppliers, community, and environment). Specifically, they emphasize the external dimensions of CSR such as their concern with the environment [26] and a sustainable supply chain [27]. McDonald's, Yum Brands, Starbucks, and Darden Restaurants are listed in the Fortune 500, suggesting they have more resources than other restaurant companies, and they have indeed actively engaged in broad range of CSR activities.

Although many researchers have found a positive effect of company size on CSR dimensions, some scholars suggest that smaller firms also tend to be involved in CSR activities. Small and medium businesses (SMEs) differ from big companies in a variety of ways including their available resources, strategies, drivers, and so on [28]. These factors impact the different ways in which CSR is perceived and practiced among small and medium enterprises. Even though SMEs have fewer resources to engage in CSR programs than do larger companies, there are advantages to their CSR programs, too [29]. SMEs act responsibly in a more personalized way because the inspiration—and perhaps intuition—for their CSR often stems from the unique influence (i.e., the personal, ethic, and religious motivations) of the owners, founders, or top managers of the SMEs themselves [30]. Since these activities are more localized, SME managers also have more autonomy over how the business approaches and manages its CSR program [31].

In addition, SMEs seem to focus more on CSR qualities such as integrity and honesty by engaging in philanthropic CSR [29] rather than in strategic-management CSR designed solely for enhancing brand image and reputation [31]. Therefore, SMEs often focus their CSR closer their corporate and home culture, such as employee management and community involvement [32]. They may delve into, for example, issues dealing with employee retention, health, welfare, equity, and participation [33]. Recently, by expanding their CSR activities, SMEs have also considered their external relations with supply-chain partners [27].

5.4 CSR ACTIVITIES

Proposition 2. Considering the uniqueness of the restaurant industry, the key attributes of CSR are food quality, supply chain, environment, employee relations, and the community.

Various CSR dimensions have been adopted from the Kinder, Lydenberg, Domini (KLD) [34] data that direct corporate attention to a wider spectrum of stakeholder issues [35]. Employee relations, product safety and quality for customers, community relations, natural environment issues, and minorities-and-diversity issues are the essential CSR dimensions often acknowledged in KLD research [36]. However, the value of CSR activities varies over time and by markets and types of industry [37]. To date, restaurants have also made clear distinctions between different types of CSR activities to relate more effectively to various stakeholders and position themselves as socially responsible companies. For example, Panera Bread has developed antibiotic-free food products, while Chipotle Mexican Grill has tried animal-welfare-related activities with a corporate vision of "Food With Integrity." McDonald's, Burger King, and Starbucks are also positioning themselves with CSR and appear to be leading communicators of various CSR practices (e.g., community support, product quality, sourcing/supply chain, employee relations, and the environment) [38].

In particular, supply-chain participants, one of the main stakeholders behind restaurants, are an increasingly important CSR issue in the restaurant industry [39]. Other than the issues of child labor and fair wages, food safety issues causing food-borne illnesses are closely related to the management or working conditions inherent in a supply chain in the restaurant industry [40]; thus, restaurants simply must observe responsible and sustainable standards in their supply chains. Consequently, as shown in Table 5.1, CSR areas of specific emphasis in the restaurant industry are product safety and quality, supply chain, environmental programs, diversity and human-resource matters, and community development.

5.5 PRODUCT QUALITY

Product safety and quality relate to customer care [41] in that they assure quality food and guarantee its safety. Restaurants have generally focused on nutritious and healthy menu offerings by considering calories, sodium levels, and fat content and food safety by monitoring inputs from their origins to restaurant. For customers' health, for example, fast-food restaurants such as McDonald's and Burger King provide menu options with fruit, vegetables, or low-fat/fat-free dairy options. Some res-

TABLE 5.1 Restaurant companies' CSR activities and channels for CSR communication

Type	Restaurant[a]	CSR Activity[b]					Channel			
		Product Quality	Supply Chain	Environment	Employee	Community	CSR Report	Website	TV Commercial	SNSs[c]
Quick Service	McDonald's	✓	✓	✓	✓	✓	✓	✓	✓	✓
	Yum Brands	✓	✓	✓	✓	✓	✓	✓	✓	✓
	Burger King	✓	✓	✓	✓	✓	✓	✓		✓
	Wendy's	✓	✓	✓	✓	✓		✓		
	Subway	✓	✓	✓	✓	✓		✓		
Fast Casual	Chipotle Mexican Grill	✓	✓	✓	✓	✓		✓	✓	✓
	Panera Bread	✓				✓		✓	✓	✓
Casual Dining	Darden Restaurants	✓	✓	✓	✓	✓	✓	✓		✓
	DineEquity			✓	✓	✓		✓		
Cafes & Bakeries	Starbucks		✓	✓	✓	✓	✓	✓	✓	✓
	Caribou Coffee		✓	✓		✓	✓	✓		
	Dunkin' Brands	✓	✓	✓	✓	✓	✓	✓		

Note: The ✓ means that the restaurant company performs the listed CSR practice or employs the communication channel indicated.

[a] Restaurants that frequently engage in CSR activities and provide public access to CSR-related information.

[b] These CSR activities were classified from restaurant CSR reports and websites.

[c] SNSs, or Social-Networking Sites, include Facebook, Twitter, and YouTube.

taurants also conspicuously use natural ingredients that are free of hormones and antibiotics. Chipotle Mexican Grill serves naturally raised meat such as chicken, pork, and beef [42], and Darden Restaurants serves seafood that is sustainably grown.

Various types of restaurants offer nutritional information on menu boards and/or on their websites; they may also offer alternate portion sizes limiting overall calorie and sodium counts (e.g., Darden Restaurants). Specifically, Dunkin' Donuts offers its DDSMART® menu, denoted by a special green running-figure logo, on its restaurant menu boards, and Baskin-Robbins offers the BRight Choices® menu, which, according to Dunkin' Brands companies, offers no-fat or sugar/dairy-free options. To assure safe menu items, some top restaurants provide the highest levels of food safety through all the levels of the supply chain by using Hazard Analysis of Critical Control Points (HACCP) systems (e.g., Darden Restaurants and McDonald's).

5.6 SUPPLY CHAIN

A restaurant's supply chain is often only as good as its supplier relations [39]. Practices important to supply chains in the restaurant setting include responsible purchasing practices, programs to ensure diversity across the supplier base, supply-support efforts, and socially responsible standards for suppliers. For sustainably responsible purchasing practices, restaurants strive to buy inputs from sources that are responsibly grown and ethically traded with respect for the individuals who grow the foods. For example, Starbucks serves fair-trade coffee certified by third-party organizations and tea and coco that are produced in a socially responsible manner (e.g., by well-treated workers earning standard wages). McDonald's also purchases a variety of its major ingredients (e.g., white fish, coffee, palm oil, poultry, fiber, and beef) via a sustainable food supply. Specifically, McDonald's distributes McDonald's Supplier Code of Conduct to every supplier, requiring them to sign the Code and ensure they provide a healthy and secure work environment [43].

Similarly, Caribou Coffee has a program to guarantee supplier diversity such as the use of women-owned, disadvantaged, and small businesses [44]. With regards to support supplier, Starbucks' farmer-support centers help coffee farmers engage in responsible growing practices and improve the quality of their produce; through the use of a farmer-loans system, Starbucks provides fiscal and technical support for small farmers to invest in fair-trade producer organizations.

5.7 THE ENVIRONMENT

Environmental issues involve the provision of eco-friendly products and services, the use of green energy, water-use efficiency, waste reduction, and recycling programs [45]. For example, Chipotle Mexican Grill uses beans that are organically grown so that they can reduce the use of the chemical pesticides that affect the environment. In an effort to keep an eye on the ocean ecosystem, Darden Restaurants continuously update a list of fish species that they do not purchase because of overfishing [46]. More generally, to conserve energy, restaurants have built high-performance green restaurants or office buildings and installed energy-efficient equipment, and employees have participated in more energy-efficient behaviors. In the case of Darden Restaurants, they installed solar energy panels on the roof of their Restaurant Support Center (RSC) to supply a portion of its annual energy needs [46]. Restaurants have used recyclable packaging for necessities such as cups, hot-cup sleeves, and napkins (e.g., Starbucks and Subway).

5.8   EMPLOYEES

Employee relations deal with all worker-related issues, such as the guarantee of employees' safety, health care, and retirement benefits [41]. Most restaurants have provided a variety of opportunity, training, and development programs for employees. They have also tried to hire and promote minority and female employees. As Darden Restaurants has recently placed on Fortune magazine's annual list of the "100 Best Companies to Work For" [47], they are an exemplary case in terms of activities for employees. Through an engagement survey, Darden Restaurants give careful attention to employees' voices in terms of their preferences related to incentives and benefit programs and how they feel toward the firm and their job. Based on this communication, Darden provides a variety of benefits and compensation such as healthcare and financial assistance. They also offer a wide range of training and development programs for all levels of employees (e.g., hourly workers, managers, senior managers, and directors). In workforce diversity, Darden excels with women and minorities comprising over half their operations managers [46].

5.9   COMMUNITY

Community relations include a company's support for local populations through charitable donations/giving, community service such as educational programs, and employee volunteer activities [45]. For example, Panera Bread created Operation Dough-Nation, making community commitments. Among their four main activities for community support, the Day-End Dough-Nation program provides unsold bread to local hunger-relief agencies. Additionally, according to an announcement on Panera Bread website, through Panera Cares "community cafes," nonprofit donation-based cafes run via shared responsibility, they help address increasing hunger in the U.S. McDonald's shows a commitment to giving back (e.g., volunteerism, communications efforts, fundraising) through the Ronald McDonald House Charities (RMHC), where the company tries to make a significant impact on the lives of children. Starbucks also engages in volunteer activities with their customers and employees, and helps younger individuals develop skills learned in order to help the next generation become leaders through their Youth Action Grants.

Proposition 3. CSR activities influence customer's internal outcomes (i.e., aware-ness, attitude, and trust) and external outcomes (i.e., purchase, loyalty, and word-of-mouth).

This proposition now argues that CSR activities have a significant influence on customer-related outcomes. Marketing research has approached CSR from different perspectives. Specific company strategies have regularly included CSR action in order to attract and retain customers. Different dimensions of CSR have different effects and consequences [35]. According to the research of Öberseder, Schlegelmilch, and Murphy (2013), consumers rated companies' responsible acts regarding employees, customers, and the environment as important, followed by those of their suppliers and community [48]. Likewise, a key challenge in designing an effective CSR strategy is understanding how to induce customers' attitudinal and behavioral changes in a positive way.

There are one of the most immediate consequences (i.e., creation of awareness, attitude change, and trust) of a company's social performance and an immediate outcome of CSR activities [49]. Additionally, CSR activities directly affect attitudes and trust [50]. Relevant research also suggests that a company's CSR positioning can positively affect consumers' behavioral outcomes such as purchasing, loyalty, and word-of-mouth [49]. Further, when practiced correctly, CSR acts to build corporate loyalty, the cornerstone of successful long-term marketing. By engaging in CSR activities, therefore, companies cannot only generate favorable customer attitudes; over the long run, they can build corporate image, strengthen stakeholder-company relationships, and enhance customers' advocacy behaviors [51] (Table 5.1).

5.10   EFFECT OF CHANNELS

Proposition 4. Channel types play a moderating role between CSR activities and outcomes.

It is clear that corporate dissemination of CSR information, which has been defined as "communication that is designed and distributed by the company itself about its CSR efforts" [52], can be achieved through a number of channels. Not all companies should advertise CSR actions in the same way [53]. Companies may disseminate their CSR actions using official documents, such as CSR reports or press releases, via official corporate websites with dedicated CSR sections, commercials in mass media, or product packaging [51]. CSR reporting and the use of corporate websites are the most common CSR channels in the restaurant industry. For example, Starbucks started issuing a CSR report in 2001 and has continued to distribute the report every year. Restaurants maintain the use of advertising channels to communicate their CSR actions. For example, Chipotle Mexican Grill, a fast-casual restaurant, introduced an animated national commercial called "Back to the Start" with a pointed message regarding sustainable farming [54], as shown in Figure 5.1. Due to the enthusiastic response of consumers, Chipotle's CSR initiative is regarded as one of the most successful among fast-casual chains in America. These corporate channels are an effective way of communicating what the restaurants do in terms of CSR; however, as these CSR communication channels are controlled by the company itself, they cause more skepticism and have less credibility than noncorporate sources.

FIGURE 5.1   Chipotle Mexican Grill's animated national commercial "Back to the Start." **Source:** adapted from Olson.; An animated Ad with a plot line and a moral. The New York Times. 2012.

Since consumers perceive corporate sources channels to be self-interested [12], restaurants have used informal communication channels such as social-media sites, blogs, and chat rooms to enhance the credibility of their CSR initiatives. Many companies engage in virtual dialogs with their customers to stimulate support for their brands, products, and services. Beyond this, companies are looking to leverage social media to design and implement their CSR for improving social welfare [55]. Informal CSR communication channels are an effective way of gathering information and sharing ideas with consumers [56]. For example, Darden Restaurants have a "Darden Citizenship" page on Facebook, as shown in Figure 5.2, where users can share opinions. Starbucks also has an online community, MyStarbucksIdea.com, where users have shared their ideas about social responsibility among a varied field of topics. Even though the popularity and power of social networking can enhance CSR communication, social media is by its nature open access. As a result, restaurants are susceptible to criticism from stakeholders who will honestly question the genuineness and legitimacy of that CSR, potentially damaging the reputation such companies have worked so hard to build [57]. Still, employing social-media channels in the CSR context of the restaurant industry is an opportunity to generate substantial value for both research and strategic management.

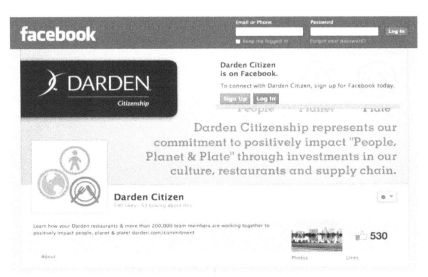

FIGURE 5.2   Darden Restaurants' citizenship page on Facebook.
Source: adapted from Darden Restaurants' citizenship page on Facebook

This proposition now turns to the debate over the effectiveness of various channels as moderators of the link between CSR activities and outcomes. As can be seen in the literature on advertising, there is a difference to be found depending on the media channel used. Information about a company's CSR initiatives can be disseminated in numerous ways. Groza and his colleagues (2011) found that the source of the CSR message had a moderating impact [58]. More than one study shows differences in consumer responses and effectiveness of advertising depending on medium [59]. For instance, Dickinger (2011) has found that users of different online information channels exhibit different levels of trust [60]. Type of channel is key in raising awareness of products and features [19]. In addition, several studies have examined the effectiveness of communication channels or media on attitudes, word-of-mouth, and loyalty [51].

5.11   INTERNAL AND EXTERNAL OUTCOMES

Proposition 5. To measure CSR, internal outcomes of CSR such as awareness, attitudes, and trust should be examined.
Proposition 6. To measure CSR, external outcomes of CSR such as purchase intentions, loyalty, and word-of-mouth should be examined.

Companies' CSR programs and practices have an impact on consumers' responses to companies [61]. CSR research has frequently focused on variables such as awareness of and attitude toward the firm, commitment and loyalty to a product, customer satisfaction, and customer word-of-mouth as potential outcomes [62]. For propositions 5 and 6, CSR awareness refers to customers' knowledge of a company's cumulative CSR engagement [62]. Communicating CSR activities is essential to enhancing CSR awareness. Consumers who receive communication about a company's CSR activities increase their CSR awareness. Attitude is one of the most extensively used concepts in social-science research; a commonly adopted definition of attitude is a learned predisposition to respond in a consistently favorable or unfavorable manner [63]. Crucially, CSR can have a positive effect on attitude responses (i.e., attitude toward the company) [64]. Homburg and his colleagues (2013) defined trust as comprising the customer's expectancy that the company is competent and can be relied on, as well as the belief that the company has benevolent intentions and motives [65]. Xie and Peng (2011) pointed out that when customers' image of a brand and their trust in the corporation converge, they result in an enduring consumer-corporate relationship [66]. CSR activities enhance that trust [67].

Some scholarship (e.g., Sen, Bhattacharya, & Korschun, 2006) [62] has stated that consumers generally have a low level of awareness about what CSR is. However, consumers showing a high level of awareness and trust in companies' CSR programs are more likely to form a good CSR mental record [61]. The theory of reasoned action has been applied in multiple studies of consumers' intentions toward CSR by businesses [68]. It is evident that several studies—all in a business-to-consumer context—have established a link between a company's CSR activities and important consumer outcomes such as purchasing, loyalty, and word-of-mouth. Through CSR activities, a company can foster consumer loyalty and even create champions who engage in advocacy behaviors (e.g., positive word-of-mouth) [69]. Outcomes from CSR include higher purchase intentions [70] and of course positive word-of-mouth [71]. As shown in Figure 5.3, this chapter suggests an extended conceptual framework for CSR activities by examining prominent factors in CSR and their outcomes.

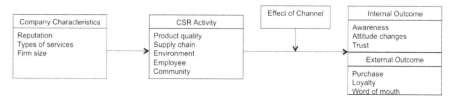

FIGURE 5.3   An extended framework of CSR activities.

5.12   IMPLICATIONS

This chapter has reviewed CSR activities and communication based on the restaurant industry's existing documents and products. With appropriate empirical studies conducted in the future, the model proposed in this chapter can be helpful to researchers setting up a fundamental framework of restaurant CSR literature. This chapter contributes to the understanding of CSR implementation in small and medium industries as well. Most literature has analyzed large manufacturing businesses while the hospitality industry and its SMEs have received less attention [72]. This chapter proposes the industry needs to adopt different strategies based on known firm-size effects. This framework proposes that a company's reputation is used to interpret its CSR communication, and hence that the industry may find a logical relationship between the corporate reputation and CSR domains. In addition, there must of course be flexibility in the design and implementation of CSR activities since consumer responses may differ among companies providing unique services.

Developing effective communication of CSR can aid in building consumers' responses. By following the proposed model, restaurants that plan the use of CSR as a part of their differentiation strategy should especially consider highlighting CSR in their communication campaigns and positioning. Reflecting their values and opinions, individuals attach different weight to CSR domains. This proposed model suggests that the restaurant industry must invest more in socially responsible initiatives because individuals tend to support and reward those companies that are perceived as socially responsible. The industry can reinforce its corporate strategies through investment in CSR initiatives and programs to reinforce customer loyalty and trust by reflecting the values and opinions of the target market. Any communication that makes CSR programs more credible, authentic, and distinct from competitors will considerably improve the company's attractiveness, both to consumers and investors. Nevertheless, any communication must be evaluated only within the extent to which the CSR-based media channels employed are actually valued by targeted individuals.

5.13   LIMITATIONS AND FUTURE RESEARCH SUGGESTED

CSR works has predominantly concentrated on consumers in different disciplines. There is increasing recognition in the marketing literature that the influence of CSR is more multidimensional. Future scholars could conduct research specifically on the effects of CSR on individuals who are part of the company or on prospective investors. In addition, there is a lack of CSR research within the business-to-business context. A limitation of this framework is that either control variables or numerous possible antecedents could be involved. There is, therefore, considerable potential for new constructs as well as other moderators to be added to our research model. Finally, antecedents employing this framework, such as corporate reputation and service type, could use these moderators or outcomes for expanding the model in future.

5.14 CONCLUSIONS

There has been increasing debate and discussion around CSR for the past several decades. Corporate social responsibility entails companies' seeking to generate profit while causing the minimal harm to society and going a step further to contribute to social improvement [28]. Sometimes, too, companies may engage in CSR activities as mere window dressing to appease various stakeholder groups [73]. Research on CSR may be approaching a mature stage, but research on consumer responses to CSR initiatives is still lacking—including within the hospitality context. As noted earlier, there is yet room for improvement in the evolving field of restaurant CSR.

In sum, this chapter has reviewed and synthesized the relevant literature on CSR and communication to present a conceptual framework for CSR communication itself. This chapter has attempted to develop a theoretical foundation for CSR within the restaurant industry. This chapter hopefully provides guidance and a useful theoretical perspective to scholars and industry members on this burgeoning topic. Further empirical studies are needed to validate the conceptual model proposed here, but until then, the discussion of the key aspects of CSR communication in this chapter should open up avenues for future research within the hospitality and tourism context.

5.15 DISCUSSION QUESTIONS

1. How do hospitality and tourism companies perceive CSR and its importance to our industry?
2. Which types of CSR activities are most common and unique in restaurant settings?
3. What are other factors (e.g., country of origin) in company characteristics?
4. Considering the five areas of social responsibility in restaurant settings, please provide examples of ways that restaurants can effectively communicate in each of these areas.
5. When considering societal change, what can be the next target area for increased sustainability in restaurant settings?
6. What are the linkages between CSR activities and outcomes, and why are they important?
7. How are other hospitality and tourism companies organized for CSR activities?
8. Beyond restaurants, are other hospitality and tourism companies engaging in CSR activities?
9. Do the CSR activities introduced in this chapter matter more to younger or to older consumers? Explain why one age group might be more sensitive to CSR initiatives than the other.

10. Do different cultures influence CSR activities in distinctive ways? Can you imagine any examples from your own experience?

5.16 SUGGESTED FURTHER READINGS

—Ihlen, Ø.; Bartlett, J.; and May, S.; The Handbook Of Communication And Corporate Social Responsibility. UK: John Wiley & Sons Ltd, **2013**.
—Sloan, P.; Legrand, W.; and Chen, J. S.; Sustainability in the Hospitality Industry□: Principles of Sustainable Operations□. New York, NY: Routledge.□□□□□□□□

5.17 USEFUL WEBSITES

—Chipotle Mexican Grill: http://www.chipotle.com/en-us/fwi/fwi.aspx
—Darden Restaurants: http://www.darden.com/sustainability/
—Green Restaurant Association: http://www.dinegreen.com
—McDonald's: http://www.mcdonalds.com/us/en/our_story/values_in_action/the_road_to_sustainability.html
—Panera Bread: http://paneracares.org/what-we-do/
—Starbucks: http://www.starbucks.com/responsibility/global-report
—Sustainable Restaurant Association (UK): http://www.thesra.org
—Yum Brands: http://www.yumcsr.com

KEYWORDS

- Channel types
- Corporate reputation
- Product quality
- Supply chain

REFERENCES

1. Brønn, P. S.; Marketing and corporate social responsibility. In: Handbook of Communication and Corporate Social Responsibility. (Eds.) Ihlen, Ø.; Bartlett, J. L.; and May, S.; Malden, MA.; Wiley-Blackwell; **2011**, pp. 110–127.
2. Pomering, A.; and Johnson, L. W.; Constructing a corporate social responsibility reputation using corporate image advertising. *Austral. Market. J.* **2009**, *17*, 106–114.
3. Elving, W. J. L.; Scepticism and corporate social responsibility communications: The influence of fit and reputation. *J. Market. Comm.* **2013**, *19*(4), 277–292.
4. de Grosnois, D.; Corporate social responsibility reporting by the global hotel industry: Commitment, initiatives and performance. *Int. J. Hosp. Manag.* **2012**, *31*, 896–905.

5. Kang, K. H.; Lee, S.; and Huh, C.; Impacts of positive and negative corporate social responsibility activities on company performance in the hospitality industry. *Int. J. Hosp. Manag.* **2010**, *29*(1), 72–82.

6. Mattila, A. S.; Hanks, L.; and Kim, E. E. K.; The impact of company type and corporate social responsibility messaging on consumer perceptions. *J. Finan. Serv. Market.* **2010**, *15*(2), 126–135.

7. Luo, X.; and Bhattacharya, C. B.; Corporate social responsibility, customer satisfaction, and market value. *J. Market.* **2006**, *70*(4), 1–18.

8. Kong, D.; Does corporate social responsibility matter in the food industry? Evidence from a nature experiment in China. *Food Pol.* **2012**, *37*, 323–334.

9. Martínez, P.; and del Bosque I. R.; CSR and customer loyalty: the roles of trust, customer identification with the company and satisfaction. *Int. J. Hosp. Manag.* **2013**, *35*, 89–99.

10. Choi, G.; Corporate social and environmental responsibility in services: will consumers pay for it? *Acad. Manag. Ann. Meet. Proceed.* **2011**, *1*, 1–6.

11. Gardberg, N. A.; and Fombrun, C. J.; The global reputation quotient project: first steps towards a crossnationally valid measure of corporate reputation. *Corp. Reput. Rev.* **2002**, *4*, 303–308.

12. Yoon, Y.; Gurhan-Canli, Z.; and Schwarz, N; The effect of corporate social responsibility (CSR) activities on companies with bad reputations. *J. Consumer Psychol.* **2006**. *16*(4), 377–390.

13. Lee, H. H. M.; Van Dolen, W.; and Kolk, A.; On the role of social media in the 'responsible' food business: Blogger buzz on health and obesity issues. *J. Bus. Ethics.* **2006**. *27*, 1–13.

14. Sheldon, P. J.; and Park, S.Y.; An exploratory study of corporate social responsibility in the U.S. travel industry. *J.Travel Res.* **2011**, *50*(4), 392–407.

15. Cowen, S.; Ferreri, L.; and Parker, L.; The impact of corporate characteristics on social responsibility disclosure: a typology and frequency based analysis. *Account. Org. Soc.* **1987**, *12*(2), 111–122.

16. Simpson, G.; and Kohers, T.; The link between corporate social and financial performance: evidence from the banking industry. *J. Bus. Ethics.* **2002**, *35*, 97–109.

17. Deegan, C.; and Gordon, B.; A study of the environmental disclosure policies of Australian corporations. *Account. Bus. Res.* **1996**, *26*(3), 187–199.

18. Ness, K. E.; and Mizra, A. M.; Corporate social disclosure: a note on a test of agency theory. *British Account. Rev.* **1991**, *12*(3), 211–217.

19. Melo, T.; and Garrido-Morgado, A.; Corporate reputation: A combination of social responsibility and industry. *Corp. Soc. Respons. Environ. Manag.* **2012**, *19*(1), 11–31.

20. Gardberg, N. A.; and Fombrun, C. J.; Corporate citizenship: creating intangible assets across institutional environments. *Acad. Manag. Rev.* **2006**, *31*(2), 329–346.

21. Camino, J. R.; Corporate environmental market responsiveness: a model of individual and organizational drivers. *J. Bus. Res.* **2012**, *65*, 402–411.

22. Baumann-Pauly, D.; Wickert, C.; Spence, L. J.; and Scherer, A. G.; Organizing corporate social responsibility in small and large firms: size matters. *J. Bus. Ethics.* **2013**, *115*(4), 693–705.

23. Elsayed, K. Reexamining the expected effect of available resources and firm size on firm environmental orientation: an empirical study of UK firms. *J. Bus. Ethics.* **2006**, *65*(3), 297–308.

24. Arvidsson, S.; Communication of corporate social responsibility: a study of the views of management teams in large companies. *J. Bus. Ethics.* **2010**, *96*(3), 339–354.

25. Branco, M.; and Rodrigues, L. L.; Communication of corporate social responsibility by Portuguese banks: a legitimacy theory perspective. *Corp. Commun. Int. J.* **2006**, *11*(3), 232–248.

26. Jamali, D.; Zanhour, M.; and Keshishian, T.; Peculiar strengths and relational attributes of SMEs in the context of CSR. *J. Bus. Ethics.* **2008**, *87*(3), 355–377.

27. Pedersen, E. R.; The many and the few: rounding up the SMEs that manage CSR in the supply chain. *SCM: Int. J.* **2009**, *14*(2), 109–116.

28. Coppa, M.; and Sriramesh, K.; Corporate social responsibility among SMEs in Italy. *Pub. Relat. Rev.* **2013**, *39*, 30–39.

29. Sarbutts, N.; Can SMEs do CSR? A practitioner's view of the ways small and medium sized enterprises are able to manage reputation through corporate social responsibility. *J. Commun. Manag.* **2003**, *7*(4), 340–347.

30. Fuller, T.; and Tian, Y.; Social and symbolic capital and responsible entrepreneurship: an empirical investigation of SME narratives. *J. Bus. Ethics.* **2006**, *67*(3), 287–304.

31. Jenkins, H.; A critique of conventional CSR theory: an SME perspective. *J. Gen. Manag.* **2004**, *29*(4), 55–75.

32. Nielsen, A. E.; and Thomsen, C.; Investigating CSR communication in SMEs: a case study among Danish middle managers. *Bus. Ethics European Rev.* **2009**, *18*(1), 83–93.

33. Vives, A.; Social and environmental responsibility in small and medium enterprises in Latin America. *J. Corp. Citizen.* **2006**, *21*, 39–50.

34. KLD Getting Started with KLD STATS and KLD's Ratings Definitions. Boston, MA: KLD Research & Analytics, Inc; **2006**.

35. Kacperczyk, A.; With greater power comes greater responsibility? Takeover protection and corporate attention to stakeholders. *Strat. Manag. J.* **2009**, *30*, 261–285.

36. Paek, S.; Xiao, Q.; Lee, S.; and Song, H.; Does managerial ownership affect different corporate social responsibility dimensions? An empirical examination of U.S. publicly traded hospitality firms. *Int. J. Hosp. Manag.* **2013**, *34*, 423–433.

37. Bird, R. G.; Hall, A. D.; Momentè, F.; and Reggiani, F.; What corporate social responsibility activities are valued by the market? *J. Bus. Ethics.* **2007**, *76*(2), 189–206.

38. Ham, S.; and Lee, S.; US restaurant companies' green marketing via company websites: impact on financial performance. *Tour. Econ.* **2011**, *17*(5), 1055–1069.

39. Maloni, M.; and Brown, M.; Corporate social responsibility in the supply chain: An application in the food industry. *J. Bus. Ethics.* **2006**, *68*(1), 35–62.

40. Murphy, J.; and Smith, S.; Chefs and suppliers: An exploratory look at supply chain issues in an upscale restaurant alliance. *Int. J. Hosp. Manag.* **2009**, *28*, 212–220.

41. Inoue, Y.; and Lee, S.; Effects of different dimensions of corporate social responsibility on corporate financial performance in tourism-related industries. *Tour. Manag.* **2011**, *32*, 790–804.

42. Ragas, M. W.; and Roberts, M. S.; Communicating corporate social responsibility and brand sincerity: a case study of Chipotle Mexican Grill's 'Food with Integrity' program. *Int. J. Strat. Commun.* **2009**, *3*(4), 264–280.

43. McDonald; McDonald's 2012 Global Sustainability Highlights. **2012**. Retrieved from http://www.aboutmcdonalds.com/content/dam/AboutMcDonalds/Sustainability/Progress%20Snapshot/2012SustainabilityHighlights.pdf

44. Caribou Coffee; Do Good Annual Report. **2013**. Retrieved from http://www.cariboucof-fee.com/page/1/social-responsibility.jsp

45. Hou, J.; and Reber, B. H.; Dimensions of disclosures: corporate social responsibility (CSR) reporting by media companies. *Pub. Relat. Rev.* **2011**, *37*, 166–168.

46. Darden Restaurants; Darden Sustainability Report. **2012**. Retrieved from http://www.darden.com/sustainability/downloads/2012-gri-full.pdf

47. Fortune; Fortune 500. **2013**. Retrieved from http://money.cnn.com/magazines/fortune/fortune500/?iid=F500_sp_header

48. Öberseder, M.; Schlegelmilch, B. B.; and Murphy, P. E.; CSR practices and consumer perceptions. *J. Bus. Res.* **2013**, *66*(10), 1839–1851.

49. Perez, R. C.; Effects of perceived identity based on corporate social responsibility: the role of consumer identification with the company. *Corp. Reput. Rev.* **2008**, *12*(1), 177–191.

50. Hillenbrand, C.; Money, K.; and Ghobadian, A.; Unpacking the mechanism by which corporate responsibility impacts stakeholder relationships. *British J. Manag.* **2011**, *24*(1), 127–146.

51. Du, S.; Bhattacharya, C. B.; and Sen, S.; Maximizing business returns to corporate social responsibility (CSR): the role of CSR communication. *Int.J. Manag. Rev.* **2010**, *12*, 8–19.

52. Morsing, M.; Corporate social responsibility as strategic auto-communication: on the role of external stakeholders for member identification. *Bus. Ethics European Rev.* **2006**, *15*(2), 171–182.

53. Schultz, M.; and Morsing, M.; The catch 22 of integrating CSR and marketing: findings from a reputation study of Danish companies, In: Conference Proceedings, MSI, Boston: Boston University, September, **2003**, 17–19.

54. Olson, E.; An animated ad with a plot line and a moral. The New York Times. **2012**, February 9. Retrieved from http://www.nytimes.com/2012/02/10/business/media/chipotle-ad-promotes-sustainable-farming.html?_r=0

55. Korschun, D.; and Du, S.; How virtual corporate social responsibility dialogs generate value: a framework and propositions. *J.Bus. Res.* **2013**, *66*, 1494–1504.

56. Rim, H.; and Song, D.; The ability of corporate blog communication to enhance CSR effectiveness: the role of prior company reputation and blog responsiveness. *Int. J. Strat. Commun.* **2013**, *7*(3), 165–185.

57. Etter, M.; Reasons for low levels of interactivity:(Non-) interactive CSR communication in Twitter. *Pub. Relat. Rev.* **2013**, *39*(5), 606–608.

58. Groza, M.; Pronschinske, M.; and Walker, M.; Perceived organizational motives and consumer responses to proactive and reactive CSR. *J. Bus. Ethics.* **2011**, *102*(4), 639–652.

59. Kim, D.-Y.; Hwang, Y.; and Fesenmaier, D. R.; Modeling tourism advertising effectiveness. *J. Travel Res.* **2005**, *44*(1), 42–49.

60. Dickinger, A.; The trustworthiness of online channels for experience—and goal-directed search tasks. *J. Travel Res.* **2011**, *50*(4), 378–391.

61. Feldman, P. M.; and Vasquez-Parraga, A. Z.; Consumer social responses to CSR initiatives versus corporate abilities. *J. Cons. Market.* **2013**, *30*(2), 100–111.

62. Sen, S.; Bhattacharya, C. B.; and Korschun, D.; The role of corporate social responsibility in strengthening multiple stakeholder relationships: a field experiment. *J. Acad. Market. Sci.* **2006**, *34*(2), 158–166.

63. Ki, E.-J.; and Hon, L.; Causal linkages among relationship quality perception, attitude, and behavior intention in a membership organization. *Corp. Commun.* **2012**, *17*(2), 187–208.

64. Brown, T. J.; and Dacin, P. A.; The company and the product: Corporate associations and consumer product responses. *J. Market.* **1997**, *61*(1), 68–84.

65. Homburg, C.; Stierl, M.; and Bornemann, T.; Corporate social responsibility in business-to-business markets: how organizational customers account for supplier corporate social responsibility engagement. *J. Market.* **2013**, *77*(6), 54–72.

66. Xie, Y.; and Peng, S.; How do corporate associations influence customer relationship strength? The effects of different types of trust. *J. Strat. Market.* **2011**, *19*(5), 443–454.

67. Vlachos, P.; Tsamakos, A.; Vrechopoulos, A. P.; and Avramidis, P. K.; Corporate social responsibility: attributions, loyalty, and the mediating role of trust. *J. Acad. Market. Sci.* **2009**, *37*(2), 170–180.

68. Yan, R. N.; Hyllegard, K. H.; and Blaesi, L. F.;Marketing eco-fashion: the influence of brand name and message explicitness. *J. Market. Commun.* **2012**, *18*(2), 151–168.

69. Du, S.; Bhattacharya, C. B.; and Sen, S.; Reaping relationship rewards from corporate social responsibility: the role of competitive positioning. *Int. J. Res. Market.* **2007**, *24*(3), 224–241.

70. Mohr, L. A.; and Webb, D. J.; The effect of corporate social responsibility and price on consumer responses. *J. Cons. Affairs.* **2005**, *39*(1), 121–147.

71. Hoeffler, S.; and Keller, K. L.; Building brand equity through corporate societal marketing. *J. Pub. Pol. Market.* **2002**.; *21*(2), 78–89.

72. Garay, L.; and Font, X.; Doing good to do well? Corporate social responsibility reasons, practices and impacts in small and medium accommodation enterprises. *Int. J. Hosp. Manag.* **2012**, *31*, 329–337.

73. Sprinkle, G. B.; and Maines, L. A.; The benefits and costs of corporate social responsibility. *Bus. Horizons.* **2010**, *53*, 445–453.

CHAPTER 6

FROM A LOVE STORY TO A SUSTAINABLE ATTRACTION: RUBY FALLS, USA

R. J. C. CHEN

Director and Professor, Center for Sustainable Business and Development, The University of Tennessee, 311 Conference Center Building, Knoxville, Tennessee 37996-4134, USA, Tel. +1 865 974 0505, Fax: +1 865 974 1838, E-mail: rchen@utk.edu

CONTENTS

6.1 INTRODUCTION

Companies understand the importance of monitoring and managing their environmental impacts and aim to integrate, with consistent quality control, effective reduce-reuse-recycle programs and risk preventions. By building an integrated sustainable management system to meet certain environmental standards, many companies/attractions are eligible to be 'green' certified. Ruby Falls was the first "green" certified attraction in the state of Tennessee in 2010. It is a 145-foot waterfall, located more than 1,120 feet beneath Lookout Mountain in Chattanooga. Millions of visitors of all ages and from all around the country have seen Ruby Falls, which was originally discovered by Leo Lambert, a cave enthusiast from Chattanooga. This chapter introduces the definitions of sustainability, addresses the importance of the tourism industry in the state of Tennessee, tells the love story of Ruby Falls through its discovery, records the sustainable journey of Ruby Falls, illustrates visitor experiences and satisfaction toward Ruby Falls visits, and provides conclusions of the case study. Meaningful discussion questions are listed at the end of this chapter for the convenience of readers.

6.2 DEFINITIONS OF SUSTAINABILITY

While researchers noted various definitions of sustainability and sustainable development [1], Prosser [2] identified four folds related to social changes, including growing environmental awareness versus cultural sensitivity, recognizing constraints of destinations' resources, growing dissatisfaction toward existing products, and increased changes in attitudes of businesses and developers. The World Tourism Organization [3] noted the definitions of sustainable tourism as "Tourism that takes full account of its current and future economic, social and environmental impacts, addressing the needs of visitors, the industry, the environment and host communities" (http://sdt.unwto.org/en/content/about-us-5).

Previous studies [4–7] aimed to highlight the positive interactions and integration of environment, economy, and society. Researchers [8–12] viewed sustainability as a venue to resolve and address conflicts among negative environmental impacts brought by businesses, interactions between businesses and tourists, and the host communities in terms of balancing natural and human resources and sustaining the quality of life.

While many studies used the terms of sustainability, sustainable tourism and sustainable development interchangeably in the literature, Butler [1], Harris and Leiper [13], and Hunter [10] sought to distinguish these terms within their studies. Liu and Jones [14: p. 217] further clarified the differences by indicating that "sustainability refers to steady life conditions for generations to come," "sustainable development" usually followed by changes and is more process of recognizing specific social and economic goals which may call for a stabilization, increase, reduction, change of quality or even removal of existing products, firms, industries, or other elements," and "sustainable tourism is defined as all types of tourism that make contributions to sustainable development." Tourism-related industries are ranked as the top-two industry, followed by manufacturing, in the state of Tennessee in terms of economic contribution and job generation. Since 2008, Tennessee has aimed to support sustainable tourism and make every effort to make contributions to sustainable development.

6.3   IMPORTANCE OF TOURISM IN THE STATE OF TENNESSEE

According to the US Travel Association, domestic and international travelers con- tributed $15.4 billion to direct effects on lodging, food, transportation, entertain- ment, recreation, and retails to the state of Tennessee in the year 2011. Hamilton County (Chattanooga region) received $893.3 million from domestic travelers' spending and was ranked fourth among the 95 counties of Tennessee.

Chattanooga, Tennessee, was named by the New York Times as one of the "Top 45 Places To Go" in the world and is one of the South's well-known top tourism destinations. Chattanooga's nick name, "Scenic City," is embraced the mountains of southeast Tennessee and flows of the Tennessee River, including numerous outdoor adventures, live events along the river bank, featured foods, and southern hospital- ity. Among all must-see attractions of Chattanooga, Ruby Falls features the deepest commercial cave and the most-visited underground waterfall in the United States with an annual visitation of more than 400,000.

6.4   RUBY FALLS DISCOVERY: A LOVE STORY

About 200 to 240 million years ago, the sediments of a shallow sea in eastern Ten- nessee formed limestone rock. The Ruby Falls Cave, which is part of the Lookout Mountain Caverns, is a limestone cave that is relatively horizontal as when it was deposited below sea level. Due to chemical weathering, slightly acidic groundwater enters subterranean streams, washes away the soluble limestone, and causes narrow cracks to widen into caves. Several well-known types of cave formations, includ- ing flowstone, drapery, columns, stalactites, and stalagmites are featured within the Ruby Falls Cave. After the cave's formation, the stream entered the cave and makes up the Ruby Falls.

At the end of the main pathway of the Ruby Falls Cave is a vertical shaft stream, 1,120 feet underground, fed by natural springs and rainwater. Ruby Falls, the verti- cal stream, collects in a pool of the cave floor and continues to flow through the mountain then join the Tennessee River at the base of Lookout Mountain Caverns. The Lookout Mountain Caverns are formed by the Lookout Mountain Cave and Ruby Falls Cave, which is the upper cavern and contains well-known geological formations, while Lookout Mountain is the lower one and does not have a variety of geological formations. The two caves are not connected.

For more than 80 years, located 1,120 feet beneath the Lookout Mountain's surface, Ruby Falls, one of top 10 most amazing underground waterfalls on the planet (Appendix), is a 145-foot deep underground waterfall, near Chattanooga in the United States. Well-trained tour guides lead visitors into the cavern by taking an elevator then walking through a paved and level pathway to view a variety of formations and Ruby Falls.

In 1905, the entrance to Lookout Mountain Cave was shut off to the public. Mr. Lambert devised a plan to reopen the cave to the public. After 5 years of planning and drilling, Mr. Lambert and a group of investors discovered a new cave. They also found a waterfall after exploring deeper into the cave. Mr. Lambert was "awestruck by its magnificence and beauty" and decided to name it in honor of his wife, Ruby Eugenia Losey. Mr. Lambert offered public tours of the new Ruby Falls. Ruby Falls has been open to the public since 1930 and became popular because of its unusual formations. It has developed into a "must see attraction in the Southeast." Ruby Falls provides a great attraction site for all to learn about its history, geology, and sustainable development.

6.5 RUBY FALLS'S SUSTAINABILITY JOURNEY

Ruby Falls is listed in the National Register for Historic Places and is now committed to sustainable business and environmentally friendliness in terms of green operations and reduction of environmental footprint. Ruby Falls was bestowed as the first green attraction in the state of Tennessee and was awarded by the Green Globe International Environmental Certification through focusing on four main initiatives, including the production of renewable energy, reduction in greenhouse gas emissions, recycling and waste reduction, and land use planning.

"Since 1928, when Ruby Falls reused the limestone excavated from the cave to build the Ruby Falls building, until today, Ruby Falls is committed to another 80 years of offering one of the most unique natural attractions in the world," according to Hugh Morrow, president of Ruby Falls, LLC. "Third-party certification is crucial to holding us to a higher standard and keeping us focused on more environmentally sensitive business practices" (Figure 6.1).

Ruby Falls received assistantships from the State of Tennessee Economic and Community Development Energy Division's Tennessee Clean Energy Technology Grant Program to purchase this state-of-the-art solar energy production equipment. Ruby Falls also had Big Frog Mountain installed an array of solar panels that produce 16,000 watts of renewable solar electricity with the full power to light more than two hundred and fifty 60-watt light bulbs. Ruby Falls utilizes a computer-controlled lighting system to reduce its annual power consumption by more than 24 percent, and, more specifically, it operates the cave with eight to 9 months of electricity power compared with the full-year consumption without the renewable energy system installation during the previous years (Figure 6.2).

FIGURE 6.1   Ruby Falls (photographer: Dr. Rachel JC Chen).

FIGURE 6.2   Solar panels (photographer: Dr. Rachel JC Chen)

Using the solar energy will replace the use of burning gasoline, oil, and coal. Reducing the burning of these of fossil fuels will lower carbon emissions, which were estimated as releasing 40,000 pounds of carbon dioxide per person annually in the United States. Ruby Falls has replaced incandescent with compact fluorescent lamps and LED bulbs in addition to changing the timing and duration of lighting while adding lighting and equipment controls. Ruby Falls has replaced its old van with a hybrid SUV, which is a more fuel-efficient vehicle.

Ruby Falls makes an effort to use environmentally friendly products, sorting waste materials, and selling waste, which could be reproduced by companies and reduce sources through altering uses of products with less or no toxicity. Ruby Falls believes that it is its responsibility to preserve the natural beauty and conserve the treasures of natural environments. In terms of land use planning and sustainable development, Ruby Falls makes an effort to capture rainwater from parking areas and basements, planting more drought-resistant shrubs, developing guide trails, conserving land, and increasing land trust donations. Ruby Falls strives to be a number-one green attraction in Tennessee, sustain its business operations, and exceed visitor expectations. Several marketing and branding-related studies have been conducted in recent years.

6.6   CASE STUDY: RUBY FALLS' VISITORS' EXPERIENCES AND SATISFACTIONS

Consented participants were invited by the Ruby Falls' marketing and customer service department directly after their Ruby Falls visit. The survey instrument was divided into several sections: (a) demographic profile; (b) quality of experience at Ruby Falls; (c) overall evaluation of Ruby Falls sustainability efforts; and (d) experiences toward Ruby Falls' various developments. On-line surveys were collected during the years of 2011 (n = 149) and 2012 (n = 90). The Ruby Falls survey is essential for assessing visitors' views and overall satisfaction during their visit. The results assist Ruby Falls to provide greater services that exceed the expectations and needs of their existing and future visitors.

6.7   RESULTS

6.7.1   APPRECIATION TOWARD SUSTAINABLE PRACTICES

The study participants of Ruby Falls appreciated the sustainable practices that Ruby Falls has made efforts toward. Forty-two percent of the study respondents were most impressed by the recycling efforts, followed by the land planning (27%), the solar panel installations (20%), and the reduction of greenhouse emissions (11%) (see Table 6.1).

TABLE 6 1 Appreciation toward sustainable practices (note: percentage indicated the effort ranked as the most important)

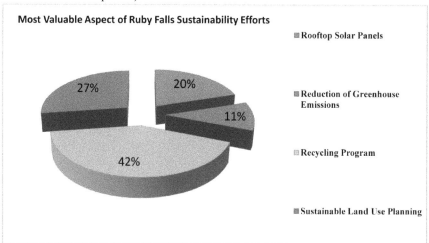

6.7.2 FACTS OF VISITING HOURS

Seventy-three percent of respondents had previously visited Ruby Falls. Only 27 percent of respondents stated that they had never visited Ruby Falls. Ruby Falls currently opens at 8:00 am and closes at 8:00 pm. No respondents stated that they arrived at Ruby Falls at 8:00 am, and only 2 percent of respondents arrived at 9:00 am. Seventeen percent of respondents arrived at 10:00 am, followed by 17 percent who stated that they arrived at 2:00 pm. Then next most popular time for respondents to arrive was at noon with 15 percent. Only 2 percent of respondents arrived during the closing hour, and 1 percent were unsure of their arrival time. A majority of respondents, 18 percent left Ruby Falls at 5:00 pm, followed by 15 percent leaving at 2:00 pm, 14 percent leaving at 3:00 pm, and 11 percent leaving at 1:00 pm. Only 6 percent of respondents left Ruby Falls at closing, 8:00 pm, and 6 percent were unsure.

6.7.3 EFFECTS OF CHANGING OPEN HOURS

Respondents were asked whether their decision to visit Ruby Falls would be effected if it opened at 9:00 am, instead of 8:00 am. An outstanding majority, 77 percent, stated that it would have no effect on their decision to visit. Twelve percent of respondents were neutral and 7 percent stated that it would have a significant effect. Respondents were asked whether their decision to visit Ruby Falls would be effected if it opened at 10:00 am, instead of 8:00 am. Half of the respondents, 50 percent, stated that the time change would have no effect on their decision to visit.

Fifteen percent of respondents were neutral and 9 percent stated that it would have a significant effect. Respondents were asked whether their decision to visit Ruby Falls would be effected if it opened at 11:00 am, instead of 8:00 am. Less than half of the respondents, 41 percent, stated that the time change would have no effect on their decision to visit. Eighteen percent of respondents were neutral, while 20 percent stated that it would have a significant effect.

6.7.4 EFFECTS OF CHANGING CLOSE HOURS

Respondents were asked whether their decision to visit Ruby Falls would be effected if Ruby Falls closed earlier at 7:00 pm, instead of 8:00 pm. Less than half of the respondents, 44 percent, stated that the time change would have no effect on their decision to visit. Twenty-three percent of respondents were neutral, while 14 percent stated that it would have a significant effect. Respondents were asked whether their decision to visit Ruby Falls would be effected if Ruby Falls closed earlier at 6:00 pm, instead of 8:00 pm. The distribution of answers was evenly spread. Only 24 percent of respondents stated that the earlier closing time would have no effect. Nineteen percent of respondents were between neutral and no effect. Fourteen percent of respondents were neutral of the earlier time. Seventeen percent stated that Ruby Falls closing at 6:00 pm would have a significant effect on their decision to visit. Twenty seven percent of respondents were between neutral and significant effect. Respondents were asked whether their decision to visit Ruby Falls would be effected if Ruby Falls closed earlier at 5:00 pm, instead of 8:00 pm. Eighteen percent of respondents stated that the 5:00 pm time change would have no effect. Thirteen percent of respondents were neutral. However, 29 percent of respondents stated that the earlier closing time would have a significant effect on their decision to visit Ruby Falls.

6.7.5 ADMISSION PRICE

Respondents were asked what amount they would feel comfortable paying for an adult admission to Ruby Falls. Majority of respondents, 77 percent, stated that they would feel most comfortable paying $17.95–$18.95 for an adult ticket, followed by 17 percent stating $19.95–$20.95 as reasonable. Only 5 percent stated that they would pay $21.95–$22.95 for an adult ticket, and 1 percent would pay $23.95–$24.96.

6.7.6 TRAVEL PARTY

Respondent were asked how many adults, including themselves, accompanied them to Ruby Falls on their visit. Eleven percent stated that they visited Ruby Falls alone. An outstanding 56 percent of respondents visited Ruby Falls with one other adults.

This was followed by 13 percent visiting in a group of three and 9 percent visiting in a group of four. One percent stated that they visited Ruby Falls with 40 other adults. One percent stated that they visited in a group of 15 and 2 percent visited with 10 other adults. Respondent were next asked how many children accompanied them to Ruby Falls on their visit. Majority of respondents, 40 percent, stated that there were no children with them on their visit. Thirty percent responded that one child came with them on their visit, followed by 16 percent stating that they brought two children, and 7 percent brought three children. One percent stated that they had 120 children accompany them to Ruby Falls. One percent stated they had 45 children on their visit to Ruby Falls and another one percent had 25 children on their visit. Respondents were asked to best describe the people who visited Ruby Fall with them. Majority of respondents, 79 percent, stated that they visited Ruby Falls with Family. Only 9 percent responded that they visited with friends, 3 percent visited with an organized group, 1 percent visited alone, and 6 percent stated other.

6.7.7   DISTANCE OF TRAVEL

The respondents were asked how far they traveled from their home to visit Ruby Falls. Less than a majority of respondents, 46 percent, traveled over 201 miles. Thirty-six percent of respondents traveled 101 to 200 miles to reach Ruby Falls, followed by 12 percent traveling between 26 and 100 miles. Only 6 percent of respondents traveled 0 to 25 miles (see Table 6.2).

TABLE 6.2   How far did you travel from your house to reach Ruby Falls?

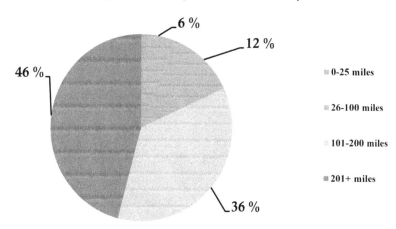

6.7.8   ENGAGED ACTIVITIES AT OTHER ATTRACTIONS

Respondents were asked what other activities they planned during their visit to Chattanooga. Fifty-nine percent of respondents stated that they planned on visiting

Rock City. Forty-two percent of respondents stated that they planned on visiting the Aquarium. Thirty-six percent of respondents planned on attending Incline Railway and 19 percent planned on attending Point Park. Seventeen percent of respondents stated that they planned on visiting other locations in Chattanooga.

6.7.9   SOURCES OF INFORMATION

Respondents were asked how they planned their trip to Ruby Falls. Forty-one percent of respondents did rely on their "previous experience in areas," and 49 percent of respondents used the "Ruby Falls Website" to plan their trip. A majority of respondents stated that they did not use an "automobile club," "rely on friends," or use the "State Welcome Center" for guidance; 92 percent, 80 percent, and 83 percent respectively. Twenty-nine percent of respondents stated that they relied on the "Chattanooga Visitor Guide" to plan their trip. Twenty-six percent of respondents used "attraction brochures" to plan their trip. Sixteen percent of respondents stated that they relied on "relatives" to plan their trip to Ruby Falls. Ten percent of respondents relied on the "Tennessee Visitor Guide." Only 9 percent stated that they relied on "Billboards." Ninety-seven percent of respondents stated that they did not use "commercial guidebooks" to plan their trip to Ruby Falls. No respondents relied on "newspaper stories and articles" or "Twitter" to plan their trip. Only 11 percent of respondents used "travel websites," and only 3 percent used "Facebook" to plan their trip to Ruby Falls. Two percent of respondents stated that they relied on "magazine advertisements." Only one percent of respondents stated that they relied on either "radio," "television," or "magazine stories and articles" to plan their trip to Ruby Falls. None of the respondents used "newspaper advertisements" to help plan their trip.

6.7.10   TYPES OF LODGING

Respondents were asked what type of lodging they used during their trip to Ruby Falls. Majority of respondents, 55 percent, stayed in a "hotel" or "motel." Thirty-three percent of respondents stated that they "did not stay overnight." Three percent of respondents stayed "with friends or relatives" and 3 percent stayed at a "campground." Five percent of respondents stated that they stayed at "other" locations.

6.7.11   TRIP PLANNING

Respondents were asked how far in advance they began planning their trip to Ruby Falls. Only 8 percent replied that they "decided to go that day." It took "less than 1 week" for 29 percent of respondents to plan their trip. Twenty percent of respondents stated that it took them "over 1 week to 13 days" to plan and 24 percent stated that it took "over 2 weeks to 4 weeks" to plan their trip. It took "over 1 month to 3 months" for 20 percent of respondents to plan (see Table 6.3).

TABLE 6 3   How far in advance did you begin planning the Ruby Falls trip?

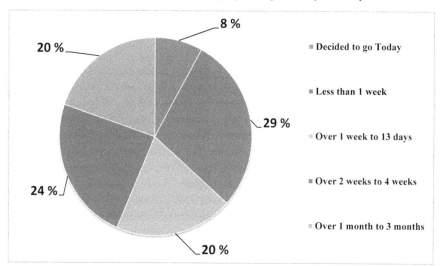

6.7.12   MOTIVATIONS

Respondents were asked to best describe their visit to Ruby Falls. Thirty-six percent of respondents described their trip for "outdoor recreation," and 23 percent stated that they visited for "other" reasons. Twenty-one percent responded that they were "just passing through." Seven percent stated that they were on a "group tour visit." Ten percent were "visiting friends or relatives" and 3 percent were visiting for "business." Respondents were given a list of statements to rank their importance on their decision to visit Ruby Falls. Majority of respondents, 58 percent, stated that it was "extremely" important for them "to observe the beauty of nature" on their trip. Only 5 percent of respondents stated that this was "not at all" important. Forty-one percent of respondents felt that planning a "peaceful vacation" was "extremely" important on their decision to visit Ruby Falls. Thirty percent of respondents stated that "escaping pressures at work" was an "extremely important" reason for planning their trip to Ruby Falls. Only 7 percent of respondents did not feel that this was an important reason for their visit. Forty-nine percent of respondents stated that it was "extremely important" for them "to experience new and different places" at Ruby Falls. Sixty-three percent of respondents stated that "seeing a geological wonder" was an "extremely important" reason for planning their trip to Ruby Falls. Only 6 percent of respondents felt like this was "not at all important" in their decision to visit Ruby Falls. Nineteen percent of respondents responded that "getting some exercise" was an "extremely important" reason for planning their trip. Majority of respondents, 51 percent, stated that "spending time with family and friends" was an "extremely important" reason for their trip to Ruby Falls. Thirty-nine percent of respondents felt that "obtaining an educational experience" was an "extremely important" reason for their visit to Ruby Falls.

6.7.13   PROBLEMS

Respondents were asked to what extent they felt the following items were problems at Ruby Falls. Eighty-eight percent of respondents did not have a problem with "litter and glass" at Ruby Falls. Sixty-six percent of respondents stated that the "lack of restrooms" was "not a problem." Only 4 percent of respondents stated that this was a "major problem." Forty six percent of respondents stated that "long lines/wait time within the cavern" were "not a problem." Twenty-two percent of respondents felt that this was somewhat of a problem. Forty-five percent of respondents stated that "hearing the tour guide" was "not a problem." Only 5 percent of respondents found that this was a "major problem." Sixty-three percent of respondents stated that, "lack of directional signs" was "not a problem." Fifty-five percent of respondents stated that "not enough parking" was "not a problem." Only 5 percent of respondents found parking to be a "major problem."

6.7.14   REVISIT

Respondents were asked if they would come back to visit Ruby Falls. An astounding 89 percent stated that they would come back to visit. Only 11 percent stated that they would not come back to visit.

6.7.15   SATISFACTION

Forty-eight percent of study respondents were extremely satisfied with their visit followed by 31 percent being significantly satisfied, 10 percent being slightly satisfied, 2 percent were neutral, 5 percent were slightly unsatisfied, 2 percent were significantly unsatisfied, and 1 percent were completely unsatisfied (see Table 6.4).

TABLE 6.4   Overall, how satisfied are you with Ruby Falls?

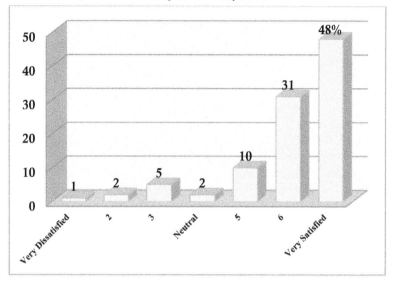

6.7.16 DEMOGRAPHICS

Six-two percent of respondents for the survey were Female and 38 percent were male. Respondents' ages ranged from 18 to 74. Only 6 percent of respondents ranged from ages 18–25. Eight percent of respondents were between the ages of 26–31. Sixteen percent of respondents were between the ages of 31–35, 15 percent between the ages of 36–40, 11 percent between the ages 41–45, and 15 percent between the ages of 46–50. Only 2 percent of respondents were between the ages of 71–74. Most of the respondents, 56 percent, attended college. Only 16 percent attended high school as their last year of school, and 28 percent attended graduate school. The respondents' occupations ranged from professional and managerial positions, students, homemakers, to retired persons. Respondents' income ranged from under $10,000 a year to more than $110,000 a year.

6.8 CONCLUSIONS

In 1928, Ruby Falls recycled the limestone excavated from the cave to build the Ruby Falls' main landmark as its main building. Since then, this natural attraction has focused on environmentally sensitive practices through business operations and its visions. As mentioned previously, because of the assistance of the State of Tennessee Economic and Community Development Energy Division's Tennessee Clean Energy Technology Grant Program, Ruby Falls was able to utilize the granted financial support to purchase the solar energy production equipment. Through an array of installed solar panels, Ruby Falls receives 16,000 watts of renewable energy that provides electricity to light more than 250 60-watt light bulbs. While combing the use of LED and compact fluorescents, the Ruby Falls Solar Panels have helped Ruby Falls reduce its power consumption by more than 24 percent.

The results of 2011 and 2012 visitor studies indicated that a majority of respondents were very familiar with Ruby Falls and believed the importance of sustaining the nature wonder of Ruby Falls. Many attributes of listed sustainability efforts of Ruby Ralls were ranked by the study participants. Two thirds of the respondents had visited Ruby Falls within the last 2 years. Almost half of the respondents traveled more than 200 miles for their visit, and the study indicated that most respondents primarily planned their trip to the Chattanooga area to see Ruby Falls. The study indicated that the respondents did not rely on newspaper ads, television, Twitter, Facebook, or travel websites to plan their trip. Fifty five percent of respondents stated that they stayed at either a hotel or a motel during their trip. Since more than half of the respondents stayed in lodging, it may be beneficial to provide discounts for admissions to Ruby Falls if staying in local hotels.

The study demonstrates areas where the marketing department can help attract tourists to Ruby Falls and how "green" and "sustainable green attraction" has become the image of this deepest underground waterfall. Most of the respondents stated that they planned their trip to "observe the beauty of nature" and "to see a geological wonder." Other respondents planned their trip as a time "to send with family and friends." Most respondents stated that they did not experience problems with litter, restrooms, long lines, or parking. The survey reported that overall the respondents were very satisfied with their visit to Ruby Falls, and 89 percent stated that they would come back and visit. Social media engagement can be used to strengthen Ruby Falls' network and to complement the attraction's sustainable business strategy by broadcasting messages to prospective markets and visitors.

Many companies that benefit from sustainability are aware of the importance and reap the benefits of incorporating sustainability as one of the main keys of organizational cultural, integrating sustainability activities into the corporate business models, generating top management support toward sustainability initiatives, investigating customer willingness to pay for a higher rate while involving sustainability issues and environmental conservations, and seeking sustainable internal and external supports among businesses, organizations, customers, public sectors, and individuals. Through the stimulations of the successful stories of Ruby Falls, this study concludes that by sustaining a high bar, extending green attraction visions toward sustainable business, motivating influential partnerships, equipping associates strategically, and capturing the impacts of sustainability on society, achievable mitigations of sustainability efforts may be structured constructively in a timely manner across the state of Tennessee.

6.9   DISCUSSION QUESTIONS

6.9.1   RUBY FALLS CASE

1. Can you suggest further good ideas for Ruby Falls to improve its green practice efforts?
2. Other than positive environment impacts, what potential advantages will Ruby Falls offer the destination (Chattanooga, Tennessee) from a destination marketing perspective?
3. As the director of sustainability division at Ruby Falls, a local journalist has asked your opinion of earth week for a story she is preparing. What are you going to tell this journalist?
4. Visit the Ruby Falls website along with other Top 10 Cave Underground Waterfalls websites. List the uniqueness and differences of these attractions.
5. For educational purposes, what kind of interactions with visitors could be provided by Ruby Falls?

6.9.2   GENERAL APPLICATIONS

1. Do you have any good or bad memories that influenced your most-visited destination's image?
2. Can you share your experiences (either on-site real visit experiences or Internet search) about any underground waterfalls globally with your team members?
3. Suggest how the "green" theme could be communicated to visitors? Brainstorm potential green/theming opportunities for your destination.
4. In your opinions, what cities in the world could be ranked as Top 10 most "green" cities? Why?
5. Are there any other underground waterfall installing solar or renewable energy equipment?

6.9.3   SUGGESTED READINGS

—Esty, D. C.; Andrew, S.; and Winston, A. S.; Green to Gold: How Smart Companies Use Environmental Strategy To Innovate, Create Value, and Build Competitive Advantage. Hoboken, NJ: JohnWiley & Sons; **2009**.

—Kellert, S. R.; Heewagen, J.; and Mador, M.; Biophilic Design: Theory, Science, and Practice of Bringing Buildings to Life. New York: John Wiley; **2008**.

—Sachs, J. D.; Common Wealth: Economics for a Crowded Planet. New York: Penguin Group publisher; **2008**.

—Wargo, J. P.; Green Intelligence Creating Environments that Protect Human Health. New Haven, CT: Yale Press; **2009**.

—Winston, A. S.; Green Recovery: Get Lean, Get Smart, and Emerge from the Downturn on Top. Boston, MA: Harvard Business Press; **2009**.

KEYWORDS

- **Green Practices**
- **Ruby Falls**
- **Sustainable Operations**
- **Visitor Experiences**

6.10   REFERENCES

1.   Butler, R.W.; Sustainable tourism: A state of the art review. *Tour. Geog.* **1999,** *1*(1), 7–25.
2.   Prosser, R.; Societal change and the growth in alternative tourism. In: Ecotourism: A Sustainable Option? (Eds.) Cater, E.; and Lowman, G.; Chichester: John Wiley; **1994,** pp. 19–37.
3.   The World Tourism Organization (WTO); **2013.** http://sdt.unwto.org/en/content/about-us-5
4.   Bramwell, B.; and Lane, B.; Sustainable tourism: an evolving global approach. *J. Sus. Tour.* **1993,** *1*(1), 1–5.
5.   Bramwell, B.; and Lane, B.; Towards innovation in sustainable tourism research? *J. Sus Tour.* **2012,** *20*(1), 1–7.
6.   Chen, R. J. C.; How can stores sustain their businesses? From shopping behaviors and motivations to environment preferences. *Sustainability.* **2013,** *5*(2), 617–628. doi:10.3390/su5020617.
7.   Fennell, D.; Ecotourism and the myth of indigenous stewardship. *J. Sus. Tour*. **2008,** *16*(2), 129–149.
8.   Butcher, J.; Ecotourism as life politics. *J. Sus. Tour*. **2008,** *16*(3), 315–326.
9.   Farrell, B.; and TwiningWard, L.; Seven steps towards sustainability: tourism in the context of new knowledge. *J. Sust. Tour.* **2005,** *13*(2), 109–122.
10.   Hunter, C.; Sustainable tourism as an adaptive paradigm. *Ann. Tour. Res.* **1997,** *24*(4), 850–867.
11.   Hunter, M.; and Chen, R. J. C.; From management to sustainability: strategies for producers, consumers, and small businesses. *J. Manag. Sus.* **2011,** *1*(1), 99–111.
12.   Meeks, M.; and Chen, R. J. C.; Can Walmart integrate values with value? From sustainability to sustainable business. *J. Sust. Develop.* **2011,** *4*(5), 62–67.

13. Harris, R.; and Leiper, N.; (Eds.); Sustainable Tourism: An Australian Perspective. Oxford: Butterworth-Heinemann; **1995**
14. Liu, Z. H.; and Jones, E.; A systems perspective of sustainable tourism. In: Proceedings of the International Conference on Urban and Regional Tourism (Ed.) Saayman, M.; Potchefstroom; **1996,** pp. 209–221.

APPENDIX 1: CAVE WATERFALLS

Cave waterfalls are notable due to their most beautiful natural forms, which are buried beneath the earth, and their shimmering streams of water flow among rocks and stones and hurtling downward to form unique underground torrents. Ruby Falls is recognized as one of the Top 10 most amazing underground waterfalls on the planet.

TABLE A1.2   Top ten of the most amazing cave waterfalls on the planet

Rank: Name of Waterfalls
1. Waiahuakua Sea Cave, Hawaii, USA
2. Ruby Falls, Tennessee, USA
3. Thunderhead Falls, South Dakota, USA
4. La Grotte aux Fees, Valais, Switzerland
5. Złoty Stok, Poland
6. Gaping Gill, UK
7. White Scar Cave, Yorkshire
8. Mine St Michel, Luxembourg
9. Smoo Cave, Scotland
10. Natural Bridge, Springbrook Park, Australia

Source: Worldreview.com

CHAPTER 7

ENVIRONMENTAL IMPACT OF COASTLINE TOURISM DEVELOPMENT IN SPAIN

ROBERTO CERVELLÓ-ROYO[1] and ÁNGEL PEIRÓ-SIGNES[2]

[1]Faculty of Business Administration and Management, Universidad Politйcnica de Valencia, Camino de Vera s/n, 46022, Valencia, E-mail: rocerro@esp.upv.es

[2]Management Department, Universidad Politécnica de Valencia, Camino de Vera s/n, 7D Building, 46022, Valencia, E-mail: anpeisig@omp.upv.es

CONTENTS

7.1   INTRODUCTION

Tourism has become one of the largest sectors of the Spanish economy, representing nearly 10 percent of Gross Domestic Product (GDP), and relegating traditional activities like fishing and agriculture to a secondary place [1]. Spain is still the second largest earner worldwide and the first in Europe (US$ 60 billion). According to the World Tourism Organization, Spain is also the fourth most visited country in the world after France, the United States and China [2]. Regarding the two key tourism indicators—international tourist arrivals and international tourism receipts—Spain ranks fourth (with 56.7 million arrivals) and second (with 59.9 million receipts) respectively.

Coastal zones are of crucial importance for Spanish Tourism Activity and, especially during the high season, there is a high concentration of population and human activity in these areas. They involve almost 52.6 million tourists, more than 164 million domestic trips, and around €49 billion ($66.6 billion). The coastal areas and archipelagos alone receive 84 percent of the inbound arrivals, representing 44 million tourists, 84 percent of the expenses, and 50 percent of the Spanish resident trips [3]. As tourism is expected to increase in Spain, which represents one of the larger destinations driving the robust growth of international tourist arrivals in Southern and Mediterranean Europe (expected to be 19 percent of world tourism), the term "sustainable tourism" has been coined as a strategy to address this challenge. As Manning et al. [4] state, sustainable tourism development meets the needs of the present tourists and host regions, while protecting and enhancing the opportunity for the future. It is envisaged that this will lead to management of all resources in such a way that economic, social, and aesthetic needs can be fulfilled, while maintaining cultural integrity, essential ecological processes, biological diversity, and life support systems.

Tourism has a unique capacity either to help preserve or destroy resources, ecosystems, and habitats. In the case of Spain, and particularly in the main coastal areas, the Mediterranean coast and the South-Atlantic Coast, a deep transformation has taken place and led to rapid urban development of these areas. Furthermore, the situation did not change over the years owing to the lack of public and management coordination, the prevalence of private interests, and the lack of integration on coastal areas. This chapter will analyze the main environmental coastal problems derived from this situation and highlight the main points of the European and Spanish initiatives. We will consider how they were carried out and can be improved in keeping with the Spanish coastline territorial and peripheral characteristics, to enhance coastal areas integration, and to avoid environmental deterioration.

7.2   SUSTAINABILITY AS A STRATEGIC FACTOR IN TOURISM

Our theoretical starting point is study carried out which focuses on environmentally sustainable tourism and the preservation of natural resources [5, 6, 7, 8, 9]. Hassan

[5] highlights how the destinations with a higher rate of growth are those whose strategies are oriented toward environmentally sustainable tourism. Budeanu [7] notes that in order to analyze how tourism can help sustainable development, it is necessary to understand the points of view of all the stakeholders of an industry in a given region. Bosch et al. [8] state that the growing sensitiveness about the landscape degrading and the environmental costs of tourism growth, has led to protection programs covering natural places, coastline strips, islands, rivers, mountains, etc.

On the other hand, models like the one by Crouch and Richie [10] and Ritchie and Crouch [11] study Destination competitiveness in line with sustainability. Physiography (landscape, natural places, climate, etc.), Culture and History, Superstructure, etc. are among the factors included within the group of "core resources and attractors" and have a strong influence on the rest (Figure 7.1).

FIGURE 7.1   Ritchie and crouch model.
Source: Ritchie and Crouch (2003)

They state that competitiveness without sustainability is momentary, even more so in the long term. Thus, a competitive Destination has to be sustainable not only in an economic way but also in an ecological, social, cultural, and political sense in order to be considered competitive. Furthermore, Dwyer and Kim [12] and Dwyer, Mellor, Livaic, Edwards, and Kim [13] also undertook studies contributing to the development of a general model of destination competitiveness based on endowed natural and heritage resources (mountains, coasts, lakes, etc.) among others, while government and industry represented the second core component of their model when considering destination management.

7.3   THE SPANISH COASTLINE

Spain has at least 10 regions (Table 7.1) which can be considered coastal areas; these regions comprise a total of 24 coastal provinces (Table 7.2) and 487 coastal towns. To those located on the mainland (Basque Country, Cantabria, Asturias, Galicia, Andalusia, Murcia, Valencia, and Catalonia), we should add the archipelagos (Balearic and Canary Islands).

TABLE 7.1   Spanish coastal regions

Region	Size (km²)	Coastline (km)
Basque Country	7,261	256
Cantabria	5,289	283
Asturias	10,565	497
Galicia	29,434	1,720
Andalusia	87,268	917
Murcia	11,317	252
Valencia	23,305	474
Catalonia	31,930	597
Balearics	5,014	1,342
Canaries	7,273	1,545

Source: Barragán [15].

TABLE 7.2   Spanish coastal provinces

Province	Size (km²)	Coastline (km)
Balearic Islands	4,992	1,428
La Coruña	7,950	956
Las Palmas	4,066	815
Tenerife	3,381	768
Asturias	10,603	401
Pontevedra	4,495	398
Cádiz	7,436	285
Cantabria	5,325	284
Tarragona	6,303	278
Murcia	11,313	274
Gerona	5,910	260

TABLE 7.2   *(Continued)*

Province	Size (km²)	Coastline (km)
Almería	8,774	249
Alicante	5,816	244
Málaga	7,308	208
Barcelona	7,733	161
Vizcaya	2,217	154
Lugo	9,586	144
Castellón	6,632	139
Valencia	10,763	135
Huelva	10,148	122
Guipúzcoa	1,909	92
Granada	12,531	81
Ceuta	19	20
Melilla	13	9

Source: INE (Instituto Nacional de Estadística-National Statistics Institute)

They can be classified into two types: erosion (cliffs) and sedimentation (beaches, sandbanks, and coastal wetlands). These two different and special ecosystems are of major importance due to their landscape, and socioeconomic and educational values. In mainland Spain, the abrupt orography, peripheral characteristics, and high average elevation produce an abundance of cliffs in several coastal regions, in total 4,021 km of cliffs, although there are also 2,000 km of beaches. The rest of the coast is low lying (1,271 km) or has been transformed as a result of artificial works (600 km). The most important coastal ecosystems of the Spanish coast include the following: sea beds (both rock and sandy), cliffs, beaches, sandbanks, and dunes, as well as coastal wetlands, including inlets, estuaries, deltas, marshlands and coastal lagoons, fens, coastal lakes, and salt flats. This highly varied range of ecosystems is further reinforced by the marked differences between Spanish Mediterranean and Atlantic coastlines:

- The Mediterranean coastline has a great abundance of beaches. The semienclosed Mediterranean Sea has a major effect on the characteristics of the area and accumulation processes are often seen in river mouths. On the Mediterranean coastline, unlike the Atlantic coastline, there are no significant tides and no large areas of low-lying coast flooded by tides. This represents the main advantage for the sun and sand tourism economy.

- The Spanish Atlantic coast has extensive cliff systems. Its sea dynamics are more pronounced and the tidal range is considerably greater, as is wave intensity (the tidal range is 10–50 times greater on the Atlantic coast compared with the Mediterranean). As a result, the sediments carried by rivers end up a long way from the coast.

The Spanish coast, both on the Mediterranean and Atlantic sides, is considered a strategic area given the many zones of great ecological, cultural, social, and economic value. There are many protected areas on the coast and, although in terms of the overall number of protected areas in Spain the number of protected maritime coastal areas may not be that high, it has increased significantly. However, it remains considerably lower than the number of protected land areas. The Spanish coastal heritage is highly valuable and recent management attention has focused on conservation of these landscapes [14].

Sun and sand tourism is considered the subsector which has most impact on the Spanish coastal environment. It is also of great social importance due to the many economic and social benefits it can bring. Fishing, industry, agriculture, and energy all benefit from tourism. However, a comparison between the two main touristic areas—the Mediterranean Coast (including the Balearic Islands) and the South-Atlantic Coast (including the Canary Islands)—shows that although tourism is perceived as the sector placing most pressure on the environment of both and also the most socially important, this opinion is more clear cut with regard to the Mediterranean (see Figures 7.2 and 7.3).

FIGURE 7.2   Example of tourism pressure on the Spanish Mediterranean coastline.
Source: Author's own elaboration

FIGURE 7.3   Example of tourism pressure on the Spanish-South Atlantic coastline.
Source: **J.** Cervelló-Royo

7.4   THE MEDITERRANEAN COAST

In Spain, there is a strong dependence on the sun and sand model and almost 84 percent of the tourist arrivals are sustained by sun and sand Tourism, which is mostly
concentrated on the Mediterranean Coast and the Balearic Islands. The Mediterranean Coast can be divided into three main subareas:

(i)   The Mediterranean Coast of Catalonia, Valencia, and Murcia

The most ecologically valuable parts of the Mediterranean coast in Catalonia,
Valencia, and Murcia are the coastal wetlands, the dunes, the rocky mountains that
produce the cliffs, the pretty coves, the small islands and islets, and some areas of
sea bed, notably the fields of oceanic Posidonia seagrass.

(ii)   The Mediterranean Coast of Andalusia

This part of the coast boasts a wide variety of natural areas, ranging from cliffs
to alluvial plains and deltas. Of particular note are the Cabo de Gata volcanic zone,
whose rich plant life is associated with the semiarid climate, and the Alborán Sea,
which hosts a range of biologically diverse Mediterranean and Atlantic species.

(iii) The Balearic Islands (the Mediterranean Archipelagos)

Compared with their overall size, the Balearic Islands have plenty of rugged
coastlines. The small continental shelf is shared by Majorca, Menorca, and Cabrera,
while Ibiza and Formentera stand separate to these three. Coastal features vary from
island to island. In Majorca, one finds rugged sectors with beaches in small inlets,
as well as abrupt coastline, beaches, and lagoons. Menorca's coast is quite homog-

enous, with beaches set in small coves. In Ibiza the coastline is dotted with cliffs and there are few beaches. The archipelago boasts a wide range of environments of great ecological importance.

7.5 THE SOUTH-ATLANTIC COAST

There is also a strong dependence on tourism on the South Atlantic Coast and archipelagos of Spain, whose main natural attractions are:

(i) The South-Atlantic Coast of Andalusia

The coastal strip of the South-Atlantic coast mainly comprises stretches of low-lying sandy coast corresponding to the plains of the mouths of the Guadiana and Guadalquivir rivers. The Doñana National Park is located in the mouth of the latter. Beaches and dune formations are common. Among the area's most important environmental treasures are the dunes and wetlands, both of which contain a vast array of animal life. The Gulf of Cadiz and Gibraltar are also of interest; however, the aforementioned Doñana National Park is the most important environmental site.

(ii) The Canary Islands (The South Atlantic Archipelagos)

The Canarian archipelago comprises seven main islands and some smaller islets. Of volcanic origin, they were formed by undersea eruptions. The many geological and topographical differences between them have increased over time due to the effect of river, marine, and wind erosion. Broadly speaking, each island has a northern coast formed by tall cliffs and a more open and sandy southern coast where most of the beaches are located. A characteristic feature of the whole archipelago is its narrow continental shelf. Due to orographic, geological, and climatic reasons, the Canary Islands' ecosystems are unique in Europe. They form part of the biogeographical region known as Macaronesia, which is part of the Mauritania sea region.

7.6 URBAN DEVELOPMENT AND TOURISM EXPANSION

One of the most remarkable aspects of the transformation process which the Spanish coast has undergone during the last 65 years is the urban development of the coastal areas. Urbanization of coastal zones is intimately bound up with tourism development in sun and sand destinations (See Figure 7.4, development of Mediterranean coastline before and after Tourism expansion). However, this development varies from region to region and, of course, some of the most affected regions are those in which tourism has experienced a faster growth. As we can see in Figure 7.5, from 2000 to 2006 most areas along both the Mediterranean coast and the South-Atlantic Coast experienced an increase ranging from 1 to 10 percent.

FIGURE 7.4   Mediterranean coastline: 1960s and 2006 (before and after tourism expansion). *Source:* Ministry of Agriculture, Food and Environment—Spain

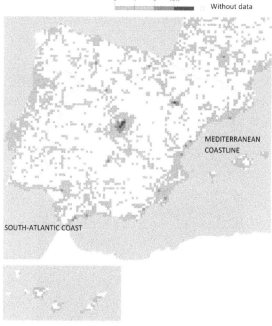

FIGURE 7.5   Increase (%) of development by areas in Spain from 2000 to 2006. *Source:* European Environment Agency

This development may produce massive alterations to the landscape, causing it to lose its natural traits and unique coastal features and turning it into an urban landscape (Figure 7.6).

On the other hand, especially on the Mediterranean coastline, Nautical Sports have had a major influence with the establishment of the first exclusive yacht clubs in a number of coastal towns and cities during the last 50 years. Small marinas became commonplace from the 1960s onwards, particularly on the Mediterranean coast, and areas to accommodate pleasure boats were also built in old fishing ports along the north coast. Additional facilities such as hotels, restaurants, pubs, cafeterias, etc. tended to be developed alongside the essentially nautical installation and the corresponding marina. At the beginning of the twenty first century, Spain ranked third in Europe in terms of marinas, behind Italy (282) and France (276). By number of berths, France leads the table with 133,000, and Spain ranks second with 78,000. Spanish marinas are at the top of the quality list: of the 729 blue flags awarded by the FEE, Spain has the highest number (96) followed by France (83) and Italy (57). Spanish marinas boast a high occupancy rate (more than 80%) and they contribute to the economies of coastal communities in a significant way, providing 3,124 direct jobs and 23,409 indirect ones. Thus, they require a high level of intangible/tangible investments such as employee training and place branding.

FIGURE 7.6   Effect of Urban and tourism development on the Mediterranean coastline.
Source: Author's own elaboration and J. Cervelló-Royo

Nautical sports, including those associated with marinas, cover a wide range of activities, from yachting to sport fishing, windsurfing, kite surfing, surfing, diving, snorkeling, etc. As a non-standardized and differentiated tourism product, nautical tourism is less dependent on climate than other types of tourism and sunshine is not in itself an indispensable requirement. Furthermore, in summer, nautical tourism can be in great demand among sun and sand clients, provided they are aware of its existence. However, this form of tourism is not exempt from problems and drawbacks. In the opinion of the main stakeholders (owners, managers, and developers), the main difficulties impeding development of the nautical sports sector are administrative and fiscal. The lack of a regulatory framework in each region, the fiscal pressure and the license expenses (VAT, registration fees, navigation charges, and local and regional taxes) represent important obstacles. However, the main disadvantages, according to developers, are the excessively short concession periods granted by law for the operation of such infrastructures, which makes a return on investment quite difficult. Furthermore, the proliferation of all these facilities can displace, or cause conflict with, the local population, who feel excluded and whose space and activities are occupied and impeded. The strong dependence on associated real estate to fund private development through a public concession to operate marinas in Spain means that the economic models for these facilities are not quite sustainable over time (see Figure 7.7).

FIGURE 7.7   Example of yacht clubs on the Mediterranean coastline.
Source: J. Cervelló-Royo

As we previously mentioned, the Mediterranean coast (including the Balearic Islands) and the Canary Islands, which together account for 84 percent of the country's regulated accommodation and receive 85 percent of all foreign tourists as well as 60 percent of domestic tourists in Spain, are the areas in which urban and tourism development has been more intensive. The uncontrolled urbanization of these zones was at its height in late 1960s and early 1970s and involved essentially the construction of hotels and apartments. Following this first boom, which affected primarily the sun and sand holiday zones, the second half of the 1990s and early part of this century have also seen an accelerated growth in the different types of construction in Spanish coastal zones, especially residential and housing developments. This situation was the result of the combination of a complex set of economic, financial, and social variables extending beyond tourism development.

The main problems faced by tourism and the associated urbanization model in these zones are the following:

(i)   Despite Spain remaining a leader in the tourism sector (it experienced a 2.7% increase from 2011 to 2012), its market share has slightly decreased as a result of competition from other countries and new emerging tourist destinations.

(ii) The habits of tourists coming to Spain have changed and the traditional chain of value has been modified, resulting in lower revenue per tourist. The two main causes behind this change are greater access to information thanks to the Internet, shorter stays, and cheaper air travel due to low cost airlines.

(iii) Domestic demand has experienced a slow down; however, and due to the economic situation, it is expected to recover, since resident tourists prefer to stay in Spain than travel abroad.

(iv) In order to be competitive, it has become necessary to look beyond pricing as the main factor of competitiveness. Therefore, business profitability in some subsectors and the socioeconomic contribution of the tourism sector in Spain are falling.

(v)   On the residential tourism demand side, until 2008, there was considerable growth in the purchase of first homes on the coast, as well as second homes by both Spaniards and foreigners.

(a) The purchase by foreigners was mainly explained by a long period of low interest rates throughout Europe. The growing confidence in the financial system was owing to the stability brought about by the adoption of the euro and the success of economic integration, as well as the improved infrastructure and new possibilities of wider connections offered by low cost airlines. Last but not least, in addition to the familiarity with Spain and a feeling of safety as a result of years of visiting the country, it was relatively cheaper to buy housing in Spain than in the tourists' home countries.

(b) The domestic market also stimulated the demand for homes on the Mediterranean coast and in the Islands until 2008. Contributing factors were: an excess of financial liquidity and the extremely favorable all-time low interest rates in Spain, which favored the loan conditions. There was growing preference for living in mild climates close to the sea and expectations of higher returns on tourism-related property compared with other financial assets given the period of continuous growth in property prices and gains until 2008.

(vi) On the supply side, property developers were extremely focused on meeting the past rising demand, and local councils allowed new developments (both residential and hotels) in their towns. The combination of these two factors nurtured an exponential process of construction and urbanization in destinations on the Spanish Mediterranean coast and the archipelagos until the crash of 2008. Thus, this massive urbanization has led to an oversupply in some coastal towns and areas.

Generally speaking, in the past decades growth and tourism management models on the Mediterranean coast and archipelagos have been based on strategies which prioritized volume and lacked initial planning. This has led to the creation of increasingly urban and crowded recreational areas with little difference between them and which are beginning to contradict new tourism trends, while also exceeding the carrying capacity of the territory. The degree of saturation due to developments is much greater, as well as sensitivity to environmental conservation and protection. The economic situation of the country is in a period of uncertainty, but legislation and regulations have to be stricter and more comprehensive with a deeper understanding of coastal processes. These conditions should be enough to prevent repeating past errors and particularly the haste with which action was taken.

7.7   EUROPEAN AND SPANISH INITIATIVES

There have been several initiatives with different scopes which have produced various outcomes when considering tourism and coastline development in Spain.

7.7.1   THE TOURISM PLAN HORIZON 2020

By means of the Tourism Plan Horizon 2020, the Spanish government has proposed several plans to improve the key factors for the destinations success. Thus, there are three strategic areas: (1) Knowledge and I + D + I, (2) a new marketing strategy, and (3) environmental destination for both companies and destinations. In the latter strategic area, a strong emphasis is placed on coastline areas and the main tourism industry stakeholders' orientation, attitude, and behavior. In fact, it enhances specific activities in those areas (mainly located in the Archipelagos and on the South-

Atlantic coast) by means of the Program for the Integral Requalification of Mature Tourism Destinations.

On the other hand, and focusing on the public infrastructures sector, the *Tourism Infrastructures Modernisation Fund (FOMIT)* also focuses on the coastline areas and puts at Municipalities' disposal €492 billion ($668.73 billion) loans to modernize infrastructures and tourism accommodations. In 2012, there were €128 million ($174 million) loans granted (38 million addressed to Consortiums and 90 million to Local Entities).

Human Resources are also recognized by The Tourism Plan Horizon 2020 as key to future sustainability, becoming a differentiation source in the coastline destinations. Thus, the Program tries to attract, develop, and retain tourism professionals, mainly young people. In this vein, the program *Avanza Formación Turismo* also included economic aid for projects and professional training for companies, employees, and professionals in the coastline tourism field. The main goal was to disseminate new e-business models and the on-line relationship with customers.

Finally, *the Blue Flag Program* is an initiative which includes simultaneous elements of environmental award (best practices in beach cleaning), information and security, environmental management of beaches, and sport ports (environmental audit, external certification, public recognition, monitoring of results, and tourist and local managers awareness). The Blue Flag is a voluntary eco-label awarded to more than 3,850 beaches and marinas in 48 countries across Europe, South Africa, Morocco, Tunisia, New Zealand, Brazil, Canada, and the Caribbean. In 2010, and thanks to this plan, Spain obtained a total of 607 blue flags in 2010 (523 in beaches and 84 in ports). One of the six of the total flags is in Spain.

The adoption of the Recommendation 2002/423/EC of the European Parliament and of the Council which concerns the implementation of integrated coastal management in Europe.

At a European level, this Recommendation calls on the Member States to adopt the following objectives:
  (i)   Protection of the coastal environment based on an ecosystem approach
  (ii) Recognition of the threat of climate change
  (iii) Ecologically responsible protection measures, including protection of coastal settlements and their cultural heritage
  (iv) Sustainable economic and employment opportunities
  (v)   A functioning social and cultural system
  (vi) Adequate accessible land for the public
  (vii) Cohesion of remote coastal zones
  (viii) Coordination of all actions

The early Coast Law 2/2013, of 29th of May, and the former Coast Law 22/1988

Both laws are at national level and rely on the concept of Public Domain. The origins of this historic concept date back to Roman Law and Public Domain status is granted to coastal zones in legal documents as old as *Las Siete Partidas del*

Rey Alfonso X, El Sabio (XIII). The importance of the Maritime-Terrestrial Public Domain is clearly relevant since over the last 60 years the Spanish coast has undergone extensive transformation and has become a strategic element of the Spanish Economy, especially due to the importance of sun and sand tourism. Over and above addressing the conflicting interests often affecting Maritime-Terrestrial Public Domains, the Coast Law is supposed to achieve two main objectives: To guarantee the domain's public status and to conserve its natural characteristics, reconciling the requirements of development with the imperatives of protection and derogating any regulations which may stand in opposition to this aim. The Law 2/2013, of May 29, for the protection and sustainable use of the Coast, modified the Coastal Law of 1988 and introduced for the first time, as regards Spanish coastline regulation, a series of preventive measures for the protection of the maritime-terrestrial public domain—the beaches and the coastline area, the territorial sea, the interior waters, the natural resources, etc.—against the effects of climate change—sea level rise, changes in swell direction, etc.,—which might have multiple negative consequences in coastal zones such as coastal erosion, flooding, flood-related health problems, property damage, and socioeconomic impacts.

The main measures contemplated, in principle, the protection of the maritime-terrestrial public domain, were:

(i)   The need for an Adaptation Strategy and/or Plan by the Ministry or the Autonomous Regions respectively, which are in charge of the management of the maritime-terrestrial public domain land and the coastline, in order to assess the risks associated with climate change that could affect the Spanish coastline. The Strategy/Plan should also propose measures to confront the potential effects of such risks.

(ii) The protection of the coastal stretches which are under serious risk due to sea level rise; furthermore, it should be considered that any new undertaking of the maritime-terrestrial public domain would not be possible. Those serious risks should be defined via scientific criteria, with details established by future regulation.

(iii) The inclusion of a new cause of extinction for public domain concessions when infrastructure, facilities, and amenities are at serious risk from the sea.

(iv) The addition of energy efficiency and water saving criteria in the rehabilitation and retrofitting of urban areas and buildings that are occupying a conservation easement and/or public domain.

As we have seen, several programs and plans have been developed, whose main goals were to develop coastline tourism destinations according to sustainable principles. However, based on the Spanish coastline situation, when considering sustainability and protection of the coastline, some important contradictions have been detected in all initiatives. For instance, focusing on the aforementioned measures, it is quite difficult to understand the reduction of the protection zone easement from 100 to 20 m for some specific areas of the coastline, especially for those which are extremely vulnerable due to tourism and urban conditions. On the other hand, it is also difficult to understand the introduction of energy efficiency or water saving criteria in the existing building stock located at coastal tourist and urban areas without taking into account any adaptation measures.

To sum up, due to the economic situation, and since sun and sand tourism remains the most valuable subsector, new efforts and ideas need to emerge in order to prevent the Spanish economy from past ecological errors. Spain should be proactive, in search of a diversifying coastline tourism economy which, at the same time, can sustain the seaside environment.

7.7.2 SUGGESTIONS FOR FUTURE MEASURES AND INITIATIVES

Future measures and initiatives might be based on the following: Command and control instruments (legislation, land use planning, regulation, licensing, and development control), voluntary instruments (guidelines and codes of conduct, reporting and auditing, certifications, eco-labels, awards, and voluntary contributions), economic instruments (taxes, fees and charges, financial incentives, and agreements), supporting instruments (infrastructure provision and management, capacity building, awareness raising, marketing, and information services), measuring instruments (benchmarking, assessments on optimal use levels, carrying capacity). All initiatives are in search of:

  (i)   *Sustainable economic prosperity*
        (a) To ensure the long-term competitiveness, viability, and prosperity of both tourism enterprises and coastline destinations.
        (b) To provide quality employment opportunities and the investments required for employee training according to the coastline complementary offer.
  (ii) *Social cohesion and integration*
        (a) To enhance the quality of life of local communities through tourism, and engage them in its planning and management.
  (iii) *Protection of the coastal environment*
        (a) To minimize the negative externalities derived from the environmental impact and the pressure exerted by tourism activities on the coastline.
        (b) To protect coastal settlements and their cultural heritage richness and biodiversity.

7.8   DISCUSSION

The tourism industry is very important in Spain, contributing directly and indirectly almost 10 percent of the Gross Domestic Product (GDP) and employing directly and indirectly one in ten employers in the country. Tourism, which has also become the main export product of Spain, is in the hands of both public bodies (the Ministry of Industry, Energy, and Tourism, Regional tourist organizations and local councils) and private bodies (Tourist Industry stakeholders). Tourism is also considered the sector which impacts most the Spanish coastal environment. As we have already seen, almost 84 percent of the tourist arrivals, 84 percent of the expenses, and 50 percent of Spanish resident trips are sustained by sun and sand Tourism, which mostly concentrate on the Mediterranean Coast and the Balearic Islands. Focusing on coastline areas, a deep transformation has taken place in last 60 years. As we noted, growth and tourism management on the Spanish coast have been based on strategies which prioritized volume rather than initial planning.

The Spanish coast, both on the Mediterranean and Atlantic sides, is considered a strategic area given the many zones of great ecological, cultural, social, and economic value. However, is Spanish coastline tourism actually sustainable? The answer to this question will depend on whether public and private bodies, institutions, local councils, and industry stakeholders, as well as residents and community members, adopt measures and initiatives which seek to maintain high ethical standards and sustainable practices at the expense of profit in the short term. The long-term preservation of the Spanish coastline seems to depend on each stakeholder realizing that sustainability and environmental proactive practices must be followed: the protection of the coastal environment based on an ecosystem approach, the protection of coastal settlements and urban heritage, the respect of the historic concept of public domain, the recognition of the threat of climate change, etc. Therefore, and despite all the aforementioned European and Spanish initiatives, it will be crucial to initiate a process which coordinates the public, private, and community strengths for the development of sustainable tourism, based on their territorial and peripheral characteristics, in order to improve the environmental, economic, and social conditions of the coastal zone and ensure the use of its resources in accordance with the principles of sustainable development.

7.8.1 IN-CLASS DISCUSSION POINTS

(i) The chapter provides insights into the environmental impact of tourism development in coastline areas. As we have seen, protective measures and initiatives can help to mitigate the negative impacts of tourism. Try to think of other helpful measures and initiatives.

(ii) Do you think a well-educated, informed, and motivated population, as well as employers and/or employees, will help to support environmental conservation and social improvements in coastline areas?

(iii) Do you is there anything to do to mitigate the effects of overpopulated touristic areas?

(iv) What kind of advantages and disadvantages may find tourists, hospitality businesses and citizens when visiting/working/living in those areas?

7.8.2 QUESTIONS FOR CLASS DISCUSSION

(i) Teamwork: Think of other natural areas in which tourism also has an impact. Try to consider the pros and cons and discuss how different they might be.

(ii) Think of two different kinds of tourism, sun and sand vs. snow and mountain, for example, and compare the protective measures and initiatives which have been adopted in each case. Once detected, try to find differences between them. Which kind of tourism seems to be more sustainable? Is it also more environmentally proactive?

SUGGESTED FURTHER READING

Aguiló, E.; Alegre, J.; and Sard, M.; The persistence of the "sun and sand" tourism model. *Tourism Manag.* **2005,** *26(2),* 219–231.

Bardolet, E.; and Sheldon, P. J.; Tourism in archipelagos: Hawai'i and the Balearics. *Ann. Tourism Res.* **2008,** *35(4),* 900–923.

Powell, R. B.; and Ham, S. H.; Can ecotourism interpretation really lead to pro-conservation knowledge, attitudes and behaviour? Evidence from the Galapagos Islands. *J. Sust. Tourism.* **2008,** *16(4),* 467–489.

KEYWORDS

- **Blue Flag**
- **Coastline tourism**
- **Maritime-Terrestrial Public Domain**
- **Urban development of coastal areas**

REFERENCES

1. IET (Instituto de Estudios Turísticos). *Balance del Turismo: Resultados de la Actividad Turísitica en España.* Madrid: Ministerio de Industria, Energía y Turismo; **2012.**
2. UNWTO (World Tourism Organization). UNWTO Tourism Highlights. 2012 Edition. Madrid: UNWTO; **2012.**
3. IET (Instituto de Estudios Turísticos). *Balance del Turismo: Resultados de la Actividad Turísitica en España.* Madrid: Ministerio de Industria, Energía y Turismo; **2011.**
4. Manning, E.W.; Clifford, G.; Dougherty, D.; and Ernst, M.; What Managers Need to Know: A Practical Guide to the Development and Use of Indicators of Sustainable Tourism. Madrid: World Tourism Organization (UNWTO); **1997.**
5. Hassan, S. S.; Determinants of market competitiveness in an environmentally sustainable tourism industry. *J. Travel Res.* **2000,** *38(3),* 239–245.

6. Mihalic, T.; Environmental management of a tourist destination: A factor of tourism competitiveness. *Tourism Manag.* **2000,** *21(1),* 65–78.

7. Budeanu, A.; Introduction and overview of the journal of cleaner production special issue on sustainable tourism. *J. Cleaner Product.* **2005,** *13,* 79–81.

8. Bosch Camprubí, R.; Pujol Marco, L.; Serra Cabado, J.; and Vallespinós Riera, F. *Turismo y Medio Ambiente.* Madrid: Centro de Estudios Ramón Areces; **2001.**

9. Huybers, T.; and Bennett, J.; Environmental management and the competitiveness of nature-based tourism destinations. *Environ. Resour. Economics.* **2003,** *24,* 213–233.

10. Crouch, G. I.; and Ritchie, J. R. B.; Tourism, competitiveness and social prosperity. *J. Business Res.* **1999,** *44,* 137–152.

11. Ritchie, J. R. B.; and Crouch, G. I.; The Competitive Destination: A Sustainable Tourism Perspective. Wallingford: CABI Publishing; **2003.**

12. Dwyer, L.; and Kim, C.; Destination competitiveness: Determinants and indicators. *Current Iss. Tourism.* **2003,** *6(5),* 369–414.

13. Dwyer, L.; Mellor, R.; Livaic, Z.; Edwards, D.; and Kim, C.; Attributes of destination competitiveness: A factor analysis. *Tourism Analysis* **2004,** *9(1–2),* 91–101.

14. Ministry of Environment. Gestión Integrada de las Zonas Costeras en España/Integrated Coastal Zone Management in Spain. Madrid: General Directorate of Coasts, Ministry of Environment; **2006.**

15. Barragán, J. M.; *Las* áreas *litorales de España. Del análisis geográfico a la gestión integrada.* Madrid: Editorial Ariel S.A.; **2004.**

CHAPTER 8

PROTECTING OUR OCEANS: SUSTAINABILITY AT HOLLAND AMERICA LINE

MURRAY SILVERMAN

College of Business, San Francisco State University, E-mail: msilver@sfsu.edu

CONTENTS

8.1 INTRODUCTION

Holland America Line (HAL) was proud of its reputation as a sustainability leader in the global cruise industry. Bill Morani, V. P. Safety & Environmental Management Systems, was responsible for ensuring that the company and fleet complied with safety and environmental regulations and policies. He had been with HAL since 2003 following a 25-year career in the U.S. Coast Guard. In light of the maritime industry's significant environmental impacts and the complex and rapidly evolving regulatory environment, Bill was thinking about the company's current initiatives in order to prioritize the areas that should be emphasized in the future. Bill's thinking was interrupted as Dan Grausz, Executive V. P., Fleet Operations, came into his office waving an article about a Stena Line ferry that claimed that the two helical turbines on the deck of one of their ferries was achieving cost-effective reductions in fuel use. Dan was the leader of the Fuel Conservation Committee, and he reminded Bill that wind turbines on the ship's deck was one of the 56 initiatives in the spreadsheet tracking their priority in being considered for adoption. However, this initiative had been assigned a very low priority, and Dan asked Bill to report back to the Fuel Conservation Committee (FCC) as to whether time and resources should be expended in reconsidering or piloting it.

Bill was particularly proud of the progress HAL had made in increasing fuel efficiency. HAL had committed to reduce its fuel use (on a per passenger berth–per nautical mile traveled basis), and thus it's associated carbon emission intensity by 20 percent between 2005 and 2015. They achieved this goal by 2011. Reductions in the quantity of fuel used to sail each guest on a voyage reduced HAL's carbon emission intensity as well as the intensity of emissions of sulfur and nitrous oxides (SOX and NOX) and particulate matter (PM). Regulations relating to SOX, NOX, and PM were becoming a major issue for the cruise industry, as there was increasing concern about their health and environmental impacts. According to Bill:

"Fuel conservation is our 'go-to' strategy. It is a win-win. By consuming less fuel, we are not emitting as much exhausts containing green house gases and other pollutants, while reducing HAL's fuel costs, and by the way, the money saved through fuel conservation can help offset the increased cost of cleaner fuel."

Bill put aside his thinking about broader sustainability priorities in order to look into the wind turbine idea.

8.2 OUR OCEANS

Holland America Line (HAL) and the cruise industry business models rely on the oceans as their most important resource. The unspoiled waters and coral reefs at port destinations are a major attraction for passengers. Our oceans cover 71 percent of the earth's surface and they provide food in the form of fish and shellfish, they are used for transportation, and for recreation, such as swimming, sailing, diving, and surfing. They are a source of biomedical organisms that help fight disease. And very importantly, the ocean plays a significant role in regulating the planet's climate. The oceans are an integral part of the world's climate system, absorbing CO_2, and heat. The oceans and the atmosphere work together in defining our weather patterns [1]. Unfortunately, our oceans face many threats:

Overfishing: More than half the planet depends on the oceans for its primary source of food, yet most of the world's fisheries are being fished at levels above their maximum sustainable yield. Furthermore, harmful fishing methods unnecessarily kill turtles, dolphins, and other animals and destroy critical habitat.

Pollution: There are numerous sources of ocean pollution. An enormous amount of oil has been accidentally spilled from ships. While this in itself is destructive to aquatic plant and animal life, the threat from land-based activities is also great. Eighty percent of all pollution in seas and oceans comes from land-based activities [2]. More oil reaches the ocean each year as a result of leaking automobiles and other nonpoint sources than was spilled by the Exxon Valdez.

Eutrophication: Another serious ocean threat is algal blooms which form and spread in coastal areas due to nutrient overloading primarily as a result of fertilizer and topsoil runoff and sewage discharges in coastal areas. As the algae die and decompose, the water is depleted of available oxygen, causing the death of other organisms, such as fish.

Black and gray water: The shipping industry, as well as recreational boats, discharge black water (human waste) and gray water (water from galley sinks and showers) at varying distances from shore. Cruise ships are outfitted with equipment that treats the black and gray water prior to overboard discharge.

Ocean acidification: Global warming is primarily driven by the increasing accumulation of CO_2 in the atmosphere due to the burning of fossil fuels. On the positive side for the earth's ecosystem, the oceans absorb about one third of this anthropogenic carbon, reducing the atmospheric warming potential. However, the CO_2 absorbed is converted into carbonic acid, which increases the acidity of the ocean. The current rate of ocean acidification is unprecedented, and the increase in acidity dissolves the carbonates needed by organisms such as corals and oysters, thereby threatening their survival. It is estimated that acidification is a major contributor along with ocean warming to the loss of 20 percent of our coral reefs, and that by mid-century; we may lose another 50 percent [3].

Ocean warming: Global warming is also increasing the temperature of the ocean. Increasing ocean temperature leads to significant marine ecosystem change, influencing the generation of plankton, which forms the base of the ocean's food web. Coral reefs are also endangered as they are extremely sensitive to temperature change. Over 90 percent of marine species are directly or indirectly dependent on these reefs [4].

Tourism: While tourism generates vast amounts of income for host countries, it can have negative social and environmental side effects. The most significant impacts are in the heavily visited coastal areas. Sewage and waste emanating from the local residents, resorts, hotels, restaurants, and the housing that supports the tourism-related employees can find their way directly or indirectly into the bays and ocean. Even when there is municipal infrastructure, the sewage system can become overwhelmed or inadequate, resulting in seepage or dumping into the ocean. Also, careless diving, snorkeling, and other tour activities can damage coral reefs.

8.3   OCEAN PROTECTION

The oceans are a global commons that is not under the control of a single nation, except for the territorial waters of coastal nations. There are a number of formal institutions and instruments that provide national governments the opportunity to cooperate in managing the ocean commons. These agreements may be bilateral, regional, or global. Examples of these agreements include the UN Convention on the Law of the Sea (UNCLOS), which is a comprehensive treaty establishing protocols for the use and exploitation of the ocean and its resources. The International Whaling Convention (IWC), which implements the International Convention for the Regulation of Whaling, regulates the hunting of great whales. There are many other agreements and conventions, but they all apply only to nations that sign them, and even then there can be variations in enforcement [5].

8.4   CRUISE INDUSTRY

According to the World Tourism Organization (WTO), tourism has become one of the largest and fastest growing economic sectors in the world [6]. Taking a cruise is a popular tourist experience and the cruise industry is one of the fastest growing sectors of the tourism industry. Prior to the mid-twentieth century, ships focused on transporting customers to a particular destination. The modern cruise industry traces its beginnings to the early 1970s in Miami, USA with cruises throughout the Caribbean. The industry created a reasonably priced opportunity for many people to experience a resort-type vacation. Sometimes, cruise ships are referred to as floating hotels or marine resorts, because like land resorts, they have rooms, restaurants, entertainment, shops, spas, business centers, casinos, swimming pools, and other amenities.

Cruise ships travel worldwide in every ocean, and frequently visit the most pristine coastal waters and sensitive marine ecosystems. Cruise packages typically include more than one destination. The most popular destinations are the Caribbean, the Mediterranean, a number of European ports, the Bahamas and Alaska. There are approximately 2000 ports capable of receiving cruise ships. The amount of time spent at a destination can vary from one-half day to many days, depending on the design of the cruise package. The length of cruises can vary from 2 days to over 2 weeks, with an average length of about seven days. Destinations vary from tropical beaches like Cozumel to nature-based destinations such as Alaska while others might feature historical and culturally rich locations such as Istanbul. The cruise product is incredibly diversified, based on destination, ship design, on-board and on-shore activities, themes, and cruise lengths. Cruise accommodations and amenities differ and are priced accordingly. A typical classification of cruise types ranges from budget to conventional to premium and lastly to luxury [7]. Exhibit 8.1 elaborates on the differences between these categories. The passenger capacity of cruise ships tends to be larger at the budget and conventional categories and varies from a few hundred to over five thousand passengers.

Budget Segment
• Low-price
• Appealing to youth and lower income population segments
• Small ships with a minimum of on-board facilities
• Leading cruise lines in this segment include Louis Cruise, Travelscope, Thompson, Island Cruises, Pullmantur, and Fred Olsen
Contemporary Segment
• Most popular and profitable segment based on application of economies of scale
• Offers resort-type facilities with a strong emphasis on on-board activities and services, such as beauty shops, golf, ice skating, etc.
• Well adapted to families with children
• Broad target market with "something for everyone"
• Cruise lines in this segment include Royal Caribbean International, Carnival Cruises, Norwegian Cruise Line, Disney, MSC, P&O, and Costa
Premium Segment
• A somewhat more sophisticated product than contemporary—better suited to repeat cruise passengers
• Clientele in the over—40 age group
• Itineraries featuring rarely visited ports
• Cruise lines in this segment include Celebrity Cruises. Holland America Line, and Oceana Cruises
Luxury Segment
• High style luxury with emphasis on the destination and on-board facilities
• Exclusivity, with fewer passengers and a much more formal atmosphere
• Spacious accommodations
• Clientele: Couples and singles with a taste for super luxury resorts on land, with no facilities for children
• Longer itineraries (10 days or more) and unusual ports and places
• Cruise lines in this segment include Radisson Seven Seas, Silversea Cruises, Seabourn Cruise Line, and Crystal Cruises

EXHIBIT 8.1   Characteristics of cruise line segments.
Source: Cruise tourism: Current situation and trends (2010), WTO.

The popularity of cruising is reflected in its growth. Since 1980, the industry has had an annual passenger growth rate of 7.6 percent. Between 1990 and 2010, over 191 million passengers have taken a cruise [8]. Twenty four percent of the American population has cruised. As demand grew, the industry responded by building more cruise ships. As of 2012, there were 256 cruise ships [9]. Newer ships tend to be bigger, they include innovative amenities such as planetariums and bowling alleys and they are being designed to conserve fuel.

The typical cruise passenger is predominately Caucasian (93%), average age is 46 years, well educated, married (83%) with an average household income between ($90–100 k) [10]. The leading factors in the customer decision to select a cruise package are the destination and the price. Customers tend to be very price sensitive. It does not appear that many customers factor a cruise line's environmental practices into their choice of cruise lines [11]. The uniqueness of the experience also ranks highly. The customer can choose from luxury, premium, conventional, and budget offerings based on the packages being offered and the price. The packages are highly differentiated based on destination and the amenities associated with the ship. Ninety percent of the bookings come through travel agents [12].

8.5   INDUSTRY STRUCTURE

The cruise line industry is a $30 billion a year global industry. Three major cruise companies dominate the industry, and in 2012 controlled 84.3 percent market share based on number of passengers: Carnival Corporation (51.6%), Royal Caribbean Cruises Ltd. (21%) and Norwegian Cruise Line (7.1%) [13]. The major cruise companies each have a number of brands, allowing them to operate within the different pricing segments. The market shares of the brands of Carnival, which includes HAL, are listed in Exhibit 8.2 along with the market shares of other cruise lines. Many of HAL's and Royal Caribbean's brands were a result of acquisitions. The resulting consolidation of the industry led to the high level of market share concentration. However, this level of concentration was not viewed as anticompetitive by the Federal Trade Commission, because cruise ships are viewed as part of the resort industry, rather than as an independent cruise industry. Carnival Corporation had 2011 revenues of $15.8 billion and averaged net income to revenue of 13.0 percent over the 3 years 2009–11. Royal Caribbean had 2011 revenues of $7.5 billion and averaged net income to revenue of 6.1 percent over those 3 years [14].

Parent Company	Brand	Share of Worldwide Passengers (%)	Number of Ships
Carnival Corporation and PLC (CCL)	Carnival Cruise Line	21.1	24
	Costa	7.2	17
	Princess	6.4	16
	AIDA	4.4	8
	Holland America	3.7	15
	Other CC Lines	6.4	23
	Total CC Lines	49.2	103
Royal Caribbean Cruises, Ltd. (RCCL)	Royal Caribbean International	17.0	22
	Celebrity	4.7	11
	Other RCCL Lines	2.1	7
	Total RCCL	23.8	40
Norwegian		7.1	11
MSC Line		5.8	12

EXHIBIT 8.2   Share of Worldwide passengers and number of ships: 2011.
Source: Cruise Market Watch (2011), http://www.cruisemarketwatch.com/market-share/

There are a number of Cruise Line Associations. The largest is the Cruise Line Industry Association (CLIA), whose membership includes 22 of the world's largest cruise line companies, accounting for 97 percent of the demand for cruises.

The cruise lines have the ability to compete with each other on the basis of a highly diversified set of offerings. Much like hotels, they offer different levels of comfort and style, all priced accordingly. In addition, cruise lines can vary destinations, cruise lengths, ship themes and amenities in the packages they offer. To the envy of traditional hotels, the major cruise lines operate at 100 percent occupancy levels. They do this through a marginal pricing strategy, adjusting prices downward as the date of departure approaches.

There are major barriers to entry and exit in the industry due to the high cost of purchasing ($300–500 million) or selling a single cruise ship and the large investment required to operate a cruise line. In terms of the supply chain, there are many sellers to choose from in terms of food, supplies, equipment, and fuel. On the other hand, ship builders are few and are in a strong negotiating position. Cruise ships need many employees. There might be as few as 2–2.5 passengers for each employee. While there is an ample supply of cabin stewards and other lower skill jobs, there is a shortage of qualified deck and engineering officers [15].

8.6   REGULATIONS

The mechanisms governing the shipping industry are complex and multilayered. Shipping activities are regulated by a mixture of the international law of the sea and the laws of various nations. The country where a ship is registered is called the flag state. The flag state is obligated to ensure that the ships it registers comply with regulations set down in international conventions and agreements to which the flag state is a signatory. The International Maritime Organization (IMO) plays an important role in developing regulations relating to shipping [16]. *The IMO is the United Nations' specialized agency responsible for improving maritime safety and preventing pollution from ships.* Their regulations relate to safety, labor standards and the environment. Even though a ship may be registered in a flag state that has not ratified a particular IMO convention, that ship must conform to the conventions adopted by nations it visits. Since almost all cruise ship ports are in nations that have ratified the IMO regulations, cruise ships must abide by IMO regulations.

8.7   SUSTAINABILITY IN THE CRUISE INDUSTRY

There is a wide range of environmental and social aspects and potential impacts associated with cruise ship operations. There are discharges to water and to air, enormous amounts of waste are generated and there are environmental aspects associated with inputs such as packaging and food sourcing. Social aspects relate to employees, cruise customers and impacts on destination communities. The environmental aspects and impacts are displayed in Exhibit 8.3.

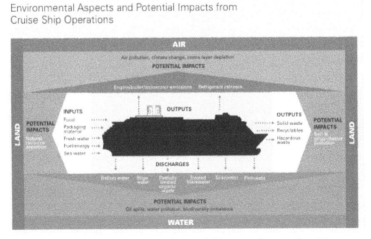

EXHIBIT 8.3   Environmental aspects and potential impacts from cruise ship operatons. *Source:* Holland America Lines.

Prior to 2000, each of the three major cruise companies listed above had been convicted of violations of U.S. water quality laws. In response to these convictions, the Cruise Line Industry Association (CLIA) developed Cruise Industry Waste Management Practices and Procedures [17]. CLIA members have adopted these voluntary environmental standards, which exceed the requirements of U.S. and international laws. Formal adoption is reflected by a cruise line including the requirements in the company's Safety Management System (SMS). As a result of these standards and an industry-wide effort to be responsible environmental citizens, the cruise industry has dramatically improved its environmental performance.

However, some cruise lines perform better than others in the environmental and social arena, because CLIA does not describe the manner in which the voluntary standards are to be implemented by their members or impose consequences for failing to incorporate them. Also, there may be a failure to adhere to an adopted voluntary standard due to equipment failure or operator error. Lastly, the standards do not address every environmental issue. In comparing performance across cruise lines, Holland America Line has been recognized as a top performer.

8.8 HOLLAND AMERICA LINE AND SUSTAINABILITY

Holland America Line (HAL) was founded as a shipping and passenger line in 1873 and offered its first vacation cruises in 1895. Over its first 136 years, HAL has carried over 11 million passengers. In 1989, HAL became a wholly owned subsidiary of Carnival Corporation. HAL maintains its own identity, operating its own fleet and managing its marketing, sales, and administrative support. In 2011, HAL operated 15 midsize ships and expected to carry 750,000 passengers to 350 ports in 100 countries. HAL operates ships with passenger capacities in the 1,200–2,100 passenger range. HAL is recognized as a leader in the industry's premium segment. HAL has more than 14,000 employees and is headquartered in Seattle, Washington, USA [18]. Holland America has received a number of awards for environmental sustainability and responsible tourism. In 2006, HAL was awarded the Green Planet Award, which recognizes eco-minded hotels, resorts, and cruise lines for outstanding environmental standards [19]. This award was based on their ISO 14001 certification and the installation of shore power plug-in systems on three ships. In 2008, Virgin Holidays awarded HAL the Responsible Tourism Award based on reducing dockside emissions by 20 percent, increasing recycling by 50 percent and instituting a training program to avoid "whale strikes" [20]. HAL was named the World's Leading Green Cruise Line at the World Travel Awards in London in 2011 [21] and they received a 2010 and 2012 Rear Admiral William M. Benkert Gold Environmental Protection Award from the U.S. Coast Guard [22]. HAL does not advertise its environmental credentials or accomplishments to potential customers, nor do any of their competitors.

In 2009, HAL released its first sustainability report covering activities from 2007 to 2009. Other Carnival Corporation subsidiaries also developed sustainability reports and were among the first in the industry to do so. Their sustainability report used the Global Reporting Initiative's (GRI) G3 Guidelines as the framework for their report. They include a GRI content index so that readers can see where GRI categories are covered in the report. The data in this baseline report was not independently verified, although this was not unusual among first time GRI reporters. Their environmental management system (EMS) was recertified in 2009 and 2012 as meeting the ISO 14001 environmental standards.

8.9   DISCHARGES TO WATER

Exhibit 8.4 diagrams the various discharges associated with a cruise ship. The primary discharges to water include black water (sewage), gray water (from showers, sinks, laundry, and the galley), and bilge water (potentially oily water leaked from engines and equipment that accumulates in the bilges). Black water is an issue because it contains pathogens, including fecal coliform bacteria that needs to be removed before being released into the environment. Untreated black water can cause serious contamination of fisheries and shellfish beds, resulting in a general contamination of the food chain and a risk to human health by transmitting infectious diseases.

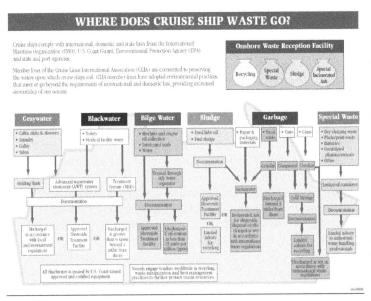

EXHIBIT 8.4   Where does cruise ship waste go?
Source: Cruise Line Industry Association

On most cruise ships, sewage is treated using a marine sanitation device (MSD) that disinfects the waste prior to discharge. While regulations require the use of marine sanitation devices (MSDs), there is a newer technology, Advanced Waste Water Purification Systems (AWWPS) that are capable of producing water effluent that is as clean or cleaner than that produced by many municipal treatment plants [23]. HAL was instrumental in developing the AWWPS technology for use in cruise ships. The first installation was on the msStatendam in 2002. These systems use a combination of screening, maceration, biodigestion, ultrafiltration, and ultraviolet light to go a quantum leap beyond MSDs. Approximately 40 percent of cruise ships have AWWPSs and more are being added every year. Holland America is a leader in this area, as twelve of their fifteen ships had AWWPSs.

MARPOL and US regulations require that treated sewage (MSD or AWWPSs) be discharged at least 3 nm (nautical miles) from shore and untreated sewage at least 12 nm from shore. In addition, there are no discharge zones (NDZs) that limit discharges in certain areas. MSD discharges by HAL are at least 12 nm from shore.

Gray water can contain a wide variety of pollutant substances, including oil and some organic compounds, detergents and grease, suspended solids, nutrients, food waste and small concentrations of coliform bacteria. In the US, gray water was not considered a pollutant until recently. Current regulations prohibit the discharge of gray water within three miles of the coast in California and Alaska. CLIA voluntary standards specify a distance of at least four miles from the coast. There do not appear to be conclusive studies as to the safest distance from shore to discharge black water or gray water [24]. Regulators require that discharged bilge water be less than 15 ppm (parts per million) while the vessel is enroute and not operating in a special area. HAL was also a leader in improving bilge water treatment prior to overboard discharge.

HAL also reduces the amount of water used and discharged through various water conservation strategies. In 2009 HAL used their EMS to set a target to use 7 percent less water than in 2008. They exceeded the target using 9 percent less water through a number of approaches, including low-flush toilets, low flow shower heads and faucets, specialized pool filters, etc. In 2010, HAL passenger growth was 9.8 percent, but overall water use rose by only 1.8 percent [25].

8.10   SOLID AND HAZARDOUS WASTE

Cruise ship waste streams can be either hazardous (chemicals from dry cleaning or photo processing, solvents, paint waste, etc.) or nonhazardous (food waste, paper, plastic, glass, etc.). The industry has grown 7.6 percent per year between 2000 and 2009, but has cut its waste almost in half [26].

The potential impact from pollution by solid waste on the open ocean and coastal environment can be significant, with a diversity of effects and consequences, including aesthetic degradation of surface waters and coastal areas, entanglement of sea birds, fish, turtles, and cetaceans, which may result in serious injury or even death by ingestion or asphyxiation, and nutrient pollution derived from continued disposal of food wastes in restricted areas.

HAL's disposition of solid waste breaks down as 26 percent going ashore primarily to landfills, 16 percent recycled to shore, 39 percent incinerated on board and 19 percent (food waste and ground glass) discharged at sea. Recycled items include glass, paper, cardboard, aluminum, steel cans and plastics. On HAL ships, paper and cardboard are shredded and are most often incinerated to reduce the fire load carried by the vessel. Food waste that has gone through a pulper is discharged more than 12 nm from shore.

In 2006 HAL set objectives to reduce solid waste offloads by 15 percent and to increase materials recycled ashore by 10 percent [27]. Between 2007 and 2008, solid waste disposed ashore increased by 5 percent and the total amount of solid waste recycled ashore increased by 86 percent attributable to fleet personnel properly segregating materials. The total quantity of waste generated by HAL during 2009 was 28 percent less than during 2008. The amount of material incinerated decreased by 27 percent in this period. Some of their waste management initiatives included replacing highly toxic perchloroethylene dry-cleaning with a nontoxic technology, developing a paint and thinner recycling program and implementing a list of approved chemicals to reduce the use of toxics. HAL donates many partially used products and reusable items (mattresses, toiletries, linen, clothing, etc.) to nonprofits.

8.11   SUPPLY CHAIN ISSUES

Exhibit 8.3 shows that the primary inputs for a cruise are food, packaging materials, fresh water and fuel. Fresh water is needed to clean and prepare food, clean kitchen equipment, wash guest and crew linens and clothes and to maintain engine room equipment. HAL used their EMS to target 7 percent less water use between 2008 and 2009 and they exceeded that target and used 9 percent less water. HAL has been working with their vendors to reduce packaging and this is reflected in their solid waste reduction.

One important supply chain issue with food is the sustainability of the seafood served. In 2010, Hal partnered with the Marine Conservation Institute (MCI) to protect marine ecosystems [28]. MCI is a nonprofit organization working with scientists, politicians, government officials and other organizations around the world to protect essential ocean places and the wild species in them. The HAL/MCI program is entitled "Our Marvelous Oceans" and includes the purchasing of sustainable seafood to be served on board, the development of a series of video programs about the oceans to be shown to guests and support for MCI to provide grants to graduate students and young scientists engaged in historical marine ecology. As part of the sustainable seafood program, MCI evaluated over 40 species of fish for HAL. MCI classified fish options within each species for HAL as best choice, good choice, not sustainable and need more information. Best choice seafood items are abundant, and caught or farmed in an environmentally friendly way. Good choice items are evaluated by MCI as acceptable although there may be some environmental concern. In those cases best choice alternatives are sought. For the "not sustainable" category, HAL discontinued purchases of those items. When more information was needed, HAL went back to the suppliers, and in many cases where there was a sustainability issue, suppliers worked hard to find sustainable alternatives for HAL. In a few instances, HAL had to eliminate specific menu items, but in some cases they were able to find an acceptable substitute for a menu item they wanted to retain (e.g., sustainably fished dover sole caught with hook and lines). HAL embraced this program because there was strong interest at the top management levels and even though purchasing costs were higher [29].

8.12   SOCIAL SUSTAINABILITY ISSUES

The cruise industry also has social aspects in the areas of guest experience, employee satisfaction and impacts on port communities visited by cruise ships. HAL's 800,000 guests are provided an opportunity to have a unique vacation, traveling by water to beautiful and interesting destinations, and they rate the cruise line very highly on follow-up surveys. In terms of employees HAL makes considerable effort to be a socially responsible employer. Their sea going workforce was 81 percent Filipino and Indonesian, who are away from home 3 to 10 months of the year, working seven days a week. All of the Filipino and Indonesian employees work under a collective bargaining agreement. The International Labor Organization in Switzerland sets standards which the CLIA supports. Benefits for HAL employees include health care, room and board, paid vacation, sick leave, compassionate leave and preparation of cuisine from their homeland. Seventy-two percent of HAL's more than 14,000 crew, officers, and shore side employees were covered by collective bargaining agreements in 2009 [30].

Community impacts associated with port visitations have complex social and environmental aspects for HAL and other cruise lines. When the cruise ship docks, thousands of passengers disembark, and it is a boon to merchants and the local economy. Many port destinations are economically dependent on tourists and cruise ships. However, the cruise line passengers can engender perceptions of income inequality and have other cultural impacts. Also, human health can be impacted by air pollution from SOX, PM, and nitrous oxides (NOX) emitted from the ship's stacks. About 9–14 percent of a cruise ship's emission occur in ports (depending on the type of ship), as some of the ship's diesel engines are used to power lights, refrigeration units, pumps, and other equipment [31].

Coastal water pollution is primarily an indirect impact associated with the cruise ships. While the cruise lines follow established regulations and voluntary standards that minimize the risk to the coastal waters, the number of passengers engaging in shore excursions in combination with tourists staying at the local resorts and hotels can place an excessive burden on the local municipal sewage treatment systems. Overflow from those systems or leaching from injection wells that are drilled to contain the sewage can enter the coastal water leading to algal blooms and pollution that degrade the coral reefs and coastal ecosystems that are the raison d'etre for visiting the destination.

Another issue is the environmental footprint of the shore side vendors and tour operators (boating, snorkeling and diving) that cater to the guests. The cruise lines responses to shore side issues are referred to as destination stewardship. In 2003, CLIA partnered with Conservation International (CI) to establish the Ocean Conservation and Tourism Alliance with the goal of addressing the shared responsibilities among cruise lines, governments, civil society, and shore operators to manage the growth of tourism in sensitive ecosystems. An example of CI's efforts in partnership with the Coral Reef Alliance is the Mesoamerican Reef Tourism Initiative (MARTI), a stewardship initiative involving Carnival and Royal Caribbean cruise lines [32]. MARTI is intended to protect the natural resources that draw tourists to Mexico, the Caribbean, Belize, and Honduras. MARTI partners meet in a multi-stakeholder format that includes private sector, government, and nongovernmental organizations to develop solutions to port-related environmental issues.

8.13   EMISSIONS TO AIR

Cruise ships generate the energy they need for propulsion as well as the electricity needed for lights, refrigeration, HVAC, and other equipment. Approximately 60 percent 0f the energy generated goes for propulsion, 15 percent HVAC, 10 percent lighting, 5 percent refrigerators and freezers and 10 percent to other systems [33]. Engine exhaust is the primary source of ship emissions. The most significant gasses are CO_2, NOX, SOX, and PM. The major concern with CO_2 is global warming. The primary concern with SOX, NOX, and PM is air pollution in coastal areas.

The primary fuel used by cruise ships is heavy fuel oil (HFO). Distillate and low sulfur fuel oil (LSFO) offer an alternative to HFO. The price of these lower sulfur fuels fluctuate, but they are expected to cost between 10 and 50 percent more than HFO [34]. Burning LSFO or distillate fuel reduces SOX and PM pollution, but the carbon footprint of these fuel is about the same as HFO. HAL relies primarily on HFO, but changes in national and international regulations in 2015, will require an increase in use of more expensive distillate fuel. In 2011, about 4 percent of fuel use at HAL was distillate [35]. (See Exhibit 8.7: Fuel Use and Efficiency). Considering that fuel costs can be on the order of 15 percent of operating expense, increases in fuel cost would have a major impact on the industry.

8.14 CO_2 EMISSIONS

There is a high level of agreement that global warming is undermining the complex web of natural systems that allows life to thrive on earth. The CO_2 emissions from the burning of fossil fuels accounts for most of the increase in GHG concentrations. Approximately 2–3 percent of the global total of CO_2 emissions comes from shipping, mostly from the 50,000 merchant ships plying the ocean [36]. The 350 cruise ships contribute in a small way to this problem. In comparison to shipping, CO_2 emissions from aviation contribute 2 percent, road transport 21 and 0.5 percent from rail [37]. According to the IMO, there is "significant potential to reduce GHG through technical and operational measures. The IMO estimates these measures could reduce emissions rate by 25–75 percent below 2009 levels-see Exhibit 8.5. Of course, not all of these measures are technically feasible and/or cost effective for the cruise lines, especially in the short term. Ship retrofit is very expensive, so design changes need to be built in up front. Some ships are getting as much as 7–10 percent fuel reduction from coatings [38]. Speed reductions can significantly increase fuel efficiency. A 10 percent reduction in speed can provide an energy saving of 19 percent [39]. Just like with driving an automobile, ship size and speed is the most critical defining parameter with respect to fuel consumption.

	Saving of CO_2	Combined within Category	Overall Combined
DESIGN (new ships)		10–50%	
Concept, speed, and capability	2–50%[a]		
Hull and superstructure	2–20%		
Power and propulsion system	5–15%		
Low-carbon fuels	5–15%		
Renewable energy	1–10%		
			25–75%
Operation (all ships)		10–50%	
Fleet management	5–50%		
Voyage optimization	1–10%		
Energy management	1–10%		

EXHIBIT 8.5   Assessment of potential reductions of CO_2 emissions from shipping using known technology and practices.

[a]Reductions at this level would require reductions of operational speed.

Source: Second IMO GHG Study 2009, UN International Maritime Organization.

Holland America Line's response to its GHG impact has been to reduce fuel use through:

(i)   More energy efficient equipment
(ii) More energy efficient ships
(iii) Energy Conservation
(iv) Shore power
(v)   Circulate monthly fuel use data to encourage competition between vessels
(vi) Sharing best practices from high performing ships
(vii) Providing monetary incentives to senior shipboard staff to encourage fuel conservation practices

These options not only conserve fuel and reduce GHG, they also reduce the amount of SOX, PM, and NOX because less fuel is burned. Exhibit 8.6 shows fuel use at HAL between 2007 and 2009. Fuel use overall increased due to an expanding fleet and passenger growth, however, on a normalized basis, the fuel used per available lower berth on the ships steadily decreased over that period.

Measure	Units	2007	2008	2009
Heavy Fuel Oil (HFO) Use	Metric Tonnes (MT)	435,806	442,362	446,765
	Kg/ALB-km[a]	0.1211	0.1163	0.1141
Distillate Fuel Use[b]	MT	5,730	5,230	4,874
		Direct GHG Emissions		
Carbon Dioxide	MT	1,395,571	1,407,527	1,420,216
Equivalent (CO_2-e)	Kg/ALB-km	0.3883	0.3862	0.3628
		Other Emissions		
Nitrogen Oxides (NOX)	MT	28,327	29,093	29,357
	Kg/mile	21.2	22.2	21.2
Sulfur Oxides (SOX)	MT	19,411	18,606	18,606
	Kg/mile	14.5	14.2	13.4
Particulate Matter (PM 10)	MT	523	537	542
	Kg/mile	0.391	0.411	0.392

EXHIBIT 8.6   Fuel Use at Holland America Line.
[a]Kg/ALB is a measure of efficiency agreed upon by all of Carnival Corporation's operating lines. It is the quantity of fuel used in kilograms divided by the available lower berths in the fleet times the number of kilometers traveled by the fleet.
[b]Distillate fuel is used in the diesel electric generators in geographic regions as specified by laws and regulations.
Source: Holland America Line 2009 Sustainability Report, p. 65.

8.15 SOX AND NOX

The maritime industry accounts for approximately 4 and 7 percent, respectively of global SOX and NOX emissions [40], of which a small proportion is attributable to the cruise industry. Combustion of HFO produces sulfur dioxide and PM Sulfur dioxide reacts with other substances in the air to form acid rain, which falls to earth as rain, fog, snow, or dry particles. Some may be carried by wind for hundreds of miles. Acid rain causes deterioration of cars, buildings, and historical monuments; and causes lakes and streams to become acidic and unsuitable for many fish. PM may cause serious human health problems, including respiratory diseases, neurological damage, birth defects, or cancer. Emissions from cruise ships are of concern while a ship is at port, close to residents of coastal communities. NOX causes a wide variety of health and environmental impacts. Ground-level Ozone (Smog) is formed when NOX and volatile organic compounds (VOCs) react in the presence of heat and sunlight. Children, people with lung diseases such as asthma, and people who work or exercise outside, are susceptible to adverse effects such as damage to lung tissue and reduction in lung function.

The health and other environmental impacts associated with SOX, PM, and NOX emissions have been under intense regulatory scrutiny. International regulations (MARPOL) in 2000 had lowered sulfur limits in fuel to 4.5 percent and by 2012 to 3.5 percent, and by 2020, global sulfur limits are set at 0.5 percent. However, certain national and regional regulations have put reduced sulfur emissions on an even shorter time line. Emission Control Areas (ECAs) are being established that impose very tight limits on sulfur, NOX, and PM for ships entering those areas. For example, sulfur limits are restricted to 1.0 percent levels already in the Baltic and EU rules will cap sulfur at 0.1 percent by 2015. Significant reductions in NOX are also being mandated. Australia, NZ, and Hong Kong have voluntary measures, likely to develop into ECAs by 2015. The industry is experimenting with seawater scrubbers in the stacks, which would remove a high level of SOX and PM. However, it is not yet clear as to whether the use of sea-water scrubbers will be a less expensive option than low sulfur fuels. In any case, increasing regulatory pressure to reduce SOX, PM, and NOX will have a significant financial impact on HAL and the rest of the cruise industry.

8.16 MANAGING FUEL CONSERVATION AT HAL

In 2005, HAL's parent, Carnival Corporation set an ambitious corporate goal of increasing fuel efficiency as measured by the amount of fuel used per lower berth per nautical mile by 20 percent by 2015. In order to address the need to reduce fuel use, HAL had established a Fuel Conservation Committee in 2007 that systematically identified and assessed fuel reduction opportunities based primarily on projected fuel savings and return on investment (ROI). The committee had been very effective in adopting successful initiatives based on established financial criteria, and HAL reached their 2015 target in 2011. (See Exhibit 8.7: Fuel Use and Efficiency).

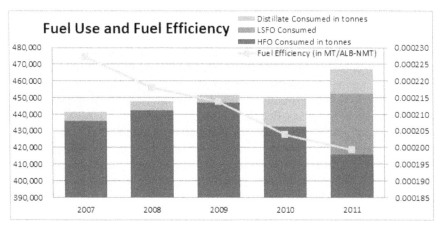

EXHIBIT 8.7   Holland America Line Fuel Use and Fuel Efficiency 2007–2011.
Source: Internal Holland America document.

Bill participated in the weekly Fuel Conservation Committee [41] meeting in Seattle, which explored and implemented various fuel conservation initiatives. In 2012 the committee was evaluating close to 50 initiatives. These initiatives fell into five broad categories, a majority of which required capital investments in new and modified equipment:

(i)   Sailing and maneuvering (six initiatives): Many of these initiatives involve the use of software to optimize speed and maneuvering.

(ii) Modifying or adding equipment (28 initiatives): A wide variety of initiatives such as upgrades of air conditioner chiller control systems.

(iii) Operational improvements (eight initiatives): Initiatives such as running one sea-water cooling pump while in port.

(iv) Monitoring various sources of energy consumption (10 initiatives): Initiatives such as installation of KWh meters in electrical substations to monitor the energy consumption of various users.

(v)   Waste Heat recovery (four initiatives): Initiatives such as adding an additional heat exchanger to reuse high temperature waste heat for potable water heating.

The committee's spreadsheet included estimates of potential savings from each initiative and the cost per ship. Typically, the estimates of savings were measured in terms of percentage of overall fuel budget. For the thirty eight initiatives for which estimates had been made, 13 would save 0.25 percent fuel or less, 16 saved between 0.26 and 0.99 percent, nine might save more than 1.0 percent. The committee also tracked whether each initiative was proven or assumed to be viable and its stage of implementation (study, funding required, implemented, or discontinued). If the committee decided that a proposed fuel conservation initiative should be implemented, it was pilot tested on a single ship. Performance was tracked and if the results met investment criteria, the initiative would be eligible to be rolled out to other ships. Finally, based on all of this information, the committee assigns a priority (1, 2, or 3) to each initiative. Because there is a limited capital budget available to pursue fuel conservation projects, even initiatives with a priority of 1, might not be implemented, or might not be implemented fleet wide.

Because of the unproven nature of the wind turbine initiative, and skepticism on the part of HAL's engineering department personnel, the Fuel Conservation Committee had long ago assigned a priority "3" and an estimated fuel savings of less than 0.25 percent. Wind turbines can be horizontal (HAWT) or vertical axis (VAWT). However it appeared that VAWT were most appropriate on ships as they can withstand much higher wind speeds, and are significantly more efficient than HAWT [42].

Bill read the article about Stena Line, a ferry line operating with travel service between Britain, Holland, and Ireland. He learned that Stena Line estimated that the two turbines installed on Stena Jutlandica would generate about 23,000 kWh per year, equivalent to the domestic electricity consumption for four normal homes during one year. (See Exhibit 8.8 for a photo of Stena Jutlandica) This was equivalent to a reduction in fuel consumption of between 80 and 90 tons per year [43]. Bill began to inquire internally at HAL about the wind turbine idea, and one of his direct reports had received unsubstantiated information from a third-party that the Stena Line installation was projected to be very cost effective and that contrary to intuition, the turbines reduced aerodynamic drag on the ferry. Bill also found another article describing how Hornblower Cruises planned to launch the Hornblower hybrid to take passengers on sightseeing, dinner, and social events in New York Harbor [44]. This 600 passenger vessel would incorporate helical wind turbines, solar panels and hydrogen fuel cells in addition to its diesel engine. The company believed the combination of alternative power generators would result in fuel savings that justified the investment.

Bill consulted with Pieter Rijkaart, former Director of New Builds, who had led the design and build of almost all of HAL's current fleet. Pieter mirrored the skepticism expressed by other engineers. For example, the engineers noted that a cruise liner is much larger and more streamlined than a ferry, raising questions about the applicability of the Stena Line performance results. There were also cost issues. A pilot test on one ship would require a large up-front investment in addition to the cost of the turbine, as it would have to be anchored to the deck and tied into the electrical grid on the ship. There were also major aesthetic concerns. Cruise ships are designed to have a beautiful appearance, and having bulky wind turbines on the deck could be an eyesore. Lastly, the amount of energy supplied by the wind turbines would account for an extremely small percentage of the ships energy needs.

EXHIBIT 8.8   Wind Turbines on Stena Jutlandica.

Bill wondered whether there were intangible benefits associated with the use of wind turbines. HAL had already demonstrated a proactive interest in alternative energy initiatives. HAL had installed heat reflective film on windows to reduce the transfer of heat to the interior, and thus reducing the load on air conditioners. At a cost of $170,000 per ship, and a projected fuel savings between 0.5 and 1.0 percent, three ships had this technology installed and other ships awaited funding [45]. Also, HAL had adopted an initiative involving the pumping of used cooking oil into the fuel line. In 2010, HAL reused 51,000 L of used cooking oil. This very low cost option resulted in both the reduction of fossil fuel and avoidance of the disposal cost of drums of used cooking oil. Wind turbines represented another opportunity for HAL to explore using alternative energy. While this could contribute to HAL's reputation as a sustainability leader in the industry, Bill did not believe that reputation should be factored into a FCC decision. According to Bill: "We don't talk about whether something will get good press." While the turbines would produce only a very small amount of the electricity used on the boat, they would contribute to reduced fuel use. Bill did not have enough information to estimate ROI or payback. Given that there were dozens of other proposed initiatives in the FCC spreadsheet, he wondered whether it made sense to expend FCC effort on this initiative. On the other hand, Bill said, "I would be concerned that we could be missing an opportunity." Bill was eager to pull together his thinking on the turbine initiative for the upcoming FCC meeting so that he could get back to longer-term thinking about the sustainability priorities facing HAL.

DISCUSSION QUESTIONS

1. From the viewpoint of the cruise line companies, do you believe that the industry will be more or less attractive in the future? Explain your thinking. How will sustainability issues and regulations impact industry attractiveness?
2. Who are the key stakeholders in relation to HAL's sustainability issues? What is the influence of each in terms of their potential impact on HAL?
3. What are the most significant environmental issues facing Holland America Line? In what ways has Holland America gone beyond compliance in its environmental initiatives?
4. What are the most significant social issues facing Holland America Line?
5. Bill Morani has asked for your assistance in assessing what action to take with respect to the wind turbine initiative. What would you recommend?
6. What are the challenges facing Bill Morani and Holland America in moving their sustainability agenda forward?

ACRONYMS USED IN THE CASE

AWWPS	Advanced Waste Water Purification System
CI	Conservation International
CLIA	Cruise Line Industry Association
CO_2	Carbon Dioxide
FCC	Fuel Conservation Committee
HAL	Holland America Lines
HAWT	Horizontal Axis Wind Turbine
HFO	Heavy Fuel Oil
HVAC	Heating, Ventilation and Air Conditioning
IMO	International Maritime Organization
IWC	International Whaling Convention
MARTI	MesoAmerican Reef Tourism Association
MCI	Marine Conservation Institute
MSD	Marine Sanitation Devices
NOX	Nitrous Oxide
PM	Particulate Matter
SOX	Sulfur Oxide
UNCLOS	United Nations Convention on the Law of the Sea
VAWT	Vertical Axis Wind Turbine
VOC	Volatile Organic Compounds
WTO	World Tourism Organization

KEYWORDS

- **Coastal water pollution**
- **Cruise industry**
- **Discharges to water**
- **Global warming**

REFERENCES

1. www.savethesea.org/resources/briefings/governance.php, accessed April 10, 2012.
2. Ibid.
3. Interview with Rick MacPherson, Conservation Programs Director at the Coral Reef Alliance on March 7, 2012.
4. www.savethesea.org/resources/briefings/governance.php, accessed April 10, 2012.
5. www.seaweb.org/resources/briefings/governance.phpImportant agreements relating to the global oceans are described here. Accessed May 5, 2012.
6. The World Tourism Organization (UNWTO) is the United Nations agency responsible for the promotion of responsible, sustainable and universally accessible tourism. www.unwto.org
7. Berlitz Complete Guide to Cruising and Cruise Ships 2011, Douglas Ward, www.berlitzcruising.com
8. 2011 CLIA Cruise Market Overview, Cruise Line International Association, Inc., p. 1, accessed on May 25, 2012 from cruise.org/regulatory/clia_statisticalreport
9. www.cruisemarketwatch.com/capacity/, accessed on April 20, 2012.
10. www.windrosenetwork.com/The-Cruise-Industry-Demographic-Profiles.html, accessed on April 20, 2012
11. http://thevacationgals.com/best-cruise-ships-of-2011/
12. Cruise Tourism: Current Situation and Trends, World Tourism Organization, Madrid Spain, 2010, Section 4.1.
13. www.cruisemarketwatch.com, accessed May 20, 2012.
14. Carnival Corporation & PLC, 2011 Annual Report and Royal Caribbean Cruises Ltd., 2011 Annual Report.
15. E-mail exchange with Tina Stotz, Manager, Sustainability and ISO Systems Management, July 20, 2012 and Bill Morani, VP Safety and Environmental Management Systems.
16. For information about the IMO, go to www.imo.org/About?pges/Default.aspx, accessed on June 15, 2012.
17. Interview in Washington, D.C, at the Cruise Line Industry Association with Michael Crye, Executive Vice President, and Bud Darr, Director of Environment and Health Programs on February 15, 2012. The CLIA Waste Management Practices and Procedures can be accessed at www.cruising.org/regulatory/cruise-industry-policies/cruise-industrys-commitment-environment

18. Holland America Line 2009 Sustainability Report. www.hollandamerica.com/about-best-cruise-lines/Main.action?tabName=Sustainability#

19. http://boards.cruisecritic.com/archive/index.php/t-457134.html, accessed August 1, 2012.

20. http://www.bloomberg.com/apps/news?pid=newsarchive&sid=aLw6DFDEovrI, accessed August 1, 2012.

21. http://www.worldsleadingcruiselines.com/about-us/press-room/holland-america-news/holland-america-line-receives-second-benkert-environmental-award.aspx, accessed August 1, 2012.

22. http://markets.on.nytimes.com/research/stocks/news/press_release.asp?docTag=201205221327PR_NEWS_USPRX____SF11884&feedID=600&press_symbol=83500, accessed August 1, 2012.

23. CLIA at 35, p. 20.

24. Post and Courier, Charleston, S. C., 2011, www.postandcourier.com

25. E-mail exchange with Tina Stotz ??????date

26. http://www.ethicaltraveler.org/2010/01/sustainability-in-the-cruise-industry/, accessed August 1, 2012.

27. Data relating to waste management can be found in Holland America's Sustainability Report (2009).

28. Interviews with Lance Morgan at Marine Conservation Institute and Tina Stotz at HAL, Fall 2011. Also, see http://www.marine-conservation.org/what-we-do/program-areas/how-we-fish/holland-america/sustainable-seafood/

29. Ibid.

30. Holland America Line 2009 Sustainability Report.

31. Internal HAL document.

32. http://www.conservation.org/fmg/articles/pages/greening_tourism.aspx

33. Holland America Line 2009 Sustainability Report

34. http://www.maritimeuk.org/2012/01/marine-fuel-sulphur-content/

35. E-mail correspondence with Tina Stotz and Bill Morani at HAL.

36. http://www.marisec.org/shippingfacts//worldtrade/index.php?SID=ca4a0dfa59eac4d7f4edc87fefd82b4d

37. Second IMO GHG Study 2009, UN International Maritime Organization, London 2009.

38. Interview with Michael Crye and Bud Darr at CLIA.

39. Second IMO GHG Study 2009, UN International Maritime Organization, London 2009, p. 176.

40. http://www.dieselnet.com/standards/inter/imo.php

41. Information relating to the FCC is based on internal documents and interviews with HAL managers.

42. http://colonizeantartica.blogspot.com/2008/01/vertical-axis-wind-turbines.html

43. http://www.stenaline.com/en/stena-line/corporate/media/press-releases/wind-power-on-board-a-ferry/

44. http://www.engadget.com/2010/12/02/hornblower-hybrid-ferry-relies-on-eco-friendly-trifecta-hydroge/

45. Internal HAL document.

CHAPTER 9

TROPICALIA: PLANNING FOR SUSTAINABILITY IN THE CARIBBEAN

NUNZIA AULETTA[1] and MARÍA HELENA JAÉN[2]

[1]Full Professor, Entrepreneurship and Marketing Departments, Instituto de Estudios Superiores en Administraciyn (IESA), Caracas, Venezuela. PhD,
IESA, Edf. Iesa, San Bernardino, Caracas, 1010,
Venezuela, Tele: 0058 2125554210, E-mail: nunzia.auletta@iesa.edu.ve

[2]Full Professor, Management and Leadership Department, Instituto de Estudios Superiores en Administraciyn (IESA), Caracas, Venezuela. PhD
IESA, Edf. Iesa, San Bernardino, Caracas, 1010, Venezuela. Tele: 0058 2125554210,
E-mail: maria.jaen@iesa.edu.ve

CONTENTS

9.1   INTRODUCTION

Tropicalia is a luxury tourism development, to be built in the North-Eastern region of Dominican Republic (DR). The project promoter is Cisneros, a family business conglomerate, which has a tradition of corporate social responsibility initiatives in Latin America. Cisneros aspires to position Tropicalia as a model for sustainable tourism with a master plan of developing not only an environmentally sound hospitality structure, but a whole sustainable tourism destination in Miches, a town in El Seibo Province in Dominican Republic. The project is conceived as a multiphase development over 30 years, expecting the opening of the first resort after 2018. In 2008, its foundation, Fundación Tropicalia (FT) was created, with the mission to design and implement community programs for stakeholders in Tropicalia's sphere of influence. Its sustainability model comprises four main initiatives: educational, well-being and culture, environmental and productivity. All of them are aimed to favor the interaction with a wide range of stakeholders, among which Miches community and potential suppliers in Tropicalia value chain. The overall Tropicalia's sustainability approach is guided by the ten UN Global Compact principles and the concept of shared value creation.

9.2   TROPICALIA: A VISION, A REALITY

Tropicalia is a luxury tourism development, to be built in an expanse of coconut groves and white beaches, in the North-Eastern region of Dominican Republic. The project promoter is the Cisneros , a family business conglomerate, which was founded in Venezuela in the early 1930s, and comprises more than 30 companies, that in over 80 years have built a family fortune of USD 4.4 billion [1].

Sharing her memories on her family settling in Dominican Republic, Adriana Cisneros, Tropicalia's CEO, has written:

"As a young girl, I had the opportunity to join my father on his trips in the Dominican Republic looking for pristine lands. After ten years, we came upon what today is Tropicalia" [2].

Her personal vision of the Tropicalia hospitality project is a mix of family style, nature preservation, and world-class luxury, as she has stated:

"When we were designing our beach front hotel we wanted to imbue it with the grace and warmth that my mother's refined taste and eye for details brings to our homes. A signature style emerges blending discreet design elements with orchids, palms, ferns, and coral stones." [2]

Close to this idyllic place of pristine natural beauty where Tropicalia will be built, Miches rises. It is a small town of 20,813 inhabitants, located in El Seibo province and surrounded by rural settlements. The people of Miches are friendly and proud of their Afro-Caribbean cultural heritage, as the annual Miches Art Festival, conceived to promote the natural and artistic Michense talents, shows. The main productive activities are agriculture (mainly cocoa, coconut, rice and root vegetables production), artisanal fisheries, and local crafts. However, the Miches community faces many social and economic challenges, starting with one of the highest poverty rates in the country, fuelled by low education levels, unemployment, and delinquency. Infrastructure is also a big concern. The town is a three-hour drive on mountain roads from Santo Domingo, the country's capital city, and the nearest airport is 60 miles away. Electricity supply is unstable and there is an environmental threat posed by unsafe waste disposal and traditional agriculture methods.

As a part of the United Nations Millennium Project in the Dominican Republic, in 2004 El Seibo, and therefore Miches, was selected as the country's first "Millennium Village" resulting in the production and circulation of an extensive analysis of base-line indicators that would set Miches on the path to tourism. However, translating findings into action has been a slow process. In 2010, the government paved local roads; and from 2008 to 2012 while the Ministry of Education invested in several local school renovations, the Ministry of Telecommunications with the support of private business improved internet and cell phone services. Despite these changes, much opportunity lies ahead for development, as these services haven't translated into breaking the poverty cycle of Miches.

Tropicalia aspires to position Miches as a haven for sustainable tourism, leading the efforts and setting a benchmark for the region. Cisneros aims to position Tropicalia as a model for sustainable tourism in the Dominican Republic, the Caribbean, and the world.

9.2.1 FROM CORPORATE SOCIAL RESPONSIBILITY TO SUSTAINABILITY

Corporate social responsibility (CSR) has been at the center of business strategy and policies discussion since the early 1950's. The seminal Bowen definition [3] referred to it as "the obligations of businessmen to pursue those policies, to make those decisions, or to follow those lines of action which are desirable in terms of the objectives and values of our society," set the pace to a "social consciousness" view of business actions, but kept it, somehow, in the realm of desirability more related to a "vague and highly generalized sense of social concern" as stated later on by Preston and Post [4].

According to Carroll [5] the evolution of the concept has incorporated new dimensions to it such as "the obligation to constituent groups" [6]; the relationship between CSR and "business ethics and corporate social responsiveness" [7]; and a "pyramid of four categories: economic, legal, ethical and philanthropic," moving up from economic concerns to philanthropy [8]. The same author introduced the idea of "the natural fit" between corporate social responsibility and an organization's stakeholders [5], which can be defined as "all those individual actors and parties, organized groups and professions, and institutions that have a bearing on the behavior of the organization as revealed in its policies and actions on the environment," in short "a stakeholder is any party that both affects and is affected by an organization and its policies" [9]. Moreover, stakeholders have been classified according to whether they have or perceived to have one, two, or three of the following attributes: power to influence, legitimacy of their claim, and urgency of their claim. As a result the stakeholders can be categorized as: dormant, discretionary, demanding, dominant, dangerous, dependent and definitive [10].

In recent years CSR has further evolved introducing the idea of business actions that focus on "social good beyond the interest of the firm" [11], and furthermore considering companies responsible "for their total impact on the societies in which they operate" taking into account both positive and negative effects they can have on society, not as an act of philanthropy or an optional add-on [12].

In analyzing the evolution of the CSR concept, beyond the idea of good corporate citizenship, Dahlsrud [13] identifies five dimensions of CSR that are present in most definitions: environmental, social, economic, stakeholders, and voluntariness, and states that the challenge for business is centered on how to construct a CSR policy in a specific context, taking into account the main drivers of the business strategy.

This view is furthered by Porter and Kramer [14] who argue that CSR should not be considered as a cost, constraint, or charitable deed. They propose a strategic approach that can turn good corporate citizenship into an opportunity to generate innovation and competitive advantages, using corporate resources and expertise to foster social benefits. Under this point of view, CSR becomes a strategy in itself, rooted in the interdependence between a company and society or environment that can produce social or external benefits and business gains as well. Furthermore, they propose to use the traditional value chain model to map social opportunities, exploring the potential contributions of business stakeholders, both in primary and support activities. Understanding of the social dimensions of the company's competitive context can be deepened by introducing Porter's diamond framework, which considers the context for: firm rivalry, the factors conditions, the local demand conditions, and the related and supporting industries. Corporate social responsibility initiatives can, therefore, become part of the firm´s strategy to enhance competitiveness or lead to product development. Under this point of view, for instance, a healthy society and an educated community can supply both a more productive workforce and an expanding demand.

Elaborating on this line of thought, more recently, Porter and Kramer [15] have introduced the concept of shared value creation that focuses on the connection between societal and economic progress, completely abandoning a redistribution-of-wealth approach. Social value is focused in three key ways of creating business opportunities: reconceiving products and markets, redefining products and markets, and enabling local cluster development.

The concept of sustainability has been simply defined by the World Business Council for Sustainable Development (WBCSD) as "meeting the needs of the present without compromising the ability of future generations to meet their own needs." However the most cited definition is the one stated by the World Commission on Environment and Development (WCED) [16], which takes into account "environmental, social, and economic aspects of sustainable development such as the notion of resource limits (energy, materials, waste, and land); equitable access to constrained resources; intergenerational and intragenerational equity; and a progressive transformation of economy and society." Following the same line of thought, the UN's Global Compact (UNGC) [17] defines corporate sustainability as "a company's delivery of long term value in financial, social, environmental, and ethical terms." In order to pursue this mission, UNGC asks companies to "embrace, support and enact, within their sphere of influence, a set of core values in the areas of human rights, labor standards, the environment, and anti-corruption actions" (Table 9.1).

TABLE 9.1 United Nation's Global Compact 10 Principles

Human Rights	Principle 1: Businesses should support and respect the protection of internationally proclaimed human rights and Principle 2: make sure that they are not complicit in human rights abuses.
Labor	Principle 3: Businesses should uphold the freedom of association and the effective recognition of the right to collective bargaining; Principle 4: the elimination of all forms of forced and compulsory labor; Principle 5: the effective abolition of child labor; and Principle 6: the elimination of discrimination in respect of employment and occupation.
Environment	Principle 7: Businesses should support a precautionary approach to environmental challenges; Principle 8: undertake initiatives to promote greater environmental responsibility; and Principle 9: encourage the development and diffusion of environmentally friendly technologies.
Anti-Corruption	Principle 10: Businesses should work against corruption in all its forms, including extortion and bribery.

Source: www.unglobalcompact.org, 2013.

A more thorough analysis on conceptualizing a sustainable business model (SBM) developed by Stubbs and Cocklin [18], proposes that "organizations adopting a SBM must develop internal structural and cultural capabilities to achieve firm-level sustainability and collaborate with key stakeholders to achieve sustainability for the system that an organization is part of." These authors propose six characteristics of a SBM. Organizations should state their purpose, mission and vision, drawing on economic, environmental and social aspects of sustainability. A triple bottom line approach- based on financial, social, and environmental indicators- is of utmost importance to set a "sustainable mindset embedded throughout the organization." This is further reinforced by moving beyond the shareholders view, connecting instead the organization's success with its stakeholders' success, through engagement and collaboration. Among these stakeholders, the organization acknowledges nature itself, with a focus on renewable resources, reducing the ecological footprint throughout the value chain and repairing environmental damage. In order for sustainability to become embedded in the organizational culture, CEO leadership and direct involvement is required, pushing the agenda throughout the entire stakeholder network, to the extent of cultural and structural changes. Finally, these changes need to appear not only at the firm level –internal capabilities- but at the whole system level, where the organization is operating [18].

9.2.2 *DOING BUSINESS IN THE DOMINICAN REPUBLIC*

The Dominican Republic (DR) (Table 9.2) is located in the Eastern Caribbean Sea, sharing the island of Hispaniola with Haiti. The country's population is slightly over 10 million inhabitants, with an estimated 1 million undocumented workers, and a poverty rate of 33.8%, mostly concentrated in rural areas. Since 2004, it is governed by the Dominican Liberation Party. Its President, Danilo Medina, was elected in 2012 for a four-year period.

The Dominican Republic is a popular tourist destination with over 5 million visitors a year, for a total revenue of over 4.5 billion dollars. By 2011, the tourism sector supported 210,000 jobs and represented 5.5% of the country's GDP. According to Euromonitor [19] tourism arrivals registered a growth of 7% in 2012, while the Dominican government is focusing on supporting the construction of infrastructure for tourism development, looking to attract 10 million tourists per year over the next 10 years.

TABLE 9.2   The Dominican Republic at a glance

Demographic Factors		Economic Factors	
Population (1)	10.1 million inhabitants	GDP per capita (US$)(1)	5,240
Urban Population (2)	66.5%	Tourism GDP (3)	5.5%
Population density (2)	203 inhabitants per km2	Unemployment (2)	14.4%
Mean age (2)	25 years	Poverty (2)	33.8%
Children completing elementary school (2)	75.8	Extreme poverty (2)	10.4%

Source: (1) TWB-IFC (2013), (2) www.paho.org (2013); (3) www.invest-indr.com (2011).

Commenting on the tourism development opportunity in DR, Adriana Cisneros declared:

> "With tourism in Latin America representing 6.6% of GDP and 12.6% of total employment in the Caribbean region, one can hardly dispute the industry's profound economic and social implications. Tourism not only acts as the driving force behind wealth creation in many countries, but when judiciously exercised, it also encourages gender equity and youth participation; protects, restores and preserves the environment; and honors local cultural heritage. This is what I know to be sustainable tourism – a model that promotes economic development, encourages business to generate progressive, innovative solutions to ever-changing social and industry demands, and allows the tourist enterprise to compete successfully over the long run by striking a careful balance between today's needs and those of tomorrow." (www.invest-indr.com, 2011)

Despite the undeniable opportunities, there are still some important challenges for a company investing in the DR, as indicated by the Doing Business Report [20], which ranks it in the 117th place among 185 countries in terms of the overall ease of doing business (Figure 9.1). Some of the critical impediments relate to the time it takes to start a business, acquire construction permits, set-up services like electricity or internet, and register property, all key factors for a company starting a tourism development.

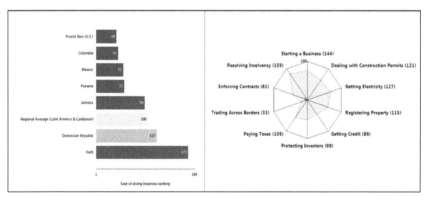

FIGURE 9.1 Ease of Doing Business in Dominican Republic
Source: The World Bank-IFC (2013).

9.2.3 MICHES AND EL SEIBO

El Seibo province is located in the northeastern of DR (Figure 9.2) and in 2010 its population was estimated at 87.680 inhabitants, of which roughly 50% lived in rural areas. The province has a land area of 1,788.4 km² and a population density of 49 inhabitants per km². It is divided into two municipalities: Miches with a population of 20,813, and Santa Cruz de El Seibo with a population estimated at 66,867 [21].

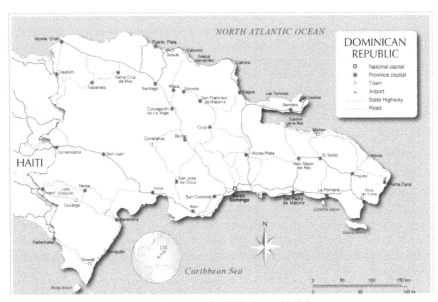

FIGURE 9.2   Dominican Republic Map with El Seibo and Miches

Source: http://www.nationsonline.org/maps/Dominican-Republic-Map.jpg.   Accessed   on February 17th, 2015.

As it is described in the 2011 Tropicalia Report, Miches is "a land of lush vegetation and fertile soil, home to cocoa, rice, and coconut production. Plentiful pastures give way to cattle-raising and its diverse ecosystem boasts wetlands, mangroves, and tropical forest. Other attractions include the natural lagoons, Laguna Redonda and Laguna Limón, whose waters filter out to the renowned Samaná Bay, a sanctuary and birthing place for the Hump Back Whale, a cetacean species famous for its acrobatic movements."

A report from the Dominican Republic's Oficina Nacional de Estadistica, cited by Tropicalia [22], indicates that 68.9% of El Seibo population lives in poverty, which includes 21% of extreme poverty. Similarly, Miches has an estimated poverty rate of 55.6%, with 9.4% in extreme poverty, well above the national average. Sixty two percent of El Seibo homes and 54.8% of Miches homes are located in rural areas. While 84% of the Miches population is literate; 29% of the heads of the household have no education and 55% have only primary education.

9.2.4 *CISNEROS AND ITS CORPORATE SOCIAL RESPONSIBILITY ACTIVITIES*

By 2013, Cisneros has gone into large organizational changes, driven by the transgenerational transition that sees Adriana Cisneros appointed as CG's CEO by her father and Chairman of the Board, Gustavo Cisneros.

For over 50 years, the CG main strategic focus has been on the entertainment industry, specializing in TV production and broadcasting. However, the group had also maintained a broad business diversification, including telecoms, beauty products, sports, education, tourism, and real estate. In 2013, Cisneros organization comprises three business divisions: Cisneros Interactive, Cisneros Media, and Cisneros Real Estate (Figure 9.3).

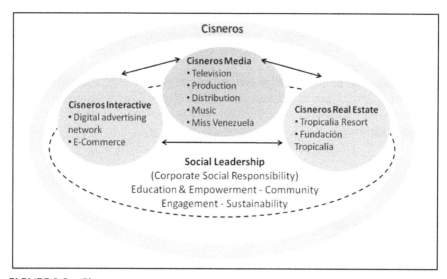

FIGURE 9.3 Cisneros
Source: Authors elaboration based upon Cisneros, 2013

CSR has always been a part of the Cisneros Family tradition, starting with philanthropic initiatives carried out since the 1970's by the Fundación Cisneros (FC). Since the very beginning, FC's mission has been to "improve education in Latin America and foster global knowledge of the region's contribution to world culture" [23]. Its most important projects have been: Patricia Phelps de Cisneros Collection (CPPC); Professional Development for School Teachers (AME); Piensa en Arte/ Think Art, and cl@se, an educational TV channel, all of which support the FC's educational mission with the ultimate vision of fostering the sustainable development of social capital in the region.

In recent years the traditional division between business strategy and the Foundation realm, started to fade out under Adriana Cisneros drives to build synergies. As Cisneros stated , it is about a "philosophy" which can be "integrated into the business strategy of all our companies, embodying a strong sense of social responsibility and providing the foundation for programs that build individual and collective human capital" [23].

9.3 TROPICALIA'S VISION AND INITIAL JOURNEY

Cisneros aspires to position Tropicalia as a model for sustainable tourism. As stated in the annual report [24], the project has a master plan of developing not only an environmentally sound hospitality structure, but a whole sustainable tourism destination in El Seibo Province in Dominican Republic. The project is conceived as a multiphase development over 30 years, expecting the opening of the first resort after 2018.

The overall design focuses on a low-density, low-impact, luxury hospitality development, which will include a boutique hotel, a well-known brand Spa, and an 18-hole golf course.

Analyzing the project timeline and milestones (Figure 9.4), the starting point can be set in 2005, when the Cisneros Family decided to buy the lands close to Miches, where they already had a family farm and a beach Palapa,[1] considered a refuge for family gatherings.

FIGURE 9.4   Tropicalia timeline and milestones

Source: Authors elaboration based upon Tropicalia reports and documents, 2013.

---

[1]Palapa is: (i) an open-sided dwelling with a thatched roof made of dried palm leaves or (ii) a structure, such as a bar or restaurant in a tropical resort, that is open-sided and thatched with palm leaves (http://www.thefreedictionary.com/palapa)

By 2007 the vision for Tropicalia began to take root and would later become the flagship project of Cisneros Real Estate, thus opening the way for this newly established business division. Concurrently, William Phelan (Vice President and General Manager of Tropicalia, and President of Fundación Tropicalia) was asked to lay the groundwork for the Fundación Tropicalia (FT), created in 2008, with the mission to design and implement community programs for stakeholders in Tropicalia's sphere of influence. Remembering the first social initiatives at that point, Phelan says: "when we arrived to Miches, we started with the traditional Fundación Cisneros education programs, such as on-line teacher training and our Think Art/Piensa en arte program before we actually created the FT with its own projects."

In 2009 a public launch of the Tropicalia project was announced at the American Chamber of Commerce in Santo Domingo, by Gustavo and Adriana Cisneros. In emphasizing their vision, Gustavo Cisneros said: "Tropicalia is expected to represent a solid balance for this beautiful country, creating profitable jobs for several generations, improving education and helping to ensure food, housing, schools, health, joy and recreation to the families of El Seibo" [25]. In that same year, Dominican Republic president, Leonel Fernández, acknowledged the relevance of Tropicalia by decreeing it a "strategic project" for the country.

Tropicalia's governance called for the creation, in 2010, of a CSR Committee (CSRC), a working group with both strategic and operational responsibilities, composed of executives from Cisneros business and or non-profit divisions, Tropicalia, and more recently the participation of representatives from Tropicalia's development partners. This board, also known as the Sustainability Committee, has the objective to "ensure a coherent strategy, maximize communications, encourage brain storming, challenge ideas and opinions, inform about Fundación Tropicalia's progress in the local community, and develop a shared vision, towards the construction phase of the project." [26]

The CSRC was also seen as a tool to "proactively guide business decisions…and continuously renew investors' confidence and our social license to operate" [26]. One of the main decisions of the CSRC, that same year, was to adopt the principles of the United Nation Global Compact (UNGC). Sofía Perazzo, Sustainability Advisor and Executive Director of Fundación Tropicalia comments on this: "thanks to our commitment to the UNGC, we began producing sustainability reports, which has resulted in a valuable communications tool for our company."

During these first years, Tropicalia also faced a twofold challenge when approaching the Dominican Republic domestic environment. On one hand they had to interact with many different local and central government regulatory agencies, in order to obtain the required environmental and operations permits. On the other hand they had to position Tropicalia's value proposition in the Miches community, communicating not only FT's commitment to the sustainable development of the region, but also find a way to empower local development initiatives so that these efforts are undertaken jointly between the foundation on the community leaders.

9.3.1 TROPICALIA'S STAKEHOLDER APPROACH

Tropicalia has undergone a thorough process of identifying individual actors and parties that may be affected by or has the power to influence the project.

The stakeholders map (Figure 9.5) reflects the complexity of Tropicalia's position inside Cisneros, and the need to consider a number of internal and external stakeholders and their demands whose urgency, legitimacy, and power can largely differ. It means that Tropicalia must take into account the different perspectives of the Cisneros family (shareholders), Cisneros business and non-profit divisions. Indeed, the CSRC, where all these parties are represented, has been an important governance tool that supports a coherent decision making process. As for external stakeholders – such as business partners, international and multilateral organizations, central and local government and Miches community, among others – given their diversity and vast scope, their potential impact on the project also adds complexity to the decision making processes taking place in the CSRC.

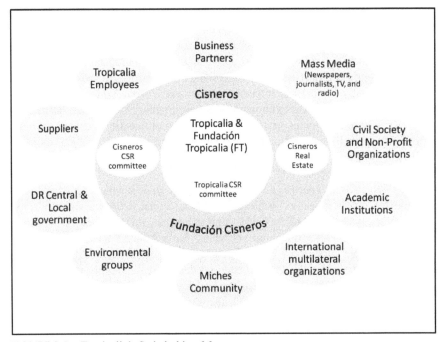

FIGURE 9.5   Tropicalia's Stakeholders Map
Source: Authors elaboration based upon Tropicalia, April 25th, 2013 and Sofía Perazzo interview (December 2, 2013).

In addition to the map, a stakeholder analysis can give a better understanding of the role, expectations and power of each actor's potential impact on Tropicalia.

Some stakeholders can be considered as dominant, some others as dependent or definitive (Table 9.3); some are classified as non-directly relevant to the project, even though they can affect the Miches community, while others have passed to a non-stakeholders group, such as potential business partners or other agents, with whom no agreement to collaborate in the Tropicalia project was reached.

Now looking inside each category it is possible to identify specific actors with different levels of power, legitimacy and urgency. The map could be even more complex by including dormant stakeholders, such as potential competitors and specific suppliers, as well as environmental groups; demanding stakeholders, like non-organized community members; dangerous stakeholders such as criminal networks, and dominants such as traditional community and local political leaders.

TABLE 9.3 Stakeholders Classification

Stakeholder	Power	Legitimacy	Urgency	Stakeholder Category
Central Government	High	High	High	Definitive
Local Government	High	High	High	Definitive
Miches community	High	High	High	Definitive
International Multilateral Organizations	Low	High	Low	Discretionary
Civil Society and NGO's	Low	High	High	Dependent
Academic institutions	Low	High	Low	Discretionary
Mass Media	High	High	Low	Dominant
Business Partners	High	High	High	Definitive
Employees	Low	High	High	Dependent

Source: Authors elaboration based upon Mitchel et al (1997).

9.3.2 TROPICALIA'S SUSTAINABILITY INITIATIVES

Fundación Tropicalia (FT) was created as the first step of Tropicalia's strategic development. Its mission is "to carry out indispensable community affairs programs in the Miches community… and to contribute to the comprehensive development and prosperity of the local community" [27]. Among initial objectives there are "the protection and restoration of the natural environment; partners and supply chain selection based on shared values, and preservation of cultural heritage."

Since its creation, Tropicalia's sustainability focus evolved from moving to a CSR and social license to operate approach, to the compliance with the UN Global Compact Ten Principles, and its incorporation as a core part of their business model.

Commenting on Tropicalia's Sustainability strategy, Perazzo says: "Tropicalia's commitment to sustainable development is two-fold, being both commercial and social, understanding the need to invest in both arenas to ensure long-term success."

When FT started to operate during the early years, it began working in the education sector bringing Fundación Cisneros' programs to local school teachers. Because the notion of Sustainable Development was the underlying theory guiding FT strategy, it initially categorized its goals under the social, environmental, and economic pillars of this theory. As FT programs grew, communicating its actions became more complex, and the organization repackaged its program areas into four distinct sectors: education, environment, productivity, and wellbeing/culture.

During their interviews, Tropicalia's managers described the sustainability initiatives, explained their motives for implementing them, clarified why or why not have they been successful, and discussed the challenges during the planning and implementing process. Annual reports, publically available reports, internal Tropicalia documents, Cisneros Group web site, and key manager's interviews were reviewed to select and prepare the initiatives' summary (Table 9.4) and timeline (Figure 9.6).

TABLE 9.4   Tropicalia's Sustainability Initiatives (2013)

Initiatives	Description
Environmental initiatives	*To promote environmental protection and civic environmental responsibility, Tropicalia and FT supports:*
Environmental impact study (EIS)	In 2009, the most robust EIS in the history of the country, involved anthropologists, archeologists, sociologists, bird experts, among others to measure the impact of Tropicalia. Investigation and Environmental impact studies to protect Wild Life Refuge Laguna Redonda and Limon (2013).
Environmental Compliance Report (ICA)	Since 2010, every six months Tropicalia submits an ICA for approval by the Ministry of Environment and Natural Resources.
Tropicalia incorporates the Inter-American Development Bank's (IDB) Sustainable Tourism Scorecard	In 2009, Tropicalia studies the IDB scorecard for sustainable tourism to ensure its considering all the aspects of sustainable tourism in the design of the project and master plan.
Costa Esmeralda Beach Rescue	Recycling and Beach Clean-up Initiatives to keep beaches adjacent to Tropicalia property limits clean. Tropicalia recycles 80% of waste collected.
Agricultural Learning Center	Agricultural Learning Center established in partnership with Estancia La Querencia (ELQ), organic certified farm, to promote best practices in the community.
Educational Initiatives	*To drive real change in the quality of education in local schools, FT implements these programs with government, NGO, and community stakeholders:*

TABLE 9.4   *(Continued)*

Initiatives	Description
Professional Development for School Teachers (AME)	Continuing professional development for primary public school teachers, in partnership with Fundación Cisneros' online education courses at www.ame.cisneros.org. Reach: 247 participants (115 of which successfully completed the program), 10 courses taught at 14 education centers.
School Renovation and Maintenance Program (PRyME)	School Renovation and Maintenance Program empowers community stakeholders to rebuild and maintain school infrastructure. Reach: 12 schools; 3,000 students; 75 teachers.
University Scholarship Program with Instituto Superior de Agricultura/ College of Agriculture (ISA) in Agricultural Sciences	ISA covers 50% of the scholarship and FT 40%, students cover 10% to give him/her a sense of responsibility for their education. Scholarship Program supports three students annually in their higher education goals and obtain a bachelor's degree in Agronomy, Natural Sciences Education, or Business Administration. Reach: 3 students per year are accepted to the program.
The League of Enterprising Farmers in Training (LEAF Program)	LEAF teaches students that farming can be profitable if done right. LEAF inspires high school students' interest in farming while teaching values and entrepreneurship skills; FT most recently partnered with Junior Achievement DR
"I'm a girl, I'm Important"	"I'm a Girl, I'm Important," an annual summer day-camp that brings girls together in a nurturing, safe environment to learn about self-esteem, career development, nutrition, exercise and safety.
Productivity initiatives	*To diversify the local economy and create opportunities for sustainable economic development, FT implements:*
Microfinance loans in partnership with "Fondo para el Desarrollo, Inc." (FONDESA)	FONDESA has vast expertise working with the banking agricultural sector; since 2008 the initiative provides access to loans. Microfinance Initiative in partnership with FONDESA. Reach: USD 2.75 million in microloans; 848 clients (39.5% female); 1,200 jobs fortified; 1,315 families benefitted. In 2014 FONDESA will benefit from the IDB/FT project by designing and launching a new financial product for project beneficiaries.
Inclusion of MSEs in the Sustainable Tourism (Tropicalia's) Supply Chain in partnership with the IDB Multilateral Investment Fund (MIF)	Inclusion of Micro and Small Enterprises (MSEs) in the Sustainable Tourism Supply Chain, in partnership with the Inter-American Development Bank's Multilateral Investment Fund, a social investment of USD 1.6 million. Reach: 300 farmers certified organic; 10 new SMEs; 10 buyer-provider contracts. http://www5.iadb.org/mif/en-us/home/news/press-releases/padominicantropicalia.aspx
Agricultural Diversification and Food Security Program in Miches in partnership with United States Agency for International Development (USAID) and the Rural Economic Diversification Program DR (REDDOM)	In 2012 USAID-REDDOM-FT worked in partnership to diversify agricultural production and promote food security in Miches via nutrition workshops. Reach: 1,580 mt2 of greenhouse infrastructure; 45 farmers trained in sustainable production; 45 women trained in health and nutrition.

TABLE 9.4   *(Continued)*

Initiatives	Description
Wellbeing and cultural Initiatives	*To promote social and cultural development in the community, FT supports:*
Copa Tropicalia	An annual baseball tournament to encourage healthy competition and recreation. Has helped position the Tropicalia/FT brand in the community and stakeholder engagement.
Artemiches' (NGO) and independent artisans	FT sponsors Artemiches' (NGO) Cultural Week. Since 2008, FT supports Artemiches one of the most important cultural NGOs working in Miches, as well as other cultural initiatives led by young artisans
Preventable diseases education and antibacterial soap distribution in schools	Since 2010, FT implements health workshops in schools and distributes antibacterial soap to raise awareness on preventable diseases, like Cholera.

Source: Authors' elaboration and quotes based on Tropicalia documents.

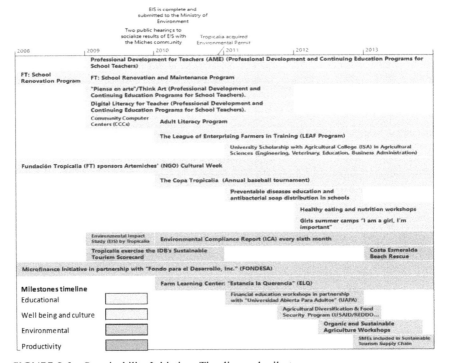

FIGURE 9.6   Sustainability Initiatives Timeline and milestones

Source: Authors' elaboration based on Tropicalia documents.

Based upon the initiatives description and the timeline, the following discussion draws out salient issues derived from the analysis.

9.3.2.1 A SUSTAINABILITY BUSINESS APPROACH GOING ALONG WITH FAMILY'S STAKES AND INTERESTS

The Cisneros Family has had ties to the Dominican Republic for nearly 50 years. Long before deciding to invest in the country, and particularly in Miches, the Family has held the Dominican Republic as a beloved place of refuge and escape.

9.3.2.2 BUILDING A BRAND AND POSITIONING A SUSTAINABILITY PROJECT

The first initiatives implemented in Miches were under the umbrella of FC, but in time the need to position Tropicalia and its own foundation was recognized. In Perazzo's words:

> "We began our social investments for sustainability in Miches, a couple of years before officially announcing the project Tropicalia. We slowly began transitioning our community programs from FC to FT, and began positioning the Tropicalia brand in the community. The Copa Tropicalia, for instance, has helped us in this effort. Along with our in-depth work in education and agriculture, gathering around the love of a national sport like baseball has had high impact in nurturing new and old friendships and partnerships."

9.3.2.3 FROM A SUPPLY-SIDE FOCUS TO A DEMAND-SIDE APPROACH

During the implementation process, FT evolved from supply driven initiatives to demand driven initiatives. As an example, the School Renovation and Maintenance Program (PRyME) considered as the FT's flagship program evolved based upon the community needs and priorities. The experience is explained by Perazzo:

> "When we arrived in Miches in 2008, we wanted to bring FC education programs to school teachers. But when we got to the schools, basic needs were more pressing. No running water, no bathrooms, unusable infrastructure abounded. So we began PRyME."

9.3.2.4   FROM A TOP-DOWN VISION TO A BOTTOM-UP IMPLEMENTATION STRATEGY

Among the educational initiatives, FT tried to implement one of the key FC's educational programs, "Think Art," but they found a gap between the social reality and their own expectations and priorities. Based on that experience, current agenda setting for initiatives has moved to a bottom-up approach, as Gustavo Román, General Coordinator of FT, explains:

> "I have a porFTolio of initiatives; this is the social offer I present. Previously, I make a survey of their needs, which is not very technical, it is just a conversation. How they are? How they feel? How many people live there? How are electricity and water services? That conversation gives me a list of needs which I can relate back to FT initiatives... Then I go to my meeting at the "long table", my superiors, and finally come back to the community..."

9.3.2.5   WORKING HAND IN HAND WITH THE GOVERNMENT

The Tropicalia experience highlights the relationships between a private enterprise and the public sector. As of 2013, FT has renovated and maintained 12 schools, but after five years developing this program, a recent public education policy has decentralized budgets for schools, enabling principals to manage their own budgets for maintenance purposes. This has allowed them to work autonomously, resolving issues that previously were attended to via the PRyME program. As Perazzo comments:

> "Thanks to a new public policy, schools now manage their own budget for minor repairs,. Today we are thinking of PRyME in terms of contributing to the 'last mile', where we can match funds with a motivated school."

9.3.2.6   LOOKING FOR STRATEGIC PARTNERS

For most of their initiatives, FT works with selected partners with which it shares the same values and commitment to socio-economic development. For instance, to implement the productivity initiatives "to diversify the local economy and create opportunities for sustainable economic development," FT works in partnership with local and multilateral institutions, such as FONDESA, Inter-American Development Bank's Multilateral Investment Fund, United States Agency for International Development, Fundación REDDOM, and the University ISA.

9.3.2.7 A MULTIPLE AND VERY COMPLEX PORFTOLIO OF SUSTAINABILITY INITIATIVES

The initiative porFTolio of FT covers a wide range of projects from educational programs including a complex effort to integrate micro and small enterprises in the value chain, under an inclusive business approach. This diversification of initiatives is explained by William Phelan:

> "When you see the Miches reality, you understand the work carried out by FT. The geographical, social, and economic conditions that people face, takes you to work and to address these social needs, in order to be a good business… I think the concept of sustainability is very broad and there are many things to do in Miches. We started to improve the social aspect, infrastructure and improvements in quality of education; that was the first step. Through improving the quality of education, we seek to attack a little the cycle of poverty and to invest in the long -term future. But we also look to the project of including small and medium enterprises in the value chain of tourism development."

9.4   PATIENT CAPITAL, IMPATIENT COMMUNITY

> "Tropicalia is a big project. We are waiting for the tourism structure to start operating. People are studying, and some are away expecting to come back and have a job in Tropicalia. Those who are now away have their homes here and they dream to come back to Miches". *José Luis, Miches community leader.*

These words confirm the urgency with which the Miches community is looking at the future of Tropicalia – mainly as a source of employment and an opportunity to grow in their own town.

However, this may clash with the long-term complexity of sustainability, which needs careful planning and calls on many players, with diverse interests, power and legitimacy. Particularly complex, has been navigating the regulatory framework in the Dominican Republic which has caused many delays, but as Phelan states: "these delays in starting the actual construction, has not always been negative, providing they gave us the opportunity to work on improving our business plans."

The time dedicated to the planning process is starting to have an impact on the business model development and appraisal. One of the main challenges Tropicalia's executives are facing is related to work out their business model, culture, and practices around sustainability concepts. This implies evolving from the current model, which has focused its sustainability efforts in the local community and the FT, to embed the sustainability strategy as more partners and employees come on board.

However, this organizational arrangement has brought positive outcomes, in terms of good will and legitimacy of Cisneros and Tropicalia, as perceived by the community. The same can be said regarding key stakeholders such as multilateral organizations and public sector as well. The creation of FT was essential to having more impact on the community and somehow to give Tropicalia more freedom to act as a business. Looking forward to an integrated organization, where sustainability is at the core of the business, William Phelan comments: "In a perfect world, I would like Tropicalia to have a Sustainability Vice President, managing one of the main business units of the company."

Among the main lesson learned during Tropicalia´s planning and implementation phase, there is the need to develop appropriate, effective, timely and sustainable initiatives through a bottom-up process, while at the same time, not fearing the dynamics of exploration, trial and error.

Fundación Tropicalia is still striving for sustainability in its programs, and faces continuous challenges related to recruiting talent, limited resources, and lack of community commitment or capability, as well as major infrastructure limitations

One of the main takeaways of the overall process experienced by Tropicalia is the need to consider people and their needs, beliefs and culture. Working in the Caribbean is not always a stroll on the beach. Centuries of "benevolent paternalism" has trained people to expect assistance and solutions from the powerful, rather than to carve out their own destiny and progress. This calls for a more assertive, although human and respectful, approach from business and social managers, who need to reinforce their empathy, honesty and humility, and become role models within the community. As Gustavo Román asserts: "Look at the fact that I live in Miches with my wife…they see me around, in the supermarket, they see me in shorts, I am here and available, I am part of the community… and it helps demystify the project.".." On the other hand, the traditional philanthropic relationship needs to be revised, as Román elaborates: "I give but I receive. To do it right you need to keep in mind that you are bringing in things but also you are taking back things. What you receive can be more relevant than what you give. It takes humility and a great deal of respect."

"Tropicalia is a business", reminds William Phelan, and at the same time it is a "social project" in the words of Sofia Perazzo. This apparent contradiction synthesizes the necessary two-fold vision of any sustainable business strategy. On one hand it calls for establishing a clear relationship between sustainability and return on investment, while measuring CSR efforts and their impact on the business. But at the same time it relies on the principles of shared value creation. Tropicalia has been working on this for five years making efforts to redesign productivity and the local value chain via economic inclusion.

As any tourism development, location is the key asset for Tropicalia, and it needs to be protected and improved. As Phelan reminds: "You need to ensure that a Tropicalia guest who would like to get out and explore the local community can do so safely, while at the same time the Miches citizen feels positively impacted by tourism." Thus, business goals can go in hand-in-hand with this so-called locational thinking, in order to create shared value. Reinforcing clusters through a comprehensive stakeholder approach and encouraging top executives, both internal and external, to agree upon common vision throughout all the phases of a business project also delivers shared value.

Finally, one must not forget that Cisneros is a family business, and as such it is influenced by the values and history of the family, who has strong beliefs as to its role in Latin American development. They also have personal feelings towards DR and Miches, a beautiful land perceived as a home away from home. To Adriana Cisneros, Miches is:

> "A place of freedom…My father taught me that the world is full of possibilities, big ideas, big projects. I have the resources, freedom and determination to continue along the path my parents began. Tropicalia is about creating the unexpected. That is the legacy of our family" [2].

9.5   DISCUSSION QUESTIONS, TEAM EXERCISES, AND ADDITIONAL READING MATERIAL

DISCUSSION QUESTIONS

1.   What are Tropicalia's main stakeholders?
2.   What is their impact on the sustainability strategy?
3.   Considering a reciprocity relationship with stakeholders, identify what are their expectations, and what Tropicalia needs from them to support its objectives.
4.   What are the main Tropicalia's sustainability initiatives?
5.   How and why did they change in time?
6.   What is the sustainability initiatives impact on shared value creation?
7.   What are the main challenges for Tropicalia future development? Why?
8.   What are the main sustainability challenges? Why?

TEAM EXERCISES

• Assuming the role of each of the main stakeholders for Tropicalia, please write down your requests and proposals for Tropicalia's Management.
• Assuming the role of Tropicalia's Management, select the most important stakeholder and write a one-page memo with your key proposals and expectations.
• Based upon the UN Global Compact principles, analyze Tropicalia's initiatives and explain how do they comply with each one of them.

- Considering Tropicalia's sustainability initiatives, analyze them under the shared value creation model.
- Compare Tropicalia's model with Stubbs and Cocklin [18] proposal of a sustainability business model (SBM). What are the main similarities and differences? What would you suggest to pursue a SBM?

ADDITIONAL READING MATERIAL

Mitchell, Ronald K.; Agle, Bradley R.; and Wood, Donna J.; "Toward a theory of stakeholder
identification and salience: Defining the principle of who and what really counts." Acad. Manag.
Rev. (October 1997), 22(4), 853–886.
Porter, M. E.; and Kramer, M. R.; "Creating Shared Value." Harvard Business School; January–
February 2011.
Stubbs, W.; and Cocklin, C.; "Conceptualizing a sustainability business model." Organization Environ. 2008, 21, 103.

WEB SITES

http://www.cisneros.com/
http://www.unglobalcompact.org/
http://www5.iadb.org/mif/en-us/home/news/pressreleases/padominicantropicalia.aspx
www.invest-indr.com/investindr/responsible-tourism/112/2
218 S ustainability, Social Responsibility, and Innovations in Tourism and Hospitality

KEYWORDS

- **Corporate social responsibility**
- **Shared value creation**
- **Stakeholders analysis**

REFERENCES

1. Forbes, 2013. http://www.forbes.com/profile/gustavo-cisneros/, accessed on December 5, **2013**.
2. Cisneros; Tropicalia, imagined by Adriana Cisneros de Griffin. Cisneros; **2012**.

3. Bowen, H. R.; Social Responsibilities of the Businessman. New York: Harper & Row; **1953**.

4. Preston, L. E.; and Post, J. E.; "Measuring corporate responsibility." *J. Gen. Manage.* **1975**, *2(3)*, 45–53.

5. Carroll, A. B.; 1999. "Corporate social responsibility; evolution of a definitional construct."*Business Soc.* September **1999**, *38(3)*, 268–295.

6. Jones, T. M.; "Corporate social responsibility revisited, redefined." *Calif. Manage. Rev.* Spring **1980**, 59–67.

7. Epstein, E. M.; "The corporate social policy process: Beyond business ethics, corporate social responsibility, and corporate social responsiveness." *Calif. Manage. Rev.* **1987**, *29*, 99-114.

8. Carroll, A. B.; "The pyramid of corporate social responsibility: Toward the moral management of organizational stakeholders." *Bus. Horiz.* July/August **1991**, *34*, 39–48.

9. Mitroff, I.; Stakeholders of the Organizational Mind. San Francisco: Jossey-Bass Publishers; Chapter 2, **1983**, 13–20.

10. Mitchell, Ronald K.; Agle, Bradley R.; and Wood, Donna J.; "Toward a theory of stakeholder identification and salience: defining the principle of who and what really counts." *Academy Manage. Rev.* (October, **1997**), *22(4)*, 853–886.

11. McWilliams, A.; and Siegel, D.; 2001. "Corporate social responsibility: a theory of the firm perspective." *Academy Manage. Rev.* **2001**, 26(1): 117–127.

12. Marsden, C.; The Role of Public Authorities in Corporate Social Responsibility. **2001,** http://www.alter.be/socialresponsibility/people/marchri/en/displayPerson (June 23, 2003).

13. Dahlsrud, Alexander, How corporate social responsibility is defined: An analysis of 37 definitions. In: Corporate Social Responsibility and Environmental Management. **2006**. Published Online in Wiley Inter Science (www.interscience.wiley.com) DOI: 10.1002/csr.132.

14. Porter, M. E.; and Kramer, M. R.; 2006. "Strategy and Society, The Link Between Competitive Advantage and Corporate Social Responsibility." Harvard Business School; December **2006**.

15. Porter, M. E.; and Kramer, M. R.; 2011. "Creating Shared Value." Harvard Business School; January–February **2011**.

16. World Commission on Environment and Development. Our Common Future. Oxford, UK: Oxford University Press; **1987**.

17. United Nation Global Compact, **2013**. www.unglobalcompact.org/abouttheGC/TheTen-Principles/index.html, accessed on November 18, **2013**.

18. Stubbs, W.; and Cocklin, C.; 2008. "Conceptualizing a sustainability business model." *Organ. Environ.* **2008**, *21*, 103.

19. Euromonitor, 2013. http://www.euromonitor.com/travel-and-tourism-in-dominican-republic/report, accessed on December 9, **2013**.

20. The World Bank-IFC, Doing Business 2014: Economy Profile: Dominican Republic. Comparing Business Regulations for Domestic Firms in 189 Economies. 11th Edition. Washington, USA: A Copublication of the World Bank and the International Finance Corporation; **2013**, 7–8.

21. Dominican Republic CENSO 2010, **2012**, 31, 44, and 59. http://www.one.gob.do/, accessed on November 20, 2013.

22. Tropicalia, 2010. Internal Report: "CSR Committee Meeting Minutes." July 9, **2010**.
23. Cisneros, 2013. http://www.cisneros.com/social-leadership. Accessed on December 4, **2013**.
24. Tropicalia, 2013. Internal Report: "Community Investment Summary." September 16, **2013**.
25. Cisneros Group, 2009. "Corporate and Social Commitment to the Dominican Republic,"presented by Gustavo Cisneros at the American Chamber of Commerce of the Dominican Republic, October 2, **2009**.
26. Cisneros Group, 2010. Tropicalia Internal Document: "Proposals for Tropicalia and Fundación Tropicalia," presented by Sofia Perazzo. March 01, **2010**.
27. Fundación Tropicalia, 2012. Sustainability Report 2011. Cisneros Group, Dominican Republic. Published on January 27, **2012**.
28. Fundación Tropicalia, 2013. Sustainability Annual Report 2012. Cisneros Group, Dominican Republic. Published on April 25, **2013**.
29. Austin, James y Coatsworth, John, 2007. "Convertir la incertidumbre en oportunidad. Las empresas y el vuelco político de América Latina hacia la Izquierda". En Perspectiva. Harvard Business Review, Edición América Latina. Febrero **2007**.
30. Beng, Geok Wee and Ivy Buche, Sustainable Tourism: Heritance Kandalama Resort of Sri Lanka, Case and Teaching Note, Publication Date: October 23, 2008, ABCC at Nanyang Tech University; **2008**.
31. Centro de Estudios Sociales y Demográficos (CESDEM) y Macro International Inc., Encuesta Demográfica y de Salud 2007. Santo Domingo, República Dominicana: CESDEM y Macro International Inc.; **2008, 46**–47.
32. Economic Intelligence Unit. Dominican Republic, Country Report, Generated on November 20, 2013. 20 Cabot Square, London E14 4QW, United Kingdom; **2013**.
33. Invest in Dominican Republic, **2011**. www.invest-indr.com/investindr/responsible-tourism/112/2, accessed on November 20, 2013.
34. Jaén, M. H.; Mogollón, D.; and y Vidal, R.; ¿Quieres cambiar tu organización? Guía práctica para conducir el cambio. Ediciones IESA; **2009**.
35. Jaén, M. H.; and y Rivas, J.; ¿Cómo se organizan las empresas para ser socialmente responsables? Revista Debates IESA; **2008**, *XIII(2)*, 54–58.
36. PAHO,   **2013**   www.paho.org/saludenlasamericas/index.php?option=com docman&task=doc_view&gid=127&Itemid=: 271-274, accessed on November 20, 2013.
37. United Nations, Global Corporate Sustainability Report. New York, USA: United Nations Global Compact Office; **2013**.
38. http://www.nationsonline.org/maps/Dominican-Republic-Map.jpg. Accessed on February 17th, 2015.

CHAPTER 10

A FRAMEWORK FOR SUSTAINABLE BUSINESS PRACTICES IN THE PRIVATE CLUB INDUSTRY

RONALD F. CICHY[1], JAEMIN CHA[2], SEUNGHYUN KIM[3], and MIRAN KIM[4]

[1]Director and Professor, 231 Eppley Center, The School of Hospitality Business, Broad College of Business, Michigan State University, East Lansing, MI 48824, 517-355-5080; E-mail: cichy@broad.msu.edu

[2]Assistant Professor, 234 Eppley Center, The School of Hospitality Business, Broad College of Business, Michigan State University, East Lansing, MI 48824, 517-884-1581, E-mail: jcha@broad.msu.edu

[3]Assistant Professor, 204 Eppley Center, The School of Hospitality Business, Broad College of Business, Michigan State University, East Lansing, MI 48824, 517-353-1928, E-mail: kimseung@broad.msu.edu

[4]Assistant Professor, 239 Eppley Center, The School of Hospitality Business, Broad College of Business, Michigan State University, East Lansing, MI 48824, 517-353-9211, E-mail: kimmi@broad.msu.edu

CONTENTS

10.1   INTRODUCTION

Private clubs are hospitality organizations where individual owners with common interests, experiences, backgrounds, and professions congregate for social and recreational purposes [1]. There are two important leaders in private club governance: nonpaid leaders (e.g., boards of directors, committee members, and other volunteers) and paid leaders (e.g., general managers, chief operating officers, department heads, and supervisors). A unique aspect of private club governance is that a private club's general manager. General Managers (GMs)/chief operating officers (COOs) collaborate closely with volunteer leaders, mainly with the board of directors and committees [2]. The board of directors represents the member owners and weighs in on important club issues such as sustainability.

Sustainability refers to "the ability of a society, ecosystem, or any such on-going system to continue functioning into the indefinite future without being forced into decline through the exhaustion or overloading and deleting of key resources on which that system depends" [3]. The term sustainability has been also used interchangeably with sustainable development, which is defined as "development that meets the needs of the present without compromising the ability of future generations to meet their own needs" by the World Commission on Environment and Development (WCED) in 1983 [4]. The definition of sustainable development has been adjusted in focus from the human being's responsibility toward future generations to the current balance of the earth's ecological systems, and the economic and sociocultural aspects were added to the definition at the United Nations Conference on Environment and Development (UNCED) in 1992 [5]. Further, the role of education that encourages values and attitudes of respect for the environment was also emphasized [6, 7, 8]. Economic sustainability means economic capital should be maintained. Social sustainability is the ability of maintaining social capital, including investments and services that create the basic framework for society. Environmental sustainability involves seeking to improve human welfare by protecting natural capital [9, 10].

According to Sloan, Joseph, and Chen [11], a sustainable hospitality business is defined as "one that manages its resources in such a way that economic, social, and environmental benefits are maximized in order to meet the need of the present generation, while protecting and enhancing opportunities for future generations" (p. 4). Both major international hospitality companies and small businesses are aware of the positive impacts in doing sustainable hospitality business on their facilities and operations [8].

Although many private clubs are showing interest in adopting sustainable business practices, there is limited understanding of what "sustainable business practices" really mean for private clubs, and how adopting sustainable practices would benefit clubs and members. It is common to find the best environmental practices in other hospitality segments, but there has been limited study to explore this topic in the private club industry [12].

10.2   STUDY OBJECTIVES

Our research into sustainable business practices (SBPs) included responses from two different studies for a total of 369 private club GMs/COOs. These two studies were a part of collaborative research projects with the Club Managers Association of America (CMAA) to identify sustainable green practices in the private club industry from the perspectives of the GMs/COOs. Furthermore, these studies also identified both benefits and challenges in adopting SBPs as well as explored who actually may push or influence private clubs to adopt the SBPs. Our research included both quantitative and qualitative approaches to analyze responses from the standardized Likert-scale and open-ended questions. To quantify content/responses, we utilized a computer-assisted content analysis program, called WordStaf from Provalis Research to run a count of word frequencies [13]. Most importantly, these analyses are the basis for the conceptualization of a new framework, consisting of management, operations, real estate, and Think Like The Owner for SBPs in private clubs. This framework is designed to have general applicability to SBPs in other segments of hospitality businesses.

10.2.1   DEFINING THE CONCEPT OF SUSTAINABILITY IN THE PRIVATE CLUB INDUSTRY

The concept of sustainability is complex, involving many different business areas and different organizational members. In defining sustainable business practices, GMs/COOs referred to words such as "recycle/reuse/renewable" most frequently, representing 15.2 percent of the comments. "Future goal/objectives/future values" and "club green initiatives/policies" were ranked second and third, representing 12.8 and 9.6 percent, respectively (Table 10.1).

TABLE 10.1   Frequency of keywords (themes) to define sustainable business practices

	Frequency	Percent[a]
1. Recycle/reuse/renewable	19	15.2
2. Future goal/objectives/future values	16	12.8
3. Club green initiatives/policies	12	9.6
4. Energy-conservation/efficiency	11	8.8
5. Water saving/waste reduction—paper, chemical	11	8.8
6. Creating staff values	11	8.8
7. Club benefits	10	8.0
8. Creating value for club members	9	7.2

TABLE 10.1   *(Continued)*

	Frequency	Percent[a]
9. Protecting environment/positive environment attitude: Less damage, reducing chemicals	8	6.4
10. Supporting community	6	4.8
11. Using green products	5	4.0
12. Natural resource use	4	3.2
13. Excellent maintenance	3	2.4
Total	125	100

Note: [a]Multiple responses, total responses are 125.

Some club members believe that sustainability includes creating opportunities for future generations to enjoy the use of the club's facilities and traditions. Sustainability is defined by other owners as doing the right things for the club members, staff, and community. A business model in place in which members participate in the long run decreases use of nonrenewable resources, gives back to the environment, or otherwise helps by decreasing the need for chemical products which damage the ecosystem.

Sustainability in a private club is a set of practices that are proven to be effective over time at building and keeping a club thriving, and doing less damage to the environment. Club members generally agree that sustainability is doing business in a manner which is good for future generations of the club and the planet earth. Clubs usually are formed with the long-term rather than the short-term in mind. For example, many private clubs have legacies that go back to their founding date, decades earlier. Long-term changes that can be maintained at a consistent level, which are mutually beneficial to both the club and community, are the core of the sustainable business practices (SBPs). Sustainability is advancement in a direction that is necessary not only for the environment but for club's own existence. Sustainability practices set the club up for future success by utilizing sound, strong business practices. These practices keep the club thriving and viable into the future.

10.2.2   PERCEIVED BENEFITS AND OBSTACLES IN ADOPTING AND IMPLEMENTING SBPS

The following two questions were asked of the GMs/COOs of private clubs:

1. At this time, what benefits/values from environmental improvements or sustainable business practices do you perceive at your club?
2. What obstacles to adopting and implementing sustainable business practices do you perceive at your club?

In terms of perceived benefits and values from environmental improvements (Table 10.2), cost savings were ranked the first, as expected, representing 27.5 percent. Most interestingly, sense of pride or member loyalty was ranked the second, representing 16.7 percent, which was even higher than improving energy efficiency (11.7%).

TABLE 10.2 Perceived benefits/values from adopting sustainable business practices

Benefits/Values	Frequency	Percent[a]
Cost savings—save money	33	27.5
Sense of pride—increased member awareness—member loyalty	20	16.7
Energy efficiency	14	11.7
Membership sales—promote club awareness/club image—public relations	14	11.7
Water conservation—water restriction	12	10.0
More recycling	10	8.3
Healthier and safe environment	8	6.7
Waste reduction—less waste cost	7	5.8
For the community	2	1.7
Total	120	100

Note: [a]Multiple responses, total responses are 128.

In terms of obstacles in adopting and implementing SBPs (shown in Table 10.3), close to 44 percent of GMs/COOs identified costs (costs for change, conversion, creating programs, and new technology) as the top challenge. Member resistance to change and staff training/staff knowledge was ranked as the second and third challenges, representing 21.9 and 19 percent, respectively. Our research shows that "cost" seems a highly important issue for GMs/COOs.

TABLE 10.3 Perceived obstacles from adopting sustainable business practices

Obstacles	Frequency	Percent[a]
Cost for change, conversion, creating program, new technology	46	43.8
Member resistant to change	23	21.9
Staff training/staff knowledge	20	19.0
Time	5	4.8
Lack of membership growth	4	3.8
Space	4	3.8
Limited accessibility	3	2.9
Total	120	100

Note: [a]Multiple responses, total responses are 120.

10.2.3 INTEGRATED FRAMEWORK FOR SUSTAINABILITY

Sustainability in a private club may be characterized in a variety of ways. Sustainability has been presented in a variety of frameworks for hospitality businesses. What makes our framework unique is the identification of Management, Operations, Real Estate, and Think Like The Owner as an integrated framework for sustainability in private clubs and perhaps other hospitality business (see Figure 10.1).

While management and operations are directly related to the day-to-day practices and outcomes achieved, strategic ties to real estate and Think Like The Owner help to realize these results in the longer term. Management includes the "ing" parts of effectiveness beginning with planning and continuing through evaluating and then planning again, in a continuous cycle of improvement [14].

Real Estate	Think Like The Owner
Management	Operations

FIGURE 10.1   A new framework for sustainability

First element, management is focused on improving operations, the melding of resources—members, staff, paid, volunteer, financial, facilities—to add value. Value emerges through innovation that is a transformation from where the resources are today to an enhanced state of resources in the future.

Second element, operations must necessarily be process-driven with improvement resulting from ongoing analysis and change in the process. Sometimes a process can be dramatically improved, other times the improvements are small incremental improvements. In either case, operation improvements in SBPs are essential if a private club is to reach its goals.

Real estate, the third element of our framework, encompasses all the physical assets that make the private club most unique—land, club house, golf buildings, golf course, natural resources, and more. Real estate is a collection of assets that must be improved each day in the form of preventive care and maintenance, as well as in the long term.

Think Like The Owner is the fourth element of our framework. Owners are the core of a private club since the members each own a stake in the enterprise. The letters are deliberately capitalized in Think Like The Owner because this results in better management and improved operations, as well as adding value to real estate.

10.2.4 WHY PRIVATE CLUBS?

Private clubs are distinctive, honor legacies and traditions, and are challenged to innovate to improve performance and protect the planet at the same time. Private clubs increasingly are being pushed by their member owners to evolve and be current, while honoring decades, and sometimes centuries, of traditions [15]. When it comes to SBPs, private clubs which are innovative recognize that it is the member owners that are the club; a club is owned in part by each person; each member who has joined, been accepted, and continues to pay monthly dues is an owner of the organization. It is Think Like The Owner that represents the collective owner in that specific private club.

Because the owners, the members, act through committees, and boards of directors in private clubs, investment in sustainable practices is determined, in large part, based on the return on the investment in the practice by the committees and/or board. This is also true for capital expenditures where the board and sometimes the relevant committee act on behalf of the other owners. Our study asked a question about who may push the private club to decide to adopt sustainable business practices. According to our study findings, executive (senior) management, board of directors, and club members are the most influential in adopting SBPs, as presented in Table 10.4.

TABLE 10.4 Influence from others: Who may push to decide to adopt SBPs?

	Mean[a]
Executive or senior management	4.36
Board of directors	4.25
Club members	3.81
Staff members	3.79
Community in which our club is located	3.6
Governmental organizations	3.73
Club Managers Association of America (CMAA)	3.3
Environmental groups (or public or social groups)	3.12

Note: [a]Mean scores are based on a scale of 5 = very influential to 1 = not very influential.

Private clubs may be viewed through a new framework of sustainability and eco-innovation by sorting green philosophes and practices into four main categories: Management, operations, real estate, and Think Like The Owner. This integrated framework of private club SBPs explains the unique character of these organizations as well as practices to better satisfy the three Ps: people, planet, and profit. Profit in a private club is often referred to as a surplus of revenues (e.g., membership dues, initiation fees, F&B revenues) over expenses (e.g., cost of sports activities, operating expenses, fixed charges) [16].

Private club members are more attached to their own clubs, compared to customers in other segments of the hospitality industry, because of the selective nature of membership. Today's club members are highly interested in understanding their club's brand image, and "green" initiatives certainly can play an important role of repositioning the club's overall value proposition. Given the members' sense of pride in belonging to a particular club, private clubs have found opportunities to make themselves more Green by adopting various SBPs.

10.2.5   MANAGEMENT OF SUSTAINABILITY

Management comes from the Latin word *"manos"* which means "hand." Managers are hands of the owners as they exercise their fiduciary responsibilities to nurture and build the private club. Managers are not owners in a private club, yet they work closely with volunteer members who represent the general ownership (i.e., membership) group on various committees and the private club's board of directors.

Club managers are charged with maintaining the club's standards and exceeding the club's members' expectations. Facilities have to be managed in such a way that the value of these assets improves over time. Managers develop SBPs as a means of being a good corporate steward that is being able to 1 day pass on the club with enhanced value to future member owners.

Managers in clubs are responsible for circulating information to members and staff about SBPs. Once the club's sustainability efforts are recognized and understood by most staff and members, the results will be seen as benefiting all. Increasingly, the club website is utilized to provide sustainability information and resulting achievements.

"Sustainable practices are business practices that help define your club's image relating to environmental issues and are supported by your membership."—a Private Club GM/COO

Managers recognize that they must encourage their department heads to be champions of sustainability in the practices that the club has to contribute its share to the planet. Department heads use the practices to train staff in the "knowing" and the "doing of" sustainability. Managers set the standards for the levels that all should and want to follow. Managers do so through their own experiences and an understanding of the sustainability directions the club's members and board of directors seek.

Sustainability many times has a positive effect on staff in addition to members. Staff sees their efforts to protect the planet and feel as they are people who are contributing their part to the effort. It is through their actions that staff delivers on the club's sustainability promises. Staff training and understanding of the shared vision for sustainability, tied to written sustainability goals that are SMARTER, ensures achievement of the planned results.

SMARTER goals are specific, measurable, attainable, reasonably high, timely, evaluated, and reevaluated [17]. A specific sustainability goal is to achieve alignment with the private club's sustainability goal to have all members of the club's management team agree that the goals are worth the effort and will improve the club for its owners. A measurable goal is to be in the top 25 percent regarding sustainability results in the "clubs of the South." An attainable goal is to develop a written mission and vision for the private club including a statement about the club's sustainability practices. A reasonably high goal for a Northern area club is to implement a set of sustainable practices for the golf course by the time the course reopens next season.

A timely goal is to evaluate and make a recommendation about the potential for solar and wind energy to power the clubhouse by the end of summer. An evaluated goal is to calculate the costs and savings of the old, current system for operating the golf course vs. the costs and savings to convert the course to meet a list of sustainable practices.

Once the listing is developed, management will review the list with the volunteer leadership and jointly decide on a course of action. A reevaluated goal might include an ongoing calculation and conversation about the costs vs. the value of sustainable practices in the clubhouse.

The management cycle (please see Figure 10.2) presents a process for a manager to innovate. Over the decades, while the identifiers of the cycle components have remained reasonable constant, the meaning behind each has evolved and can be applied to SBPs in a private club.

Planning is short term and long term. Generally top management and unpaid boards and committees are responsible for planning in a private club. Usually the board of directors plans more at the strategic levels, and committees plan at the operating levels. Both levels are integrated so they are aligned and mutually contribute to the goals. Once plans are put into place, SMARTER goals that are monitored and recorded by managers are developed.

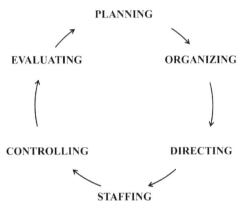

FIGURE 10.2   The management cycle [14]

Organizing is a set of activities that orient the resources (people, facilities, equipment, dollars) toward realizing the desired outcomes that is the SMARTER goals. Organizational charts are a tool for management to show the formal reporting relationships in an organization. The informal relations are very important as well because they represent a shared vision across the club.

Directing is a manager's use of human resources scheduling, product production scheduling, equipment usage procedures, standard recipes and portion sizes, and standard purchasing procedures, among others. Directing necessarily includes staff development and retention.

Staffing begins with a written position description. Attraction of talented staff often makes the difference between a club that is thriving and another that is struggling to stay in business. Staff members are selected, rather than hired. They are staff or associates, not employees. They are the key to exceeding members' expectations, because it is the staff who create and deliver products, services, and experiences for the owners, the club members.

Controlling is management's responsibility that management hopes to give to each member of the staff. Each staff member should be in control of achieving the goals. By understanding what it is that is worthwhile that particular staff member does, the staff member can control her or his own behavior and response to helping to make the club's mission and vision come alive for the owners, as well as other staff.

Evaluating ends the cycle and the cycle begins again with planning. Each time the cycle begins; there is more information available to evaluate the effectiveness of the sustainability plans and practices. This measuring stick evaluates where it currently is and provides needed information for where it might go.

Private club managers are challenged to be catalysts for innovation. Innovation often stems from curiosity about the possibility for the future. Curious managers search for understanding with veracity and tenacity. The steps toward sustainability innovation begin with the truth, the truth about the present and the truth about where the club is going. Once the truth is understood, it takes persistence, stick-to-itiveness, and the contributions of as many staff and owners as possible, because the power of innovation comes from the shared commitment of the people.

Since this management cycle was conceptualized, leading has been added to the cycle. Some believe leading begins the cycle just before planning. Other would insert leading in the middle of the cycle. In any case, leading includes several practices: knowing self, leading self, knowing others, leading others, and leading change, innovations and continuous improvement (CI).

10.2.6   SUSTAINABILITY IN OPERATIONS

Operations in a hospitality business, and particularly a private club, have as its core managing for quality. Managing for quality considers three various sets of expectations: staff, members, owners/investors, which could be thought of as a triangle. The staff, the first angle of the triangle includes full-time, part-time, everyone from an hourly position to the GM/COO position. Categorizing them all as staff highlights the belief that no position is unimportant when managing for quality and utilizing SBPs. Staff must be recruited, selected, oriented and initially training. This is followed by ongoing training, coaching, and evaluation.

The second angle of the triangle references the owners, the members, those who have purchased a stake in the private club during initiation and those who have ongoing monthly dues for membership and products and services. The owners are the club members who voluntarily gather together to be in an organization whose operations meet or exceed the members' expectations in a positively delightful way, so the recipient of this "hospitality magnum" is reaffirmed for his or her desire to join the club. The third angle of the triangle could be pictured as the community in which the club operates.

Operations vary from club to club. Most private clubs have a golf course. The golf course and its structure, golf course maintenance and improvement, are an important part of operations. Food and beverage (F&B) operations may include an *a la carte* restaurant, banquet and catering facilities, pool-side food and beverage, and more. Operations are best managed by looking at each area and writing a process flow from beginning to end. For example, in a F&B operation, the process begins with menu planning, then purchasing, receiving, storing, issuing, preparing, and serving. This is the F&B process. When mistakes happen in F&B, it is critical that managers examine the process steps for areas to be improved. This written, disciplined problem solving is the key to operations delivering on what is promised to members.

The selection of an operation's (i.e., F&B, rooms, golf, marina, fitness facilities) suppliers who are eco-environmental can assist the manager of the operations with products and procedures that will, for example, clean a room but also be friendly to the ecosystem in terms of low or no pollution.

Suppliers today are more often local suppliers than in the past. Each vendor in a local purchasing situation can better understand the product needs and recommend a product that will work yet not damage the planet. In addition to golf course pesticides, this would also include a local vegetable grower. Different questions are asked of suppliers depending upon the unique needs of that particular club operation.

Members are attracted to private clubs, in part, because the other members share similar values and participating in similar activities preferably together. Member attraction is a critical focus each day, as is member retention. Members are attracted by the level of services, products, and experiences provided by their club. As owners, members have the right to request that operations evaluate and continuously improve (CI) to make the member experience more memorable.

Retention of members is based on the belief that it is easier, more effective, and less costly to keep a member than it is to recruit a new member. Member retention is based on the perceptions of these owners as to their satisfaction and delight. Satisfaction is the minimum as unsatisfactory operations are not acceptable by member owners. It is better to go for the maximum and retain members by delighting them. One of the components of delightful operations, and, thus retention of members, is the process for welcoming members and their guests when they arrive in the dining room. Here are some suggestions: employees should smile often, use the member's name, and make the member feel welcome and special, and thank the member for utilizing their club.

"SBPs are a marketing opportunity because they increase pride and membership attraction and retention. SBPs are a unique aspect of the club that separate us from the competition. There is also a potential reduction in operating costs."—Private Club GM/COO

SBPs in operations, according to our study, fall into five categories: (1) chemicals, (2) energy, (3) environment, (4) water, and (5) work procedures. Chemicals are specific to areas and to applications and usage. Chemicals should cause no harm and leave little or no trace in the environment. Energy conservation and recycling are very helpful contributors as SBPs. Some clubs do regular energy audits to find ways to improve the operations and waste less or save more energy. The environment concern is that SBPs must stand the test of time and across the operations of the club. By doing so, the environment of the community in which the club is located also improves.

Water conservation is a very important sustainability practice particularly when a private club is located in a desert (e.g., Tucson, AZ). Golf courses can use vast amounts of water in their irrigation systems. This operation of the club should be the responsibility of a golf professional with knowledge in turf management and eco-environmental practices.

Work procedures begin with training management, supervisors, and staff members how to follow each written process in each area of the operations. Training takes place after orientation and is not a one-time occurrence. Rather, training and coaching are ongoing and vital to the continued development of each individual at all levels of the private club. Training is designed, in part, to foster understanding of work procedures, practices, and standards. When a staff member understands and puts into practice standards based on members' expectations, the operations and its component systems, deliver on the promise to the owner.

Selection of staff members is different from hiring employees. Selection begins with an up-to-date written position description of the skills, knowledge and attitudes (KSAs) of the individual who will be selected to be in that particular position. Once the description is developed, hopefully with input from those who are currently in the position and performing famously well, and then it can be posted and advertised. Selection cannot take place unless there is a pool of candidates from which to choose.

Training is in service of process improvement, a daily goal in operations in hospitality businesses. Without training, there is no understanding about how each individual can contribute to the overall shared vision of the private club. Training starts with values, the values of the trainee and the values of the club. We are seeking alignment of the majority of the person's values with the values of the club. Values are the rocks, the foundations, and the platform upon which all else is built. Understand employee values and club's values and, if there is alignment of the majority of values, an individual will never work another day in his or her life. Rather, the manager will go each day to the club where she or he can live into personal and club values like a melodious chord of musical notes. That is, in harmonious alignment.

Following a discussion of values, training must proceed to explaining the club's mission (its purpose, its distinctive source of value added to the planet) and its vision (what the club members want to create). Values, mission, and vision in writing, but more importantly in action by those who are in positions to make these come alive, are the starting point of a training program that seeks learners' understanding and ability to deliver with the right behaviors and actions.

Someone once wrote: "*What gets rewarded gets done.*" Rewards for behaviors that advance the mission of a private club, and improve its processes and various operations are utilized to call out actions that are vital to the club's operations sustainability goals. Some staff members prefer to be recognized one-on-one with a simple "THANK YOU" and a handshake and that is enough. Others clamor for recognition among peers for a task well done. It is important for the manager to come to know each individual so the recognition that achiever is given is personalized and makes the recognition even more meaningful and special.

Individual recognition is needed. Those who are achieving sustainability goals on their own are to be applauded. So, too, teams of staff who are perhaps cross-functional (i.e., from different areas—golf course, club house, kitchen, dining room), usually are able to improve operations processes more effectively since they see the needed improvements from a variety of vantage points in the club. To refer to one operation in a private club oversimplifies the interdependence that all operations have, for example, the irrigation system with the sewage system on a golf course. The interdependence sometimes makes the analysis and identification of improvements more complex and takes greater time to solve.

The interdependence of systems within operations would speak in favor of cross-functional teams to continuously improve operations. Improvement ideas that come from staff usually are better thought out because staff are the ones creating and delivering the products, services, and experiences. They are at the point of interaction in an interpersonal way with the members and with each other.

10.2.7   REAL ESTATE

As one might expect, the real estate varies by club type, location, and members' needs. Some golf clubs are rimmed with condos and private residences that form a community. Yacht clubs have marinas and may have buildings on-site to service their members' ships. Athletic clubs consider indoor real estate when deciding where to place workout equipment, and may also have outdoor facilities such as pools and tennis courts. A social club in a metropolitan area likely will be multistory real estate due to the land cost in such a prime location.

"In our club, water, energy, and clubhouse in general are most in need of established sustainable business practices (SBPs). Working with local, regional, and national agencies is helping to develop such programs. A commitment from members and staff is also required."—Private Club GM/COO

The club house is an asset owned by the members. Energy cost savings in the club house are good for Mother Earth as well as the community. Members who live in the community will have reinforced that their club is doing something for the environment locally, and thereby linking with those who are using similar practices (e.g., sustainable selection and application of herbicides, pesticides) around the globe.

The golf course practices of water conservation, caring for the environment when applying chemicals, and maintaining the course are SBPs. Golf course drainage as well as improvements of the asset over time are usually led by the golf committee, a group of volunteer leaders who are also owner members in the club.

Other athletic facilities can range from very small fitness centers, to spas, to fitness centers with a full staff of trainers, exercise class instructors, and a pool facility. Each of these has defined operations that the manager utilizes to enhance the value of the real estate today and into the future for the owners.

Landscape around the grounds of a private club adds to the enjoyment through an ambiance that must be created. Once again, there are a series of operations: for example, plant care, tree care, annual flower planting and care, perennial flower planting, and more. Tree care is based on the type of tree, the soil in which it is planted, and the watering and nutrients required to keep the tree healthy and thriving. Just like a legacy of generations of a family who are members of a private club, a tree can grow over generations and provide enjoyment for decades or centuries if there is an operation for tree care in the club.

More clubs are moving toward nurturing the natural environment and the ecosystem(s) present. The benefit is at least two fold: native natural plants and trees and ground cover tend to thrive when cared for in the soil in which they were "born," and the operation shows that the club is trying to be environmentally friendly. Some say that the long-term environmental benefits need to be identified relative to the cost savings or expense for the practice.

One club has joined focus with the National Audubon Society and has installed duck houses and houses for other native birds on specific areas of the golf course. This same club also created butterfly gardens, most popular with the members' children. The third visible environmental design was to plant fresh herbs so the chefs can harvest and use these herbs in food preparation.

Ecosystems are fragile in some locations. They require a dedicated commitment by the club and the community to protect them. One club helps its local community by maintaining nearby public parks for use by the community. This same club does not apply fertilizer chemicals on the grass or the grounds, even though it is not a golf club. Rather the club uses eco-environmental applications to not damage the planet. Being a good environmental steward for the golf course and other natural real estate protects the ecosystem and enhances the long-range value for the owners. Some clubs have a written commitment to being environmentally friendly and protecting the ecosystem; these clubs tend to do a much better job with sustainability practices than those who do not have such SBPs in place.

The community is likely the source for new members. Existing members may also live in the community. In both cases, the owners of the real estate are more frequently in the club than owners of equity stock in, say, Marriott International. The latter are passive owners. Club members are onsite owners who tend to utilize their clubs more frequently.

SBPs are right for the community, staff, and members. Local municipalities' taxes continue to rise because of EPA, and other issues. Long-term energy deregulation had a negative effect as club budgets driving money away from capital improvements, maintenance of real estate assets, and repairs.

Working with local, regional, and national agencies to develop a sustainability program for the club makes a lot of sense. Also, suppliers are usually quite knowledgeable, and have experts on staff, who can coach a club on practices and products to use. Community good citizenship is important even though environmental practices sometimes are not attractive in the short-term because of the costs and, simply put, because staff, just as other people, sometimes resist change and innovation. Community interaction to develop environmental practices to implement today and continue to improve over the long-term is essential. Every decision in the club, whether it is an investment or an operations practice, has a link to environmental friendliness in the community.

Environmental organizations are local, state, regional, and national. These resources can assist with the development of sustainable management, operations, and real estate practices that provide a cleaner, safer, and a healthier work environment. The organizations can also provide recommendations for the club to reduce the carbon footprint. Joining forces with an environmental organization can sometimes lead to media interest. Media exposure in a positive way for a club's sustainable management operations and real estate practices results in being placed in front of prospective members who may share similar environmental values and then take little convincing to join the club. Working with environmental organizations also helps ensure that the club is up on the latest techniques and practices. For current members who feel a need to emphasize sustainability at the club they own, these efforts will result in member pride for what their club is doing for the community and for the environment.

10.2.8 THINK LIKE THE OWNER

Think Like The Owner issues a challenge to management. The charge is to view management utilizing operations to enhance the value of the real estate both now and in the future. Think Like The Owner is a responsibility that is accepted by managers who do not necessarily intend to create and own a new hospitality business. Rather, they manage and operate the one they have fiduciary responsibility for by understanding, thinking, and acting like the owner members.

The owners in a private club are the club members who are represented by the club's board of director and committees. These assemblies of owners are charged, along with the GM/COO and the other paid leaders, to create the member experience for the various demographics of membership while being fiscally responsible as fiduciaries. These actions create value and member retention, as well as sustainability and stability for both club members and club staff.

Think Like The Owner in terms of sustainability is a series of business practices that help define the club's image relative to environmental issues. These must be supported by member owners. The practices in a private club relate to the long-term. Clubs are a rare segment of hospitality with long legacies of operations and generations of family members participating in "their" club over the decades. Sustainability makes sense from the standpoint of the owner because the SBPs are not only good for the club environment, they help the club reach its planned levels of sustainability objectives and assist the club in lasting long into the future.

"Sustainable practices create opportunities for the future generations to have the use of our facility and traditions."—Private Club GM/COO

Sustainability practices, if known by members, have the ability to enhance member relations, satisfaction, and delight. Additionally, for those staff members who are personally committed to eco-environment behaviors, the sustainability practices at the club where they are employed help the staff realize their own personal missions regarding sustainability, in whole or in part. This alignment strengthens the club's shared sustainability vision and the commitment that all staff and managers and volunteers (owners) will work together to become more sustainable whenever possible regardless of the costs. Now that is member-driven Think Like The Owner behavior!

Boards of directors are charged with the governance of their club. Boards in clubs help by monitoring policies and rules with consistency and longevity. Boards adopt practices that are current and recognizable to the members, staff, and managers. As members of the board, the only way that a sustainability plan will work is if these volunteer leaders endorse, promote, and communicate the plan to others and the staff, management team, and other owners. Boards of directors are fiduciaries of their clubs; they are also stewards of the environment in the communities in which they operate.

Some clubs have sustainability committees who help the paid managers and staff with golf course, club house, tennis, fitness, pool, and F&B operations by implementing SBPs in a country club. The practices must be beneficial to the owners, staff, club, real estate, and environment both financially and physically. A sustainability committee could study water usage rates, energy savings possibilities, paper and plastic recycling, and chemical selection and usage both inside the facilities and on the grounds of the club. The committee could examine the costs and compare them to the benefits of the sustainable actions.

The goal is not to just save money. It is to show owners that sustainability matters and the club members care about the environment today and for future generations. Clubs are managed by a team of senior managers, department heads, supervisors, and the GM/COO. This team is expected to advance the club's sustainability commitment. This team of owners in consultation with the other club owners could decide to provide future capital improvements regardless of economic downturns via an investment that yields an annual spendable amount for CAPEX projects. Dues increase and/or capital fund monthly assessments may also be necessary to fund the sustainability goals. No pun intended, but sustainable practices are not sustainable without the financial, emotional, managerial, and operational resources allocated by the team of senior managers and the GM/COO. This, of course, is done with owner approval but it is management typically that prepares and presents the sustainability plan to the board of directors for approval.

Innovation in sustainable practices is the hallmark of private club leaders who Think Like The Owner and also lead in their communities. Innovation continues when the club's members, staff, and managers feel the sense of worth and value for sustainable efforts. In addition, there are cost savings that go beyond the community goodwill of green practices, and member acceptance of eco-environmental operations. The owners are thinking like good stewards of planet Earth, good stewards of the environment, and fiduciaries of the club.

Innovation comes about via sustainability in the ways that the image and brand of the club are viewed by community members, owner members, and prospective members. To innovate, people have to be willing to change beginning with the mindset that sustainability does not cost as much as it pays. And the payoff is now as well as into the future.

Innovation takes consistent efforts on the part of managers, staff, and members. It may require reengineering facilities and other components (e.g., golf course) of the real estate. Innovation is an education process for all. The more innovation takes place, the more likely it will continue to take place if it is an important element of the private club.

In closing, Think Like The Owner includes many characteristics that we have identified over the years. It is this "collective" owner that a private club represents [18]. The list includes:

(i)   Accounting
(ii)   Fiduciary
(iii)   Finance
(iv)   Global (in international members and locations)
(v)   Human Resources
(vi)   Information Systems
(vii)   Management
(viii) Marketing
(ix)   Operations
(x)   Real Estate
(xi)   Relationships
(xii)   Service
(xiii) Strategy

10.2.9   GOLF ENVIRONMENTAL ORGANIZATION (GEO)

The Club Managers Association of American (CMAA), a professional association for general managers and chief operating officers (COOs) of membership clubs, has in the past endorsed the Golf Environmental Organization (GEO) certification [19]. GEO certification is an international eco-label verifying credible eco-minded golf clubs by conducting several evaluation procedures [20]. GEO certification sets golf sustainability standards, which consist of six themes: (1) nature, (2) water, (3) energy, (4) supply chain, (5) pollution control, and (6) community. Its standards have been created through collective knowledge and experience of sustainability related to golf courses in academic, research, government, nongovernmental organization (NGO), and practitioner input in order to have a wider understanding of sustainability and apply the knowledge across the industry. Obtaining GEO certification is based on three procedures: (1) standard-setting; (2) recertification and monitoring; and (3) evaluation.

Once a golf club has decided to be evaluated, a standard development step initiates the process and consultants conduct the review following International Social and Environment Accreditation and Labelling (ISEAL) Alliance code. ISEAL is the global organization committed to defining credibility in sustainability standards. After a standard has been set, the club is under GEO's standard monitoring. In this process, there are five major elements covered: participation in the program (registration and certification), checking club performance, on-site visits, reviewing, and reports, Determination process for award by ensuring all the criteria are met, oversight of the verifier network, and industry support. Even if golf clubs are certified, the evaluation procedure is completed every 3 years from the date of its approval. Each evaluation assesses that the club continues to implement and utilize the standards since it had been certified. Evaluation is divided into steps of scoping, review and consultation, information and data requirements, standard evaluation report, and approval and publication [20].

With the high interest in SBPs issues and GEO certification in eco-friendly golf clubs, country clubs with golf clubs are pushing to adopt the GEO certification to be nationally and internationally recognized as a leader. One of the golf clubs that successfully adopted GEO certification is Mirimichi, Tennessee. This property is the first golf course to become GEO certified in the United States. The certification signifies Mirimichi has met all comprehensive and advance sustainability criteria, and applies the standards to manage and operate the real estate. It shows the club's efforts in order to maximize resource efficiency, reduce waste, and conserve cultural heritage and landscapes [21].

10.3   CONCLUSION

This book chapter described two collaborative research projects with the CMAA to explore SBPs in the private club industry from the perspectives of the GMs/COOs. These two studies also helped identify both benefits and challenges in adopting SBPs, as well as explored who actually may push or influence private clubs to adopt the SBPS, based on both qualitative and quantitative approaches. So where does the pressure come from to implement sustainable practices in a private club? In our study, we asked that question and 24 percent of the GMs/COOs who responded told us that there was no pressure to become more sustainable in their private clubs. This percentage will likely decline in the future; that is, there will be a greater push to adopt SBPs. Pressure to innovate in sustainable ways may come from local/city regulations, owner members, the community, environmental agencies, the general public, government, the sustainability or eco-environment committee, the board of directors, staff, and/or management. Sustainable practices set the club up for future success by implementing sound practices that fit with the club house, golf house, golf course, food and beverage, fitness facilities, and other such services offered to members. Sustainable practices help the club thrive to be more viable in the future. This creates opportunities for future generations to have use of the club.

Qualitative responses and our analyses also contributed to developing the new framework, consisting of management, operations, real estate, and Think Like The Owner for SBPs in private clubs. Management of SBPs requires shared information among member owners and staff members. This information prompts the implementation of SBPs for the good of the environment, the private club, its owner members, and staff. SBPs in operations encourage the attraction of new members because they clearly show the organization's commitment to sustainable practices. Operations and SBPs are intimately linked because the practices are specific to the club house, golf course, and other areas of operations.

In terms of retention of members, there is pride in having their club be sustainable. They retain members and communicate to the community that the SBPs are in place. SBPs that impact today's and the long-term value of the club's real estate are helped along by suppliers who have knowledge of the unique needs and goals regarding sustainability for that particular private club. Real estate values contribute to the overall image in the community in which the members live, specifically the financial value of the property/assets of the club. The Owner is the aggregation of all the member owners in the club. The Owner looks out for the future not only of the club but of planet earth. The Owner is a steward of the club's operations and real estate and as such the totality of effort represents in SBPs.

Clubs that have a sustainability model in place, focused on the long run and decreases in the usage of nonrenewable resources, give back to the environment, and otherwise help by decreasing the usage of damaging chemicals. But this is not as supremely necessary for the environment as it is for the clubs' long-term viability and existence. Sustainability behavior may be first and foremost for the preservation of planet Earth, but additionally there is a sense of pride in the ownership, management, staff, and community. This is a positive way to approach management, operations, real estate, and Think Like The Owner in a private club. This integrated framework is likely to have general applicability to SBPS in other segments of hospitality businesses.

10.3.1   CLASS DISCUSSION QUESTIONS FOR BOOK CHAPTER (PRIVATE CLUB)

Question 1: In all the ways in which sustainability can be defined, what common thread applies to all segments of hospitality businesses? Alternatively, what unique aspect of sustainability would apply to the private club industry?

Question 2: How should a club reposition itself and improve its image in the community by adopting sustainable business practices (SBP)?

Question 3: Given the structure of private club governance, what are the roles of GMs/COOs in initiating and adopting SBPs? How are their roles similar to, or different from, volunteer leaders such as directors and committee members? In formulating your response, consider the management cycle discussed in this chapter: Planning, organizing, directing, staffing, controlling, and evaluating.

Question 4: What would be *your* concerns in implementing SBPs, if you were a staff member at a private club which had not implemented such practices? What kinds of support and resources would be necessary for management and the owner to involve staff in successful SBPs implementation?

Question 5: This chapter explores benefits and obstacles in adopting and implementing SBPs in clubs, as perceived by *paid management* (GMs and COOs). How would *staff members'* perceptions of benefits and obstacles be different?

Question 6: Focusing on Think Like The Owner improves management and operations, as well as adds value to the real estate. How do you integrate together to promote SBPs in private clubs?

Question 7: How do GMs, COOs integrate "Management, Think Like The Owner, Real Estate, and Operations"?

10.3.2 FURTHER SUGGESTIONS—CLASS EXERCISE ACTIVITIES

1. Arrange a field trip to local private clubs to see their SBPs.
2. Divide students into four teams; ask each team to develop action plans to execute SBPs for each of four aspects of integrated framework for sustainability. Categorize into Management, Think Like The Owner, Real Estate, Operations, then develop action plan with SMARTER goals to improve SBPs.
3. Have students visit the Golf Environment Organization (GEO) website at www.golfenvironment.org, and review GEO certification's guidelines and criteria.
4. Ask students to develop sustainable training programs and marketing strategies, which can be helpful for overcoming perceived obstacles from adopting SBPs.
5. Have students make a list by working in groups on how a club would communicate and implement SBP with club members who may have limited understanding about SBPs.
6. Ask students to do a role-playing about how a club would communicate and collaborate with club members who may have limited understanding in implementing SBPs.

7. Share with students some examples of private clubs that successfully adopted SBPs and ask students to discuss how these clubs executed SBPs from the management, operations, real estate, and Think Like The Owner perspectives.

SUGGESTED FURTHER READINGS

Cha, J. M.; Kim, S.; Cichy, R. F.; Kim, M.; and Tkach, J.; General Managers' and Chief Operating Officers' Evaluations of Private Club Boards of Directors. *Int. J. Hospit. Manage.* **2013,** *32(1),* 245–253.

Cichy, R. F.; Singerling, J. B.; Kim, S.; Cha, J.; Kim, M.; and Tkach, J.; Financial performance linked to board size and involvement in strategy. *Club Manage.* **2013,** 74.

Cichy, R. F.; Cha, J. M.; and Kim, S.; Private club leaders' emotional intelligence: Development and validation of a new measure of emotional intelligence. *J. Hospit. Tourism Res.* **2007,** *31(1),* 39–55.

Cichy, R. F.; Kim, M. R.; Cha, J. M.; and Kim, S. H.; GMs and COOs evaluations of green practices in their private clubs. *Board Room.* (May/June 2013), *17,* 36.

Cichy, R. F.; Kim, S. H.; Cha, J. M.; Tkach, J.; and Kim, M. R.; Who is the leader of your club? *Club Manage.* (November/December 2010), *88(6),* 15.

Cichy, R. F.; Kim, S. H.; Cha, J. M.; Tkach, J.; and Kim, M. R.; Volunteer board and committee members' roles in private club communication. *Club Manage.* (September/October 2010), *88(5),* 14–15.

Cichy, R. F.; Singerling, J. B.; Cha, J. M.; and Kim, S.; Emotional intelligence and your feelings about your volunteer board leadership in your club. *BoardRoom.* (July/August 2006), 10, 26, 28, 74.

Cichy, R. F.; Singerling, J. B.; Cha, J. M.; and Kim, S. H.; Fresh insights into private club board and committee members. *BoardRoom.* (July/August 2008), *12,* 68–71.

Kim, S. H.; Cha, J. M.; Cichy, R. F.; Kim, M. R.; and Tkach, J. L.; Effects of board size and board involvement in private club financial performance. *Int. J. Contemp. Hospit. Manage.* **2012,** *24(1),* 7–25.

KEYWORDS

- **Framework for sustainability**
- **Private clubs**
- **Sustainable business practices (SBPs)**
- **Think Like The Owner**

REFERENCES

1. Perdue, J.; and Koenigsfeld, J.; Contemporary Club Management. East Lansing, MI: Educational Institute of the American Hotel & Motel Association; **2013.**

2. Cha, J. M.; Cichy, R. F.; and Kim, S. H.; Commitment and volunteer-related outcomes among private club board and committee member volunteer leaders. *J. Hospit. Tourism Res.* **2011,** *35(3),* 308–333.

3. Gilman, R.; Sustainability, from the 1992 UIA/AIA. Call for Sustainable Community Solutions. 1992, retrieved from Context Institute website: http://www.context.org/about/definitions/#sustainability

4. WCED (The World Commission on Environment and Development). Our common future. World Commission on Environment and Development. Oxford: Oxford University Press; **1987.**

5. UNCED (The United Nations Conference on Environment and Development, Earth Summit). Agenda 21 and the UNCED Proceedings. Dobbs Ferry, New York: Oceana Publications; **1992.**

6. Chalkley, B.; Education for sustainable development: Continuation. *J. Geogr. High. Edu.* **2006,** *30(2),* 235–236.

7. Reid, A.; and Petocz, P.; University lecturer's understanding of sustainability. *High. Edu.* **2006,** *51,* 105–123.

8. Sloan, P.; Legrand, W.; and Chen, S.; Sustainability in the Hospitality Industry: Principles of Sustainable Operations. 2nd Edition, New York, NY: Routledge; **2013.**

9. Barber, N.; Deale, C.; and Goodman, R.; Environmental sustainability in the hospitality management curriculum: Perspectives from three groups of stakeholder. *J. Hospit. Tourism Edu.* **2011,** *23(1),* 6–17.

10. Dyllick, T.; and Hockerts, K.; Beyond the business case for corporate sustainability. *Bus. Strategy. Environ.* **2002,** *11,* 130–141.

11. Sloan, P.; Joseph, W.; and Chen, S.; Sustainability in the Hospitality Industry: Principles of Sustainable Operations. Oxford: Butterworth-Heinemann; **2009.**

12. Kim, M.; Kim, S.; Cha, J.; Cichy, R. F.; Koenigsfeld, J.; and Perdue, J.; (In Press). An exploratory study of perceived innovation characteristics influencing sustainable business practices in the private club industry. Accepted for publication in *J. Tourism Res. Hospit.*

13. Peladeau, N.; WordStat Content Analysis Module for SIMSTAT. Montreal, Canada: Provalis Research; **2003.**

14. Minor, L. J.; and Cichy, R. F.; Foodservice Systems Management. Westport, CT: AVI Publishing Company; **1984.**

15. White, D.; Sustainability grows. The Boardroom. May/June 1, **2012.**

16. Schmidgall, R. S.; Contemporary Club Management: Club Financial Management. **2007,** retrieved from CMAA website: http://www.cmaa.org/CCMBook2/Chap12.pdf

17. Doran, G. T.; There's a S.M.A.R.T. way to write management's goals and objectives. *Manage. Rev.* **1981,** *70(11),* 35–36.

18. The Leader. The School of Hospitality Business Alumni Magazine. 231 Eppley Center, Michigan State University, East Lansing, MI 48824; (Summer **2013**).

19. Club Managers Association of America. Golf Environment Organization. **2013,** retrieved from CMAA Online website: http://www.cmaa.org/sustainability.aspx

20. GEO. (n.d.). *GEO Certification.* Retrieved from GEO website: http://www.golfenvironment.org/about/certification

21. Mirimichi. (n.d.). *GEO Certified.* Retrieved from Mirimichi website: http://www.mirimichi.com/geo-certified.html

CHAPTER 11

SUSTAINABLE TOURISM CERTIFICATION: A FRENCH PERSPECTIVE

KAREN DELCHET-COCHET[1], THIERRY DELECOLLE[2], SARAH GOUDEAU[3], and RAPHAËL DORNIER[4]

[1]ISC Paris, 22 Bd du Fort de Vaux, 75017 Paris, France, Tele: (33) 1-40-53-99-99, E-mail: karen.delchet-cochet@iscparis.com

[2]ISC Paris, 22 Bd du Fort de Vaux, 75017 Paris, France, (33) 1-40-53-99-99, E-mail: tdelecolle@iscparis.com

[3]Alumni ISC PARIS, 22 Bd du Fort de Vaux, 75017 Paris, France, (33) 1-40-53-99-99, E-mail: sarah.goudeau@iscparis.com

[4]ISC Paris, 22 Bd du Fort de Vaux, 75017 Paris, France, (33) 1-40-53-99-99, E-mail: rdornier@iscparis.com

CONTENTS

11.1 INTRODUCTION

According to the barometer of the World Tourism Organization (UNWTO), 980 million tourists traveled around the world in 2011 when they were only 528 million in 1995. UNWTO has recently released its forecast for the next two decades and asserts that the annual growth in the number of international tourists will reach 4 percent. Therefore, there should be around 1.8 billion international tourists in 2030. On the economic side, the tourism industry represents 10.4 percent of the global Gross Domestic Product (UNWTO, 2006) and 8 percent of international employment but, in contrast, tourism alone represents 4–10 percent of the greenhouse gas issued by industry worldwide. It should be noted that 89 percent of CO_2 emissions are generated exclusively by public transport between the home and the tourist destination.

Considering these alarming data some professionals have created so-called alternative tourism forms, including sustainable tourism and its three pillars environmental, economic, and sociocultural. In ten years tour operators (TO) have included in their brochures sustainable tourism packages and have developed charters, labels, standards, and certifications aimed at legitimizing the "sustainable" discourse to the clients. Some of these forms are more compelling than others for companies and associations: a simple communication approach (charter) vs. audit by an independent third organization (certification).

The purpose of this study is to focus on the impact of the certification process "Agir pour un Tourisme Responsable" (ATR), founded in France in 2008 on the initiative of several adventure tour operators, on their organization. First we will examine the standards and their challenges in terms of sustainable development. Then we will contextualize the development of the so-called sustainable tour operators before presenting our research methodology, the results of our qualitative study and a discussion.

11.2 LITERATURE REVIEW

11.2.1 FROM THE STANDARD TO THE CERTIFICATION

According to ISO, "a standard is a document that provides requirements, specifications, guidelines or characteristics that can be used consistently to ensure that materials, products, processes and services are fit for their purpose." Standardization means the development of shared principles from a consensus between stakeholders [1]. These principles are in coherence with the very notion of Corporate Social Responsibility (CSR) as defined by the European Commission (EC, 2001) "being socially responsible means not only fulfilling legal expectations, but also going beyond compliance and investing more in human capital, environment and relationships with stakeholders."

The role of standardization to define sustainable development and its integration in organizations is emphasized by many authors, due in particular to the limits of the traditional legal regulation when dealing with the global environmental and social issues of the twenty-first century (Quairel & Capron, 2004). According to Pesqueux [2], these standards are used to produce qualifying information (certifications, accreditations, assessments) with a view to create a regulation (not rules).

Nevertheless the proliferation of standards in terms of CSR leads us to be especially vigilant about documents. Indeed, it should be noted that the term "standard" includes various types of documents. Delchet-Cochet and Vo [3] show that analyzing standards in terms of CSR should take into account different aspects:

(i) Firstly the field of CSR covered by the repository. In some cases just one pillar such as the environment is covered. In other cases we find a more comprehensive and integrated approach involving the three pillars.

(ii) Secondly, the purpose of the standard (implementation of a global approach or reporting instrument). According to Delchet-Cochet and Brodhag [4], approaches to the implementation and recognition of sustainable development practices in organizations can be diverse: management system certification, product certification or system of indicators. If the interest of each of these approaches is not questioned, the performance issues for sustainable development are not systematically guaranteed by each of these approaches.

(iii) At least the legitimacy of this reference document, based on stakeholders' representation in particular.

Even if the repository forms a shared base for work, the need to recognize its progress is regularly discussed. The aim is thus to obtain a recognition following the recommendations of the standard through a certification. Following Debruyne [5], certification, as defined by ISO as a given written insurance by a third party (in the form of a certificate) that a product, service or system meets specific requirements, appears to be at present "the most successful trust form."

Savall and Zardet [6] showed that the standard is not only an "idea principle" but also a "product" sold by economic actors. These actors engage in an increased competition partly responsible for the expansion of normative documents and associated labels. The standard is therefore both a contribution to an inadequate regulation, a content emerging from a consensus between stakeholders [1] and a purpose in terms of recognition: the certification.

11.2.2   SUSTAINABLE TOURISM: AN OVERVIEW

According to Font [7] the lack of methods to implement sustainable management and to evaluate the ecological character of practices in tourism has led to a growing number of voluntary initiatives in the form of codes of conduct, manuals, rewards, and ecolabels. These charters are intended to promote principles and rules of conduct for members of the organization [8, 9, 10].

By the way, these tools do not guarantee the genuine responsible character of practices. Some scholars have tried to evaluate to what extent ethical commitments in tourism are actually applied by different actors [11]. A charter may not be more than a list of the legal responsibilities of the organization and the behaviors it expects from its employees and customers, rather than an actual reflection of the ethical principles and aspirations of its management team [12]. In addition, ethical charters may appear to be a way for management teams to reject their responsibilities to their employees and customers [9]. Fisher [13] distinguished superficial and deep approaches to ethics to understand the differences between rhetoric and actual practices. He noted that most organizations seem to adopt a superficial and "opportunistic" approach to ethics. Fennel and Malloy [14] on the other hand assume that tourism organizations should adopt a more structured and functional ethical vision. Evaluation and control should therefore be important components of the formulation of ethical codes. They also point out that for a code of ethics to be fully implemented there must be compatibility between the value systems of the organization and individuals.

Some tourism professionals then felt the need to control their operating modes and engage in a "social contract" governing the moral character of relationships and behaviors between organizations, tourists, and local communities [14]. Three principles of codes of conduct, following the principles of sustainable tourism, have often been put forward: understanding the culture visited, respecting and having sensitivity towards the local population and reducing the negative impacts on the local environment [12].

11.2.3   THE INVOLVEMENT OF TOUR-OPERATORS IN SUSTAINABLE TOURISM

It is only recently that tour operators have begun to assess the environmental impact of their operations and those of their suppliers [15]. Since the study of Tapper [16] that showed a disparity between the long-term commitments of tour operators of different sizes, the average commitment has increased significantly as the majority of UK tour operators are employing one or more persons responsible for sustainable development [15]. Currently, among operators, there is more evidence of good practice regarding the environment rather than socioeconomic issues [17]. For example, TUI, LTU Touristik, MyTravel Northern Europe, and Hotelplan have implemented environmental manuals for their suppliers and evaluate them focusing on energy, waste, and water reduction (TOI, 2003). On the contrary, socioeconomic performance criteria were generally perceived as potentially increasing costs, as more difficult to implement and measure and as expected to be covered through labor law [18].

Béji-Bécheur and Bensebaa [19] for their part highlighted four types of positioning of French tour operators in terms of corporate social responsibility (1) CSR as a quality certification process, (2) CSR as relationship marketing strategy with business partners, (3) CSR as ecotourism approach, and (4) CSR as a global approach to sustainable development.

11.2.4 THE CERTIFICATION PROCESS OF TOUR-OPERATORS

In the field of tourism there are many certification programs taking into account environmental, sociocultural, and/or economic criteria [20]. We can mention for instance the Ecolabel for tourist accommodation that takes into account environmental issues or the Green Globe certification.

Some tour operators have effectively engaged in this type of approach. In general, the firms involved in a process of recognition of their sustainable development strategy must pass a certification process to ensure that their products, services, production processes or management systems meet or exceed the standards set by the certification body [21]. These certification processes also represent support tools for business managers allowing them to integrate different criteria or methods for reducing waste, protecting of biodiversity or promoting local supply [21]. These processes are therefore effective ways to turn abstract principles of sustainable development into concrete actions [22].

But then what certification to choose between the ones shared by different sectors, the ones specific to the tourism industry or the ones developed for SMEs? EMAS and ISO systems are generally accessible only to large companies. Therefore the tourism industry, consisting mostly in small operators, has often opted for its own certification systems on a less restrictive basis. This orientation enables them to integrate the accreditations more directly their own specificities, as evidenced by ATR.

11.2.5 ATR: A CERTIFICATION OF THE TOUR-OPERATORS' SERVICES

In France there are two main sustainable tourism certifications for tour-operators: "Association pour le Tourisme Equitable et Solidaire (ATES)" for associations and "Agir pour un Tourisme Responsable (ATR)" for private firms. AFNOR Certification accompanied the founding members of ATR in the formalization and the measurement of the standards to make them auditable. In addition, the ATR Association provides members many tools: strategic advice, training and provision of documents in order to obtain the certification, communication (press and public relations, events, trade shows and website), or partnerships and recognition at the national and international level.

Through the association, members support since 2010 four associations of social and environmental development. These associations implement at the local level projects whose values are close to those of ATR members. In addition, each certified member supports its own development projects. A major project of the ATR association is the creation of country profiles. This profile is made by members who wish to participate and are specialists of the chosen destination. It consists of three areas: regulation of the country regarding tourism business, consumption and waste management, and the social aspect (minimum employment age, minimum wages, accommodation, food, and equipment for local staff welfare ...). ATR certified operators will then use these forms to require their suppliers to respect the different criteria. The country profile is also adapted to be integrated into travel diaries published by tour operators for their customers.

Moreover ATR is a member of EARTH (the first European network of sustainable tourism actors supported by the European Commission) network and has received the accreditation of the Global Sustainable Tourism Council (GSTC). The purpose of this organization is to accredit current certification programs for sustainable tourism that exist throughout the world. ATR is therefore involved in the working group of GSTC standardization that is studying and reconsidering the global criteria for sustainable tourism in order to make this concept evolve.

When the company member of ATR feels sufficiently prepared to apply for certification, it must file an application for the certification body AFNOR Certification. During the audit, skilled and independent auditors analyze customer satisfaction records collected by the company throughout the year, administrative documents proving that the company is indeed promoting sustainable tourism and respecting all repository criteria and discussions between auditors and employees. Certification is granted for a three years period and controls are performed by auditors each year. During the two intermediate annual audits, inspections focus on the criteria that require improvements.

Regarding the cost of certification, the company must first pay its membership to the association which is proportional to its sales turnover. The price of the audit depends on the size of the company, the number of sites to be audited and the time spent in the premises. This cost can range from €1.600, when there is only one site to be audited, to €4.500 for larger structures.

11.2.6 LIMITS OF OPERATORS' COMMITMENT IN SUSTAINABLE TOURISM

Some authors have highlighted the limits of tour operators' sustainable engagement, even certified ones. These limits may be related to particular characteristics of the sector, the certification system or the tour operator. According to Schwartz and Font (2009) divergent goals and priorities of suppliers and tour operators, focus on low prices on the European market and the complexity of the supply chain for tour operators make it difficult to put into practice the sustainable tourism "theory."

The literature suggests a number of problems limiting the ability of suppliers to meet the sustainability requirements of operators. First, sustainable activities can be expensive, or at least be perceived that way [23]. As part of a process of labeling or certification, the setting of the application file, the normalization and the monitoring generate spending and require resources that are not always available to businesses, especially tourism suppliers from poor countries.

Added to this are human barriers: some resistance to change, lack of qualified personnel and training programs and an inability to plan [24, 23, 25]. Resources of tour operators and their suppliers may be too limited to engage in assistance or investments programs (Schwartz & Font, 2009).

The third frequently mentioned problem is the weak demand for sustainable travel [15]. A gap exists in fact between the results of studies showing that consumers want sustainable products and their actual purchase behavior. Moreover, hotels have often been forced by European directives to invest in the field of health and safety. They were therefore reluctant to implement new "green" practices that go against these aspects. The 1990 Directive of the European Union on package travel consider that the tour operators are responsible for the "performance" of their suppliers. This factor in itself is a barrier to environmental sustainability (Schwartz & Font, 2009)[17, 16]. The tour operator is indeed responsible for the compliance with contractual obligations [26, 27]. Baddely and Font [13] stress that tour operators top managers are often reluctant to make suggestions to their suppliers on environmental. Some authors have also highlighted the complexity of effective stakeholders management [28, 29, 30]. Stakeholders are particularly diverse in sustainable tourism. Cooperation is made difficult by the existence of different views and interests between the organizations involved [31, 32]. As Robson and Robson [33] have noted, the method of application of sustainable tourism has not been fully explored and although the concept is widely used, routes and directions for its implementation remain unclear [34]. Pioneering studies have highlighted problems with mistrust vis-à-vis public policy, poor administration and the failure to involve local communities [35](Ioannides, 1995). Subsequently other studies have outlined a lack of stakeholders involvement, government support, leadership, awareness, and coordination [36, 37]. To better understand the issue of sustainable tourism, it is necessary to examine more specifically the issues and impacts of the ATR certification on the organizations involved in its implementation.

11.2.7   METHODOLOGY

On February 17, 2012, thirteen French tour operators were granted the ATR certification. Given the exploratory purpose of this research, a qualitative approach by semistructured interviews was preferred. The opinions of six certified TO top managers, one AFNOR Certification auditor in charge of the ATR certification and one sustainable tourism expert who participated in the development of a concurrent labeling were collected to understand the context of the standard and its potential shortcomings. These interviews were recorded to facilitate the subsequent treatment of responses. With an average duration of 44 min, they took place from April to June 2012. Table 11.1 shows the profile of the interviewees.

TABLE 11.1   Respondents' profile

Respondents	TO-1	TO-2	TO-3	TO-4	TO-5	TO-6	Auditor	TO-7
Function	Director	Vice Director	Co-founder	Sustainable tourism manager	Quality manager	Director of sustainable development and customer relations	Auditor	Vice-director
Status / ATR	Certified fonder member	Certified fonder member	Certified fonder member	Certified member	Certified fonder member	Certified member	Afnor Auditor	Non-member involved in a competing association
Sales Turnover 2011	<10 M€	11–20 M€	11–20 M€	31–40 M€	41–50 M€	151–160 M€ (2010)	N/A	N/A
Duration	38 mn	29 mn	30 mn	50 mn	44 mn	67 mn	41 mn	53 mn

To facilitate the confidence of respondents, the interview was starting with a presentation of the research context, a presentation of the investigator and a guarantee of anonymity, before asking respondents their definition of sustainable tourism. The following of the interview was organized around an interview guide that sought to understand the motivations that led the company to implement the AFNOR standard, the certification process and its issues and impacts on the organization and the management of the repository within the ATR association.

A thematic analysis was performed. In order to assess its reliability the qualitative material was double-coded [38]. The inter-coder reliability reached the desirable range of 91 percent agreement, thereby allowing us to examine the cases where disagreements were observed with the advices of a third researcher.

11.3 RESULTS

11.3.1 INTRA-ORGANIZATIONAL CONSEQUENCES

The tour operators top managers interviewed did mention the four limitations to the commitment to sustainable tourism identified by the literature.

11.3.2 CERTIFICATION IS COSTLY

The first criticism mentioned by the TO interviewed is the financial (association membership and audit fees) and human (amount of work) cost of the certification process. In fact, it takes about six months to a year for the company to gather all internal and external documents (from suppliers) which will be used to demonstrate its commitment to the ATR repository.

One way to limit the wage inflation induced by the certification process involvement is to recruit trainees. A second one is to share resources. The TO-4 associated with another TO belonging to the same group to create a joint post of project head. His mission is to follow the local suppliers throughout the year, train staff and new recruits and make quality manuals to explain to everyone how the company applied the different sustainable criteria within the organization. Only the larger tour operators have created specific full-time positions: the TO-6 created a position of ATR project chief. In smaller organizations like TO-1 and TO-5, many employees now spend part of their time working on the ATR criteria.

11.3.3 A DIFFICULT CHANGE

The problem that faced some companies is the lack of involvement or understanding of the subject from a few employees or services. Indeed, the certification process creates extra work for employees and some may feel less involved than others in the process. In general, it is complicated to make it clear to teams and TO-6 noted that a significant number of employees do not understand why so many documents are required. It is therefore important to explain to employees the motivations, the benefits and the importance of the certification for the company. The challenge is to do so in an intelligent manner so as not to create "gasworks" and not to make complicated and grunt work for those who will carry them out.

It is also the work of the auditor who spends much of his time at the controls to discuss with counselors, production managers, destination managers and other services to observe how each one applies the principles of sustainable tourism within its function. This concept is important because these employees are the bridge between clients, with whom they have direct contact, and destination management companies (DMC), with whom they are in regular contact to guide them in their development.

11.3.4   A COMPLEX STAKEHOLDER MANAGEMENT

Certified TO must ensure that their local suppliers (agencies, hotels, etc.) apply the principles of social and environmental management in accordance with the certification. This control is complex, in a sector that is not used to the proof and where suppliers are numerous. The first step was to develop country profiles (repository of good practices and good economic, social, and environmental policies to be implemented in each of the different countries). Members and suppliers have an obligation to refer to these country profiles. As explained by the TO-5 the credibility of the process lies on the country profiles. They oblige local agencies to comply with the laws and reality of the country.

As it is necessary to justify everything to the auditor, the TO had to be much more organized, impose a stricter monitoring and collect various documents that were not previously requested. Indeed, in the tourism sector, most professional relations were based on trust. Today, companies must collect many documents from the local agencies. This notion of control and formalization is alien to the culture of many local agencies. It is therefore very difficult to convince them of the importance of procedures related to the certification: "Some of our local agencies are still following an oral tradition. It is difficult for the employees who are in charge of that part of the process in our organization to impose their local partners this change in the mode of relationship without hurting. It is complicated in human terms. There is a problem of implementation beyond a possible underlying problem" (TO-5).

At first, relations were altered by the fact that the local agencies were not used to be monitored and controlled. Then progressively they were able to understand it as a process of evolution and progress that could be beneficial for them. As explained by the TO-4, a focus on working with larger local agencies can increase the awareness of a greater number of customers towards sustainable tourism.

The ATR repository provides a support for local agencies on these issues. Thus, the criterion 2.2 states that the tour operator must "implement a transfer of skills to local providers." This transfer is, for the moment, very difficult to implement and then monitor. Some members work with local agencies in almost every country in the world. It is therefore difficult to compel all to set up training but member companies can encourage and advise. The local agencies will decide what they will put in place or not in their business. TO-4 says: "we offer training when we fail to find tour guides. These courses are beneficial for us and for them as they gain skills and they can also have customers from other French-speaking agencies." The idea is to share the cost of training with local teams for a common benefit but in no case to force and therefore not gain any real benefit.

11.3.5   A WEAK DEMAND

Another disadvantage of the certification is that it is still very little known by the general public whereas it is recognized in the workplace. Most loyal customers have not seen the change between "before ATR" and "after ATR." Moreover "no client comes because we are part of ATR" (TO-4).

Some TO have even raised the question of the weight of this standard in the customer decision making process. According to TO-5, "the fact that we are involved in this process of sustainable tourism and certified reassures our customers. It is a kind of moral comfort for them. They go on a trip and in addition it is ethical, so it's good for them. [...] However, will they consider that it is a criterion of choice? It is not obvious. It is rather something that reassures them in their orientation, in their personal ethics vis-à-vis the travel they do, but that does not mean they would be willing to give up something or willing to pay more to choose a tour operator really involved in sustainable tourism. It's a bit the whole issue of sustainable development. Everyone finds it great, but when he must push the air conditioner button in the car they do. It runs exactly the same thing in the travel industry." TO-7 slightly tempered these comments and wants to be more optimistic about the future: "Even if customers are not very demanding, even if it does not change their mind, even if they are not ready to pay more for that, it is important. It reassures them and it will one day become a criterion of choice."

It is important to point out, first, that the weak demand is minimized by members who declare unanimously that the question of the value of the repository for the customers is secondary (the initial engagement in the certification process did not have as primary purpose the attraction of new customers) and secondly it is explained by the weak weight of adventure TOs (3% of the French tourism market) which cannot invest much on communication around this norm.

11.3.6   BENEFITS IN TERMS OF LEARNING AND STRUCTURING

It is interesting to note that respondents find it more difficult to identify the real contribution of the certification for the company beyond legitimizing the discourse of companies that were already working for sustainable tourism before ATR: "If we did not have the certification, we would surely have lost something but when the certification is granted, we do not really realize the benefit" TO-2). However, the commitment to the process provides structuring methods that benefit the entire firm.

The benefits seem therefore more oriented towards the internal organization rather than towards customers.

11.3.7   THE ANNUAL CERTIFICATION AUDIT: A CONTRIBUTION TO LEARNING

Pivotal moment for companies engaged in the certification process, this moment seems to be lived positively and constructively by respondents. The contribution is at two levels: on the repository itself and on a benchmark of what is done elsewhere. About the repository, the TO-2 notes that "it was searched. Every year it highlights things that can be improved and others that we have a little passed by the wayside." TO-1 summarizes quite well the general opinion on the contribution outside the repository: "I found it well to the extent that the person auditing was not there just to control, but gave much examples of other companies. It was quite rich in terms of management and what we could learn. [...] There has been much discussed outside the repository and it was very rich."

11.3.8   THE CERTIFICATION PROVIDES STRUCTURING TO THE COMPANY

Before obtaining the certification, commitments, actions, and concerns for sustainable tourism among members were generally the same, but without making the formalization required by the ATR certification. Certification involves putting in place procedures and responses and thus provides member companies with a certain rigor. Certification has also enabled companies to grow and deepen their approach to sustainable tourism. Thus, in the TO-6, this rigor developed by the ATR certification is now being applied to other projects of the company. Tour-operators must enter into a rational of "I say then I prove it." Audits also allow companies to have concrete evidence of what they do well, to reassure themselves about their actions and consider the progress to be made.

11.3.9   CHANGING THE CORPORATE CULTURE

When a company embarks on a heavy task like a certification process, it is necessary to involve all employees. Certification also helps support the internal approach of a company ("it helps to involve all employees, it is highly structuring and it makes us enter a process of progress; so far it goes like this, but how could we do better?" TO-5) and implement a change in corporate culture.

The changes are more easily detectable in some companies than in others: It depends on the size of the company, its management style and the profiles of its employees. Three years after obtaining the certification, TO-4 is pleased to see that within his company ATR is really rooted in the language and spirit of each employee. These took reflexes and habits that allow the company to be more efficient "when employees go on eductours, they come to me asking me "I will see such local agency, is there any missing document? Is there a need to do something?"

11.3.10 THE CONSEQUENCES AT THE INTER-ORGANIZATIONAL LEVEL

The certification also provides several lessons regarding the steering of the repository and the proof tools within the ATR association.

11.3.11 A COLLECTIVE LEARNING

The adventure TOs that were sending groups to fragile destinations (e.g., deserts) have decided to discuss the behavior to be taken vis-à-vis these ecosystems and host populations in order for customers to adopt an adequate attitude during the trip. "As our wish was to do something in common, the idea that came fast was to ensure that this approach was communicable to our customers and recognized. And there indeed the discussion focused on the form to give to the process: A label, a certification, a shared charter? The association was accompanied in its efforts by the Tourism Ministry, met AFNOR and the choice fell on a certification" (TO-5).

Hence the association got structured and the creation and management of the repository was at the center of its activity. From the outset the members wanted to ensure the openness of the certification and their first task was to define criteria that could be opened to TOs that are not adventure TOs. The control of the repository and particularly the creation of the country sheets are now the most important according to the members interviewed. Another related issue is security: "It's really a big problem because we work on a large number of fragile destinations. Sometimes there is a gap between our teams on the ground who need to work, our clients who want to leave and security. This is a big question. For instance ATR has decided to stop in Mauritania" (TO-5). The impact of this work has resulted in both a collective learning and a questioning of certain collective choices.

This learning has had an impact in relation to the quality and sustainable development approach: "The repository is a collective approach. We built it together from scratch. This is a strong limit as it was made by beginners. We spend a lot of time on it. With time we will make it to simplify, get right the first time. Today it is a little more confusing, complex, as we are in a process of compromise, made by beginners. Neither of us had employees specialized in quality processes in his teams" (TO-5) but also in more general terms.

It is a process of consultation with the various companies that are on the market. You must accept to "open with competitors and say: "Is it really an improvement. […] The problem is to agree without falling into banality." The exchange between members can also address businesses issues: "It has allowed us to meet the CEOs of the biggest TO and see what was happening elsewhere and on a larger scale" (TO-1).

11.3.12   A COLLECTIVE CALLING INTO QUESTION AND THE SEARCH FOR CREATIVE SOLUTIONS

The ATR certification has been widely criticized by both members (when setting the operational implementation of certain criteria of the repository) and by outside observers. As the human and financial resources of the association are limited, it has sought to develop creative solutions.

11.3.13   THE INABILITY TO EXTEND THE CERTIFICATION TO COUNTRIES

As noted by TO-2, "the concern today is that we do not have the means to extend the certification to countries themselves. The control principle is that our product managers go to the ground and do on-site verification." Indeed, since 2010, it is possible for the local agency to be "certified" provided the audit is performed by the French company. It is then the product managers or travel counselors who are in charge of this audit. They check on-site all documents (ATR criteria, declared commitments by the local agency …). One of the main limitations of this system is that the local agency often outsources its guides. The questions that arise are firstly whether these sub-contractors are within the scope of the repository or not, and then whether it is necessary to verify that all subcontractors have their licenses."

To partially offset this problem, the TOs try to take into account the clients perceptions of quality to identify breaches in the certification principles and thus published a country profile for customers (traveler sheet). This sheet gathers all the information that may be necessary to the traveler during his stay: tip level, local minimum wage, accommodation of guides and drivers... the idea being that if a customer notices a problem, he must bring the information when completing the customer satisfaction survey. This raises the following question: "What customers really know about local wages, the future of guides ... and especially will they bother to discuss and question local suppliers compliance with the specifications of their country profiles that were distributed?" (TO-7) This limit is one of the main topics of discussion of the association to continue to legitimize its repository.

11.3.14   THE ISSUE OF THE WEIGHT OF STAKEHOLDERS

In the words of TO-1: "The credibility of the certification will go through representativeness. Adventure tourism is barely 3% of tourism." What weight then has the association in the tourism industry? To illustrate this lack of weight in the negotiations, the TO-6 takes as an example one of the environmental requirements of the standard: "Signaling degraded sites." Even if TOs, local agencies and customers actively participate in this criterion, sometimes it is difficult to change things: "For example, cruise ships that degas in the Nile. Very quickly, we realized that we could not act when facing these situations. Indeed, how much weight has a small French Association against the Egyptian government or multinationals that owns the boats that degas in the Nile?"

It is the same with the country profiles. TO-5 explains that companies are not masters of the territories concerned. The steps are implemented with local agencies but it is impossible to impose at all costs something. Indeed, even if in some areas adventure tourism can weigh heavy, at the national level the weight is quite different. How can they implement cleanup actions or even discuss wages with ministries …?

Moreover, even if all the members interviewed praised the work of the people at the head of the association, the size of the association induces its lack of weight. Certainly things are moving and progressing but it would be possible to move more quickly with more financial and human resources. One solution would be to make the nonspecialized TOs enter the certification process, with adapted sustainable criteria. On this point, the TO surveyed are aware of the importance of gaining weight in the negotiations: "The credibility of the certification depends on its representativeness" (TO-1), but "with different criteria so we can keep our legitimacy" (TO-2). This search for recognition should "not make us fall in the shortcomings of greenwashing and social-washing" (TO-1).

11.4   DISCUSSION

This study illustrates a certain number of points raised in the literature review. This certification is being criticized by some external professionals (TO-7). The internal members far from complaining of the shortcomings already identified in the literature (cost of certification for example) are actively involved in the life of the ATR association to see it evolve into an effective sustainable tourism.   While the previous research put forward a predominantly environmental approach to the issue (Schwartz & Font, 2008), the ATR standard is very committed to the implementation of economic and social principles to ensure decent working conditions for employees of its service suppliers in the host country.

Moreover regarding the financial, organizational or human barriers to reach certification, the ATR repository appears to answer several limitations. By offering local agencies the possibility to be certified by the members themselves, the tourist actors of poor countries can access the certification with low cost (which responds partly to the criticisms by Cañada & Gascón, 2008). By proposing to fund the training of local staff and investing in economic development projects at the local level, certified members of ATR also answers the criticism by Schwartz and Font (2009).

This approach specific to the ATR certification therefore partly compensates for the limitations identified by the literature on the implementation of certification in sustainable tourism. The only limit that really seems to be a problem for the profession is the lack of demand for ethical travel or at least the lack of willingness to help finance the ethical aspects of travel.

This is all the more important as when is raised the question of improving the certification, the discourse of some interviewees refers to the concept of critical mass on a more economic level. So far, the approach involves relatively small TOs in the French market that have limited resources. Therefore, even if they are aware of the limits and develop creative approaches to address them a TO notes: "To make the certification more legitimate, there should be money in it—but no one is willing to do this today—it is an additional constraint in a period of crisis." Therefore certification, initially envisaged as an idea of principle in the meaning of Savall and Zardet [6], also proves to be a product that must be valued and sold.

The question of the future of the certification is at the heart of their thinking: should it remain only French? (the association has already initiated a rapprochement with international organizations on these matters), how to integrate nonspecialized tour operators? Indeed, developing communication and integrating new tour operators could increase the weight of the group in the negotiations. As such, ATR members might try to lobby the Ministry of Tourism to find a French ally in the negotiations with foreign governments.

The issue of stakeholders is also a possible route of action for the association. On the issue of control of the implementation of economic, environmental, and sociocultural at the level of destinations, involving more the clients, guides, and NGOs appears to be a desirable development axis to triangulate the measuring means. The question then is how to encourage customers to consult the Code of Ethics of the traveler and especially to apply it.

Although this research has raised the opinion of almost half of the certified TOs at the end of February 2012, it received a single viewpoint by company. The study of changes in the internal organization could be richer if it was based on a case study with several respondents by company or participant observation. Similarly it would be interesting to interview top managers at the beginning of the certification process and therefore not yet certified or develop a more critical approach to identify the reasons why some TOs do not engage in the certification.

It seems that the grouping of certified members in an association can assure a greater adaptability of the repository. The nature of the organization "structuring" the creation and maintenance of the certification could also be the subject of further research.

11.5 CONCLUSION

In conclusion, it seems important to note that since the creation of the ATR certification no study had examined its impact on tour operators engaged in the process. This work has shown that this certification is facing the major limitations identified in the literature, but its associative nature allows companies to circumvent these limits and work on ways to improve it in a positive and proactive way.

This is a compelling approach within the company that makes practices change. But the cost of certification remains a challenge for small firms. In addition, some results are more directly related to the peculiarities of the tourism sector and the principles of sustainable development such as the culture of research evidence, founding principle of the certification process that is foreign to the tourism sector but also the difficulty of assessing partners. The issue of the ATR recognition by other certifications with more communication such as the eco-label for sustainable tourism, Earth Check or Green Globe label, asks for a more international standardization of sustainable development within the tourism industry.

Teaching Notes:
  (i) It could be interesting to consider the focus of the certification: certification of a trip versus certification of a tour-operator or a hotel. A specificity of the ATR certification is to consider the overall service provided to customers and not the only characteristics of a "place." Moreover, the choice of a sustainable development certification is not a neutral one. Indeed there is no certification of the standard ISO 26000 on the social responsibility of organizations, published in 2010. Different factors explain this positioning. One factor is that the experts defining this standard considered that for a system certification, an obligation of means is not the right answer. On these issues, the notion of "results" more than the one of "process" should be taken into account.

 (ii) Students could discuss to what extent the standards of ATR are more focused on the processes or the results, cover the whole aspects of sustainability and are more or less "easy" to measure. The very "nature" of the criteria used in the certification could also be discussed. Some criteria are more qualitative and others are more quantitative. It could be outlined to what extent each criterion really "measure" what it aims at measuring, and how the criteria could be "improved" to improve the measure.

(iii) It could be interesting to compare the ATR certification (a certification for French adventure tour operators) with the Travelife certification (a certification for tour operators and travel agents from different countries). The students could compare the criteria of each one, and assess the main differences and similarities. These two associations are now engaged in discussions for a future cooperation.

The main criteria of the ATR certification are the following ones:
1. Involve and respect the local people in the development:
1.2. Focus at all levels, in the case of equal skill levels, on direct local jobs.
1.3. Favor the use of local resources for design of travel.
1.4. Promote the transfer of skills

1.5. Ensure the proper respect of decent social minimum

1.6. Comply with local administrative and legal rules, the local suppliers must provide decent working conditions for their employees

1.9. Actively and financially support the local development of destinations

1.10. Inform and educate visitors to respect cultures and host populations

2.   Minimize our impact on the environment:

2.1. Apply a policy of waste management and natural resources management based on the sensitivity of the environment

2.2. Promote the preservation of local heritage

2.3. Promote the establishment of a policy for managing flows across destinations

2.4. Inform and educate visitors to respect the natural environment

2.5. Actively contribute to the environmental protection of destinations

3.   Be respectful of our customers:

3.1. Have a responsible marketing policy

3.2. Having a mobilized and trained staff

3.3 Working with skilled, involved, trained, and sharing the same values and working principles local suppliers

4.   Apply self what you preach to others:

4.4. Moving towards a policy of environmental management for its business

4.5. Having a formalized quality control processes in its business

4.7. Ensure a fair sharing of the benefits of the activity

(iv) It could also be interesting to compare ATR (a "process" certification focusing on tour operators) with Earthcheck or Green Globe ("destination" certifications covering a wide range of tourism sectors). The comparison could be based on the criteria used or on the "general" impact of these two types of certifications. We may also consider the possible cooperation between these two certifications. We noticed for instance that for ATR that there is a lack of control at the local level. We could then consider the possibility to overcome this lack by developing some form of partnership with organizations granting a destination certification. ATR could therefore focus on the tour operators of the outgoing country, obliging them to work with destinations and local suppliers that were granted the Earthcheck or Green Globe certification.

(v) The issue of the "cost" of certification seems to be a crucial one, above all for small organizations like adventure tour-operators. We should consider the cost of engaging in the certification process and the cost of keeping the certification. As a limit of the certification may be the lack of control at the local level, an increase in this control may result in higher costs. The cost of the certification is now based mostly on the sales turnover of the tour-operator, but it could take into account also the number of destinations it offers.

(vi) The sharing of information between ATR members seems to be at the same time an advantage and a disadvantage of the certification. In a sector where developing and keeping a competitive advantage

(vii) The general sensitivity of French tourists regarding sustainable development does not turn yet in a responsible behavior. We notice that according to top managers most tourists do not consider sustainability as a choice criterion. This issue is found in other industries. We could therefore in the class describe and explain some initiatives taken in other industries to promote a more responsible behavior from consumers, and consider the possibility to "import" these initiatives to the tour operating industry.

Points for Class Discussion:

(i) To what extent the limitations of the ATR certification are specific to the tourism industry? Will we find the same limitations of certifications on sustainable development in other industries, and to what extent the ways to overcome them?

(ii) What should be the nature of the governance of ATR? To what extent the different types of stakeholders should be directly involved in this governance?

(iii) To what extent the standards of ATR should evolve in order to certify more diverse tour-operators? The ATR certification was "designed" by adventure tour-operators, and the only organizations that were granted so far this certification are adventure tour-operators. Now nonspecialized tour-operators are engaged in discussions with ATR members to make the criteria evolve and be granted later on the certification.

(iv) The issue of the certification of local suppliers is to be considered. Now the local suppliers can be certified by the certified French tour-operators. To what extent an independent body should be also involved in this process of local certification?

(v) The ATR certification is well-known by tourism managers but not by tourists. Tourists do not indeed really notice and understand the differences in terms of sustainable tourism involvement between a tour-operator that has the ATR certification and another one that is just communicating on its sustainable travel packages. Should ATR communicate more on its specifications to the general public and if so how?

(vi) Some adventure tour-operators have a positioning based on the sustainable trips they offer. To what extent such a positioning is relevant for an organization that is "sharing" with its competitors a sustainable tourism certification? In other words to what extent a differentiation based on sustainability is relevant when your more direct competitors implement a marketing strategy based on the same type of differentiation?

(vii) One of the main limitations of sustainable tourism is to ensure that tourists do adopt a "sustainable" behavior. Some top managers pointed out that there is often a gap between the "discourse" and motivations of tourists before their trip and their actual behavior during their trip. One issue is therefore how the certification should take into account the tourist behavior that is essentially difficult to control and measure.

(viii) Students could consider the possibility to weight each criterion of the certification, and discuss the elements that should be taken into account to perform this task.

(ix) As ATR consists mainly in small organizations, it is difficult for them to have an impact on destinations at a macro level. More particularly their capacity to influence a government policy is limited. Students could discuss then the "lobbying" capacity of a group of small organizations, and how to increase this capacity.

(x) The aim of a certification like ATR is not only to change the practices but also to change the culture of the organization as a whole. A discussion could then take place on the general ways to change a culture, and more specifically on the ways to implement a culture based on sustainable development values.

(xi) A debate could take place on the limitations of the ATR certification identified in the research. It could be discussed whether these limitations are specific to the tourism industry or shared by other industries. Students could identify the limitations that are inherent to any certification, whatever be the industry involved, and the ones that are inherent to a certification type (focusing on processes or on results).

Further Readings:

(i)   The website of the ATR certification (unfortunately the website is not translated into English): http://www.tourisme-responsable.org/

(ii)   The website of the EARTH (European Alliance for Responsible Tourism and Hospitality) network:http://earth-net.eu/

(iii)   The website of EarthCheck: http://www.earthcheck.org/

(iv)   The website of the Green Globe certification: http://greenglobe.com/

(v)   The website of Travelife:http://www.travelife.info/

(vi)   The ISO website, and more particularly the pages on ISO 26000. http://www.iso.org/iso/home/standards/iso26000.htm

(vii)   UNEP, 2011, Tourism investing in energy and resource efficiency. http://www.unep.org/greeneconomy/Portals/88/documents/ger/11.0_Tourism.pdf

(viii) Betker A., 2012, Certification in Sustainable Tourism: Factors influencing their emergence and development, AV Akademikeverlag.

(ix)   Brebbia C. A. and Pineda F. D., Sustainable tourism, WIT Press.

(x) Castka, P. and Michaela, A. Balzarova, M. A. (2008), Social responsibility standardization: Guidance or reinforcement through certification, *Human System Management*, 27, *3*, 231–242.

(xi) Chen, J. S., Sloan, P. and Legrand, W., (2009), Sustainability in the hospitality industry: Principles of sustainable operations, Butterworth-Heinemann.

(xii) Leslie, D., (2009), Tourism enterprises and sustainable development: International perspectives on responses to the sustainability agenda, Routledge.

(xiii) Terlaak, A., (2007), Order without law? The role of certified management standards in shaping socially desired firm behaviors, *Academy of Management Review*, *32(3)*, 968–985.

(xiv) Weeden, C., (2013), Responsible tourist behavior, Routledge.

KEYWORDS

- **Certification**
- **French tour operators**
- **Sustainable tourism**

REFERENCES

1. Borraz, O.; "Les normes, instruments dépolitisés de l'action publique," In: Lascoumes P. Les Politiques Publiques et Leurs Instruments. Presses de Sciences Po, Paris; **2004**.

2. Pesqueux, Y.; Pour une évaluation critique de la théorie des parties prenantes. La Découverte. **2007**.

3. Delchet-Cochet, K.; Vo L-C.; Classification of CSR standards in the light of ISO 26000. *Soc. Bus. Rev.* **2013**, *8(2)*, 134–144.

4. Delchet-Cochet, K.; and Brodhag, C.; Le DS 21000 un regard international croissant le BNQ 21000, HAL; **2012**.

5. Debruyne, M.; La certification, substitut ou complément de la confiance dans les relations entre agents économiques? Revue Des Sciences De Gestion. **2011**, *252*, 47–57.

6. Savall, H.; and Zardet, V.; Tétranormalisation: défis et dynamiques. Editions Economica, Paris, **2005**.

7. Font, X.; Environmental certification in tourism and hospitality: progress, process and prospects. *Tourism Manage*. **2002**, *23*, 197–205.

8. Hultsman, J.; Just Tourism: An ethical framework. *Ann. Tourism Res.* **1995**, *22(3)*, 553–567.

9. Malloy, D. C.; and Fennell, D. A.; Codes of ethics and tourism: An exploratory content analysis. *Tourism Manage*. **1998**, *19(5)*, 453–461.

10. Payne, D.; and Dimanche, F.; Towards a code of conduct for the tourism industry: An ethics model. *J. Bus. Ethics*. **1996**, *15*, 997–1007.

11. Garrod, B.; and Fyall, A.; Beyond the rhetoric of sustainable tourism? *Tourism Manage.* **1998**, *19(3)*, 199–212.

12. Hall, D.; and Brown, F.; **Finding a Way Forward: An agenda for research.** *Third World Quart.* **2008**, *29(5)*, 1021–1032.

13. Fisher, J.; Surface and deep approaches to business ethics. *Leadership Organ. Dev. J.* **2003**, *24(2)*, 96–101.

14. Fennell, D.; and Malloy, D. C.; Codes of Ethics in Tourism: Practice, Theory, Synthesis. Channel View Publications; **2007**.

15. Baddelley, J.; and Font, X.; Barriers to tour operator sustainable supply chain management. *Tourism Recreat. Res.* **2011**, *36(3)*, 205–214.

16. Tapper, R.; Tourism and Socio-Economic Development: UK Tour Operators' Business Approaches in the Context of the New International Agenda. *Int. J. Tourism Res.* **2001**, *3(5)*, 351–366.

17. Schwartz, K.; Taper, R.; and Font, X.; A sustainable supply chain management framework for tour operators, *J. Sust. Tourism.* **2008**, *16(3)*, 298–314.

18. Font, X.; and Harris, C.; Rethinking standards from green to sustainable. *Ann. Tourism Res.* **2004**, *31(4)*, 996–1007.

19. Béji-Bécheur, A.; and Bensebaa, F.; Les stratégies de positionnement responsable: le cas des tour-opérateurs. *Décis. Market.* **2009**, *54*, 39–49.

20. Otis, J.; and Barabé, A.; Programme de labellisation en développement durable du tourisme: le cas de la Réserve mondiale de la biosphère du Lac-Saint-Pierre, Actes du colloque *Sites du patrimoine et tourisme*. Québec, Canada; **2011**.

21. Marcotte, P.; Bourdeau, L.; and et Leroux, E.; Branding et labels en tourisme: réticences et défis. *Manage. Avenir.* **2011**, *47*, 205–222.

22. Woodland, M.; and Acott, T.-G.; Sustainability and Local Tourism Branding in England's South Downs. *J. Sust. Tourism.* **2007**, *15(6)*, 715–734.

23. Bohdanowicz, P.; Zientara, P.; and Novotna, E.; International hotel chains and environmental protection: An analysis of Hilton's we care! programme (Europe, 2006–2008), *J. Sust. Tourism.* **2011**, *19(7)*, 797–816.

24. Amoah, V.; and Baum, T.; Tourism Education: Policy Versus Practice. *Int. J. Contemp. Hospit. Manage.* **1997**, *9(1)*, 5–12.

25. Dong, B.; and Wilkinson, S. J.; Practitioner Perceptions of Sustainability in the Building Code of Australia. Paper presented at the AIBS Transitions International Conference. Adelaïde, Australia; **2007**.

26. Grant, D.; and Mason, S.; Holiday Law: The Law Relating to Travel and Tourism (Fourth Edition), London: Thomson; **2007**.

27. Saggerson, A.; Travel Law and Litigation (4th edition). St. Albans. XPL Publishing; **2007**.

28. Friedman, A. L.; and Miles, S.; Stakeholders: Theory and Practice. Oxford: Oxford University Press; **2006**.

29. Jamal, T.; and Getz, D.; Community roundtables for tourism related conflicts: The dialects of consensus and process structures. *J. Sust. Tourism.* **1999**, *73(4)*, 290–313.

30. Mowforth, M.; and Munt, I.; Tourism and Sustainability. London: Routledge; **2003**.

31. Ladkin, A.; and Bertramini, A. M.; Collaborative tourism planning: a case study of Cusco, Peru. *Curr. Iss. Tourism.* **2002**, *5(2)*, 71–93.

32. Markwick, M. C.; Golf tourism development, stakeholders, differing discourses and alternative agendas. *Tourism Manage.* **2000**, *21(5)*, 515–524.
33. Robson, J.; and Robson, I.; From shareholders to stakeholders: Critical issues for tourism marketers. *Tourism Manage.* **1996**, *17(7)*, 533–540.
34. Wall, G.; and Mathieson, A.; Tourism: Change, Impacts and Opportunities. Harlow: Pearson Education Limited; **2006**.
35. Berry, S.; and Ladkin, A.; Sustainable tourism: A regional perspective. *Tourism Manage.* **1997**, *18(7)*, 433–440.
36. Dodds, R.; Sustainable tourism and policy implementation: lessons from the case of Calvia Spain. *Curr. Iss. Tourism*. **2007**, *10(4)*, 296–322.
37. Timur, S.; and Getz, D.; Sustainable tourism development: How do destination stakeholders perceive sustainable urban tourism? *Sust. Dev.* **2009**, *17(4)*, 220–232.
38. Miles, M. B.; and Huberman, A. M.; Qualitative Data Analysis: An Expanded Sourcebook. 2nd edition, Newbury Park, CA: Sage Publications; **1994**.
39. Nash, D.; and Butler, R.; Towards sustainable tourism. *Tourism Manage.* **1990**, *11(3)*, 263–264.
40. OMT, *Vers un tourisme durable, Guide à l'usage des décideurs.* **2006**.

CHAPTER 12

NATURAL ENVIRONMENTAL SUSTAINABILITY AND MICRO-TOURISM DESTINATIONS: THE CASE OF SOUTHERN ITALY

ANGELO A. CAMILLO[1], ANTONIO MINGUZZI[2], ANGELO PRESENZA[3], and SVETLANA HOLT[4]

[1]Associate Professor, School of Business – Woodbury University, 7500 – Glenoaks Blvd - Burbank, CA 91510, Ph: 818-394 3314, Fax: 818 – 394 3311, E-mail: angelo. camillo@woodbury.edu

[2]Associate Professor and Director of the Tourism Research Center, University of Molise, Via Duca Degli Abruzzi, 86039 Termoli, (CB), Italy, Ph: +39 0874 404840, Fax: +39 0874 404814, E-mail: minguzzi@unimol.it

[3]Assistant Professor, University "G. D'Annunzio" of Chieti-Pescara, Tourism Research Center, University of Molise, Via Duca Degli Abruzzi, 86039 Termoli, (CB), Italy, Ph: +39 0874 404840, Fax: +39 0874 404814, E-mail: presenza@unich.it

[4]Associate Professor , Department of Management - School of Business, Woodbury University - 7500 Glenoaks Blvd. Burbank, CA 91510, Ph: 818-394-3359, Fax: 818-394-3311, E-mail: svetlana.holt@woodbury.edu

CONTENTS

12.1   INTRODUCTION

Scholars of tourism studies posit that sustainable tourism needs to be developed in a way that all tourism activities, especially those involving the natural environment, be carefully managed in order to avert/minimize possible negative impacts on its existence, tourists' satisfaction, and the local community at large [1, 2]. Environmental sustainability, therefore, is no longer a distant factor when analyzing tourism destinations; in fact, the concept of sustainability in general has become an integral part of most tourism businesses and destinations' strategic planning, especially in emerging tourism destinations. Environmental sustainability concerns, however, can have double causality: Tourists seek destinations that are well preserved; while local communities are concerned with the impact tourism has on the natural environment. The latter is not part of this investigation; along with the emphasis on the importance of sustainable environment, the focus of this investigation is on tourists' satisfaction in emergent microtourism destinations using the concept of customer satisfaction within the framework of consumer behavior. Therefore, the main purpose of this investigation is on testing the factors that influence tourist behavior to determine if the quality of the natural environment is of major concern to tourists.

Countless theories explain customer behavior and determinants that influence customer satisfaction [3]. Consumer choice is usually understood as a problem-solving and decision-making sequence of activities, the outcome of which is determined principally by the buyer's intellectual functioning and rational, and goal-directed processing of information [3]. Within this context we can define tourist satisfaction as a function of the perception of consumption [4, 5]. Cole and Scott [6] argue that tourist perception is influenced by factors related to the emotional sphere, such as personal expectations and experiences. Customer satisfaction within the study of tourism continues to be a research topic of interest to many scholars. One of the paradigms most used to study customer satisfaction has been the expectation-confirmation theory [7].

Supporting findings identified in the literature reveal a direct relationship between customer satisfaction and customer expectations [8, 9] and that satisfaction is determined by expectations [10]. Therefore, according to these arguments, "expectations" can be interpreted as performance of establishment, ideal performance, or desired performance [11] and as "anticipation of future consequences based on prior experience, present circumstances, or other sources of information" [12]. Customer expectations can also be defined as the needs, wants, and preconceived ideas of a customer about a product or service. Customer expectations, in turn, are influenced by many factors, for example, customer's perception of the product or service being offered and related attributes such as perceived value [13, 14].

Tourist destinations strive to gain market share by competing for customers/tourists based on this information. Consequently, this increasing global competition in the tourism landscape compels tourism destinations' managers to constantly measure and analyze all tourism related activities, especially in emerging microtourism destinations. Hence, in the analysis process, customer expectations and satisfaction are the focal points for determining the influential factors related to activities, attractions, services, and pricing policies. For example, the critical variable that influences a destination's comparative advantage is the quality of the natural environment [15, 16]. Based on the Learning Curve and Experience Curve theories [17, 18] established destinations use competitive pricing strategy and cost leadership to gain and sustain competitive advantage. However, their competitive edge is affecting customer satisfaction.

Advances in Information Technology (IT) are also of utmost importance [19, 20, 21]. Tourist destinations with advanced Information Technology and Information Technology—Electronic Commerce (IT-EC), Social Commerce (SC), and Mobile Commerce (MC) infrastructure benefit from greater competitive advantage. Social media presence especially increases exposure allowing the tourists to immediately compare and contrast the destinations' offerings—especially the sustainable environment—on interactive platforms.

This study investigates the role of the environmental quality/sustainability and focuses primarily on identifying the rank of the factors that have significant effect on tourist satisfaction in three specific microtourism locations. Particularly, the study endeavors to determine, compare, and contrast the influential factors that affect tourist satisfaction in emerging microtourism destinations by investigating the tourism activities of three uniquely characteristic cities in Southern Italy (Appendix I). These three emerging tourist destinations have until now been able to attract tourists during three summer months only: June, July, and August. Contrary to what is important for other destinations, for instance, those in mountain regions, factors such as climatic conditions and accessibility are not dominant factors here.

APPENDIX 1

Based on our findings, we propose an interpretative and descriptive model capable of measuring of the factors that create and maintain tourists' satisfaction. This model will help determine the ranking tourists assign to the factors that influence expectations and satisfaction and the role the importance of the factor "environmental quality" plays in the evaluation. By understanding tourist perception, management can make appropriate changes in how their businesses are promoted. This strategic approach supports effective marketing strategies, which position products/destinations into the desired target markets. Del Bosque and Saint Martin [22] concur that, "If expectations are appropriately communicated, tourists will be more satisfied and consequently more loyal" [22]. In the pursuit of finding answers as to what matters in tourists' satisfaction, previous studies largely ranked satisfaction factors in order of the means, from high to low [23].

APPENDIX 1: Southern Italy Coastline.

Overall, while there is abundant literature published on "sustainable tourism," topic-specific literature on "Environmental Quality and Sustainability" within the concept of tourism destinations and satisfaction is scarce. Within the scope of this research we do not investigate the Environmental Sustainability or its quality of a destination, rather the importance a tourist gives to it compared to other determining factors that contribute to tourist satisfaction. This study differs from previous studies in two major ways: first, it investigates the factors that contribute to tourist satisfaction in three "emerging micro tourism destinations" simultaneously.

Second, it ranks the factors in the order of importance from the point of view of the tourist. It is hoped that the factor "Quality of the Natural Environment" will rank the highest. It is critical to consider, however, that during the emerging phase, a microtourism destination may not have the same offerings as an established destination, especially when it operates on a macrolevel, (e.g, transportation and recreational facilities). A microtourism destination may be able to have the same offerings once the destination is well structured and tourism matures. Indeed, the characteristics of the three destinations investigated are unique in nature, thus making this study a compelling one. Finally, this study will provide worthwhile information and guidance for tourism related strategic decisions, appreciated by tourism professionals, destination managers, government officials, and academicians engaged in all related tourism activities.

12.1.1   DEFINITIONS OF MICROTOURISM

Within the microgeographic context of this research, we define *Microtourism* as the "undertaking of travel activities for specific purpose such as recreational, leisure or business purposes to a "*narrow*" geographic area of the country. *Emergent Microtourism* can be defined as "all the activities in a micro zone where tourism is in the developmental stage which, if fully developed, can play a significantly dominant and economical role in the future development of the tourist activities of the aggregate macro tourism zones [24]. Also within this context we define *Microtourism Enterprises* (MTEs) as "the aggregate supporting organisms made—up of Small Business Enterprises (SMEs) that deliver all products and services to inbound tourism activities, described as "business enterprise having 10 employees or less with limited capacity and a current revenue or balance sheet total of $\leq \text{€}$ (Euro) 2 million" [25].

12.1.2   NATIONAL AND REGIONAL HISTORICAL BACKGROUND

Within the scope of assessing the importance of sustainability using the quality of the environment as the main factor, this study focuses on investigating and comparing additional determining factors that affect customer expectations—satisfaction in three emergent microbeach tourism destinations in South Central Italy. Two of the destinations, Termoli and Campomarino, are located in the Molise region, and the third, Vasto, is located in the adjacent Abruzzi region. They have a shared coastline of 35 km or 21.8 miles [26]. Tourism in these two regions is considered an emerging industry at a microlevel. These destinations are of note to tourists due to their presence on the internet through various government promoted websites and social media pages. In fact, these destinations have received the Blue Flag Award from the Foundation for Environmental Education [27] for excellent water quality, environmental quality, service quality, security, and environmental education. The Abruzzi region is rich in natural attractions and history and is growing in popularity with first-time tourists. During the emerging phase these two regions attract largely local and regional tourists and only a smaller percentage of tourists from other regions. As a result, the State Tourism Development Agencies of both regions are striving to put their emerging tourist destinations on the world map as the "Green Regions of Europe" in order to attract additional tourists [28].

These three cities investigated in the study have a unique and compelling tourist operation: they attract tourists during a short period of approximately 3 months a year, from June to August. Consequently, the extreme seasonality of incoming tourism with high demand during these 3 months poses serious challenges but also great opportunities in regards to tourist expectations/satisfaction. During this short period of heightened competitiveness, however, tourism managers face a difficult task in delivering the perceived quality expectation customers believe they 'should get' from the provider [29].

Italy is a well-established macro tourism destination. As such, the macro tourism market serves as benchmark for the management of these emerging tourism destinations. Thus local tourism managers hope to benefit from the touristic patrimony, knowledge, and experience Italy has, and try to integrate the well-established strategies into their destinations' marketing activities. In terms of its key performance indicators (KPIs), Italy ranked 5th worldwide by number of international tourist arrivals and fourth worldwide by total of international tourism receipts [30]. In 2012, however, Italy only ranked 27th in the World Economic Council's Travel & Tourism Competitiveness Index.

Obviously, Italian tourism faces unique challenges, including pressure from its regional competitors, among which it is ranked 20th. Compared to its main European competitors, France and Spain, Italy has been able to extract more value per visitor. While France and Spain receive more international tourist arrivals, Italy generates higher receipts per tourist. On average, each tourist who visits Italy spends about $1,141 USD, while averages in France and Spain are $664 and $1,019, respectively [31]. The World Economic Forum 2013 Travel & Tourism Competitiveness Index ranked Italy first in the number of World Heritage Cultural Sites and tourism infrastructure, and second in creative industries export [31].

The Italian travel and tourism industry aggregate tourism revenues for 2012 accounted for $40.25 billion, 9.4 percent of its total Gross Domestic Product, and 2.49 million jobs, or 10.9 percent of the total Italian workforce. Despite these positive factors Italian tourism industry enjoys, The World Economic Forum 2013 Travel & Tourism Competitiveness Index ranked Italy 78th in natural environment quality [31]: a serious concern for tourism management. Another concern to emerging destinations is the economy of scope of competitive destinations within and outside Italy in terms of marketing activities and effectiveness. Nevertheless, despite the global economic downturn, the Italian Travel & Tourism Economy is expected to grow by 1.9 percent per annum in real terms between 2010 and 2019 and travel & tourism totals are expected to reach $389 billion [31].

12.1.3 LITERATURE REVIEW

Research on tourist satisfaction has interested scholars for a number of years. In an increasingly competitive marketplace, tourist satisfaction becomes the most important factor in developing a better destination image, attracting more tourists and generating repeat business [32]. While scholars continue their scientific inquiry within the context of "tourist satisfaction," there is hardly any significant literature on tourist satisfaction in "micro tourism destinations," especially in the areas of their environmental quality and sustainability. In fact, a global search in scholarly literature on tourist satisfaction about "micro tourism destinations" within the framework of environmental quality and sustainability did not return useful results except for related terminology and brief references [33, 34, 35, 36, 37]. Most literature available is based on nonscientific research by local governments and organizations in the pursuit of developing local tourism to boost economic growth. Published scholarly literature shows that tourist satisfaction creates loyalty and leads to repeat visits, thus generating destination competitiveness [38, 39, 40].

Destination competitiveness can be defined as the result of the interaction of components that characterize those conditions of unity and inimitability. This is based on Hassan's theory of competitive advantage and on Leiper's proposed interpretation of mechanisms that draw tourists to a destination [38, 39, 40]. The literature also suggests that the tourist product is "experiential in nature" and seeks the active participation of the tourist [41, 42]. Rispoli and Tamma [43] refer to the tourist product as *"the ensemble of factors of attraction in which the user translates, interprets, and processes, through his/her motivation, the culture, system of values, personality, socio-economic conditions, behavior, and the individual demand"* [43]. The product is the result of the interaction between the process of the offer of an area and the process of purchasing/consumption of the tourist. Accordingly, tourist satisfaction is a function of the quality of the bundle of activities offered to the consumer at a touristic destination [44]. Golinelli [45] stresses that a destination requires the development of a cohesive and coherent development plan across the region as a whole.

Tourism is a system of complex consumption, and its success depends on a sustainable delivery mechanism. Destinations can achieve competitive advantage through increasing the value of core competencies the tourist seeks to enjoy, especially the value of the immediate natural environment [46, 47]. The distribution of services and the constant control of the customer satisfaction are widely recognized as keys to the success of the tourism industry [48, 49]. Consequently, customer satisfaction has become a principal unit of measurement for the analysis of the tourist's experience [50]. Previous studies on customer satisfaction have contributed greatly to tourism organizations. Yüksel and Yüksel [51] have demonstrated that research into customer satisfaction enables an organization to reach prospective customers, to achieve consumer driven improvement, to evaluate processes devised for continuous service improvement, and to understand competitive strengths and weaknesses [51]. Casarin [52] argues that tourism enterprises often make the mistake of considering that "the satisfaction of the tourist" is directly and exclusively tied to satisfaction relating to their own product and not to aggregate products. Previous studies have neglected the role of added critical components, such as sustainable environment, to overall satisfaction [52].

Published literature shows evidence that tourist satisfaction is a function of the perception of consumption [53, 54]. Cole and Scott [55] summarize the findings of several authors and argue that tourist perception is influenced by other factors, most of them related to the emotional sphere such as personal expectations and past experiences. For these reasons the tourists may not be influenced exclusively by their individual activities during their stay, but also by the experience and satisfaction of other activities such as pretrip services, services at the destination and satisfaction with transit route services. From a subjective point of view, the satisfaction of the tourists may be tied directly to the tourists' expectations (pretrip) and to the experience (posttrip). Intrinsic and extrinsic factors such as spending potential, types and price level of amenities and services offered have a direct effect on satisfaction. Ultimately the degree of overall tourist satisfaction is affected by the level of services and types of amenities delivered by the service provider [56, 57]. Wait time for any service delivered during the tourists' stay is also of ultimate importance [58]. Franch, Martini, Novi-Invernardi, and Buffa [59] argue that tourists are influenced by two categories of factors: *Permanent amplifiers* (constant, prevailing factors influencing consumer expectations) and *temporary amplifiers* (those factors that can temporarily raise the acceptable minimal quality of a service).

Additional elements that can considerably influence tourists are those factors that cannot be attributed to the individual supplier—especially the conditions attributed to climate and environment. Overall there is substantial research into the formation of consumer satisfaction [60]. The study of emotional factors like experience [61] and ego-based consumption [62] have also greatly contributed to the field of customer satisfaction. However, current trends on sustainable tourism show that the concept of sustainable environment will be another major contributing factor for the tourist to decide on specific destination.

12.1.4 TOURISM MODEL

This empirical analysis focuses on the investigation whether the environmental quality factor is of primary concern to tourists when they choose a destination. The study also focuses on identifying other major factors that affect the tourist satisfaction of unique emergent microtourism destinations and on comparing them with the environmental quality factor. Based on published literature, the study also develops and presents an interpretative and descriptive model and a "Matrix of Actions," useful for evaluating the destination's system of emergent tourism as well as the systems of established tourism destinations similar to those investigated. The model can be used to evaluate the effectiveness of the tourism system and to measure how it affects the relationship between expectations-satisfaction and/or dissatisfaction and perceived quality, especially during the emergent phase.

The matrix can be used to evaluate the positive factors that should be capitalized on and the negative ones that require a specific set of actions. The study describes "overall satisfaction" perceived by the tourist. The methodology applied measures tourist satisfaction through a subjective evaluation of the importance of each variable in the proposed model. The criteria for this evaluation is based on previous theories that examined tourist satisfaction by assessing responses to the natural environment compared to the quality of the public and the quality of commercial services offered [63]. Figure 12.1 shows the structure of the proposed empirical investigation model, and Figure 12.2 depicts the structure of the proposed matrix of actions. The factors included in our model were also compared and contrasted with determinants and indicators presented in various studies and based on the Dwyer—Kim Integrated Model and Crouch—Ritchie model [64, 65, 66, 67]. The proposed model includes factors that have an effect on the tourism experience in three main groups: (1) Tourist Natural Environment and sustainability; (2) Public Services; and (3) Commercial Services. The third group is subdivided into a further three subgroups, which measure the variables that have an effect on the following: (a) Professionalism of the Operators and (b) Cleanliness and Liking of Tourist Structures; and c. Convenience.

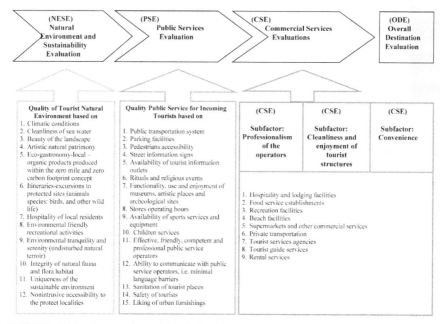

FIGURE 12.1 Proposed model of the determinants of tourist satisfaction. Various determinants and indicators have been adopted from Dwyer—Kim and Crouch—Ritchie models [68, 69].

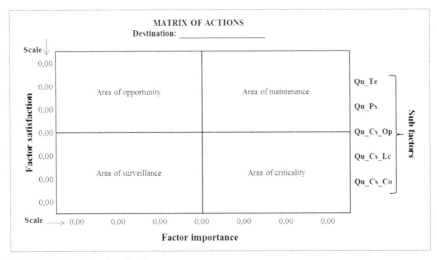

FIGURE 12.2 Matrix of actions.

The measurement of satisfaction relating to all quality factors is integral to the evaluation of their importance by the tourist. The main objective of this study is to measure total tourist satisfaction as it relates primarily to the quality of the natural-sustainable environment and also to the determinants identified in the literature review, focus groups, and face-to-face interviews. In the process, it is expected that the data collected could indicate insignificant effect if the factors isolated and evaluated by tourists are truly important. Hence, the effects of a single factor could produce a high level of individual statistical significance; however, it may be of lesser value or even irrelevant when related to the results of a large set of items in the construct. Consequently, we posit that in order to achieve an accurate interpretation of the results, it is necessary to rank the importance that the tourist assigns to each variable. We constructed a hierarchy of the degree of importance that the tourist associates with each variable prior to assigning a specific weight to each variable.

12.1.5 HYPOTHESES DEVELOPMENT

The development of the hypotheses is based on previous tourist satisfaction theories within the context of the natural environment sustainability and the quality of the public and the quality of commercial services offered [68]. We determined that the individual models of Dwyer-Kim and Crouch-Ritchie [69, 70] are mutually exclusive, but if fully exploited, can be jointly exhaustive. We then summarized the items in both models and through recursive abstraction adopted several determinants and indicators which we included in our model, as well as in the formulation of the hypotheses. Specifically, we divided the determinants into three main groups and subgroups. We posit that it is necessary to construct a hierarchy of the importance of tourist evaluations in order to rank their importance and provide valuable results. As such, the total tourist product is characterized as a "bundle of determinants" of predominantly cognitive and individual value. Accordingly, we can hypothesize that the total satisfaction of the tourist is a function of all expectations and the overall quality the tourist experiences. These expectations, however, depend on the intensity of the vacationers' needs, past experiences, and on the promise made or implied by the tourism supplier. The levels of appreciation by tourists can further depend on situational factors that cannot be controlled by the single supplier (e.g., climatic and environmental conditions).

In addition, literature shows that the quality of the overall sustainable environment contributes to economic growth and is considered primary expectation by the tourist. In fact, empirical findings from economic studies related to tourism in Southern Italy reveal that there is a causal relationship between the environmental quality and economic growth. The causal relationship existing between tourism demand and supply supports the concept that the quality of the environment is a major aspect of attractiveness for tourists [71, 72]. Considering this assertion, we hypothesize that the Quality of Tourist Environment scores highest among all factors leading to tourist satisfaction, since it is the principal influential determinant of choice tourists consider when selecting a destination.

Hypothesis 1: Tourist satisfaction is a function of the expectation and experience of the "Quality of Tourist Environment" (QTE) and the level of importance the tourist assigns to it.

This can be explained as QPS is expected to be a secondary influential determinant of choice tourists consider when selecting a destination. Also, because there may be no competition to choose from, the tourist may have no other alternative but to use public service provider.

We then anticipate that for the tourist, the "Quality of Public Service" (QPS) is a significant influential factor but is not a primary influential determinant in selecting a destination. One of the reasons is that the "Quality of Public Service" can only be experienced once the tourist arrives at the destination and uses the services. Also, emergent microtourism destinations may not have a wide selection of services available due to lack of competition, thus leaving the tourist at a disadvantage and compelled to use the only service provider.

Hypothesis 2: Tourist satisfaction is a function of expectation and experience of "Quality of Public Service" (QPS) and the level of importance the tourist assigns to it.

In the present case, QPS is expected to be a secondary influential determinant of choice tourists consider when selecting a destination. Also, because there may be no competition to choose from, the tourist may have no other alternative but to use public service provider.

The "Quality of Commercial Services" (QCS) is determined by the level of quality of all possible subfactors (convenience, availability, accessibility, etc.) of the services offered by various providers (e.g., gas stations, stores, accommodations). However, because competition in this cluster may exist, the tourist might have a wider range of services to choose from. Thus, we anticipate that tourists consider (QCS) a tertiary influential factor when selecting a destination.

Hypothesis 3: Tourist satisfaction is a function of expectation and experience of the "Quality of Commercial Services" (QCS) and its sub factors: Professionalism of the Operators, Cleanliness and Liking of Tourist Structures, and Convenience and the level of importance the tourist assigns to it.

In the above scenario, QCS is expected to be a tertiary influential determinant of choice tourists consider when selecting a destination. In addition, because services may be provided by many different competitors, such as accommodations and car rentals, the tourist may have a variety of choices as to which commercial service to use.

Government agencies at all levels (Local, Provincial, Regional, National, and at European Union, and Federal) level in charge of tourism development and environmental sustainability continuously offer support and conduct survey studies both with tourists and service providers to assess the level of overall satisfaction of the tourists and the possibility of a return visit [73]. Using scale measurement for the surveys, these agencies can assess the level of overall satisfaction of the tourists and be able to make future predictions, financial forecasts, etc.... useful for all stakeholders (EC, 2003). According to conventional wisdom, higher score across the spectrum always means better. Hence, these studies reveal that the higher the score the tourist assigns to a factor (services, accessibility, awareness, etc.), the higher the satisfaction [73].

Hypothesis 4: There is a direct and positive relationship between tourist satisfaction and the importance score the tourist assigns to each factor.

12.1.6   MATRIX OF ACTIONS DEVELOPMENT

Within the framework of hypotheses development and testing, we also propose and develop a "Matrix of Actions" to be generated from data analyzed through the multivariate statistical techniques. We subdivide the matrix into four areas, or "quadrants" (see Figure 12.2), and assign to each the type of action required according to the results of the data analysis. These areas are: (1) Maintenance (M); (2) Opportunity (O); (3) Surveillance (S); (4) Criticality (C) [MOSC], hence the MOSC Matrix of actions. These four areas in the matrix correspond to the various combinations of the value of the variables "importance and satisfaction." In the axis of the same quadrants, the matrix allocates a point for each variable of "importance and satisfaction." Following the analysis, the four quadrants highlight the value of all factors according to the results of the analysis. The interpretation of the matrix is as follows:

(i)   Area of maintenance (M) (if importance high, satisfaction is high)
(ii) Area of opportunity (O) (if importance low, satisfaction is high)
(iii) Area of surveillance (S) (if importance low, satisfaction is low)
(iv) Area of criticality (C) (if importance high, satisfaction is low)

Accordingly, the matrix suggests which factors require maintenance, which factors need surveillance, which factors are critical to satisfaction, and which factors offer an opportunity to capitalize on and improve tourist satisfaction. Because each variable in the questionnaire measured the factor "quality," this factor is further broken down into a subset of variables (components) and analyzed. The correlation coefficients between the variables in the subset and the first principal components identify the variables determining tourist satisfaction levels. In the analysis, we use both, the coefficients of correlation between the original variables and those of the components identified in the principal component analysis. The sign preceding the coefficients indicates the type of linear relationship (direct or reverse) between the components and the variable to which it refers, while the numerical value in the module indicates its identity and the link between them.

12.1.7 METHODOLOGY

This study uses a mixed method research design—both qualitative and quantitative. To collect the data, a survey was conducted using a multipart questionnaire that consists of three parts, with a total of 30 qualitative and quantitative questions: yes or no, scaled, ranked, and open-ended. In Part A, the questions investigate the degree of importance tourists assign to three microfactors: (1) Quality of the environment, (2) Quality of Public Service, and Quality of Commercial service. Each factor is made-up of several subquestions (variables) which investigate the level of satisfaction relative to them. The factor "Commercial Service" is further subdivided into three subgroups that test the satisfaction as it relates to the Professionalism of the Operators, Cleanliness and Liking of the tourism structures, and Convenience. Part B analyzes various aspects of the activities the tourist is involved in (e.g., choice, booking/reservations, and fruition of the stay). Part C is dedicated to the collection of demographic data.

The questionnaire was constructed using data from the literature review, sample questionnaires used in previous studies, for example, Cracolici and Nijkamp [74], secondary stratified-time series data from the Italian Statistical Institute [75], and results of three focus group interviews with city officials, tourism operators, travel agents, and representatives from other supporting tourist services, such as retailers, tour guides, etc.… The aim of the focus group interviews was to gather information about the destinations aggregate tourists products from an inclusive sample of participants who are involved in daily activities related to the tourism offerings (e.g., traffic, accessibility to banks, bedroom capacity, overall quality and efficiency of the services, etc.). In this way, it was possible to develop an instrument that together with those used in previous studies would be most inclusive. The design included perceptual measures that were rated on 10-point Likert scales: 1 representing the lowest and 10 representing the highest level of importance and satisfaction.

We purposely chose a 10 point scale to obtain more detailed results providing an exhaustive explanation of the phenomenon being investigated. Hence, we were able to design a questionnaire that was able to collect all possible data necessary to measure the importance that tourists attribute to three destinations' microfactors: Quality of the Tourist Environment, Quality of Public Services, and Quality of Commercial Services. It surveyed the satisfaction of the tourist relative to the single components (variables) from which quality is composed. Through the investigation, the model proposed in the study empirically tested the items in the construct and the results of the analysis were used to generate the Matrix of Actions.

12.1.8   DATA COLLECTION AND ANALYSIS

The large sample of participants interviewed (1,488) and the detailed questionnaire provided a significant amount of data. In an attempt to keep the study concise, we will not be able to show all tables and figures that have been developed. Nevertheless, despite these omissions, an exhaustive report of the analyses and results is presented. As described in Figure 12.1, this study investigates the determinants of tourist satisfaction regarding emergent tourist destinations based on three main factors: (1) Natural Environment, (2) Public Services, and (3) Commercial Services and three sub-factors of the latter: Professionalism of the Operators, Cleanliness and Liking of Tourist Structures, and Convenience."

The design is based in part on previous studies on customer satisfaction and service quality [76, 77, 78]. The data were collected using face-to-face interviews during the months of June, July, and August of 2012. Participants were randomly selected and interviewed at their beach tourism destination by a team of graduate students and doctoral candidates of the University of Molise, Italy, who were familiar with research methodologies and data collection process. They were recruited specifically to interview the participating subjects and collect data. A total of 1,488 usable questionnaires were received from interviews with tourists on location. The aggregate data was transcribed, checked for errors and missing values, and was then analyzed by applying multivariate statistical techniques using the statistical software SPSS Version 18.0. The first step of the analysis was to test the reliability of the data using Cronbach's alpha value investigation [79]. According to Peterson [80] and Kopalle and Lehmann [81], a value of 0.7 can be considered as cut-off point for evaluating the research reliability, even if also lower value (between 0.65 and 0.7) can be considered reliable for preliminary research. The alpha for each dimension of the collected data measured a value ranging from .90 the lowest to .94 the highest. The results of the reliability testing imply that the measurement scale is very reliable.

The questionnaire asked respondents to evaluate their satisfaction of all variables and to assign an importance score to each factor. It included related perceptual measures that were rated on 10-point Likert scales, 1 representing the lowest and 10 representing the highest level of importance and satisfaction. Other measurement techniques such as frequency, ranking, and multiple choices were used to investigate choice of services, lodging reservation, usability, and demographics of the tourists. In processing the data we first analyzed the frequency of the answers in order to identify the profile of the respondents and the main characteristics of their style of vacation. Then the data were elaborated using the statistical techniques of Principal Component Analysis (PCA) followed by a Conjoint Analysis (CA). Conjoint analysis is a quantitative decompositional model used to understand consumer choice behavior. Tourism is composed of a bundle of product attributes, which differ in perceived quality, value, and importance to tourists [82].

This analysis of the tourist choices determines the relative importance the respondent assigns to each attribute at a specific level [83]. In other words, it portrays consumers' decisions more realistically as tradeoffs among multi-attribute products or services. Principal Component Analysis (CPA) is similar to Factor Analysis (FA); however, they differ in the fact that FA's assumption is to test a theoretical model of latent factors causing observed variables, while PCA's assumption is to simply reduce the correlated observed variables to a smaller set of important independent composite variables. These statistical techniques are widely used in consumer, hospitality, and tourism study research [84, 85, 86, 87, 88]. Based on the previous discussion, the following construct was used to analyze the relationship and effect of the independent variables on the dependents variables (factors) satisfaction: (Qu_Te; Qu_Ps; Qu_Cs_Op; Qu_Cs_Lc; Qu_Cs_Co)

Where:

Qu = Quality

Te = Tourism environment

Ps = Public services

Cs = Commercial services and subfactors: (Op) professionalism of tourism operators, liking and cleanliness of tourist structure (Lc), and convenience (Co)

Op = Operators' professionalism

Lc = Liking and cleanliness

Co = Convenience

In the construct, variables were measured and the two components with the most meaningful account of the variances were analyzed. We used Principal Component Analysis to identify which variables have a negative or positive effect on the variable "satisfaction" as it relates to each factor of quality through the interpretation of the coefficients of correlation between the original variables and the extracted components to obtain an accurate measurement of "tourist satisfaction." In step two, the data were analyzed to evaluate the results of the principal components. We then analyzed the dimensions importance-quality, quality, and satisfaction to determine which one showed the highest statistical significance in measuring the tourists' satisfaction. From the data analysis, we generated the MOSC Matrix of Actions.

12.2 RESULTS AND DISCUSSION

A breakdown of distinctive demographic characteristics of the study participants is presented in Figure 12.3. From the 1,488 participants interviewed, 803 or 53.9 percent were female and 685 or 46.1 percent were male. The respondents' ages ranged from <21 to >65. About two thirds of the participants' average ages fell in the ranges of 21–40 and 41–50, an equivalent of 40.7 and 26.4 percent respectively, for a total of 67 percent. The participants' nuclear group composition was represented largely by friends and extended family, 19.11 and 28.56 percent respectively.

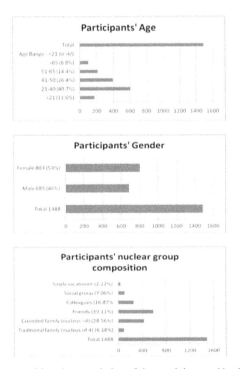

FIGURE 12.3 Demographics characteristics of the participants, $N = 1,488$.

According to the results, most participants prefer to spend their vacation with someone, rather than alone. In fact, single vacationers represented only 2.22 percent of the participants. Interestingly, the sample is represented predominantly by Italian tourists from Central and Northern Italy. Participants indicated their intention for a return visit to be 32.49, 39.84, and 60.87 percent for the cities of Termoli, Vasto, and Campomarino, respectively. About 99 percent of the tourists who have chosen Termoli visited this destination for the first time; tourists who had chosen Vasto and Campomarino had visited the destinations up to four times prior.

The results also suggest that the motivations underlying the choice of destination are different among respondents in the three cities. However, the reasons why they had chosen each particular destination are very similar: visitors relied on suggestions or accepted invitations from friends and relatives (see family nucleus make-up in Figure 12.3). The average length of stay of the respondents was about 7 days. Although the choice of lodging appears to be the use of a second private home in the city of Campomarino, the percentage of tourists choosing a hotel in the cities of Termoli and Vasto is relatively low as well: 28.99 and 31.90 percent respectively. For the purpose of this study, the factors affecting the decision of whether to stay at a hotel or to choose alternative accommodation were not investigated. In terms of tourist spending, those tourists who took advantage of services in Vasto and Campomarino ($3,335 per week) are willing to spend far more money than the tourists in Termoli ($1,334 per week).

For these data analyses, the variables were measured on a scale from 1 (lowest level) to 10 highest level), producing values sufficient to the significance of the analysis; however, the values are not as high as expected. On a scale of 1–10, the total average of the factors analyzed for the dimension "importance" across the three cities is 7.4 and the average for the dimension "satisfaction" is 6.37.

The analysis of the individual results presented in Table 12.1 illustrate that "Quality of Tourism Environment" scores the highest average in all cities: 8.33, 8.08, and 7.99 for Termoli, Vasto, and Campomarino, respectively. The highest value is for Termoli, with 8.33. This means that the factor "Quality of Tourist Environment" is the most important factor for tourists—as it was anticipated by researchers, followed by "Quality of Public Services."

TABLE 12.1   Factors and dimensions "Satisfaction" and "Importance"

Hierarchy of the Factors	Destinations					
	Termoli		Vasto		Campomarino	
	Impor-tance	Satis-faction	Impor-tance	Satisfac-tion	Impor-tance	Satisfac-tion
Quality of the tourist environment (Qu_Te)	8.33	7.32	8.08	7.29	7.99	6.98
Quality of public services (Qu_Ps)	7.99	6.45	7.37	6.55	7.72	5.84

TABLE 12.1   *(Continued)*

Hierarchy of the Factors	Destinations					
	Termoli		Vasto		Campomarino	
	Impor-tance	Satis-faction	Impor-tance	Satisfac-tion	Impor-tance	Satisfac-tion
Quality of commer-cial services						
(sub factors)	7.77	6.53	7.31	6.64	7.77	5.46
Operators Profes-sionalism						
(Qu_Cs_Op)						
Likeliness & cleanli-ness	7.77	6.71	7.31	6.61	7.77	5.90
(Qu_Cs_Lc)						
Convenience	7.77	6.11	7.31	6.15	7.77	5.07
(Qu_Cs_Co)						
	7.93	6.62	7.48	6.65	7.80	5.85
Average						

The results also indicate a direct correlation between "Quality of Tourism Environment" and the dimensions of "Importance" and "Satisfaction." The score for the dimension "Satisfaction" is the highest in the construct with 7.32, 7.29, and 6.98 for Termoli, Vasto, and Campomarino, respectively. By comparing and contrasting the results of all three cities, the city of Vasto scores highest in terms of tourists' satisfaction: 6.65 compared to 6.62 and 5.85 for Termoli and Campomarino, respectively. When the results for all three cities are compared, the city of Termoli, however, scores highest in terms of importance: 7.93 compared to 7.80 and 7.48 for Campomarino and Vasto, respectively. Overall, the tourist judgment in respect to the dimension "satisfaction" did not score highest, as one would have expected: tourists seemed to place more emphasis on other important attributes. Evidently, a gap between the dimensions Importance and Satisfaction does exist: Mean averages 7.93 − 6.32 = 1.31 for Termoli; 7.48 − 6.65 = 0.83 for Vasto; 7.80 − 5.85 = 1.95 for Campomarino). Campomarino shows the widest gap compared to the other two cities.

For each destination being investigated, a MOSC matrix for the evaluation of the factors related to quality was generated. To illustrate the true significance and the application of the matrix, we present the matrix with the results relative to the city of Termoli: see Figure 12.4. Analogous matrices have been constructed for the cities of Vasto and Campomarino; however, due to space limitations of this publication, other MOSC matrices are not presented at this time. Figure 12.4 shows the quadrants representing the four areas with the combinations of the values related to the dimensions "importance" and "satisfaction of the tourist in correlation with the factor "quality."

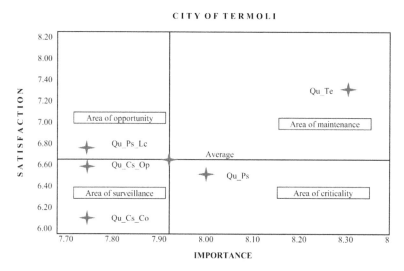

FIGURE 12.4   MOSC Matrix for the evaluation of quality for the City of Termoli.

The criteria demonstrate important components for which there is a need to intervene and to formulate strategies to increase the overall satisfaction through improvements to the tourism destinations. In the areas where the factor "satisfaction" is high (maintenance and opportunity) it is necessary to act on the variables that are negatively correlated, because the variables that are positively correlated already have a high level of satisfaction and the margin for improvement is limited. Conversely, in the areas of low "satisfaction" (surveillance and criticality) it is necessary to act on the variables that are positively correlated since these variables have a low evaluation that could diminish the total satisfaction of "quality" (see Figure 12.4).

In the inquiry process, we have analyzed the direct and reversed correlations of each variable compared with the factors that constitute the axes of the matrix. The significance of each quadrant of the MOSC matrix suggests the necessary action to be taken. The variables that are negatively correlated with the factors are located in areas with above-average satisfaction (maintenance and surveillance). In those areas, the variables adequately meet the tourist expectations. Although they show a certain level of satisfaction, these variables need to be monitored and worked on to improve tourist satisfaction.

The variables negatively correlated suggest a high potential for improvement and are, therefore, the best target for intervention of destination management activities in order to increase consumer satisfaction. With the same approach, in quadrants representing a satisfaction lower than the average (criticality and surveillance) it is appropriate to intervene with actions that influence the variables with the highest positive correlation because these cause the highest increase in tourist satisfaction.

As anticipated, the quality of the "tourism natural environment" is the element of greater satisfaction for all three destinations. Table 12.2 shows the results of the Principal Components Analysis grouping for each variable in relationship to the Quality of Tourist Environment for all three cities. The components (see Table 12.2) which have contributed to increased satisfaction for Termoli specifically are as follows: its uniqueness (0.80), integrity of the natural environment (0.79) and the hospitality of the local people (0.78). In the city of Vasto, the variables with the highest satisfaction, ranked in order of significance, are the uniqueness of the territory (0.74), and integrity of the natural environment (0.74) and the attributes itinerary and excursions (0.73). Lastly, for Campomarino the variables that significantly satisfy the tourists are artistic patrimony (0.69), followed by the integrity of the natural environment (0.68), and the uniqueness of territory (0.66). The preservation of resources is, therefore, key to maintaining tourist satisfaction. The values which are negatively correlated, especially in the second components, indicate that the corresponding factors are indeed areas that require action for improvement.

TABLE 12.2 Matrix of the principal components related to "Quality of the Tourist Environment" (Qu_Te)

Attributes	Destinations					
	Termoli		Vasto		Campomarino	
	1st compo-nent	2nd compo-nent	1st compo-nent	2nd compo-nent	1st compo-nent	2nd compo-nent
Climatic conditions	0.63	0.58	0.57	0.15	0.36	0.59
Cleanliness of the seawater	0.62	0.60	0.50	0.01	0.38	0.63
Beauty of the landscape	0.71	0.50	0.69	0.07	0.58	0.36
Artistic natural patrimony	0.72	-0.05	0.66	-0.48	0.69	0.15
Eco-gastronomy-local products	0.59	0.04	0.46	0.00	0.61	0.22
Itineraries/excursions	0.68	-0.03	0.73	-0.40	0.62	-0.10

TABLE 12.2 *(Continued)*

Attributes	Destinations					
	Termoli		Vasto		Campomarino	
	1st	2nd	1st	2nd	1st	2nd
	compo-nent	compo-nent	compo-nent	compo-nent	compo-nent	compo-nent
Recreational Activities	0.69	-0.18	0.60	-0.33	0.53	-0.25
Hospitality of lo-cal residents	0.78	-0.09	0.53	0.60	0.64	-0.37
Tranquility-serenity	0.53	-0.21	0.36	0.74	0.58	-0.11
Integrity of the natural	0.79	-0.34	0.74	0.26	0.68	-0.14
Environment						
Uniqueness of the destination	0.80	-0.36	0.74	0.08	0.66	-0.19
Accessibility to the locality	0.65	-0.30	0.57	-0.33	0.63	-0.27

Tables 12.3 and 12.4 show the results of the analyses for the "Quality of Public Service" (Qu_Ps) and the "Quality of Commercial Service" (Qu_Cs), respectively. In Table 12.3 we determine that the factors with highest value, meaning that they are positively correlated, are evident in the first components, although the factors differ in each city. In addition, the values that are negatively correlated show similarities in several factors in all three cities.

Table 12.4 shows the analysis of the "Quality of Commercial Service" (Qu_Cs). The results for the extraction of additional components are missing. There was an error in the printing of the questionnaire which was actually used to collect data in all three cities. This critical error was not evident until the data was transcribed and entered into SPSS. Consequently, the interpretation is ambiguous. Nevertheless, all values are generally high, which means that tourists rate the quality of commercial service rather satisfactorily.

TABLE 12.3 Matrix of the principal components related to "Quality of Public Service" (Qu_Ps)

	Destinations					
	Termoli		Vasto		Campomarino	
Attributes: Quality of Public Service	Components					
	1	2	1	2	1	2
Public transportation systems	0.59	0.11	0.44	0.66	0.58	-0.32
Parking	0.53	0.72	0.42	0.74	0.62	-0.43
Pedestrians islands	0.56	0.71	0.36	0.82	0.66	-0.17
Street and information signage	0.68	-0.32	0.29	0.29	0.68	0.02
Availability of tourist information	0.41	0.16	0.43	-0.57	0.57	0.04
Festivals and religious events	0.53	-0.26	0.32	0.16	0.45	-0.08
Functionality of museums, artistic and archeological sites	0.71	-0.45	0.63	-0.25	0.39	-0.42
Stores' operating hours	0.71	-0.14	0.27	-0.01	0.34	0.06
Availability of sports' services and equipment	0.80	0.05	0.62	-0.20	0.37	-0.35
Children's services	0.80	-0.02	0.57	-0.11	0.58	-0.09
Effective and professional public service operators	0.84	-0.07	0.58	-0.21	0.67	0.24
Ability to communicate with public service operators	0.79	-0.04	0.64	-0.09	0.66	0.15
Sanitation of tourist places	0.82	-0.08	0.75	-0.23	0.48	-0.17
Safety of tourists	0.71	-0.07	0.67	-0.02	0.49	0.49
Liking of urban furnishings	0.66	0.15	0.63	-0.18	0.48	0.45
Availability of sports' services and equipment	0.76	-0.08	0.58	0.07	0.39	0.65

As previously discussed, there is a gap between the factors of Importance and Satisfaction (see Table 12.5). The mean averages and the gap between the three cities are as follow: 7.93 − 6.32 = *1.31* for Termoli; 7.48 − 6.65 = *0.83* for Vasto; 7.80 − 5.85 = *1.95* for Campomarino). Campomarino shows the widest gap compared to the other two cities. Table 12.5 also shows the ranking of the factors "Quality of the Tourist Environment" (Qu_Te), "Quality of Public Service" (Qu_Ps), and "Quality of Commercial Service" with the subfactors of Professionalism, Cleanliness, and Convenience [Qu_Cs(Op_Lc_Co)].

TABLE 12.4 Matrix of the principal components related to "Quality of Commercial Service" (Qu_Cs)

Attributes	Destinations								
	Termoli			Vasto			Campomarino		
Quality of Commercial Service	Components								
	Professionalism	Cleanliness	Convenience	Professionalism	Cleanliness	Convenience	Professionalism	Cleanliness	Convenience
Hospitality and lodging facilities	0.81	0.88	0.84	0.63	0.82	0.787	0.721	0.679	0.593
Food service establishments	0.76	0.89	0.88	0.42	0.86	0.447	0.675	0.679	0.696
Recreation facilities	0.82	0.88	0.87	0.77	0.88	0.792	0.550	0.693	0.760
Beach facilities	0.88	0.86	0.88	0.04	0.06	0.585	0.504	0.710	0.617
Supermarkets services	0.86	0.89	0.90	0.38	0.66	0.729	0.310	0.599	0.540
Private transportation	0.87	0.84	0.87	0.75	0.83	0.877	0.737	0.446	0.629
Tourist services agencies	0.77	0.83	0.90	0.69	0.74	0.819	0.546	0.622	0.601
Tourist guide services	0.75	0.77	0.76	0.74	0.81	0.749	0.595	0.250	0.129
Rental services	0.81	0.88	0.88	0.79	0.79	0.775	0.605	0.438	0.533

TABLE 12.5 Ranking and gap analysis between the factors importance and satisfaction

City of Termoli	Importance	Satisfaction	City of Vasto	Importance	Satisfaction	City of Campomarino	Importance	Satisfaction
Qu_Te	8.33	7.32	QU_Te	8.08	7.29	QU_Te	7.99	6.98
Qu_Ps	7.99	6.45	QU_SP	7.37	6.55	QU_SP	7.72	5.84
Qu_Cs_Op	7.77	6.53	QU_SC_PO	7.31	6.64	QU_SC_PO	7.77	5.46
Qu_Cs_Lc	7.77	6.71	QU_SC_PP	7.31	6.61	QU_SC_PP	7.77	5.9
Qu_Cs_Co	7.77	6.11	QU_SC_CO	7.31	6.15	QU_SC_CO	7.77	5.07
Mean average	7.93	6.62	Mean average	7.48	6.65	Mean average	7.80	5.85

12.2.1   HYPOTHESES TESTING

In our proposition and within the scope of the study, we hypothesized that the Quality of natural Tourist Environment would score highest in terms of "importance and satisfaction" since we strongly anticipated it to be the principal influential determinant of choices tourists consider when selecting a destination. Accordingly, Table 12.5 shows that the Quality of the Natural Tourist Environment ranks the highest for both factors in all three cities; hence, *hypothesis 1* is supported. We then proposed that the "Quality of Public Service" would score lower than Quality of the Tourist Environment in terms of "importance and satisfaction." This is because Quality of Public Service is expected to be a secondary influential determinant of choice tourists consider when selecting a destination. Indeed, Table 12.5 shows that the Quality of Public Service ranks second across the three destinations. Hence, *Hypothesis 2* is supported.

We then proposed that the "Quality of Commercial Services" (QCS) and its sub-factors, *Professionalism of the Operators*, *Cleanliness and Liking of Tourist Structures*, and *Convenience*, would score lower than the Quality of Public Service in terms of "importance and satisfaction." This is because Quality of Commercial Services is expected to be a tertiary influential determinant of choice tourists consider when selecting a destination. Indeed, Table 12.5 shows that the Quality of Commercial Services and its subfactors rank third across the three destinations. Accordingly, *Hypothesis 3* is supported.

Lastly, we proposed that there is a direct and positive relationship between tourist satisfaction and the importance score the tourist assigns to each factor: the higher the importance scores, the higher the satisfaction. Table 12.5 shows that in all occurrences the factor "importance" to each variable is higher than the factor "satisfaction." Thus, *Hypothesis 4* is also supported: the higher the importance, the higher the satisfaction. In sum, *Hypotheses 1, 2, 3, and 4* are supported and have confirmed our assumption of the hierarchy of tourists' satisfaction with the factors in the model and with the dimension "importance" as assigned to each variable.

12.2.2   QUALITATIVE DATA ANALYSIS

Using open-ended questions, we asked respondents to add anything they felt would have enhanced the scope and quality of our research. Not surprisingly, we received more negative than positive comments. From these suggestions, we summarize that pedestrian zones, parking, cleanliness, easy access to heritage sites, competence of operators, modernization, maintenance of facilities, entertainment, and staff knowledge are major factors of dissatisfaction. Less impactful factors for dissatisfaction were the convenience offered by the operators (price/performance ratio) and professionalism. Clearly, these results show the management's lack of experience in meeting the expectations of the tourists—a true reflection of an emergent microtourism destination.

12.3   CONCLUSIONS

Environmental Sustainability has become an integral part of most tourism businesses and destinations' strategic planning—especially in emerging tourism destinations. In this investigation, the focus was customer satisfaction within the framework of consumer behavior and the importance of the sustainable natural environment. Therefore, the emphasis was on testing the importance of factors impacting tourist behavior—with a hypothesis that the quality of the natural environment is of major concern to tourists. This study synthesizes quantitative and qualitative data to transform the great variability of the collected information into hierarchical system that is useful in the analysis of the determinants of tourist satisfaction within the concept of environmental sustainability. Although these factors are not considered "discovery" in the broader sense, they must be evaluated on a case-by-case basis, especially in emergent micromarkets, and are crucial in the investigation in relationship to the overall tourist offering, as well as expectations and satisfaction from the point of view of the tourist.

The data illustrate the findings related to the most critical customer satisfaction factors for these three destinations. Based on literature review, a model for the analysis was designed to help synthesize the results of the Multivariate Analysis, which revealed important information and validity of single factors representing the offer of the tourism system. The analysis of the components extracted for the evaluation of the dimensions "importance and satisfaction" relative to the single elements of the tourism offer has provided valuable insights in measuring the satisfaction of the tourists.

12.3.1   LIMITATIONS

Although the sample was randomly chosen, the researchers assumed the participants who were approached for the study were all tourists. The instrument was constructed on the basis of stratified secondary data obtained from the Italian Institute of Statistics [89] and from the literature review. The validity and reliability of the secondary data rests with the accuracy of the Institute from which the data were obtained. The time series data obtained from ISTAT [89] may not be a true representation of the specific demographics of the emergent tourist cities investigated. Because only three cities in two emerging tourism regions in a microgeographic area were surveyed, the results of the study cannot be generalized to the entire population. The sample was limited to those cities and tourists who participated in the study. The timing of the survey could have delivered biased results because the tourists were already at the destination. The results might have been more comprehensive if the tourists had been interviewed before and after the vacation. A further observation is that the tourists who owned a second home in the destination could have been part of a population that had migrated outside its place of origin for professional reasons and therefore may not necessarily be classified as tourists.

12.3.2 RECOMMENDATIONS

The results of this study clearly indicate that tourists around the world are concerned with the environmental sustainability and preservation of the natural environment. Therefore, the topic of environmental sustainability in general will be the main driver of tourism development and be a crucial component in creating and maintaining tourism destination's competitive advantage. Using the results from this study, tourism planners have at their disposal clear references for crafting future tourism policies within the framework of environmental sustainability in order to meet tourist expectations and to deliver a superior package to enhance satisfaction levels. Such references contribute to the body of knowledge of *consumer behavior* as it relates *to tourist satisfaction.* The critical factors analyzed in the study are emotional in nature and have an effect on the processes of selection and purchase by tourists through their expectation/ satisfaction/ dissatisfaction.

The empirical results have confirmed how important it is to consider tourism destinations as networks of various influential factors/determinants. Some very important factors identified in the qualitative data analysis are parking, cleanliness, access to heritage sites, and competence of operators. Also, we found that the enterprise development (new services, modernization of service facilities, varied entertainment, technological upgrades), the improvement of knowledge and know-how, improving training and the hospitality of the residents can be considered as a network of factors relevant to creating heightened tourist satisfaction. Hence we suggest that future studies on sustainable environment could also consider including comparative analyses of tourists at multiple destinations that target specific consumers (young, elderly, business travelers or leisure travelers), with different type of governance (public or private), and emergent microtourism destinations in different countries or cultures. The techniques used in this study could be enriched by theoretical and operational results of such studies [90, 91]. From a marketing strategy point of view, tourism managers should play special attention to the demographic make-up of the tourists identified in this study (see Figure 12.3). Knowing who the customer is helps marketers target potential tourists who may have different values, different expectations, and who may need a diversified approach to the overall satisfaction.

This study should be replicated in different destinations where emerging tourism is prevalent with similar environmental microtourism characteristics to determine potential similarities found in this study. Application of the proposed model would be beneficial to future researchers of the topic. Future investigations should include foreign tourists, and the potential variability of the factors "satisfaction" and "importance" between Italian and foreign tourists could deliver valuable insights.

During literature review, the topic of "Tourist Experience" was identified, but it was not possible to investigate this dimension concurrently. Therefore, we suggest that tourist experience is not only a factor that needs attention but a crucial component that should be included in the investigation of "tourist satisfaction"—especially when researching into authenticity of a tourist destination, which could be a factor that influences both the experience and satisfaction, thus creating loyalty leading to repeat visits.

KEYWORDS

- **Sustainability**
- **Natural environment**
- **Tourism marketing**
- **Destination management**

REFERENCES

1. Ceballos-Lascurain, Tourism, Ecotourism, and Protected Areas: The state of nature-based tourism around the world and guidelines for its development, UK: IUCN Publication Services Unit; **1996.**
2. Buultjens, J.; Ratnayake, I.; Gnanapala, A.; and Aslam, M.; Tourism and its Implication for Management in Ruhuna national Park (Yala), Sri Lanka, *J. Tourism Manage.* **2005,** *26,* 733–742
3. Foxall, G.; "Consumer Psychology in Behavioral Perspective." New York, NY: Routledge; **1990, 8.**
4. Neal, J. D.; and Gursoy, D.; A Multifaceted Analysis of Tourism Satisfaction. *J. Travel Res.* **2008,** *47(1),* 53–62.
5. Lee, C. K.; Youn, Y. S.; and Lee, S. K.; Investigating the relationships among perceived value, satisfaction, and recommendations: The case of the Korean DMZ. *Tourism Manage.* **2007,** *28(1),* 204–214.
6. Cole, S. T.; and Scott, D.; Examining the mediating role of experience quality in a model of tourist experiences. *J. Travel Tourism Market.* **2004,** *16(1),* 77–88.
7. Oliver, R. L.; A cognitive model of the antecedents and consequences of satisfaction decisions. *J. Market. Res.* **1980,** *17(4),* 460–469.
8. Marzo, J. C.; Martínez-Tur, V.; Ramos, J.; and Peiró, J. M.; La satisfacción del usuario desde el modelo de la confirmación de expectativas: Respuesta a algunos interrogantes. *Psicothema.* 202, *14(4),* 765–770.
9. Ngobo, P. V.; The standards issues: An accessibility-diagnosticity perspective. *J. Consumer Satisfact. Dissatisfact. Compl. Behav.* **1997,** *10,* 61–79.
10. Ferrer, C.; Structural equation models for predicting customer expectation, satisfaction and perceived-quality relationships. *Int. J. Acad. Res.* **2009,** *1(1),* 147–152.

11. Teas, R. K.; Expectations as a comparison standard in measuring service quality: An assessment of a reassessment. *J. Market.* **1994,** *58(1),* 132–139.
12. Tryon, W. W.; Expectation. In: Ramachandran, V. S.; ed. Encyclopedia of Human Behavior. San Diego, CA: Academic Press; **1994,** *2,* 313–319.
13. Andriotis, K.; Agiomirgianakis, G.; and Mihiotis, A.; Measuring tourist satisfaction: A factor-cluster segmentation approach. *J. Vacat. Market.* **2008,** *14(3),* 221–235.
14. Ross, E. L. D.; and Iso-Ahola, S. E.; 'Sight-seeing tourists' motivation and satisfaction.' *Ann. Tourism Res.* **1991,** *18(2),* 226-37.
15. Ritchie, J. R. B.; Crouch, G. I.; and Hudson, S.; Assessing the role of consumers in the measurement of destination competitiveness and sustainability. *Tourism Analy.* **2000,** *5(2),* 69–76.
16. Dwyer, L.; and Kim, C.; Destination competitiveness: Determinants and indicators, *Curr. Iss. Tourism.* **2003,** *6(5),* 369–414, Routledge, London.
17. Hax, A. C.; and Majluf, N. S.; "Competitive cost dynamics: the experience curve." *Interfaces.* October **1982,** *12,* 50–61.
18. Hirschmann, W.; "Profit from the learning curve." *Harvard Bus. Rev.* (January–February 1964 issue).
19. Buhalis, P.; and O'Connor, P.; Information communication technology revolutionizing tourism. *Tourism Recreation Research Volume,* **2005,** *30(3),* 7–16.
20. Paraskevas, A.; and Buhalis, D.; Information communication technologies decision-making: The asp outsourcing model from the small hotel owner/manager perspective. *Cornell Hotel Restaur. Administ. Quart.* **2002,** *43(2),* 27–39.
21. Fodor, O.; and Werthner, H.; Harmonize: A step towards an interoperable e-tourism marketplace. *Int. J. Electr. Commerce.* **2005,** *9(2),* 11–39.
22. Del Bosque, I.; and San Martin, H.; Tourist satisfaction. A cognitive-affective model. *Ann. Tourism Res.* **2008,** *35(2),* 551–573.
23. Ibrahim, M.; and Moradi, L.; A model of e-tourism satisfaction factors for foreign tourists. *Aust. J. Basic Appl. Sci.* **2011,** *5(12),* 877–883.
24. UNWTO, UNWTO Tourism Highlights 2013 Edition. United Nations World Tourism Organization Report, (September 2013), **2012.**
25. EU, Model declaration on the information relating to the qualification of an enterprise as an SME (2003/C 118/03), replacing recommendation 96/280/EC of April 3, 1996. *Off. J. Euro. Union.* Retrieved May 15, 2013, **2003** from: http://ec.europa.eu/enterprise/policies/sme/facts-figures-analysis/sme-definition/index_en.htm
26. ISTAT, Data banks and information systems. *Istat—Istituto Nazionale di Statistica,* accessed March 23, **2013** at http://www.istat.it/english/databanks.html
27. FEE, Report Blue flags—Italian Beaches. Foundation *for Environmental Education,* retrieved September 26, 2013 from http://www.blueflag.org/menu/awarded-sites/2013/northern-hemisphere/italy/molise
28. Regione Abruzzo, Data banks and information systems, *Tourism in Abruzzo,* accessed March 23, 2013 at http://www.regione.abruzzo.it/turismo/en/index.html
29. Khan, M.; ECOSERV. Ecotourists' quality expectations. *Ann. Tourism Res.* **2003,** *30(1),* 109–124.
30. UNWTO, UNWTO Tourism Highlights 2013 Edition. United Nations World Tourism Organization Report (September 2013), **2012.**

31. World Economic Forum, The Travel & Tourism Competitiveness Report 2013, Data banks and information systems, accessed August 23, 2013 at http://www.weforum.org/en/initiatives/gcp/TravelandTourismReport

32. Meng, F.; Tepanon, Y.; and Uysal, M.; Measuring tourist satisfaction by attribute and motivation: The case of a nature-based resort. *J. Vacat. Market.* **2008,** *14(1),* 41–56.

33. Reid, S. D.; and Reid, L. J.; (1994). Tourism marketing management in small island nations: A tale of micro-destinations. *J. Int. Consumer Market.* **1994,** *6(3, 4),* 39.

34. Woodside, A. G.; and Martin, D.; Applying ecological systems and micro-tipping point theory for understanding tourists. *J. Travel Res.* **2008,** *47(1),* 14.

35. Campo, S.; and Yagüe, M. J.; Exploring non-linear effects of determinants on tourists' satisfaction. *Int. J. Cult. Tourism Hospit. Res.* **2009,** *3(2),* 127–138.

36. Paige, R. C.; Educational promotion strategies: Brokering culture between tourists and tourist destinations. *J. Promot. Manage.* **2009,** *15(1/2),* 286–301.

37. Martin, D.; and Woodside, A. G.; Tourists. *Int. J. Cult. Tourism Hospit. Res.* **2011,** *5(2),* 195.

38. Hassan, S.; Determinants of market competitiveness in an environmentally sustainable tourism industry. *J. Travel Res.* **2000,** *38(3),* 239–245.

39. Leiper, N.; Tourist attraction systems. *Ann. Tourism Res.* **1990,** *17(2),* 367–384.

40. Leiper, N.; Tourism Management. 2nd ed. Sydney: Pearson Education; **2003.**

41. Leemans, H.; The Multiform Book: Using Information in Purchasing Hedonic Products; Delft: Eburon; **1994, 23.**

42. Schmitt, B.; Experiential Marketing. New York: The Free Press; **1999.**

43. Rispoli, M.; and Tamma, M.; L'impresa alberghiera nell'industria dei viaggi e del *turismo*. Padova: Cedam; **1996.**

44. Casarin, F.; La soddisfazione del turista tra ricerche quantitative e qualitative. *Sinergie.***2005,** *66,* 113–135.

45. Golinelli, C. M.; *Il territorio sistema vitale. Verso un modello di analisi.* Torino: Giappichelli; **2002.**

46. Minguzzi, A.; Network activity as critical factor in development of regional tourism organization. An Italian Case Study. In: Lazzaretti, L.; and Petrillo, C. S.; eds. Tourism Local Systems and Networking. Series Advances in Tourism Studies, London: Elsevier; **2006.**

47. Petrillo, C. S.; Risorse ambientali e sviluppo delle attività turistiche. *Studi monografici CNR-IRAT.* **2001,** 10.

48. Hui, T. K.; Wan, D.; and Ho, A.; Tourists' satisfaction, recommendation and revisiting Singapore. *Tourism Manage.* **2007,** *28(5),* 965–975.

49. Presenza, A.; Sheehan, L.; and Ritchie, J. R. B.; Towards a model of the roles and activities of destination management organizations. *J. Hospit. Tourism Leisure.* **2005,** *13(3),* 1–16, http://www.hotel.unlv.edu/res_journalPubsArticle.html

50. Tonge, J. M.; and Moore, S. A.; Importance-satisfaction analysis for marine-park hinterlands: A Western Australian case study. *Tourism Manage.* **2007,** *28(3),* 768–776.

51. Yüksel, A.; and Yüksel, F.; Measurement and management issues in customer satisfaction research: Review, critique and research agenda. Part 1 and Part 2. *J. Travel Tourism Market.* **2001,** *10(4),* 47–111.

52. Casarin, F.; La soddisfazione del turista tra ricerche quantitative e qualitative. *Sinergie.***2005,** *66,* 113–135.

53. Neal, J. D.; and Gursoy, D.; A multifaceted analysis of tourism satisfaction. *J. Travel Res.* **2008**, *47(1)*, 53–62.
54. Lee, C. K.; Youn, Y. S.; and Lee, S. K.; Investigating the relationships among perceived value, satisfaction, and recommendations: The case of the Korean DMZ. *Tourism Manage.* **2007**, *28(1)*, 204–214.
55. Cole, S. T.; and Scott, D.; Examining the mediating role of experience quality in a model of tourist experiences. *J. Travel Tourism Market.* **2004**, *16(1)*, 77–88.
56. Pencarelli, T.; Betti, D.; and Forlani, F.; L'attività di ricerca di informazioni per la scelta del prodotto turistico. *Sinergie.* **2005**, *66*, 27–54.
57. Milman, A.; and Pizam, A.; The role or awareness and familiarity with a destination. *J. Travel Res.* **1995**, *33(3)*, 21–31.
58. Zeithaml, V. A.; and Bitner, M. J.; Il marketing dei servizi. Milano: Mc Graw Hill; **1993**.
59. Franch, M.; Martini, U.; Novi Inverardi, P. L.; and Buffa, F.; Comportamenti e scelte del turista fai-da-te nelle Dolomiti. *Sinergie.* **2005**, *66*, 153–180.
60. Tsiros, M.; Mittal, V.; and Ross, W. T.; The role of attributions in customer satisfaction: A reexamination. *J. Consumer Res.* **2004**, *31(2)*, 476–483.
61. Hamilton, R. W.; and Thompson, D. V.; Is there a substitute for direct experience? Comparing consumers' preferences after direct and indirect product experiences. *J. Consumer Res.* **2007**, *34(4)*, 546–555.
62. MacCannel, D.; The ego factor in tourism. *J. Consumer Res.* **2002**, *29(1)*, 146–151.
63. Neal, J. D.; and Gursoy, D.; A multifaceted analysis of tourism satisfaction. *J. Travel Res.* **2008**, *47(1)*, 53–62.
64. Dwyer, L.; and Kim, C.; Destination competitiveness: Determinants and indicators, *Curr. Iss. Tourism.* **2003**, *6(5)*, 369–414, Routledge, London.
65. Dwyer, L.; Livaic, Z.; and Mellor, R.; Competitiveness of Australia as a tourist destination. *J. Hospit. Tourism Manage.* **2003**, *10*, 60–78, Sage Publications, London.
66. Crouch, G. I.; and Ritchie, J. R. B.; "Application of the analytic hierarchy process to tourism choice and decision making: A review and illustration applied to destination competitiveness." *Tourism Analy.* **2005**, *10(1)*, 17–25.
67. Omerzel, G. D.; and Mihalic, T.; Destination competitiveness□applying different models, the case of Slovenia. *Tourism Manage.* **2008**, *29(2)*, 294–307
68. Neal, J. D.; and Gursoy, D.; A multifaceted analysis of tourism satisfaction. *J. Travel Res.* **2008**, *47(1)*, 53–62.
69. Dwyer, L.; and Kim, C.; Destination competitiveness: Determinants and indicators. *Curr. Iss. Tourism.* **2003**, *6(5)*, 369–414
70. Crouch, G. I.; and Ritchie, J. R. B.; "Application of the analytic hierarchy process to tourism choice and decision making: A review and illustration applied to destination competitiveness." *Tourism Analy.* **2005**, *10(1)*, 17–25.
71. Lanza, A.; "Is specialization in tourism harmful to economic growth?" *Statistica*, **1997**, *18*, 123–35.
72. Pigliaru, F.; "Economia del turismo: crescita e qualità ambientale." Paci, R.; and Usai, S.; eds. L'Ultima Spiaggia-Turismo, Economia e Sostenibilità ambientale in Sardegna, CUEC, Cagliari; **2002**.
73. EC,Supporting European Tourism. European Commission Enterprise and Industry DG, B—1049 Brussels (Belgium), **2012**. Accessed June 1, 2013 at: http://ec.europa.eu/enterprise/sectors/tourism/index_en.htm

74. Cracolici, M. F.; and Nijkamp, P.; Attractiveness and effectiveness of the attractiveness and competitiveness of tourist destinations: A study of Southern Italian regions. *Tourism Manage.*, **2009**, *30(3)*, 336–344. The questionnaire in this study was developed and administered by AC Nielsen, ACNielsen SITA, A division of ACNielsen Customized Research, Via Napoleone Colajanni, 4—00191 ROMA—Tel. 06/36306489-36306472

75. ISTAT, Data banks and information systems. *Istat—Istituto Nazionale di Statistica*, accessed March 23, **2013** at: http://www.istat.it/english/databanks.html

76. Jacobucci, D.; and Ostrom, A.; Distinguishing service quality and customer satisfaction: The voice of the consumer. J. *Consumer Psychol.* **1995**, *4(3)*, 77–303.

77. Andaleeb, S. S.; and Conway, C.; "Customer satisfaction in the restaurant industry: An examination of the transaction-specific model." *J. Services Market.* **2006**, *20(1)*, 3–9.

78. Neal, J. D.; and Gursoy, D.; A multifaceted analysis of tourism satisfaction. *J. Travel Res.* **2008**, *47(1)*, 53–62.

79. Cronbach, L.; and Shavelson, R.; My current thoughts on coefficient alpha and successor procedures. *Edu. Psychol. Measure.* **2004**, *64(3)*, 391–418.

80. Peterson, R. A.; A meta-analysis of Cronbach's coefficient alpha. *J. Consumer Res.* **1994**, *21(2)*, 381–391.

81. Kopalle, P. K.; and Lehmann, D. R.; Alpha inflation? The impact of eliminating scale items on Cronbach's alpha. *Organiz. Behav. Human Decision Proc.*, **1997**, *70(3)*, 189–197.

82. Carmichael, B. A.; Conjoint analysis of downhill skiers used to improve data collection for market segmentation. *J. Travel Tourism Market.* **1996**, *5(3)*, 187–206.

83. Timmermans, H.; Decompositional multi-attribute preference models in spatial choice analysis: some recent developments. *Prog. Human Geography.* **1984**, *8(2)*, 189–221.

84. Cattin, P.; and Wittink, D. R.; "Commercial use of conjoint analysis: A survey." *J. Market.* **1982**, *46*, 44–53.

85. Dellaert, B.; Borgers, A.; and Timmermans, H.; A day in the city: Using conjoint choice experiments to model urban tourists' choice of activity. *Tourism Manage.* **1995**, *16(5)*, 347–353.

86. O'Rourke, N.; Hatcher, L.; and Stepanski, E. J.; A Step-By-Step Approach to Using SAS for Univariate and Multivariate Statistics. 2nd Edition. Cary, NC: SAS Institute Inc.; **2005**.

87. Jinman, K.; and Nobuyuki, O.; Importance analysis on hotel components from a manager's perspective: Using conjoint analysis. *Asia Pacific J. Tourism Res. 11(3)*, **2006**.

88. van Zyl, C.; A conjoint analysis of festival attributes for successful positioning of selected arts festivals in South Africa. *Southern African Bus. Rev.* **2008**, *12(3)*, 2008.

89. ISTAT, Data banks and information systems. *Istat - Istituto Nazionale di Statistica*, accessed March 23, **2013** at http://www.istat.it/english/databanks.html

90. Dwyer, L.; Forsyth, Rao, P.; The price competitiveness of travel and tourism: A comparison of 19 destinations. *Tourism Manage.* **2000**, *21(1)*, 9–22.

91. Kozac, N.; and Kozac, M.; Information sources available to visitors: A segmentation analysis. *Tourism Rev.* **2008**, *63(4)*, 4–12.

CHAPTER 13

LUXURY TOURISTS VALUE PROPOSITIONS THROUGH NATURAL ASSET PROTECTION: A STUDY OF SMALL ISLAND DEVELOPING STATES

BLANCA DE-MIGUEL-MOLINA[1], MARÍA DE-MIGUEL-MOLINA[2], MARÍA-DEL-VAL SEGARRA-OÑA[3], and VIRGINIA SANTAMARINA-CAMPOS[4]

[1]Associate Professor, Globalisation, Service Economy, Tourism and Heritage Microcluster, Management Department, Universitat Politиcnica de Valиncia, 7D Building, Camino de Vera s/n, 46022 Valencia, Spain, Tele: 0034963877680, E-mail: bdemigu@omp.upv.es

[2]Associate Professor, Globalisation, Service Economy, Tourism and Heritage Microcluster, Management Department, Universitat Politиcnica de Valиncia, 7D Building, Camino de Vera s/n, 46022 Valencia, Spain, Tele: 0034963877680, E-mail: mademi@omp.upv.es,

[3]Associate Professor, Globalisation, Service Economy, Tourism and Heritage Microcluster, Management Department, Universitat Politиcnica de Valиncia, 7D Building, Camino de Vera s/n, 46022 Valencia, Spain, Tele: 0034963877000, E-mail: maseo@omp.upv.es,

[4]Associate Professor, Globalisation, Service Economy, Tourism and Heritage Microcluster, Department of conservation and Restoration of Cultural Heritage, Universitat Politиcnica de Valиncia, 3N Building, Camino de Vera s/n, 46022 Valencia, Spain, Tele: 0034963879314, E-mail: virsanca@crbc.upv.es

CONTENTS

13.1   INTRODUCTION

Sustainable tourism is officially acknowledged as an important tool for achieving objectives such as the conservation of biodiversity. However, tourism literature is more focused on protecting environmental health (i.e., through environmental management tools) rather than on the vitality of ecosystems (i.e., the protection of valuable natural assets). In the case of some Small Island Developing States (SIDS), biodiversity is one of their main tourist attractions, although not all resorts and hotels include it in their customer value proposition (CVP).

The natural assets of SIDS make them different and more exclusive than other tourist destinations as their flora and fauna normally create unique ecosystems. The United Nations recognizes the native biodiversity of some islands, like the Seychelles, which have been included in the UNESCO World Heritage List. Additionally, eco-labels such as Green Globe and Earth Check evaluate the contribution of businesses to biodiversity conservation, including support for natural protected areas and areas of high biodiversity value.

Furthermore, the idea of offering a luxury destination has led some SIDS to focus on unique resorts and hotels, which provide a peaceful and exotic atmosphere. In this context, biodiversity can add more value to a deluxe target when conservation is included in the customer value proposition, as it shows that hotels and resorts are sensitive toward biodiversity protection.

This chapter analyzes deluxe resorts and hotels in the Seychelles, and sets out which ones include conservation programs for native biodiversity in their customer (tourist) value proposition. Three types of resorts have been established based on their value propositions. The first type includes resorts whose CVP is based on luxury but which do not include conservation programs. Moreover, customers are not encouraged to participate in them. The second type features resorts whose CVP is based on luxury and includes conservation programs; however, customers are not encouraged to participate in them. The third type includes resorts whose CVP is based on luxury, which do incorporate conservation programs. In addition, customers are encouraged to participate in them.

Additionally, we have characterized the factors that determine differences in resorts and hotels' CVP in terms of their conservation programs and the participation of guests in these programs. Does inclusion come as a result of the existence of a protected area or national park on the island where the resort is located? If this is not the case, is there a protected area or national park on a nearby island? Or is inclusion conditioned by the species that exist on the islands? What other reasons explain the differences in resorts and hotels' CVP? We aim to answer these questions by analyzing the information that resorts and hotels use to publicize their CVP.

13.1.1   LUXURY TOURISTS VALUE PROPOSITION

The concept of *value proposition* refers to what a firm provides to its customers. It is an essential element in business model design. A *business model* represents how a hotel creates, delivers, and captures value [1]. Thus, a hotel's value proposition will appear in the description of what it creates and delivers to its customers.

Likewise, the value that customers perceive they have obtained will affect the price they are willing to pay. Hotels that offer a luxury value proposition use a differentiation strategy, which involves providing their services with superior and different attributes [2]. However, as business models need to be profitable, hotels have to determine their prices in relation to their costs. This is the reason that justifies the relationship in luxury tourism between the number of rooms and the customer segment targeted by the hotel. When hotels set a premium price for their accommodation, they can offer fewer rooms, but when they establish a lower price they need more rooms. We provide an example in Section 4, where hotels that set a price of about €3,000 per night have a reduced number of rooms (less than 25). However, those charging €500 have a greater number of rooms because lower prices require more volume.

Tourist destinations have some common resources that hotels tend to include in their value proposition. In some cases, this common resource is an important attracting force for tourists. Cultural heritage is a critical attraction in cities like Paris, Rome, Venice, Florence, or Barcelona. Yet natural heritage, such as marine biodiversity, flora, fauna, beaches, are also essential factors in attracting tourists. SIDS include their natural heritage in their value proposition, which appears on the websites of these hotels to attract tourists willing to pay a premium price to stay in a luxury hotel, located on a small island and which offers them activities that involve natural heritage.

13.1.2   SMALL ISLAND DEVELOPMENT STATES AND TOURISM

There is no common definition for SIDS [3]. For example, McElroy and Albuquerque [4] included islands that have less than 500,000 inhabitants and a surface area of less than 2,000 km². However, over time the concept has evolved: in 2006, McElroy included islands with a population of less than 1 million inhabitants in a land area of less than 5,000 km².

These small islands have rich biodiversity as well as other characteristics, such as a good climate and sandy beaches [5], which are in high tourist demand. These tourists are also attracted by activities like scuba diving and snorkeling, which can harm coral reefs [6, 5], use large amounts of water and energy, and produce large amounts of waste [7]. This is also a threat that makes their biodiversity vulnerable to tourism, and this needs to be balanced alongside the sustainability of their natural assets [8, 9, 10]. Balance is an important issue because some of these islands have few economic alternatives to tourism [10, 5]. One solution adopted on some of these islands has been to focus on luxury tourisms this segment is willing to pay a higher price in exchange for privacy. However, the example included in Section 4 reveals that they need more than luxury tourism if they want to conserve their source of income.

The following table (Table 13.1) includes the names of the SIDS, islands which share a series of characteristics including their small size, remoteness, isolation, fragile ecosystem, low intensity and volatility of human capital, diseconomies of scale, limited local markets and lack of diversification activities [11].

TABLE 13.1   The SIDS

Unesco Sids Member States					Unesco Sids Associate Members
1. Antigua and Barbuda	9. Cuba	17. Jamaica	25. Palau	33. Seychelles	1. Anguilla
2. Bahamas	10. Dominica	18. Kiribati*	26. Papua New Guinea	34. Solomon Islands*	2. Aruba
3. Bahrain	11. Dominican Republic	19. Maldives	27. Samoa*	35. Suriname	3. British Virgin Islands
4. Barbados	12. Fiji	20. Marshall Islands	28. São Tomé and Principe*	36. Timor-Leste*	4. Cayman Islands
5. Belize	13. Grenada	21. Mauritius	29. Singapore	37. Tonga	5. Curaçao
6. Cape Verde	14. Guinea-Bissau*	22. Federated States of Micronesia	30. St. Kitts and Nevis	38. Trinidad and Tobago	6. Sint Maarten
7. Comoros*	15. Guyana	23. Nauru	31. St. Lucia	39. Tuvalu*	7. Tokelau
8. Cook Islands	16. Haiti*	24. Niue	32. St. Vincent and the Grenadines	40. Vanuatu*	

*These are also the least developed countries.

Source: **UNESCO**   (http://www.unesco.org/new/en/natural-sciences/priority-areas/sids/about-unesco-and-sids/sids-list/)

13.1.3   SEYCHELLES: LUXURY TOURISTS VALUE PROPOSITIONS THROUGH NATURAL ASSET PROTECTION

In this section, we explain how hotels transmit their value proposition to their potential customers through the information they include on their websites. They try to influence customers' decisions to choose the Seychelles as their travel destination by using sentences and words that send messages with a symbolic content. The effect they want to communicate is related to the senses the visitors may enjoy, like the sound of the birds, the turtles, the blue pigeons, the sight and smell of the sea, the sight of the vegetation, and the feel of the white sand under foot on a beautiful beach.

13.1.3.1   THE SEYCHELLES

The Seychelles is a Small Island Developed State located in the Indian Ocean, comprising 115 islands, some of which are uninhabited. It has two natural parks which are included in the UN's World Heritage; the raised coral atoll of Aldabra, with the world's largest giant tortoise population, and the forest of Vallée de Mai, home of Coco de Mer trees. Some of the flora and fauna are endemic to the islands. Examples of these species are the Black Parrot and the Blue Pigeon.

The maps included in Figures 13.1 and 13.2 show where the islands and the hotels included in this chapter are located. It is obvious that hotels tend to be located near the capital and close to good transport links.

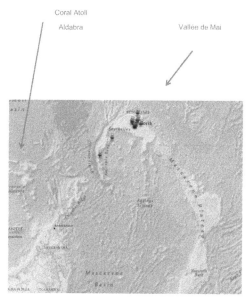

FIGURE 13.1   The Seychelles.

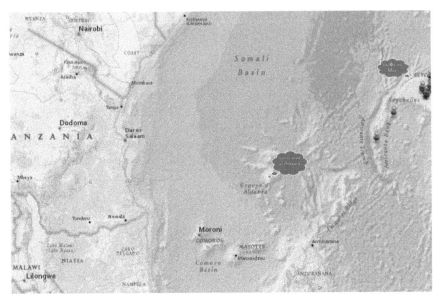

FIGURE 13.2   Location of Seychelles.

13.1.3.2   DATA AND METHOD

Data was taken from the 18 luxury hotels located in the Seychelles. We obtained the hotel names from the Tourism Board website. This website also provided us with information about the number of rooms in each hotel and their price list. We used the number of rooms as a variable to measure their size, and the price as a variable to differentiate between customer segments depending on the level of luxury. Table 13.2 includes information about the data obtained from the Seychelles Tourism Board.

TABLE 13.2   Luxury Hotels in the Seychelles

File	Hotel Name	Island	Size*	Segment*
S1	Alphonse Island Resort	Alphonse Island	<25	>3,000
S2	Banyan Tree	Mahé	51–75	1,000–1,500
S3	Constance Ephelia	Mahé	>150	500–999
S4	Constance Lemuria Resort	Praslin	101–125	500–999
S5	Cousine Island Resort	Cousine	<25	1,000–1,500
S6	Denis Private Island	Denis Island	26–50	1,000–1,500
S7	Desroches Island Resort	Desroches	<25	1,000–1,500

TABLE 13.2   *(Continued)*

File	Hotel Name	Island	Size*	Segment*
S8	Four Seasons	Mahé	51–75	500–999
S9	Frégate Island Private	Frégate	<25	2,501–3,000
S10	Hilton Seychelles Labriz	Silhouette	101–125	500–999
S11	Hilton Seychelles Nor-tholme	Mahé	26–50	500–999
S12	Kempinski Seychelles Re-sort	Mahé	>150	<500
S13	Le Méridien Fisherman's	Mahé	101–125	500–999
S14	Maia Luxury Resort	Mahé	26–50	1,000–1,500
S15	North Island Resort	North Island	<25	>3,000
S16	Raffles	Praslin	76–100	500–999
S17	Saint Anne Resort	Saint Anne	76–100	500–999
S18	Round Island Luxury Villas	Praslin	<25	1,501–2,500

*The data was divided into groups for the purposes of analysis.
Source: Seychelles Tourism Board (www.seychelles.travel/en/home/index.php)

Hotel websites provide information about what they offer their customers. This is called their Value Proposition. However, this data is mostly qualitative and needs to be analyzed objectively. For this purpose, we used Provalis Research's QDA Miner and WordStat software for qualitative data analysis. The steps taken to analyze the data were the following: First, we created a Word file for each hotel, where we introduced all the information available on their websites. Then, we inserted these files in the QDA Miner software, and created a document variable with the nonstructured qualitative information. Finally, we undertook a content analysis of the information, using both QDA Miner and WordStat.

The content analysis process included the exploration of word frequencies by counting the words which appear in the variable "document," to obtain the words that hotels used to explain their value proposition. Accordingly, we analyzed the content with WordStat, and obtained the frequencies of the words included on the websites (Table 13.3). Then, we used these words as expressions of the value proposition that hotels wanted to transmit to their potential guests. Finally, we analyzed this qualitative and quantitative data and obtained the results which are explained in the next section.

The data in Table 13.3 is expressed in Figure 13.3 but in this case represents the number of times (as a percentage) that each code (word) appears on every hotel website. It is clear that the important features included by hotels in their sales pitches are the fact that they are on an island, are located in the Seychelles, that guests will be able to relax and enjoy themselves, that they offer a luxury, private experience, and that the islands offer a beautiful natural environment which is unique. The words most repeated on the websites are islands, Seychelles, relax/relaxation, ocean, beach, enjoy, activities, private, pool, sea, natural and nature, luxury, and unique. However, conservation appears as a less important word.

TABLE 13.3   Frequency of codes in counts and cases when they appear

Code	Count	Codes (%)	Cases	Cases (%)
Island	266	12.00	18	100.00
Seychelles	155	7.00	17	94.40
Spa	98	4.40	15	83.30
Private	112	5.00	15	83.30
Ocean	83	3.70	18	100.00
Beach	102	4.60	17	94.40
Pool	49	2.20	16	88.90
Activities	53	2.40	17	94.40
Luxury	57	2.60	15	83.30
Enjoy	49	2.20	18	100.00
Natural	57	2.60	14	77.80
Sea	47	2.10	16	88.90
Nature	42	1.90	14	77.80
Unique	40	1.80	15	83.30
Tropical	37	1.70	14	77.80
Marine	35	1.60	12	66.70
Discover	37	1.70	12	66.70
Conservation	32	1.40	8	44.40
Paradise	33	1.50	13	72.20
Beauty/beautiful	65	2.90	14	77.80
Fishing	27	1.20	12	66.70
Exotic	27	1.20	9	50.00
Turtle	45	2.00	11	61.10
Diving	23	1.00	13	72.20
Exclusive	26	1.20	12	66.70
Explore	23	1.00	11	61.10
Bar	22	1.00	10	55.60
Environment	24	1.10	8	44.40

TABLE 13.3   *(Continued)*

Code	Count	Codes (%)	Cases	Cases (%)
Coral	23	1.00	11	61.10
Cuisine	43	1.90	14	77.80
Fitness	20	0.90	9	50.00
Flora	22	1.00	11	61.10
Garden	39	1.80	15	83.30
Granite	22	1.00	12	66.70
Yoga	19	0.90	7	38.90
Spectacular	21	0.90	11	61.10
Birds	34	1.50	10	55.60
Rare	20	0.90	12	66.70
Relax/relaxation	51	2.30	18	100.00
Sports	20	0.90	8	44.40
Trees	18	0.80	10	55.60
Sanctuary	19	0.90	11	61.10
Fauna	18	0.80	10	55.60
Tennis	17	0.80	9	50.00
Snorkelling	17	0.80	9	50.00
Sun	16	0.70	11	61.10
Escape	15	0.70	8	44.40
Vegetation	13	0.60	9	50.00
Comfort	13	0.60	9	50.00
Haven	13	0.60	10	55.60
Kayaking	13	0.60	9	50.00
Massage	12	0.50	8	44.40
Adventure	11	0.50	7	38.90
Jungle	12	0.50	5	27.80
Leisure	12	0.50	8	44.40

Source: Own source compiled from information on hotel websites

FIGURE 13.3   Appearance of words on hotel websites.

The data obtained from the content analysis also enabled us to undertake a network analysis method to get more information about the value proposition patterns offered by luxury hotels in the Seychelles. In the network analysis, the 2-mode networks were represented by UCINET and NETDRAW software.

13.1.4   RESULTS

This section shows the results obtained from the analysis of data collected through both qualitative and quantitative information. Quantitative data about prices per room and number of rooms allowed us to determine the hotels' target customers, and is shown in Figure 13.4. In terms of hotel size, Table 13.2 shows that 9 hotels had less than 50 rooms and 9 more than 50. Of those with less than 50, 6 hotels had less than 25 rooms and 3 hotels more than 25 rooms. In the case of hotels with more than 50 rooms, four hotels had between 50 and 100 rooms, and 5 hotels had more than 100 rooms. When the hotel price segments are added for every hotel, we can see that in Figure A the prevailing segments are those whose prices are between €500 and €1,000. In this group hotels with more than 50 rooms prevail, while in premium segments the smallest hotels predominate, that is, those with less than 25 rooms. Therefore, we can affirm that great privacy implies higher prices.

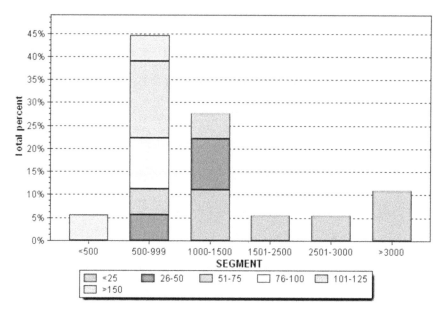

FIGURE 13.4   Hotels' target customers: size and segments in Seychelles luxury hotels.

Once we had defined the hotels' target audience, we analyzed their use of words and how the choice of these words determined the message they were transmitting to potential clients. For this purpose, we have included two figures; Figure 13.5 refers to every word and how many hotels use them, while Figure 13.6 refers to every hotel and which words are most used by them. For example, Figure 13.5 can be used to make comparisons between hotels, because the figure shows the hotels where a word appears more than in the rest of the hotels. Thus, the term *conservation* is most used by the Cousine Island Resort, the Frégate Island Private and the Desroches Island Resort. The word *exclusive* is most used by the Desroche Resort, which is also the hotel that uses the terms *birds* and *environment* the most. Thus, tourists who want to visit the Seychelles and go to a hotel that values conservation would probably choose the Cousine Island Resort. In fact, the resort's mission is "To promote and practice nature conservation and the wise use of natural resources of the island and its surroundings and to share this philosophy with our guests." Those looking for a spa in a hotel would probably go to the Saint Anne Resort, which has a spa managed by *Clarins*, or to the Raffles hotel.

FIGURE 13.5   Words used by the hotels.

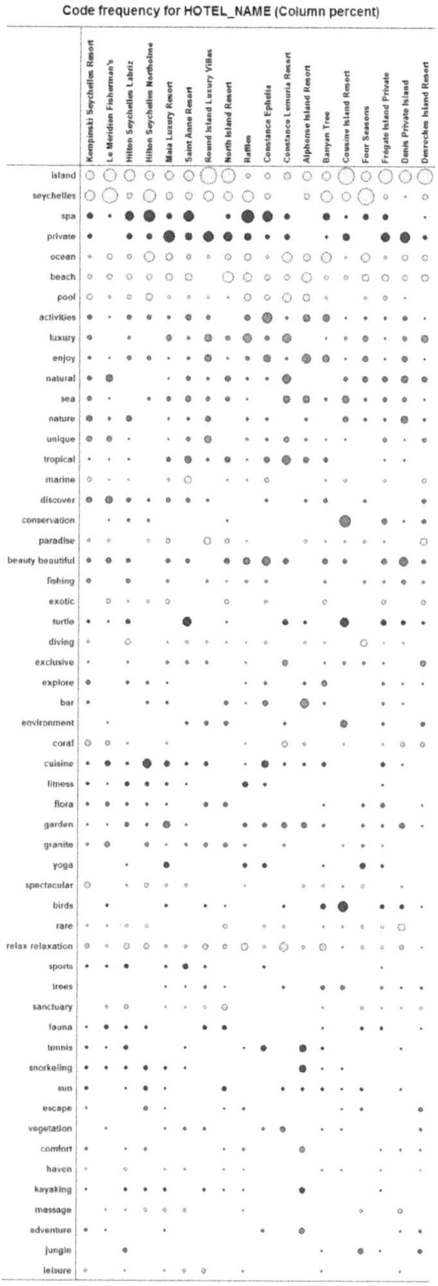

FIGURE 13.6   Hotels and the words they use.

In Figure 13.5, the words most used on the Cousine Resort website are *island, conservation, turtle,* and *birds*. These words transmit the resort's mission, which prioritizes nature conservation. Table 13.4 shows that resorts mainly used the words *island, Seychelles,* and *spa*.

TABLE 13.4   Centrality, closeness, and betweenness for rows (hotels)

	Degree	Closeness	Betweenness	Eigenvector
Kempinski Seychelles Resort	**0.818**	**0.817**	0.059	0.286
Le Meridien Fisherman's	0.691	0.724	0.044	0.239
Hilton Seychelles Labriz	**0.800**	**0.802**	**0.062**	0.271
Hilton Seychelles Northolme	0.564	0.650	0.028	0.197
Maia Luxury Resort	**0.855**	**0.848**	**0.069**	0.293
Saint Anne Resort	0.673	0.712	0.038	0.241
Round Island Luxury Villas	0.564	0.650	0.026	0.203
North Island Resort	0.636	0.690	0.035	0.222
Raffles	0.691	0.724	0.040	0.248
Constance Ephelia	0.582	0.659	0.027	0.212
Constance Lemuria Resort	0.491	0.614	0.017	0.186
Alphonse Island Resort	0.509	0.622	0.020	0.186
Banyan Tree	0.745	0.761	0.051	0.260
Cousine Island Resort	0.582	0.659	0.028	0.208
Four Seasons	0.545	0.640	0.025	0.197
Frégate Island Private	**0.818**	**0.817**	**0.063**	0.282
Denis Private Island	0.655	0.701	0.037	0.233
Desroches Island Resort	0.691	0.724	0.046	0.237

It is important to review the qualitative information that we have included in the file for each hotel. In some cases, these give us information about which customers are not the target of a hotel, and the hotel expresses its stance. For example, the Alphonse Island Resort indicates that "because this is a multi-adventure destination, it is not suitable for people with severe health problems or disabilities." If we look at the results in Table A for this hotel, we can see that they offer *activities* like *tennis, kayaking* and *snorkeling*.

The next step consisted of trying to detect patterns in the value propositions offered by hotels. We thus prepared a 2-mode network, where the rows were the hotels, and the columns were the words obtained from the content analysis of the hotels websites. Firstly, we represented the entire network in Figure 13.7. It became obvious from our first attempt that some hotels used a number of words more than others.

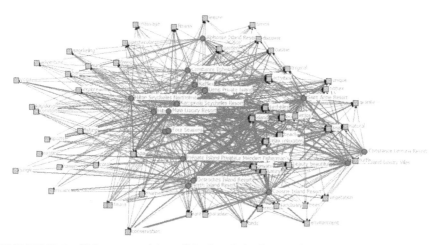

FIGURE 13.7   Value proposition of the hotels in the Seychelles.

Because our aim was to determine patterns in the value propositions, we calculated density, degree, closeness, and betweenness. However, we first had to dichotomize the network because these measures required binary data. Density indicated that 66.2 percent of potential relations were achieved in this network. However, the standard deviation was 1.88, representing high inequality in the distribution of the relations. In the degree column, the highest values were obtained by the Maia Luxury Resort, Frégate Island Private, Kempinski and Hilton Seychelles Labriz. These hotels appeared at the center of the network in Figure Y. In terms of closeness, the hotels that were most likely to coincide with other hotels, as they incorporated the same words in their value proposition, were also the Maia Luxury Resort, Frégate Island Private, Kempinski and the Hilton Seychelles Labriz. With respect to betweenness, the hotels with the highest values in the column were the Maia Luxury Resort, Frégate Island Private and the Hilton Seychelles Labriz. These hotels include words that are both important nodes and are also used by other hotels, and words that few hotels use in their value proposition. These hotels are in a better position to obtain information from other hotels. In the correspondence analysis, these hotels appear as being of the same type in terms of the design of the value proposition.

Finally, we used QDA Miner to represent the code and hotel data resulting from the correspondence analysis. The Figure 13.8 shows that the Cousine Hotel, which is the most conservation-aware, is not close to the other hotels. The figure also shows a group on the left that is close to words related to activities, while hotels in the center and at the top are close to words related to biodiversity and luxury, but conservation only appears near the Cousine Resort. Therefore, we can conclude that there are three different types in the definition of hotels' value propositions. The first includes hotels whose value is based on luxury and activities; the second group includes hotels whose value centers on luxury and biodiversity but do not mention conservation, whilst the third are hotels for which conservation and luxury go hand in hand with their value proposition.

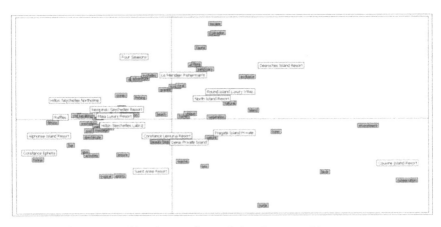

FIGURE 13.8   Groups of hotels according to their value proposition.

13.2   CONCLUSIONS

Value propositions are an important issue in the design of a business model. When we want to compare the value proposition of different hotels there are several tools that enable an objective analysis. This chapter tries to set out how we can obtain interesting data through the information included on websites or in any other type of advertising.

To apply our ideas, we used the case of luxury hotels in the Seychelles as an example, and analyzed the 18 luxury hotels located there. We used content analysis and network analysis to detect differences and patterns in the value proposition. Our analysis has confirmed that the use of different methodologies provides us with information that we would not be able to obtain without using them.

Our results have confirmed that, although the Seychelles have an important natural heritage that needs to be protected, the term conservation is little utilized in the value proposition of luxury hotels in the Seychelles.

The use of software to analyze and represent both qualitative and quantitative data enables more detailed results to be obtained. The different software programs we have chosen to explain how to obtain hotels' value propositions are available free of charge or for a small fee. For example, QDA Miner has a free version named QDA Miner Lite. Ucinet is not expensive, and there is also a trial version available for a few months.

13.2.1 IN-CLASS DISCUSSION POINTS

(i) The chapter provides a different approach to detect the value proposition of firms (hotels) in a particular location. The limitation of this technique is the risk of losing information that may be relevant, such as the mission of the hotel. Try to think of other limitations of this technique.
(ii) To what extent do the words that identify a company on its website correspond to the values it aims to transmit?

13.2.2 QUESTIONS FOR THE CLASS TO DISCUSS

(i) Teamwork: Think of goods and services that firms try to sell using symbolic messages. Try to think of similar articles and discuss how differently these messages get your attention.
(ii) Think of two firms in the same industry and compare the words that appear on their websites. Once you have detected the differences between them, which firm do you identify most with? Is it a firm you buy a lot from?

13.2.3 SUGGESTED FURTHER READING

We encourage you to read the following books. The first book we suggest is the work by professors Kim and Mauborgne, who use the Blue Ocean Strategy to create innovative customer value propositions. Second, the work by Osterwalder and Pigneur is very useful to connect customer value propositions and business models.

Kim, W. C.; and Mauborgne, R.; Blue Ocean Strategy. United States: Harvard Business Press Books; **2005**.

Osterwalder, A.; and Pigneur, Y.; Business Model Generation. United States of America: John Wiley & Sons; **2010**.

KEYWORDS

- **Cultural heritage**
- **customer value proposition (CVP)**
- **Small Island Developing States (SIDS)**

REFERENCES

1. Osterwalder, A.; and Pigneur, Y.; Business Model Generation. United States of America: John Wiley & Sons; **2010**.
2. Thompson, A. A.; Peteraf, M. A.; Gamble, J. E.; and Strickland, A. J.; Crafting and Executing Strategy. The Quest for Competitive Advantage. Concepts and Cases. 19th Edition. New York: McGraw-Hill Irwin; **2013**.
3. De Miguel, B.; De Miguel, M.; and Rumiche, M.; Does luxury indicate sustainability? An analysis of the Maldives. *EJBO Elect. J. Business Ethics Organ. Studies*. **2011,** *16.1,* 21–31.
4. McElroy, J. L.; and Albuquerque, K.; Tourism penetration index in small Caribbean Islands. *Ann. Tour. Res.* **1998,** *25.1,* 145–168.
5. Belle, N.; and Bramwell, B.; Climate change and small island tourism: Policy maker and industry perspectives in Barbados. *J. Travel Res.* **2005,** *44,* 32–41.
6. Nurse, L.; and Moore, R.; Adaptation to global climate change: An urgent requirement for Small Island Developing States. *Rev. Euro. Commun. Int. Environ. Law*. **2005,** *14.2,* 100–107.
7. Scheyvens, R.; and Momsen, J.; Tourism in Small Island States: From Vulnerability to Strengths." *J. Sustain. Tour.* **2008,** *16.5,* 491–510.
8. Fry, I.; Small Island Developing States: Becalmed in a sea of soft law. *Rev. Euro. Commun. Int. Environ. Law*. **2005,** *14.2,* 89–99.
9. Zubair, S.; Bowen, D.; and Elwin, J.; Not quite paradise: Inadequacies of environmental impact assessment in the Maldives. *Tour. Manag.* **2011,** *32 2,* 225–234.
10. Clampling, L.; and Rosalie, M.; Sustaining social development in a Small Island Developing State? The case of Seychelles. *Sustainable Dev.* **2006,** *14,* 115–125.
11. Blancard, S.; and Hoarau, J. F.; A new sustainable human development indicator for small island developing states: A reappraisal from data envelopment analysis. *Economic Modell.* **2013,** *30,* 623–635.
12. McElroy, J. L.; Small Island tourist economies across the life cycle. *Asia Pacific Viewpoint.* **2006,** *47.1,* 61–77.

CHAPTER 14

THE SLOW TOURISM: AN INDIRECT WAY TO PROTECT THE ENVIRONMENT

LLUÍS MIRETPASTOR[1], ÁNGEL PEIRÓ-SIGNES[2],
MARÍA-DEL-VAL SEGARRA-OÑA[3], and JOSÉ MONDÉJAR-JIMÉNEZ[4]

[1]Assistant Professor, Social Sciences Department, C/ Paraninf, 1, 46730 Grau de Gandia, Universitat Politиcnica de Valиncia, Valencia, Spain, Tele: 0034963877000 E-mail: luimipas@esp.upv.es

[2]Assistant Professor, Management Department, 7D building, Camн de Vera s/n, 46022, Universitat Politиcnica de Valиncia Valencia (Spain), Tele: 0034963877000 E-mail: anpeisig@omp.upv.es

[3]Associate Professor, Management Department, 7D building, Camн de Vera s/n, 46022, Universitat Politиcnica de Valиncia Valencia (Spain), Tele: 0034963877000, E-mail: maseo@omp.upv.es

[4]Associate Professor, Dean of the Social Sciences School, Edificio Cardenal Gil de Albornoz. Avda. de los Alfares, 44-16.071, Cuenca Universidad de Castilla La Mancha, Tele: 0034969179125, E-mail: Jose.Mondejar@uclm.es

CONTENTS

14.1   INTRODUCTION

This paper presents applications and opportunities to explore what the so-called "Slow Tourism" may have for tourism in general and tourism in small towns in particular. Slow tourism derives from the Slow food movement, founded at the eighties decade by Carlo Petrini. At the crossroads of ecology and gastronomy, ethics and pleasure stand the Slow Food movement, opposing to the standardization of taste and culture, to Fast Food and to the power of the food industry multinationals and industrial agriculture. The slow-food movement involves a commitment to local cuisine, for the recovery of traditional productions, the plant and animal species in danger of extinction, and likewise, seeks to promote a new model of agriculture, less intensive and cleaner founded on knowledge and savoir faire of local communities.

The Slow Food movement began to develop in Europe, but since the late nineties has been expanding its global dizzying and is currently present in more than 160 countries. Slow Food USA was founded in 2000.

The Slow Food emerged as an alternative to Fast Food, but has been drifting into a philosophy of life that does not refer only to food but also many other aspects of life. Thus, in terms of food has led to thematic movements as slow fish (linked to sustainable seafood) or the slow cheese (linked to artisanal cheeses) or km0 Restaurants. In other areas, the slow movement encompasses such different fields as the slow architecture, slow schooling, slow money, slow work and the two that concern us in this work: the slow tourism and slow cities.

The Slow Cities Movement groups, towns, and cities committed to improving life quality of its citizens especially, but not only in relation to food (Slowfood.es, 2010). Although many authors find it difficult to talk about quality of life in cities [7], the Slow Cities Movement arises to ensure the best quality of life in their populations, some authors have called to create a city of sensations (sensory city) [23].

As for slow tourism, appears as an alternative to scheduled trips, the "all inclusive" or "low cost" tourism. Faced with superficial, fast, and stressful tourism, the slow tourism searches a calmed and relaxed tourism. Slow tourism intends tourist to become a part of local life and to connect with the destination, its people, and culture. The trip purpose is not simply to visit a city or a territory, but to figure it out. The travel experience goes beyond the "visit" and includes the local cuisine as motivation [27], or the discovery of idiosyncrasies, cultural, and social history of the territory [8].

In this paper we review the concepts of slow tourism and slow city, aiming to analyze the potential of these new concepts for tourism in small towns. Once the initial concepts have been presented, a second section will analyze the concept of slow city and its potential applications not only in the tourist field but in the development of small towns, in a third section we propose the concept of slow tourism its connection with other forms of tourism and it is compared with the traditional model, in a fourth section we describe current status, potentialities, and synergies that this tourism model presents, ending with a final chapter that sets the main conclusions and future lines of research.

14.2   THE SLOW CITY AS TOURISM PRODUCT AND OPPORTUNITY FOR LOCAL DEVELOPMENT

As a result of the prevailing economic and social model [26], small towns face many problems such as poor communications, lack of job opportunities or lack of leisure for young people. This situation leads many municipalities to end up becoming bed towns or to lose population [6]. To address this problem, many municipalities are making considerable efforts to attract industries and businesses that often are owned by multinational corporations, with no roots in the territory, and that are installed in exchange for significant tax advantages and that normally offer low pay jobs. This ends up causing what some authors have called "clone towns" [21].

Given this approach, some authors have worked on the opportunities that small towns may find offering the "second modernity" [4, 5]. These opportunities are based on the search for sustainable growth that is capable of combining economic development with environmental respect and town's peculiarities, with special emphasis on the quality of life.

As suggested by Mayer and Knox (2007), the slow movement of the cities may be small populations' response to pressures and opportunities of the second modernity. This is not to numb towns, but to set the basis for them to achieve sustainability, entrepreneurialship, and creativeness (Mayer and Knox, 2007). It aims to promote economic development, but it must be done endogenously, creating "alternative economic spaces" [18]. The small towns should take advantage of their culture, traditions, and specificities to generate creativity, since much of the new postindustrial economy is based on knowledge.

Slow city movement began in 1999 and originally composed of four Italian towns (Greve-in-Chianti, Orvieto, Bra, and Positano). In 2001 there were 29 slow cities already certified and in 2013 included more than 180 cities in 28 countries. At the United States of America, only three cities join the international network, Fairfax, Sebastopol, and Sonoma, all of them in California (http://www.cittaslowusa.org/, 2011). Note that the key areas to be considered a slow city are the same worldwide, although some of the performance indicators may vary depending on each country's regulatory framework. Urban planning policies of all slow cities are based on the same principles, but each city will find their own solutions.

As an example, we note that the Italian town of Bra has the main square´s clock thirty minutes delayed and all shops are closed on Thursdays and Sundays. Cars have denied access to the city center and hundreds of snails (the slow movement symbol) are scattered around the city.

The Spanish network was certified as official network in March 2008. The official name is "Cittaslow—Red Nacional de ciudades por la Calidad de Vida," short version "Cittaslow." Cittaslow is linked to the international Slow Food association with which it shares the philosophy. The first Spanish towns to show interest in this subject in 2003 was Palafrugell, Begur, and Pals. Along the same lines, other towns in other regions, namely, Mungia and Lekeitio (Vizcaya), Rubielos de Mora (Teruel), and Bigastro in (Alicante), undertook efforts to integrate themselves into the network. Thus, these seven towns started Cittaslow movement in Spain, although Palafrugell has quitted and, actually, now only 6 towns are running.

Some of these cities such as Begur, Pals, or Bigastro are located near some of the busiest tourist areas in Spain, but they have been able to differentiate themselves from the mass tourism and offer a much more relaxed and authentic alternative betting on slow movement philosophy.

Town applicants must meet a number of requirements among which it could be highlighted:

• The implementation of an environmental policy based on promotion of recovery and recycling of waste.
• Urban policy must serve to improve the territory, not to occupy it.
• The use of technological advances to improve environmental quality and urban areas.
• Promoting the production and use of food products obtained using natural and environmentally compatible methods, not including biotech products and implementing, where appropriate, services of defense and development of autochthonous productions.
• The empowerment of autochthonous productions linked to the territory: the most ancient traditions remain and the relationship between consumers and producers of quality is promoted.
• Hospitality and convenience empowerment between inhabitants and tourists.
• Both people and tourist's operator's awareness about what it means to live in a slow city and its impact, with particular attention on raising young people concern through specific training plans.
• The population of the cities in the network cannot exceed 50,000.

Cittaslow movement is an alternative approach to sustainable urban development (Mayer and Knox, 2007). Small-scale local production, handicrafts, rural work and family retail is sought. Compared to competitive models, here cooperation is awarded. One of the key aspects of the slow city is building a strong local community.

14.3   THE SLOW TOURISM AS AN ALTERNATIVE TO TRADITIONAL TOURISM

There is no doubt that we are in a time of major changes in the tourism industry. Different variables affect general tourism and, therefore, offer a variety of alternative touristic models. These factors lead to a new tourism increasingly based on products and services and more focused on the experience. Moreover, another big trend in tourism is the growing concern for sustainability. Some authors such as Ioannides and Debbage [17] have pointed a "post-Fordist tourism industry" where sun and beach tourism correspond to the so-called second-generation tourism, characterized by homogenization of the tourist packages and the search for economies of scale (Miret et al., 2011). This model is considered by many authors as unsustainable and outdated [2, 1]. These authors argue the emergence of a third generation tourism, characterized by the heavy use of new technologies and a product based on quality and environmental respect criteria [25].

In any case, much of current tourism is based on scheduled trips, all inclusive packages, or "low cost" hotels and travel that follow this pattern. This model search helps to visit the most at the lowest cost. In this way, without having to leave work stress, a visit only includes "must-visit" places and these visits are very fast and shallow. An extreme example would be the Caribbean resorts where you can travel to a country without knowing anything of it. As an alternative to this way of traveling, different forms of tourism have emerged, characterized by environment and social respect of the territory.

Traditional tourism is seen as a resource-intensive sector and that leaves a significant mark on the environment [16], [14], in fact the UN is warning of significant environmental impact of tourism [28]. However, it was in the 1980s and since Brundtland report (1987) when concepts like "sustainable tourism" [15]; and Joppa, 1996) or "eco-tourism" [12] came up. By the turn of the millennium, new ways of understanding tourism as the "pro-poor tourism" [3] or "low-carbon tourism" [22] have continued to emerge.

The slow tourism would be framed in these new forms of tourism that are not trying to move from the current model but to break dramatically with the traditional concept of tourism. The slow tourism aims tourist to be a part of local life and to connect with the destination, its people and culture [11]. The trip purpose is not to visit a city, but to discover it.

It is difficult to establish a Decalogue with the main features of the slow tourism, but its main features to highlight are (slowtrav.com, 2010):

- Spend at least a week in one place. Avoid superficial traveling, get to know a place takes time.
- Instead of staying in hotels or resorts, vacation rentals accommodation is used. Vacation rentals have different names depending on the country ("Self-catering" in England and Australia, "gites" in France, "agriturismos" in Italy, "ferienwohnungen" in Germany, etc.) and in Spain correspond to what we know as "turismo rural."
- See what is near. Avoid spend the holidays locked in the car. A recommended technique is to draw concentric circles from the chosen base. It's about seeing what is near, rather than spend days traveling to see the "must sees."

The main differences between traditional tourism and slow tourism, has been displayed on Table 14.1.

TABLE 14.1   Differences between the standard model of tourism and slow tourism.

Standard Model	Slow Tourism
Global	Local
Miles	Sensations
You buy the journey	You make your own journey
Standard	Authenticity
Hotels, resorts	Vacation rentals
Replicable	Unique
Indifferent to the local culture and history	Committed to local culture and history
Stressful	Quiet
Treat tourist as a visitor	Treat the tourist as a temporary resident
See	Joining
Visit	Discover
As much is possible	As best is possible

Source: Compiled by Authors.

14.4   CREATION, EXPANSION, AND POTENTIAL FOR A NEW TOURISM MODEL

Slow tourism appears as an alternative to the traditional touristic approach, just as slow city appears as an alternative to traditional urban planning approach that prevails in small towns. The purpose of this work is to show the potential synergies that can be created between both.

It is clear the growing importance of hiking and sightseeing in small towns [24]. In fact, in many cases, tourism is presented as the panacea for job creation and wealth in small local economies, but tourism can also lead to serious problems for the local community. There is extensive literature that studies the impact of tourism in rural areas [10], [20], [29], [13]. Studies show how complicated is the management of a historic center, which is a major challenge for urban design. These centers often face strong historical architectural constraints, traffic, and loss of privacy and functionality due to excessive tourism support have been highlighted already. Therefore, it is necessary for a sustainable development to preserve the architectural heritage without avoiding its transformation into a modern and functional city.

Slow tourism and slow city concepts, as they share the same philosophy, may address urban development and tourism growth from the same perspective and seek common goals.

Moreover, "slow city" label can create important synergies with the "slow tourism" concept, although very new, it is making its way into the overall tourism market, as its presence is growing in touristic forums and blogs, as well as various initiatives in several fields.

In fact, slow tourism has inspired new ways of doing business. Www.slowtrav.com could be an example. It has over 8,000 members and 4,000 reviews of hotels and restaurants and is consulted daily by between 20,000 and 30,000 visitors from around the world. Spanish level initiatives such as belonging to the www.slowtravelling.es that belongs to IMS consulting group are also opening this emerging market.

Another initiative from the gastronomic point of view but that shares the same "slow" philosophy are Km0 restaurants. This "eco-gastronomy" label is awarded by the slow-food movement itself and brings together 66 chefs and 59 Spanish restaurants.

14.5   CONCLUSIONS

The Slow Food philosophy has been expanding into Europe originally from Italy, but today is present in worldwide. Similarly, if the movement initially focused on food, today includes aspects as diverse as tourism or urban planning.

This work applications and opportunities to explore the so-called "slow Tourism" might have on tourism in general and on tourism in small towns in particular have arisen. It is difficult to quantify the economic impact of this type of tourism, since it is an emerging market. In any case, the number of slow movement members, its variety (urban planning, culinary, etc.) and its rapid international growth, does augur important opportunities for those towns with a slow city certification, as well as restaurants, hotels, or agencies seeking a position in this market.

The importance of the slow movement lies not only in the business opportunities it presents, but also in the way that it can restate the existing tourism and urban development models, in line with current and important concepts for the touristic industry such as sustainable tourism or sensations tourism [30]. In this sense, the present study was a descriptive introduction that opens the door to future work with quantitative or qualitative methods to explore different aspects of "slow tourism." Eventually, this concept will have to strengthen and social, environmental, or economic profitability can be explored.

SUGGESTED RESEARCH QUESTIONS

www.slowtrav.com

The slow tourism movement has inspired new business models; www.slowtrav.com is a good example. This is an independent website and online community where everyone can learn about Slow Travel with more than 8,000 affiliates and 14,000 touristic information worldwide websites. Every day, between 20,000 and 30,000 tourists enter the site.

Considering this,
- How could you use this site as a tool for promotion and positioning of a touristic product?
- Analyze the different sections of this tourist site and its relationship with the new tourism model of the speaker this work (forums, blogs, trip reports, guides, webcams, members photo albums, travel services, etc.).

www.cittaslowusa.org

At the United States there are only three slow cities. It would be interesting o analyze what's supposed to be in the town Cittaslow network: advantages, difficulties, problems, etc. and also the potential of this certification and the transferal possibilities to other municipalities.

http://www.slowtravelberlin.com/

Although the slow city movement focuses on municipalities with less than 50,000 inhabitants and small towns, the slow travel movement can be a new way to develop also big cities. To analyze its potential application in large cities still remains pendant.

SLOW TOURISM REFERENCES

http://www.slowfood.com/
http://www.slowfoodusa.org/

http://www.slowmovement.com/
www.cittaslowusa.org
www.slowtrav.com

KEYWORDS

- **Second modernity**
- **Traditional tourism**
- **Km0 restaurants**

REFERENCES

1. Aguiló, E.; Alegre, J.; and Sard, M.; The Persistence of the Sun and Sand Tourism Model. *Tour. Manage.* **2005**, *26*, 219–231.
2. Argawal, S.; Restructuring Seaside Tourism: The Resort Lifecycle. *Ann. Tour. Res.* **2002,** *29*, 25–55.
3. Ashley, C.; Roe, D.; and Goodwin, H.; Pro Poor Tourism Strategies: Making Tourism Work For The Poor: A review of experience. *Pro Poor tourism Report* vol. 1, Overseas Development Insitute, The Russel Press, Nottingham; **2001**.
4. Beck, U., Bonss, W.; and Lau, C.; The Theory of Reflexive Modernization. Problematic, Hypotheses and Research Programme. *Theor. Cult. Soc.* **2003**, *20*(2), 1–33.
5. Beck, U.; Cosmopolitan Vision. Cambridge, UK, **2006**.
6. Beck, U.; and Lau, C.; Second modernity as a research agenda: theoretical and empirical explorations in the 'meta-change' of modern society. *Br. J. Sociol.* **2005**, *56*(4), 525–557.
7. Bellet-Sanfeliu, C.; and Llop-Torném, J. M.; Ciudades intermedias. Entre territorios concretos y espacios globales," en *Ciudad y territorio. Estudios Territoriales* (CYTET). **2004,** *XXXVI*, 569–558.
8. Brunori, G.; and Rossi, A.; Synergy and coher03nce through collective action: some insights from routes in Tuscany. *Sociologia. Rurales.* **2000**, *40*(4), 409–423.
9. Bruntland, G.; (ed.) Our Common Future: The World Commission on Environment and Development. Oxford: Oxford University Press; **1987**.
10. Delgado, C., Gil, C., Hortelano, L. A.; and Plaza, J. L.; Turismo y desarrollo local en algunas comarcas de la montaña cantábrica: recursos y planificación. *Cuadernos de Turismo.* **2003,** *12*, 7–34.
11. Dickinson, J.; and Lumson, L.; Slow travel and tourism. Ed Lavoisier; **2010**
12. Fennell, D.; Ecotourism. Ed Routledge; **1999.**
13. Ferrari, G.; Mondéjar-Jiménez, J.; and Vargas-Vargas, M.; Environmental sustainable management of small rural tourist enterprises. *Int. J. Environ. Res.* **2010**, *4*(3), 407–414.
14. Goessling, S.; Global environmental consequences of tourism. Global Environment Change, **2002**.
15. Hunter, C.; Sustainable tourism as an adaptive paradigm. *Ann. Tour. Res.* **1997**, *24*(4), 850–867.

16. Hunter, C.; and Shaw, J.; The ecological footprint as a key indicator of sustainable tourism. *Tourism Management.* **2007**, 28(1), 46–57.

17. Ioannides, D.; and Debbage, K.; Neo-Fordism and Flexible Specialization in the Travel Industry. Dissecting the Polyglot, in D. Ioannides and Debbage K. (Eds) Economic Geography of the Tourist. London: Routledge, 99–122; **1997.**

18. Leyshon, A.; Lee, R.; and Williams, C. C.; Alternative Economic Spaces. London:Sage; **2003.**

19. Mayer, H., & Knox, P. L. (2009). Pace of life and quality of life: The slow city charter. In *Community Quality-of-life Indicators: Best Cases III* (pp. 21-40). Springer Netherlands.

20. Miret-Pastor, L., Segarra-Oña, M., & Peiró-Signes, A. (2011). Environmental certification as a tool to measure and promote ecoinnovation in the tourist sector. *Research Studies in Tourism and Environment*, Nova Publishers, Hauppauge, NY, USA.

21. Mondejar Jimenez, J. A.; Mondejar Jimenez, J.; and Vargas Vargas, M.; Análisis del turismo cultural en Castilla la Mancha (ESPAÑA): El impacto de los programas europeos de desarrollo rural LEADER y PRODER. *Estud. perspect. tur.* [online], **2008,** *17*(4), 364–378.

22. New Economics Foundation.; Clone Town Britain. The survey results on the bland state of the nation; **2004.**

23. Peeters, P.; Gössling, S.; and Lane, B.; Moving towards low-carbon tourism: new opportunities for destinations and tour operators. In: Gössling, S, Hall, C. M., Weaver D. B. (eds) Tourism Futures: perspectives on Systems, Restructuring and Innovations. Routledge, New York, USA; **2009.**

24. Pink, S.; Sensing Cittaslow: Slow living and the constitution of the sensory city. *Sense. Soc.* **2007,** *2*(1), 59–77.

25. Royo, M.; and Serarols, Ch.; El turismo rural-cultural: un modelo de gestión del marketing turístico a nivel local basado en la medida de la imagen del destino. *Cuadernos. de. turismo.* **2005,** *16*, 197–222.

26. Segarra-Oña, M.; Miret-Pastor, L.; and Peiró-Signes, A; Identificación y Análisis de Clústers Turísticos: ¿Influye la Localización en los Resultados Empresariales?, *Restma, revista de economia, sociedad, turismo y medio ambiente (in Spanish).* **2011,** 13, 9–16.

27. Segarra-Oña, M.; Miret-Pastor, L.; Peiró-Signes, A; and Verma, R.; The effects of localization on economic performance. Analysis of Spanish tourism clusters, *European Planning Studies.* **2012,** *20*(6), 4–24.

28. Stewart, J. X.; Bramble, L.; and Ziraldo, D.; Key challenges in wine and culinary tourism with practical recommendation. *Int. J. Contempor. Hospital. Manage.* **2008.** *20*(3), 303–312.

29. UNWTO; Climate change and tourism—responding to global challenges. UNWTO Publications, Madrid; **2008.**

30. Vargas-Vargas, M.; and Mondéjar-Jiménez, J.; Environmental Impact And Business Management In Rural Tourism. *J. Appl. Bus. Res.* **2010.** *26*(3), 93–98.

31. Wang, N.; Rethinking authenticity in tourism experience. *Ann. Tour. Res.* **1999**, 26(2), 349–370.

CHAPTER 15

MANAGING TOURISTIC CULTURAL HERITAGE FROM A SUSTAINABLE POINT OF VIEW

FRANCISCA RAMÓN FERNÁNDEZ[1], LOURDES CANÓS-DARÓS[2], and CRISTINA SANTANDREU-MASCARELL[3]

[1]Associate Professor, RE-FOREST Research Group, Escuela Técnica Superior de Ingenierнa Agronymica y del Medio Natural (ETSIAMN), Universitat Politècnica de València, Camino de Vera, s/n. 46022, Valencia-Spain, Tele: 0034963877000, E-mail: frarafer@urb.upv.es

[2]Assistant Professor, ROGLE Research Group, C/ Paranimf, 1, 46730, Grao de Gandia, Valencia, Spain, Universitat Politècnica de València, Tele: 0034962849407, E-mail: loucada@omp.upv.es

[3]Assistant Professor, IGIC Research Group, C/ Paranimf, 1, 46730, Grao de Gandia, Valencia, Spain, Universitat Politècnica de València, Tele: 0034962849407, E-mail: crisanma@omp.upv.es

CONTENTS

15.1   INTRODUCTION

Cultural heritage is an asset that attracts a large numbers of tourists. Tangible and intangible heritage of cultural interest (from here referred as BIC because of the acronym in Spanish) are protected by law. However, heritage management has to be oriented also to be sustainable: cultural tourism often results in an increase of visitors in certain locations that cause an irreversible damage. Attention must be paid to the type of heritage and its entailment to tourism together with the number of visitors, to prevent resources deterioration.

In this paper we study some of these cases and how the law provides measures to avoid such a situation. About the methodology, we analyze the laws that protect the resources that comprise the cultural heritage of Valencian Region in Spain (see Figure 15.1), distinguishing between interesting cultural property with specific protection and going deeply into immovables and intangibles (cultural traditions).

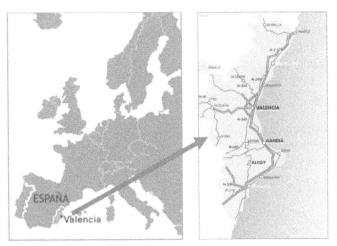

FIGURE 15.1   Location of Valencia (Spain).

15.2   HERITAGE PROTECTION IN SPANISH NATIONAL LAWS

In the field of heritage protection, the Spanish Constitution establishes different ideas in different precepts:

- (a)   Art. 46 indicates that public authorities shall guarantee the preservation and will promote the enrichment of historical, cultural, and art heritage from the peoples of Spain and property within it, whatever their legal status and ownership. Criminal law will punish any offenses against this heritage.
- (b)   Art. 132.3 points out that, by law, state heritage and national heritage will be regulated, along with their administration, protection, and conservation.

(c) Art. 148.1 items 15th and 16th enunciate that the Autonomous Communities (different regions in Spain) may assume competences over the following matters: Museums, libraries, music conservatories and monuments of interest.

(d) Art. 149.1 item 28 a) denotes that the State has exclusive competence over the following matters (although they can be managed by regional governments): Defense of cultural, artistic, and monumental Spanish heritage against exportation and spoliation; museums, libraries, and State archives.

On the other hand, in the Statute of Autonomy for the Valencian Region, art. 12 indicates that corresponds to the Valencian Government to ensure the protection and defense of identity, values, and interests of the Valencian people and the respect for the cultural diversity of Valencia and its heritage. Art. 49.1 item 5th points at the exclusive competence of the Valencian Government in terms of historical, artistic, monumental, architectural, archeological, and scientific heritage.

The main cultural heritage regulation is formed by the next laws:

1. Law 4/1998, June 11, about Valencian Cultural Heritage (BOE no. 174, July 22, 1998).
2. Law 7/2004, October 19, amending Law 4/1998, June 11, about Valencian Cultural Heritage (BOE no. 279, November 19, 2004).
3. Law 5/2007, February 9, amending Law 4/1998, June 11, about Valencian Cultural Heritage (BOE no. 71, March 23, 2007).

15.3 BIC IN VALENCIAN CULTURAL HERITAGE LAW

As required by art. 45 of Law 4/1998, June 11, we can consider BIC the activities, knowledge, practices, and techniques that constitute the most representative and valuable manifestations of culture and traditional lifestyles of Valencia. Immaterial goods may also be declared as BIC because they are expressions of the traditions of the Valencian people in their musical, artistic, gastronomic, and leisure manifestations, especially those that have been orally transmitted, which preserves and enhances the use of Valencian language.

The art. 26.2 of Law 4/1998, June 11, of the Valencian Government, about cultural heritage, provides that the declaration of a BIC shall be made by Decree of the Council, on a proposal from the Counselor competent for culture. Without prejudice to the competences that have the State Administration reflected in art. 6 of Law 16/1985, June 25, about Spanish Historical Heritage, Valencian legislation aims to protect, conserve, disseminate, promote, research, and enhancement cultural heritage.

The resources which constitute the cultural heritage have movable and immovable property. Those with historical, artistic, architectural, archeological, paleontological, ethnographic, documentary, literary, scientific, technical or any other cultural nature value, which exist in the territory of Valencia or, if they are outside of it, constitute a representative example of the history and culture of Valencia [2]. Intangibles also include ethnological heritage, creations, knowledge, skills, practices, and representative uses and valuable ways of life and traditional culture from Valencia [4], [5].

BIC are declared: movable and immovable property, collection or a part of museum collections; documents and bibliographic works, cinematographic or audiovisual recordings, individually declared as collection or as archival and library funds; immaterial goods and intangible technological goods that constitute relevant events or milestones in the technological evolution of Valencia [1], [11].

Immovables have one of the following categories: Monument (engineering and architectural productions, and colossal sculptures); historical set (continuous or dispersed group of immovables, clearly distinguishable and with a separate and distinct cultural entity different from the value of the unique elements that form it); historic garden (delimited space with ordered natural elements, supplemented or not with factory structures and appreciated because of historical or aesthetic, sensory or botanical values); ethnological space (construction, installation or both linked to lifestyles and traditional activities that are, by their significance, especially representative of the Valencian culture; historical site (linked to past events, popular traditions or cultural creations with historical, ethnological or anthropological value); archeological site (place where there are resources whose study requires archeological methods, whether or not extracted and therefore are in the outside, underground or under water); paleontological area (where there is a set of fossils scientifically or educationally significant); cultural park (contains significant elements of cultural heritage embedded in a physical environment relevant for its scenic and ecological values).

15.4   DIFFERENT IMMOVABLE BIC PROTECTION IN VALENCIAN CULTURAL HERITAGE LAW

Immovable BIC, as noted above, may have the categories of monument, historical set, historic garden, ethnological space, historical site, archeological area, paleontological area, and cultural park.

Some protection measures about them (see Casar, 2008), using the previous categories, focusing on the protection measures that consider different decrees, can be seen in Appendix. In the following Figures 15.2, 15.3 and 15.4 we can see the location of them according to different categories.

FIGURE 15.2   BIC—Category: Monument.

FIGURE 15.3   BIC—Category: Historical set.

FIGURE 15.4   BIC—Category: Historic garden (*in black*); Ethnological space (*in red*); Archaeological area (*in green*).

We want to indicate that, depending on the nature of the resource, protection measures are different but always aimed at preserving it, together with the delimitation of its environmental protection. Measures allow the use of them according to: their historical associated uses (agriculture, forestry, tourism, etc.), uses that are compatible with any stated research, enhancement and enjoy, and uses that contribute to the achievement of those purposes. For example, there are properties in the protected environment they cannot be demolished. Also note that to be a good resource for tourism enjoyment, advertising signs are prohibited and any obstacles to view it. Similarly, the discharge of waste, earthworks, and excavations with landscape impact are prohibited. It also extends to motor vehicles, being allowed in some cases agricultural vehicles. Especially in areas of excavations, tillage work is prohibited at a depth indicated in the law, as well as plantations, but exceptional cases and prior authorization.

15.5   DIFFERENT IMMATERIAL BIC PROTECTION IN VALENCIAN CULTURAL HERITAGE LAW

In Appendix, we can see a list of different immaterial BIC declared in Valencian Region by decree. In all cases, depending on the nature of their elements, in accordance with its cultural manifestation and the preservation of traditional values, protection measures are:

(a) Any change exceeding the normal development of the elements has to be communicated. An administrative approval and a modification of the corresponding decree is required. Moreover, improvement of the protected values has to be justified.

(b) Generic protection of activities, knowledge, and techniques in the case of manual touches of bells do not have to interfere their routine or even extraordinary concerts. Any machining, bells or facilities modification, as well as displacement or variation of the set must be authorized by presenting a project.

(c) Fallas are managed by Junta Central Fallera; Tamborada in Alzira by Junta de Hermandades y Cofradías de la Semana Santa; drumbeat in L'Alcora by Hermandad del Santísimo Cristo del Calvario; Santantonada in Forcall by the City Council and members of Cofradía de San Antonio; bulls and horses running in Segorbe by the City Council of the town; Festivity of Our Lady of Health by Patronato de la Fundació per a la Festa de la Mare de Déu de la Salut i el Crist de l'agonia, who will decide on the material and immaterial aspects, and the development acts of the annual festival; in the case of the Solemnity of Corpus Christi civic management is for the City Council and the Metropolitan Council, regardless of the liturgy that correspond to the Roman Catholic Church.

The use or promotion of roman catholic festivities as a whole or those tangible or intangible elements (even allegorical) are reserved exclusively to the City Council of Algemesí, to St. James parish Church and the Patronato de la Fundació in Algemesí. In the case of Corpus Christi in Valencia, the use and promotion is exclusively reserved to the City Council and the Metropolitan Council, without prejudice to the right of information media about various events related to the solemnity.

In the case of the Water Court of Valencia Vega, as stated in decree, the values that determine this immaterial BIC are based on ritual representation, linked to a temporary space in which are carried the public meetings, and linked to a concrete physical space, which is the Apostles Door of the Cathedral, and the territory of the Valencian orchand, as well as its unique and defining elements. Moreover, following the contents of arts. 28 and 45 of Law 4/1998, June 11, about Valencian Cultural Heritage, Regional Government will assist in the preservation of customary and traditional values. General Manager responsible for cultural heritage in Regional Government has to ensure the study (by using scientific criteria) and documentation of this cultural activity, and incorporate available evidence through different support materials to ensure its survival. The conservation of the Court is subject to the maintenance of some Irrigation Communities, and the traditional practice of irrigated agriculture in Valencia Orchard. Regional Government, in coordination with local authorities and involved communities will arbitrate appropriate measures to ensure the survival of so ancient institution. These measures will be coordinated through the Regional Action Plan for the Protection of Valencian Orchard as seen in art. 22 of Law 4/2004, June 30, about Spatial Planning and Landscape Protection.

In the case of Tirisiti Betlem, the protection of this intangible implies that representations are developed in spatial and temporal original context, which is in the town of Alcoy at Christmas. The City Council is responsible for the protection of this event.

(d) Ensure the maintenance and dignity of Festivities.

(e) Institutional support by providing financial and human resources.

(f) Development by Public Administration of promotion, guaranteeing their study and documentation with scientific criteria, and incorporating the available evidence to ensure their survival.

Today, bullfighting and traditional bullfights "bous al carrer" have been included as a BIC through Resolution, February 20, 2012, of the Spanish Ministry of Tourism, Culture and Sport, throughout the region of Valencia (DOCV no. 6720, February 23, 2012).

15.6 MONUMENTAL TREE HERITAGE PROTECTION

Monumental tree heritage protection is regulated in Law 4/2006, May 19, of Monumental Tree Heritage of the region of Valencia (BOE 154, June 29, 2006). In particular, this law considers the protection of this cultural heritage that has as main figures outstanding, monumental or singular trees that constitute a potential for the region of Valencia, through their special protection and cataloging.

The main reasons for tree heritage to be object of a specific regulation have been the special environmental and historical characteristics of the region of Valencia, since there exists a great deal of biodiversity of native ligneous vegetal and allochthonous species, that are part of the vegetation of the Valencian forests—being some of them introduced within our spaces in remote times, and others are part of our culture, as they are considered ornamental. All these indicators have determined the existence of botanical groups and specimens that are unique and that have an historical, cultural, scientific, and recreational value that constitutes what has been called tree heritage, a singular part of the environmental Valencian heritage and very important to be object of protection and conservation for future generations [12].

As the law states, this living tree heritage, formed by trees of spectacular measures, also includes shrubs or other nontree specimens of remarkable dimensions; those that include an important historical or symbolic meaning and those that represent religious or social traditions or a high ethno-agrarian or ethnobotanical value. Likewise, this section includes specimens of extremely rare ligneous species, whose presence implies an outstanding scientific value and those which society enjoys their contemplation.

The trees that correspond to these characteristics have reached unusual dimensions and forms for their respective species and are indebted to the effort of the human being in their care and multicentennial maintenance; in fact, the great majority of this hoisting corresponds to specimens that have been planted and improved throughout time. Many of them are located in historic gardens, town and city squares, resting areas of cattle routes and other surroundings near rural constructions or farms. Multicentenary specimens of some agricultural species particularly longevous also survive.

Protection measures in the law are the following [7, 8, 9, 10]:

(a) Conservation of the species, including the development of fruiting and mild pruning, phytosanitary treatments or other traditional activities for maintenance, if not threat the tree.

(b) Technical support to facilitate the enhancement of the species.

(c) Various planning tools are included to ensure proper management and supervision of the health of trees.

A generic protection (without resolution) is established for trees that exceed one of the following parameters (350 years old; 30 m high; 6 m perimeter (trunk) at a height of 1.30 m from base; 25 m diameter (cup)). Moreover, there is a specific protection for monumental or unique trees.

On one hand, the protection and cataloging of the tree heritage located in forest land will correspond to the Department of environment (Order 22/2012, November 13, about the catalog of monumental and unique trees in Valencian Region—DOCV num. 6909, November 23, 2012). It will also be responsible for the protection and cataloging of the tree heritage located in nonforest land, regarding trees of generic protection, and those that correspond to city councils considered to be protected. On the other hand, city councils will be responsible for the protection and/or proposal of cataloging of the trees of all species that are in forest and nonforest land. In addition, protection and cataloging of the monumental tree heritage is subject to regulation by means of the current Law 4/2006, May 19, which promotes the consideration of the natural heritage and culture of unique trees.

15.7 PROTECTION AND REVIVAL OF HISTORICAL SET IN VALENCIA CITY

Protection and revitalization of the historic set in Valencia is regulated by Law 2/2010, March 31 (BOE no. 100, April 26, 2010). This law substitutes Decree-Law 1/2010, January 7 (DOCV no. 6180, January 8, 2010). The protection of the historic set was established by Decree BIC 57/1993, May 3, which was defined for the purposes of specified protection in three different areas in Valencia: the walled city (Ciutat Vella), the first extension bounded by major roads and the Turia riverbed, and the original core of the extension of Cabanyal neighborhood.

The reform done by Law 7/2004, October 19, had as one of the principal axes the enhancement of cultural assets, focusing on those whose value is based largely on the existence of a social use, the maintenance of traditions and the activities that characterize it. In this context, art. 39.2 has generated a legal controversy about the validity of the Special Plan of Protection and Internal Reform Cabanyal-Canyame-lar, allowing public responsible to authorize special protection plans of historic locations. These plans can include changes in the urban and architectural structure if an improvement in relation with the environment and urban land uses occurs, or to avoid degrading the set itself, or when activities of general interest for the municipality or relevant unique projects are present.

Spanish Supreme Court ruled on the matter, with different judgments (March 12 and 13 and December 16, 2008), stating that in the case of Cabanyal neighborhood of Valencia, the reproach of spoliation is directed against a planning instrument, Special Protection Plan, that has been the result of a complex process. Special Plan for the Protection Cabanyal-Canyamelar do not endanger any loss or destruction of the values of the historic city. Actions and interventions on urban and architectural structure are authorized, considering that the plan produces an improvement of the relationship of the neighborhood with their local environment and avoid degrading purposes.

15.8 CONCLUSIONS

The regime of protection by law in the case of BIC is large and adapted to the characteristics of resources. It is laudable the auditor character from the administration to authorize activities for the protection of BIC [6]. It should be noted that after different legislative changes [14], mainly in the Valencian Cultural Heritage Law, the so-called intangible resources are important, represented by those that reflect Valencian culture. So, their protection is increased in the field of preservation for future generations [11].

Protection afforded to alive heritage is also emphasized. This is a pioneering Law in the Valencian Region to protect monumental tree heritage. This Law considers landscape and location of resources very important, not only the resource itself as happens with other kind of heritage (buildings, for instance). In the field tourism, this Law is an important milestone as through the trees protection it encourages the visitor to contemplate peculiar specimens and revitalizes the importance of the city as a destination.

Special mention deserves the historic quarter of the city of Valencia, because of protective measures and actions developed also allowing interventions of urban character.

IN-CLASS DISCUSSION POINTS

1. Historic heritage. Search information about protection laws of elements discovered in the progress of a restoration. You can take as an example the case of a renaissance picture covered by a baroque dome (a real case happened in Valencia Cathedral). Which element has preference to be protected? Can the experts protect both in some specific circumstances?
2. Do you think Cabanyal neighborhood has enough protection for its historic set?

QUESTIONS FOR CLASS DISCUSSION

1. Immovable resources attract tourists. Order these four antecedents of tourist satisfaction -most of them related to the characteristics of destination- according to tourist preferences: (1) Tourist expectations: Consumer satisfaction/dissatisfaction is a result of a comparison between a consumer's prepurchase expectations and their postpurchase evaluation; (2) Destination image: An individual's mental representation of the knowledge, feelings, and overall perception of a particular destination. It is a driving factor in the formation of consumer expectations; (3) Perceived quality: Overall evaluation made by consumers regarding the excellence of a product; (4) Perceived value: Consumer's overall assessment of product utility based on perceptions of what is received and what is given [15].
2. Millenarian olive trees. Read the next example and search some protected trees near your home, workplace, etc. Within these trees, and as an example, are the centennial and multicentennial olive trees located in the region of Valencia and compliant with the Law under consideration. The existence of magnificent specimens older than 500 years motivated their protection by means of the Law under study, in article 4 of Law/2006, to the trees that exceed 30 years of age. The presence of the olive grove in the region of Valencia goes back to the time of the Romans, more than 2,000 ago. There is certainty of its culture in zones of the province of Valencia, in the regions of the Maestrazgo of Castellon, in areas near the August Route, that communicated the capital of the Roman Empire with Cadiz. It is in that region

where numerous specimens older than 2,000 years, being easy to verify the presence of millenarian olive trees thanks to the effort of the cooperatives and their relaunch as the so-called routes of tourist interest of the "millenarian oil." Favorable decision to the request of registration in the community registry of protected denominations of origin and protected geographic indications is adopted, foreseen in Regulation (EC) 510/2006, of the Council, 20 March, Protected Denomination of Origin Oil of the region of Valencia and its conditions are published, according to Resolution of 24 June, 2008, of the Department of Agriculture, Fishing, and Food (Ramón et al. 2012).

SUGGESTED FURTHER READING

Canós, L.; and Sutinen, O.; Opportunities for Northern-Finland sustainable leisure tourism: case Liminganlahti birdwatching. *4th Tourism Industry and Education Symposium*, Jyvaskyla (Finland), **2009**.

Cuccia, T.; and Rizzo, I.; Tourism seasonality in cultural destinations: Empirical evidence from Sicily. *Tour. Manage.* **2011**, 32, 589–595.

Judgements (in Spanish): STSJ CV 7753/2012, December 4, 2012; STSJ CV 398/2013, February 6, 2013.

Lew, A. A.; A framework of tourist attraction research. *Ann. Tour. Res.* **1987**, *14*(4), 553–575.

Ramón, F.; Canós, L.; and Santandreu, C.; Monumental tree heritage as urban tourist attraction. Research Studies on Tourism and Environment, José Mondéjar-Jiménez, Guido Ferrari, Manuel Vargas-Vargas; Hauppauge: New York, **2012**; 133–143.

Russo, A. P. and Van der Borg, J.; Planning considerations for cultural tourism: a case study of four European cities. *Tour. Manage.* **2002**, *23*, 631–637.

KEYWORDS

- **Monumental tree heritage**
- **Immovables**
- **Tangibles**
- **Valencian Region**

REFERENCES

1. Azuar, R.; Los museos en la dinámica territorial del patrimonio cultural valenciano. *Braçal: revista del Centre d'Estudis del Camp de Morvedre*. **2005**, *31–32*, 17–36.
2. Carrera, J. C.; La Ley del Patrimonio Cultural Valenciano: Del patrimonio arqueológico. *Arse: Boletín anual del Centro Arqueológico Saguntino*. **2002, 36**, 177–189.

3. Casar, Mª. E.; Las diversas categorías de bienes inmuebles de interés cultural, con especial referencia a la Nueva Ley de patrimonio cultural valenciano de 2007. *Práctica urbanística: Revista mensual de urbanismo.* **2007**, *73*, 23–34.

4. Ferré, C.; La Ley del Patrimonio Cultural Valencian. Derechos civiles de España, coord. por Julián Martínez-Simancas Sánchez y Rodrigo Bercovitz Rodríguez-Cano, 5, Madrid.: Editorial Sopec; 2033–3048; **2000.**

5. López, C.; La Ley valenciana de patrimonio cultural: Ley 471998, de 11 de junio, del Patrimonio Histórico-artístico, normas reguladoras del patrimonio cultural valenciano. Valencia: Tirant lo Blanch; **1999.**

6. Montiel, A.; La legislación protectora del patrimonio cultural valenciano: una mirada crítica. *Braçal: revista del Centre d'Estudis del Camp de Morvedre.* **2004**, 28–29, 49–60.

7. Ramón, F.; La protección del paisaje y del patrimonio arbóreo monumental en la Comunidad Valenciana. *Libro de Ponencias y Resúmenes. Congrés Forestal Català*, Centre Tecnològic Forestal de Catalunya, 299, Tarragona; **2007**.

8. Ramón, F. La catalogación del patrimonio arbóreo monumental como instrumento de reputación de la Comunidad Valenciana. *Artículos y Comunicaciones 2007 y 2008, Congreso Internacional de Gestión de Eventos.* **2008,** 128–135. Depósito Legal: 3955–2008. Castellón.

9. Ramón, F.; Aspectos jurídicos del Patrimonio Arbóreo Monumental. *La influencia del Derecho valenciano en las disciplinas tecnológicas*, Coordinadora Francisca Ramón Fernández, monografías Tirant lo Blanch. Valencia; **2009**; 99–122.

10. Ramón, F.; Los olivos centenarios y milenarios y su protección en la Ley de Patrimonio Arbóreo Monumental de la Comunidad Valenciana. Actas del Simposium Científico-Técnico de EXPOLIVA 2009, tomo II, 471–475. Jaén; **2011.**

11. Ramón, F.; El patrimonio cultural. Régimen legislativo y su protección. Ed. Tirant lo Blanch.Valencia; **2012.**

12. Ramón, F., Canós, L.; and Santandreu, C.; Monumental tree heritage as urban tourist attraction. Research Studies on Tourism and Environment, José Mondéjar-Jiménez, Guido Ferrari, Manuel Vargas-Vargas, Hauppauge, 133–143. New York; **2012.**

14. Sirvent, C.; Luces y sombras de la nueva ley de patrimonio cultural valenciano. *Recerques del Museu d'Alcoi.* **2000**, *9*, 11–16.

15. Wang, X.; Zhang, J.; Gu, C.; and Zhen, F.; Examining antecedents and consequences of tourist satisfaction: a structural modelling approach. *Tsinghua. Science. Technol.* **2009**, *14*(3), 397–406.

APPENDIX

(a) BIC—Category: Monument.

BIC—Category: Monument	Decree or Order
Polop Castle in La Marina	Decree 126/2012, August 3 (DOCV no. 6834, August 6, 2012)
The Farmhouse of the Duke	Order 4/2011, October 25 (DOCV no. 6682, December 30, 2011)
The Fortified Farmhouse Tower of the Fathers	Order 2/2011, October 25 (DOCV no. 6643, November 3, 2011)
Maçanes Tower in Torremanzanas	Order 11/2011, June 21 (DOCV no. 6552, June 27, 2011)
The remains of the Roman aqueduct in Altea	Decree 41/2011, April 15 (DOCV no. 6504, April 18, 2011)
Arches Aqueduct in Manises	Decree 55/2006, April 28 (DOCV no. 6413, December 9, 2010)
Royal Monastery of the Visitation of Holy Mary in Orihuela	Decree 42/2010, March 5 (DOCV no. 6222, March 9, 2010)
Aledua Castle in Llombai	Decree 6/2010, February 12 (DOCV no. 6220, March 5, 2010)
Castle and City Walls in Vistabella del Maestrazgo	Order 5/2010, February 11 (DOCV no. 6220, March 5, 2010)
Boi Castle in Vistabella del Maestrazgo	Order 4/2010, February 10 (DOCV no. 6220, March 5, 2010)
Alfauir Tower	Order 3/2010, February 9 (DOCV no. 6219, March 4, 2010)
Fort or "Grau Vell" Tower in Sagunto	Order 2/2010, February 8 (DOCV no. 6219, March 4, 2010)
Walled Iberian and Roman village La Carencia in Turis	Order, October 20, 2009 (DOCV no. 6172, December 24, 2009)
Walled Iberian village La Seña in Villar del Arzobispo	Order June 17, 2009 (DOCV no. 6061, July 21, 2009)
St. Nicholas of Bari Church in Requena	Decree 171/2008, November 14 (DOCV no. 5895, November 18, 2008)
Monastery of San Miguel de los Reyes	Decree 142/2008, October 3 (DOCV no. 5865, October 7, 2008)
Palau de la Generalitat	Order, July 29, 2008 (DOCV no. 5832, August 21, 2008)

Assumption of Our Lady parish Church in Utiel	Decree 111/2008, July 25 (DOCV no. 5817, July 30, 2008)
Town Hall in Liria	Decree 110/2008, July 2, (DOCV no. 5816, July 29, 2008)
Our Lady of the Angels parish Church in Castielfabib	Decree 20/2008, February 29 (DOCV no. 5716, March 4, 2008)
Columbus Market building in Valencia	Decree 134/2007, July 27 (DOCV no. 5567, July 31, 2007)
Real Sanctuary of Our Lady of the Health Fountain in Traiguera	Decree 20/2007, February 16 (DOCV no. 5454, February 20, 2007)
Vall de Crist carthusian building in Altura	Decree 1/2007, January 12 (DOCV no. 5429, January 16, 2007)
Morella Aqueduct	Decree 190/2006, December 22 (DOCV no. 5419, January 2, 2007)
Portaceli carthusian building in Serra	Decree 164/2006, October 27 (DOCV no. 5378, October 31, 2006)
Saint Andrew Church in L'Alcúdia	Decree 146/2006, October 6 (DOCV no. 5368, October 17, 2006)
Our Lady of the Angels Archpriest Church in Chelva	Decree 147/2006, October 6 (DOCV no. 5365, October 11, 2006)
Irrigation ditch historic section from Mislata to Quart de Poblet	Decree 133/2006, September 29 (DOCV no. 5359, October 3, 2006)
Town Hall in El Toro	(Decree 86/2006, June 16 (DOCV no. 5285, June 21, 2006)
Santa Quiteria bridge between Almazora and Villarreal	Decree 87/2006, June 16 (DOCV no. 5284, June 20, 2006)
Saint Michael Archangel Church in Enguera	Decree 158/2005, October 28 (DOCV no. 5126, November 2, 2005)
Channel from Bellus to Xativa	Decree 95/2005, May 20 (DOCV no. 5014, May 26, 2005)
Bosquet de Moixent dam	Decree 54/2005, March 11 (DOCV no. 4968, March 17, 2005)
Arches Aqueduct in Alpuente	Decree 53/2005, March 11 (DOCV no. 4968, March 17, 2005)
Assumption of the Virgin of Vallibona parish Church	Decree 263/2004, December 3 (DOCV no. 4901, December 13, 2004)

Pcña Cortada aqueduct in Tuéjar, Chelva, Calles and Domeño	Decree 159/2004, September 3 (DOCV no. 4837, September 8, 2004)
Saint James Archpriest Church in Villarreal	Decree 27/2004, February 20 (DOCV no. 4699, February 25, 2004)
Saint Luke the Evangelist parish Church and Bell Tower in Cheste	Decree 26/2004, February 20 (DOCV no. 4699, February 25, 2004)
the Farmhouse of the Moor in Valencia	Decree 25/2004, February 20 (DOCV no. 4699, 25 February, 2004)
Serena or Sirena House in Alfara del Patriarca	Decree 17/2004, February 13 (DOCV no. 4693, February 17, 2004)
Royal Monastery of the Assumption or Santa Clara in Xativa	Decree 136/2003, July 18 (DOCV no. 4552, July 25, 2003)
St. Vincent Martyr Church in Guadassuar	Decree 14/1997, January 28 (DOCV no. 2921, February 3, 1997)
Ara Christi carthusian building in Puig	Decree 129/1996, of July 4 (DOCV no. 2801, July 29, 1996)
Monastery of San Jeronimo de Cotalba in Alfauir	Decree 93/1994, May 24 (DOCV no. 2286, June 10, 1994)
Tibi dam	Decree 84/1994, April 26 (DOCV no. 2268, May 17, 1994)

(b) BIC—Category: Historical set.

BIC – Category: Historical set	Decree or Order
Bastion and Renaissance enclosure in Altea	Decree 69/2013, June 7 (DOCV no. 7044, June 12, 2013)
Chelva and its orchard	Decree 168/2012, November 2 (DOCV no. 6895, November 5, 2012)
Ares del Maestrat	Decree 64/2012, April 20 (DOCV no. 6759, April 23, 2012)
The area called "Gothic walled Teulada"	Decree 232/2007, December 7 (DOCV no. 5657, December 11, 2007)
Molinar de Alcoy	Decree 105/2005, June 3 (DOCV no. 5025, June 10, 2005)
Vilafamés	Decree 80/2005, April 22 (DOCV no. 4993, April 26, 2005)
Palms Desert in Benicassim	Decree 38/2005, February 25 (DOCV no. 4956, March 1, 2005)

Jérica	Decree 273/2004, December 10 (DOCV no. 4905, December 17, 2004)
Catí	Decree 231/2004, October 22 (DOCV no. 4871, October 27, 2004)
Alzira with a historical category and Santa Catalina Church with the category of monument	Decree 126/2004, July 30 (DOCV no. 4811, August 3, 2004)
Culla	Decree 83/2004, May 21 (DOCV no. 4761, May 26, 2004)
Villajoyosa	Decree 237/2003, November 28 (DOCV no. 4643, December 3, 2003)
Sant Mateu	Decree 166/2002, September 24 (DOCV no. 4347, October 1, 2002)
Segorbe and its Cathedral Basilica	Decree 163/2002, September 24 (DOCV no. 4347, October 1, 2002)
Valencia	Decree 57/1993, May 3 (DOCV no. 2020, May 10, 1993)

(c) BIC—Category: Historic garden.

BIC – Category: Historic garden	Decree or Order
The Botanical Garden of the University of Valencia	Decree 134/2006, September 29 (DOCV no. 5360, October 4, 2006)

(d) BIC—Category: Ethnological space.

BIC – Category: Ethnological space	Decree or Order
Mills Canyon in Ares del Maestre	Decree 67/2009, May 15 (DOCV no. 6016, May 19, 2009)

(e) BIC—Category: Archaeological area.

BIC – Category: Archaeological area	Decree or Order and Resolution
El Molón archeological deposits in Camporrobles	Decree 93/2013, July 12 (DOCV no. 7067, July 15, 2013)
Solana de las Pilillas in Requena	Decree 161/2012, October 19 (DOCV no. 6886, October 22, 2012)
The Saint Michael Hill Iberian settlement in Liria	Decree 130/1994, July 5 (DOCV no. 2322, August 1, 1994)
L'Alcúdia and its monographic museum in Elx	Decree 100/1992, June 22 (DOCV no. 1816, July 1, 1992)

Sagunto	Decree 78/1992, May 11 (DOCV no. 1784, May 18, 1992)
The "Solar" in Xàtiva (ancient city)	Decree 2371992, February 17 (DOCV no. 1730, February 24, 1992)
Plaça de l'Almoina in Valencia	Resolution, February 23, 1988 (DOCV no. 792, March 25, 1988.

(f) BIC—Category: Paleontological area.

BIC – Category: Paleontological area	*Decree or Order*
Footprints in Morella, Bicorp, Bejís, Alpuente, Dos Aguas and Millares	Decree 29/2006, March 3 (DOCV no. 5213, March 7, 2006)
Torrelló de Boverot in the municipality of Almazora	Decree 297/1997, December 2 (DOCV no. 3151, December 29, 1997)

(g) Immaterial BIC.

Inmaterial BIC	*Decree or Order*
Manual touches of bells in Assumption of Our Lady parish Church in Albaida, in Castellón de la Plana, in Cathedral Basilica Assumption of Saint Mary in Segorbe and in Metropolitan Cathedral of Saint Mary in Valencia	Decree 111/2013, August 1 (DOCV no. 7082, August 5, 2013)
Fallas in Valencia	Decree 44/2012, March 9 (DOCV no. 6738, March 12, 2012)
"Tamboradas" (drumbeat) in Alzira and in L'Alcora	Decree 11/2012, January 13 (DOCV no. 6692, January 16, 2012)
Santantonada in Forcall	Decree 10/2012, January 5 (DOCV no. 6688, January 10, 2012)
Cavalcade of Three Wise Kings in Alcoy	Decree 199/2011, December 23 (DOCV no. 6678, December 26, 2011)
Bulls and horses running in Segorbe	Decree 6/2011, February 4 (DOCV no. 6454, February 7, 2011)
Festivity of Our Lady of Health in Algemesí	Decree 117/2010, August 27 (DOCV no. 6345, September 1, 2010)
Solemnity of Corpus Christi in the city of Valencia	Decree 92/2010, May 28 (DOCV no. 6280, June 2, 2010)
Water Court in Valencia	Decree 73/2006, May 26 (DOCV no. 5269, May 30, 2006)
Tirisiti Betlem in Alcoy	Decree 192/2002, November 26 (DOCV no. 4389, November 29, 2002)

INDEX

For Product Safety Concerns and Information please contact our EU
representative GPSR@taylorandfrancis.com
Taylor & Francis Verlag GmbH, Kaufingerstraße 24, 80331 München, Germany

www.ingramcontent.com/pod-product-compliance
Ingram Content Group UK Ltd.
Pitfield, Milton Keynes, MK11 3LW, UK
UKHW021623240425
457818UK00018B/703